Token Ring

Principles, Perspectives and Strategies

Data Communications and Networks Series
Consulting Editor: Dr C. Smythe, Surrey University

Selected titles

X400 Message Handling: Standards, Interworking, Applications
B. Plattner, C. Lanz, H. Lubich, M. Müller and T. Walter

Network Management: Problems, Standards and Strategies
Franz-Joachim Kauffels

Token Ring

Principles, Perspectives and Strategies

Hans-Georg Göhring
Franz-Joachim Kauffels

Translated by Stephen S. Wilson

ADDISON-WESLEY
PUBLISHING
COMPANY

Wokingham, England · Reading, Massachusetts · Menlo Park, California · New York
Don Mills, Ontario · Amsterdam · Bonn · Sydney · Singapore
Tokyo · Madrid · San Juan · Milan · Paris · Mexico City · Seoul · Taipei

Translated from the German edition *Token Ring: Grundlagen, Strategien, Perspektiven* published by Datacom-Verlag.

Cover designed by Chris Eley and
printed in Great Britain by The Bath Press, Avon

First printed 1992.

ISBN: 0 201 56895 0

British Library Cataloguing in Publication Data
A catalogue record for this book is available from the British Library.

Library of Congress Cataloging-in-Publication Data
A catalog record for this book is available from the Library of Congress.

For simplicity, the pronoun 'he' is used to relate to both male and female throughout the book.

Preface

With the aid of international standardization and open interfaces, Token Ring networks, once a relatively IBM-specific solution, have developed into universally usable, flexible and powerful local area network (LAN) systems. Thus, Token Ring is now, together with Ethernet, the dominant LAN system.

The IEEE 802 standard and the ISO 8802 standard for LANs have led to hybrid implementations of Token Ring, Ethernet, Token Bus and FDDI LANs under a common logical link control. Thus, in principle all LAN operating systems and protocol stacks are equally usable on all systems.

The ever increasing degree of PC networking and the basic concept of workgroup computing within modern commercial networks provide a new qualitative and quantitative impetus to the use of Token Ring. Diskless workstations with built-in LAN connections in practice represent the status quo of professional workstation hardware.

The use of Token Ring networks requires thorough strategic and technical consideration. This book is intended to assist those interested in networks of this type.

The collaboration of two very different authors provides for ample coverage of both the technical and the strategic aspects. One author is a Business Consultant, with many years experience, from the initial development of LANs; the other author was one of the first pilot users of Token Ring in a mainframe computer centre and is now responsible for the overall data processing within a major authority.

We could have written a book on Token Rings before now. It would have been easy to summarize the comprehensive IBM manuals. However, we decided to wait until major extensions of the basic IBM scheme and the participation of other firms in the Token Ring market were well established. In the book, these extensions and alternative schemes are compared with IBM products and critically analyzed and their practical importance is assessed.

A year after the publication of the first edition of the book, we may be proud of the fact that our ideas have caught on. The book has become a leading text on Token Ring in the German-speaking market, of which DATACOM Verlag has a large share. Thus, it seemed natural to prepare an international edition in English. We believe that we have found the right partner in Addison-Wesley Publishers Limited, and would like to thank them for their faithful cooperation.

Euskirchen and Troisdorf-Bergheim bei Bonn Winter 1991 The Authors

Contents

Chapter 1

Introduction

1.1 Token Ring: history and perspectives

1.2 Communications technology in distributed data processing

1.3 The development of network system architectures

1.4 LAN summary

1.5 Areas of application of Token Ring networks

This book is devoted to Token Ring networks, which together with local area networks (LANs) of the established Ethernet type largely determine the networking of terminals in the local area. While today only 10–15% of installed LANs are Token Ring networks, it is estimated that within the next five years Token Ring and Ethernet will each account for half the systems.

This is simply because the introduction to the market of Token Ring networks, with IBM as forerunner, was delayed for too long and now the need for the (by no means few) IBM users to catch up must be met.

In the meantime, considerable competition to the IBM solutions has developed; around 45% of LAN products adhere to the Ethernet concept and more than 35% to Token Ring. This is encouraged by international standardization (which includes Token Ring as a LAN subsystem) and by the lack of prospects for Ethernet-type networks.

In Ethernet-type networks, the CSMA/CD access algorithm restricts further development, as far as higher transmission speeds are concerned. This fact has been known in research for ten years. When one wants to go above the standard data rate of 10 Mbps, in order to maintain the same level of efficiency as at the standard data rate, one has to increase the average packet length to an uninteresting figure (almost 100 kbytes).

Token passing, based on the popular procedure of control of mutually exclusive access to a shared transmission medium, is the prime candidate for the control of networks with data rates greater than or equal to 100 Mbps.

Today, the fields of application of Token Ring networks are different from those of Ethernet systems. Token Ring networks, in their slow form, form SNA subsystems in the IBM world, for PC networking, which, in IBM's strategic view will slowly but surely supersede terminals and cluster controllers. Fast Token Rings link medium systems, controllers and communications front ends and also, in the future, mainframe channels. Ethernet systems are designed for use in a heterogeneous environment of PCs, workstations, minicomputers and larger systems from various manufacturers.

It is possible to hold highly polarized discussions as to which LAN type is the better. These usually come to nothing, since what one should install depends on the application and the objective. Fortunately, the manufacturers and international standardization allow us tackle these points more calmly through corresponding system gateways.

Beyond the IBM propaganda, this book is intended to help readers to get to know Token Ring as an open system and as a flexible basis for the distributed data processing of the next decade. It is not meant for insiders only, but also for anyone with a certain basic knowledge who wishes to get to grips with the Token Ring network.

In addition to an overview, which is mainly contained in this chapter, the reader will learn much about Token Rings in the IBM world and also about compatible alternatives.

Whether for cabling, adaptor cards or the operation of the necessary network software, there are alternatives to IBM, which may even be cheaper, more effective or more flexible.

The reader will also learn a lot about practical aspects, which may be useful in planning, constructing and handling the system.

Of course, a book cannot be as topical as a periodical. Thus, more emphasis is placed on important infrastructural information than on transient details which the user can find out for himself if he really needs them.

One of the authors sees Token Ring and other networks primarily from a strategic perspective and each year coorganizes (with the DATACOM Congress and Seminar Department) a congress on Token Rings at which the latest facts are presented. The other author is more technically and information technology oriented and was one of the very first major users of Token Ring. He has over five years experience with this system, which experience he also brings to bear in many public seminars.

With these different perspectives, some sections of the book inevitably come down more clearly on one side than on the other. The alert reader will sometimes be able to identify a particular author. This provides for variety, which distinguishes this book from other publications and was a reason for the joint authorship.

In this chapter we first introduce the main protagonist, the Token Ring of yesterday, today and tomorrow. We then turn primarily to the infrastructural, logical and strategic problems of the further development of computer network-based information processing. Then we outline the development of the network system architectures. The chapter ends with a summary of LANs for readers with less experience of this area.

This book does not lay down the bases of data communication or LANs. For this, we recommend the books listed in the bibliography.

The subsequent chapters give a detailed description of hardware and software for Token Ring networks. The book ends with considerations of network management, planning and operation together with aspects of future development.

1.1 Token Ring: history and perspectives

The Token Ring control principle for LANs was developed as early as 1972 by von Willemjin. It has taken more than a decade for IBM to have this network ready for production. A large part of this delay can be put down to the fact that IBM did not see any urgency in forcing such a system. Indeed, for several years, Mr Willemjin was very successful in conducting patent and licence claims against IBM, which made him a rich man. He is now working with raw materials, so we cannot expect him to come up with any more radical LAN concepts.

1974 was the time when SNA began. The sole objective of SNA, the hierarchically oriented control concept for terminal subnetworks, was to systematize the interworking between terminals and transaction-oriented applications. There was no place for a LAN between hosts, communications front ends, trunk lines, cluster controllers and dumb terminals, particularly in the case of IBM's traditional clients.

At that time, IBM had previously done everything in its power to disrupt or hinder distributed data processing based on small networked computers, which was then coming to the fore, at least in research. In particular, this type of data processing was not officially supported.

Others such as DEC and Xerox had done this earlier. They developed smaller machines with the basic idea of adapting the solution to the problem rather than the problem to the host. They were soon successful, but in different areas such as scientific and technical computing and manufacturing.

The basic idea for LANs was then primarily to create a common peripheral environment for smaller computers (not PCs, which only came later!). Examples of such, then very futuristic, computers include the Altos and Dorados from Xerox. These were standalone multitasking systems with an impressive performance. The concept of the PILOT operating system, developed at that time, survives in OS/2 today. Another new development in the operating system area at that time was UNIX, which is less bound to particular computers and thus correspondingly widespread today. As part of this trend, the Ethernet LAN concept was developed at the beginning of the seventies by DEC, Intel and Xerox (the 'DIX group') and brought relatively rapidly to the stage of pilots and production readiness in the mid seventies. The original message transfer speed of around 3 Mbps of the series zero was soon raised to 10 Mbps. Today, it is said that the Ethernet concept has reached its limits. This is not because the original concept of this type of network was flawed, but rather because, with the LAN boom, the network must now satisfy requirements, in terms of numbers of stations, traffic types and overall performance, which could not have been predicted by its forebears.

When considering LAN performance, it should not be forgotten that the LAN is only a type of transport subsystem which, in the context of a network system architecture, has relatively subordinate tasks to perform. The conceptual basis of a network system architecture is fundamentally much more crucial to the final assessment of a communication-based application system solution than the LAN access algorithm.

Here too it was DEC which set completely new standards two years after IBM's announcement of SNA. The *Digital Network Architecture* (DNA) and the DECnet product line have brought communication between two peer entities (operating systems on small computers) into the foreground. Unlike control in the transaction-oriented SNA, the control of the system network is not located at a central point but is distributed across the subscribers. File transfer and program-to-program communication were quickly supplemented by network management, remote file access, network terminals and downline loading. In 1982, Phase IV of DECnet (which is still ongoing) extended the communication capabilities by including Ethernet. Thus, for the first time, a LAN was an integral component of an important network system architecture. What about OSI? This was certainly a topic at that time, although it was then much further from implementation than today and totally uninteresting commercially (except for developments of the lower layers such as X.25).

At the end of the seventies quite hardened fronts existed between purely centrally oriented data processing with SNA and relatively decentralized data processing, for example, with DECnet. There was also much support for the so-called office computers with small (usually low performance) networked systems. In the meantime, at the beginning of the eighties a device which was to revolutionize completely the whole of data processing became increasingly popular, namely the personal computer (PC). Although one might never think it, the PC was not developed by IBM either. In fact, a large number of small and medium-sized companies developed an immense variety of peculiar devices based first on 4-bit then on 8-bit microprocessors. These devices were scarcely ever compatible and contributed to the lack of uniformity amongst operating systems.

In the same way that the Beatles became socially acceptable because the Queen listened to them, the breakthrough for the PC came with its introduction by IBM. The open architecture made it possible to bring clones to the market quickly at bargain prices and the victory parade of these continuously improving devices is unstoppable, despite the many data-protection problems associated with them. Once again, a non-IBM man Bill Gates, who put together DOS (the giant among operating systems) and is now one of the richest men in the world and head of Microsoft, could rub his hands together with glee. Even though DOS certainly has major failings, this 'operating system' (actually, it is only an improved keyboard driver which has the nice ability to fetch and store data on floppy and hard disks) must certainly be credited with the fact that it was well suited to PCs for a long period. Alternatives to DOS are only now being sought, with the greatly increased performance of PCs. The outcome, if the development were to be left to IBM alone, can be seen in OS/2 Extended Edition (EE) – a tiny mainframe!

However, as far as the development and introduction of PCs is concerned, IBM still clearly sees no urgent need for action in the LAN direction. The PC is a standalone device; if it is connected to something, that something must be an SDLC line to a cluster controller. The PC may then behave like an SNA terminal.

Others have a totally different view of things. Small PC LAN schemes such as Omninet and PLAN 2000 are growing like mushrooms. The resource sharing of the DEC and Xerox experiments is realized with PCs and XTs, not with Altos and Dorados. Hard disks and laser printers are so valuable that connection to a 'real' LAN, such as Ethernet, is a worthwhile expense. The first PC LANs had message transmission rates of 1–2 Mbps on simple hardware. Network software is needed on PC networks since DOS 2.x knows nothing of networks. This gave manufacturers such as Novell (which first implemented the idea) the chance to banish the crippled DOS from server machines and replace it with a multitasking operating system optimized for access to hard disks (NetWare).

Between 1980 and 1984, the spread of LANs outside the PC area was slowed down by fears of choosing a LAN system which might not be supported later by IBM. These fears of the users were also shared by, for example, the standardization bodies, which, on the one hand, could not ignore a concept such as Ethernet which had in the meantime become an industry standard and, on the other hand, were awed by the power of IBM which could make whole international standards unusable. At the same time, IBM had not made many friends, since even its traditional clients, including banks and insurance companies, saw a requirement for action in the PC direction. In addition, increasingly elegant solutions were being released on a mixture of small multiuser systems and PCs. There were also heated debates (now totally irrelevant) about topics such as 'LANs or PBXs: which will survive?' or 'PC LANs or multiuser systems?'. History has shown what happens to companies that maintain that PCs are a 'bicycle with a motor' ('we don't build mopeds').

In 1984, together with its announcement of the PC-AT and DOS 3.x, IBM produced its first LAN. This was the (broadband) PC Network, a conglomerate of components bought from Sytek, which could be used to network together approximately 70 PCs. This is what happens when IBM makes a push forward. 2 Mbps was available for the price of an ordinary LAN. This also came with the *PC Network Program* (PCNP). Instead of removing DOS from the server, the whole file/print service was made into an application under DOS. This was disappointing as far as performance was concerned, but very pleasing to Novell. Sadly, unlike the PC LAN itself, the PCNP has survived in the form of the *PC LAN Program* (PCLANP). Multitasking on file/print server machines was only introduced with the LAN server under OS/2 EE in 1988–89. PC Cluster was another IBM system with a 300-kbps CSMA/CA algorithm, which is almost completely unknown in this country (Germany).

Finally, in 1985 (much too late for the waiting market) came the Token Ring network. Using the APPC concept (which had been developed since 1982 and was more widely publicized around 1985–86), the PC was conceptually accepted as a peer partner in an SNA network. Strategically, this is ultimately more important for the development of the LAN in the commercial application environment than Token Ring itself.

We interrupt this historical review to introduce the 1985 Token Ring. Readers to whom certain terms are unclear are referred to the LAN summary in Section 1.4.

1.1.1 The IBM Token Ring, 1985

IBM introduced the IBM Token Ring network at the end of 1985. IBM's development objective was to produce the cheapest, extensible, high-speed network with a baseband transmission technology. IBM envisaged (then as now) that this would mainly be used in the area of office communications.

The IBM Token Ring network corresponds to the ECMA and IEEE international standards for Token Ring LANs (IEEE 802.2 and 802.5). It is an open network which permits access from IBM and non-IBM devices.

Even in 1985, IBM offered hardware and software products which enabled all PCs of the IBM family (PC, PC-XT, PC-AT, 6150) to connect to Token Ring. The network software for PCs was based on the DOS operating system from version 3.2. Front-end processors of the IBM 3720/25 family, IBM 3174 cluster controllers (remote and local) and 9370 departmental computers could also be connected directly to the ring.

Here, the front-end processors (or preprocessors) and the cluster controllers or terminal controllers may take on the role of a high-speed gateway for PCs to the mainframe. A prerequisite for this is the implementation of the IBM PC 3270 emulation software on the PCs (this was only officially available in Germany from the beginning of 1987).

The IBM Token Ring network is a star-shaped ring; in other words, for reasons of security, fault tolerance and redundancy, it is formed from a number of ring-coupled stars, but logically, it behaves like a ring.

Access to the shared ring is controlled by the standardized token access procedure. Data is transmitted in a single direction within the ring. There is only one token (single-token procedure) in the ring at any given time. Each of the terminals attached to the ring regenerates the incoming signal (with interim storage of a data stream bit in each attached terminal) and forwards the data to the next station. IBM offers passive repeaters for its cable system if large distances must be traversed.

When fibre-optic cables are used, with the appropriate converters, there are practically no restrictions on distance, since the corresponding optical converters can be cascaded as necessary.

Up to 260 terminals (processors, controllers, peripheral devices) may be attached per ring. The ring transmission speed of just 4 Mbps is sufficient for office communications and similar applications.

Terminals are connected to Token Ring by *Multistation Access Units* (MSAUs). Each contains connection points for up to eight connectable terminals and forms an internal ring for these eight devices. The cables connecting the terminals to the MSAUs are generally called *lobes*.

The MSAU does not need its own power supply. Its functions, which amongst other things, ensure that terminals are automatically introduced into or removed from the ring, are activated by the attached terminals. It is either built into a 19-inch rack cabinet with other components of the IBM cable system or may be installed in a table- or wall-mounted housing

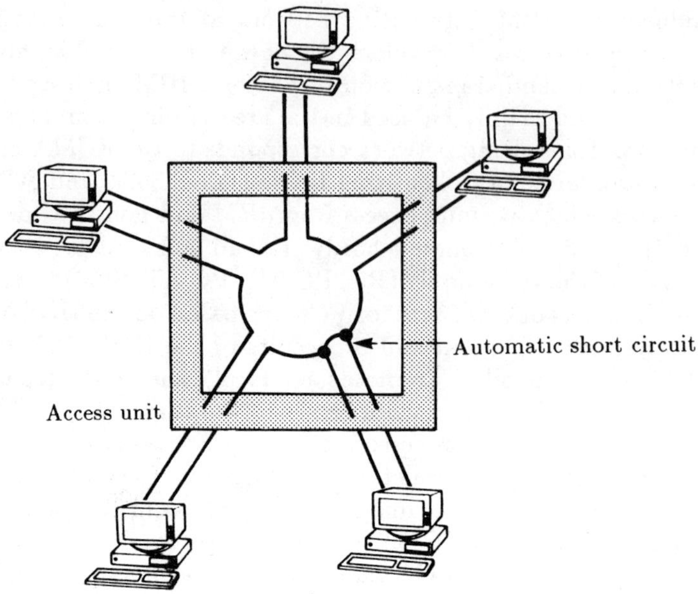

Figure 1.1 Token Ring 1985.

delivered separately by IBM.

To enlarge the network, up to 33 MSAUs may be interconnected in a ring. In this case, the output socket of one MSAU is connected to the input socket of the next MSAU. The functional description of these sockets differs from that of the terminal connection points.

When all the MSAUs are interconnected in a ring, there is an extra connection which is not necessary for operation, but which serves as a back-up line in the case of line outage.

IBM type 1 cables are used for the lobes and to connect the MSAUs. Alternatively, data cables of type 3 or 5 may be used. The maximum coverage of a ring using standard cables (type 1) is limited. In Chapter 2, we discuss cable types in more detail.

The maximum distance (around 300 m) between two MSAUs using IBM type 1 cables (screened 4-wire cables) may be increased in two ways: using fibre-optic cables with appropriate converters or using passive repeaters for the IBM type 1 cables. Both solutions are offered by IBM.

With the use of line repeaters, the maximum distance between two MSAUs increases to around 750 m. Since both the main bus and the secondary bus must be boosted and the ring line repeater only operates in one direction, four line repeaters per section are needed. If fibre-optic cables and the necessary converters are used, this distance increases to 2 km

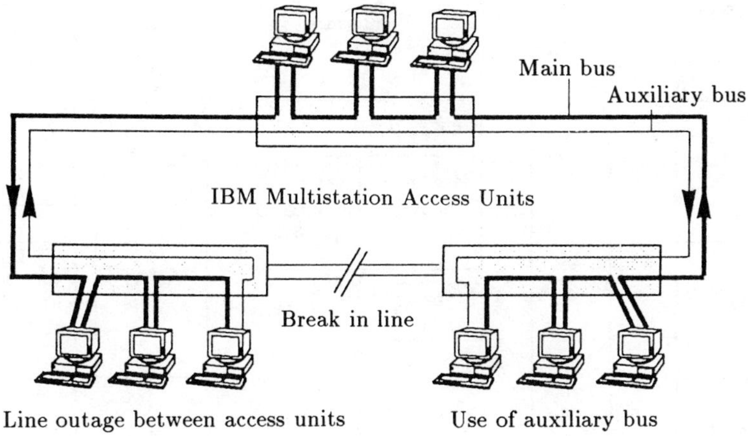

Figure 1.2 Token Ring 1985: configuration.

for IBM type 5 cables (multimode 100/140-micron fibre-optic cables). Other cables types such as the 50/125-micron cables primarily used in Europe may also be used. The fibre-optic cables are cascadable. Thus, there are no longer any theoretical restrictions on the distance between two MSAUs. Since a fibre-optic cable can cater for both the main and the secondary bus, only two fibre-optic cables are needed per section.

Since 1975, IBM has provided Token Ring network adaptor cards for access of the IBM PC family to Token Ring. The PC adaptors execute logical control according to IEEE 802.2 and support the IEEE 802.5 physical interface with a speed of 4 Mbps.

The address under which the adaptor identifies itself in the LAN is preset by the manufacturer and is unique worldwide. It may be altered by the user. On switch-on, the adaptor executes a series of test and diagnostic functions. These check the adaptor functions and the cabling to the MSAU (the lobe). The adaptor is only switched automatically into the ring once the tests have been executed. IBM provides a corresponding diagnosis program with the adaptor.

Since 1986, four user interfaces have been available for the development of application programs:

(1) Direct access

(2) Data Link Control – IEEE 802.2 (DLC)

(3) Network Basic Input/Output System (NetBios)

(4) Advanced Program-to-Program Communications Interface (APPC)

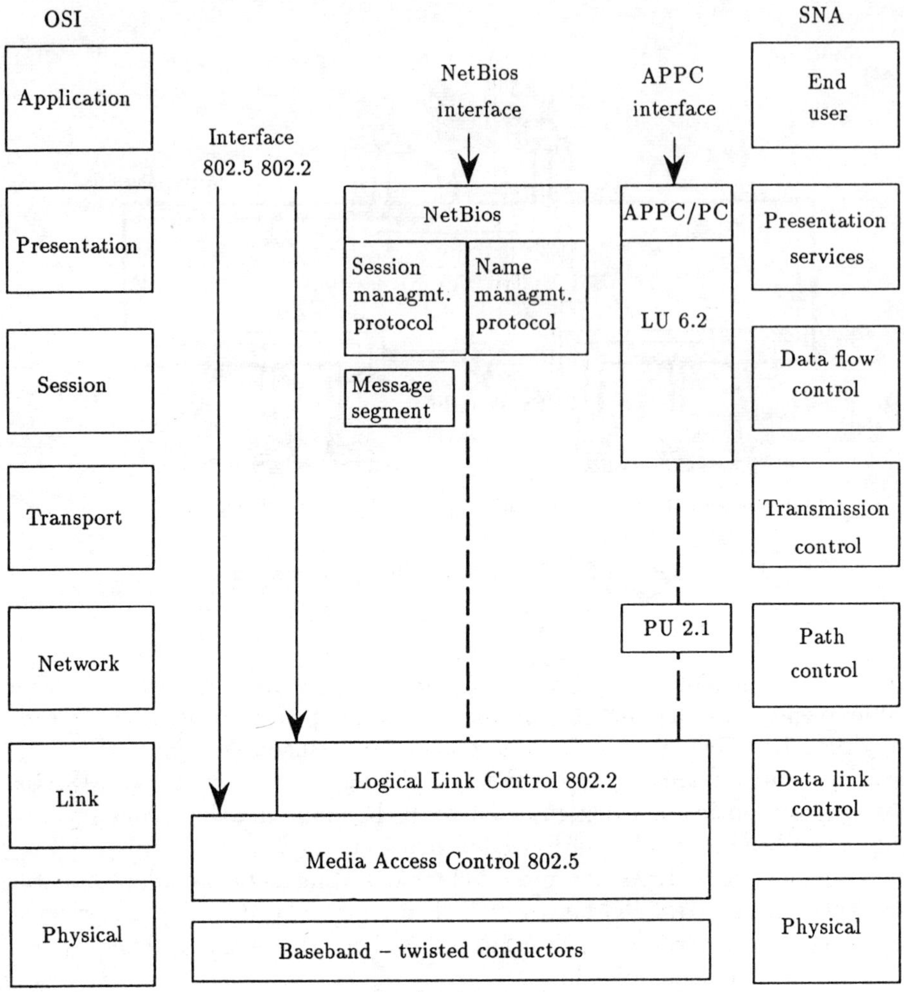

Figure 1.3 Token Ring 1985: interfaces and standards.

Interfaces 2 and 3 are mainly used by software houses as interfaces for their software products. The above interfaces may be accessed using assembler macros. These may be used or included in higher-level languages.

Since 1986, APPC and NetBios have remained standalone software products which must be separately bought and implemented. They permit the generation of device-independent programs. Figure 1.3 shows the embedding of software associated with the IBM Token Ring in the SNA architecture and the ISO reference model.

Since we shall discuss these interfaces in detail in later chapters, we bring this discussion of the 1985 Token Ring to an end.

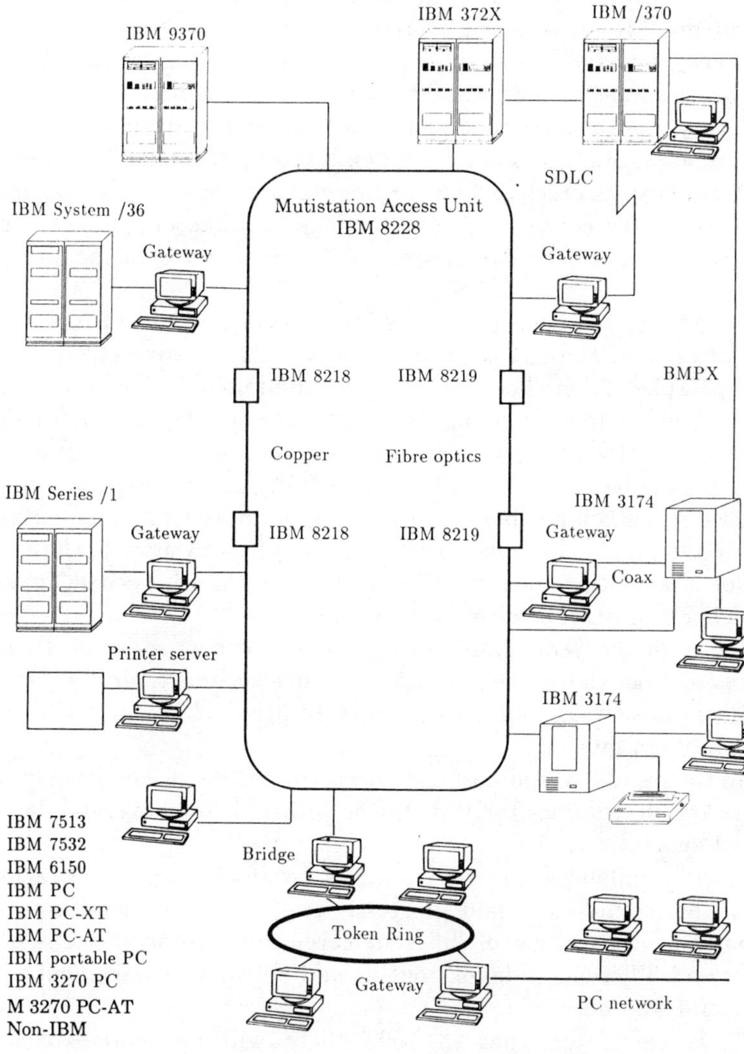

Figure 1.4 Token Ring 1985: overview.

1.1.2 The world of the IBM Token Ring today: compatibility and communication

Together with Ethernet, Token Ring is one of the most important standardized LAN schemes. When Token Ring networks were announced by IBM in 1985 and Texas Instruments (TI) introduced the first Token

Ring chip set, both companies promised programmes and efforts to secure the compatibility of future product series. In the meantime, IBM has considerably developed Token Ring and a number of other manufacturers are producing TR cards based on the TI chips. Thus, currently, there are many hardware and software differences which do not contribute directly to easing the problems of compatibility and interoperability.

Every month new connection facilities are introduced. These involve new controllers, communications front ends, host connections and bridges to Token Rings just as much as new cabling variants or network management improvements. We consider all these things in Chapter 2. Here, we wish to turn our attention to the process of token *perestroika* including IBM *glasnost.*

In 1989 there were a number of innovations for Token Ring networks. Firstly (already at the end of 1988) there was IBM's announcement of the 4/16-Mbps Token Ring. Then, the competition introduced a number of new cards which now effected the interworking between adaptor cards and PCs, not through a shared storage area or DMA, but using the bus master ring, which is particularly well suited to the MCA architecture. A number of manufacturers of compatible adaptor cards, such as Ungermann Bass and Schneider and Koch, also announced their intention to support the 16-Mbps version of Token Ring during 1990–91. This was much needed, in view of IBM's delivery problems with the new card.

Later in the year, Apple brought out the new series of TokenTalk products, so that the numerous Macs could also find their LAN home in Token Ring. Lastly, TI announced a new 16-Mbps chip which should soon be deliverable in quantity.

In the past, it was almost dangerous to consider Token Ring hardware and software alternatives to IBM. In the future, it may even be dangerous to neglect such alternatives.

Early problems with signal voltages, timing and the access algorithm can now be confidently laid to rest. The main problem area today concerns the interworking of different cards and protocol stacks in large networks and different bridging, routing and network management schemes in interconnected networks.

It is calculated that in 1992 there will be more Token Ring installations than Ethernet installations. When the new TI chip with variable data rates of 4 and 16 Mbps is available in quantity, Token Ring will be able to penetrate the world of high-performance PCs and workstations (a domain of Ethernet) at widely acceptable prices. Companies such as Sun Microsystems are today reviewing whether Ethernet is still useful and whether clients may already reasonably expect FDDI. 16-Mbps rates on shielded or unshielded twisted pairs from independent manufacturers such as Ungermann Bass or Proteon are certainly an interesting alternative. In addition to the pure IBM clients who buy Token Ring precisely because nothing else is suitable, there will soon be a new host of purchasers who have waited a long time to be able to install this robust LAN without an IBM label. Token Ring is and will remain the only simple LAN which is based on a redundant topology with a low susceptibility to interference.

However, over the last five years, it is not only the physical and logical Token Ring device environment which has changed markedly but also the background conditions (for example, through standardization under IEEE 802). IEEE 802.5 has progressed and will progress further. Internetworking, higher data rates and other transmission media (such as unshielded twisted pairs (UTPs)) serve to renew the discussion about waveforms, timing, frame structure and algorithms.

In the same way, the openness of the concept and its standardization are increasingly turning Token Ring into an intercompany campaign.

However, it should be said that nowadays the use of non-IBM equipment in Token Rings is not an adventure with an imponderable outcome. Product interworking is largely achievable. IBM's current market share of 80% of Token Ring cards will certainly not last long. Other alternatives are now available, particularly for cabling.

1.1.2.1 The IEEE 802.5 standard

The development of Token Ring networks by IBM and TI dates back to the early eighties. IEEE 802 work on this topic began around 1982. In 1985, the main elements of the 802.5 access procedure were laid down in a Blue Book. This document contains a description of the MAC frames for connection establishment and connection execution but not necessarily for control and management of the ring. Since 1985, IEEE has released a series of amendments and extensions of the standard.

As always, 802.5 leaves great freedom of interpretation as far as implementation of the functions is concerned. However, there have been few problems with this in the past, since two other documents were used for consultation prior to standardization, namely the IBM Token Ring Network Architecture Reference and the user's guide for the TI Token Ring chip set.

Currently, the standard refers to transmission speeds of 4 and 16 Mbps although there were other speeds in the past. The standard is an abstraction which leaves much freedom for the design itself (for example, the bit order of Token Ring addresses at different interfaces). Such problems are well known from the Ethernet area, where they have been satisfactorily solved, despite a large number of manufacturers.

The call for a manufacture-independent forum to secure the compatibility of Token Ring products and for controlled and deliberate distribution of technical information to guarantee the openness of the Token Ring concept was only heard in 1988, when it led to the foundation of the *Open Token Foundation* (OTF). The goal of the OTF is not to define standards but to act as a common mouthpiece for the manufacturers in dialogue with the standardization bodies.

ANSI/IEEE Standard 802.5 (1985) was extended by a Common Reference Document (1988) with:

- A. Station management. Defines 16 management MAC frames.
- E. Management entity specification. Defines link to 802.1 management.
- F. 4/16 Mbps operation. Defines physical layer for 16 Mbps.
- H. LLC III support. Defines LLC III.
- I. Early token release. Defines early token release.

Other IEEE drafts concern:

- B. Voice-grade media attributes. Defines use of telephone cables.
- C. Reconfiguration. Defines two rings with opposite directions.
- D. Multiple ring networks. Defines source routing.
- G. Conformance testing. Defines appropriate tests.
- J. Fibre optics. Defines fibre-optic cables.
- K. Token Ring media. Defines unshielded/shielded twisted pair media.

Figure 1.5 IEEE 802.5.

The combination of a stronger organization of the manufacturers in the OTF and the ongoing work of the IEEE bodies should guarantee that open Token Ring technology meets the highest expectations of the users.

1.1.2.2 Communication and coexistence

For a better understanding of the characteristics of Token Ring networks based on technologies from different manufacturers, one should be aware that there are at least two types of interworking between components (mainly adaptor cards and devices) of Token Ring networks: coexistence and communication.

Communication between two devices in Token Ring means the meaningful exchange of data between applications. For this, both nodes must involve similar implementations of all the layers of the ISO/OSI reference model and, in particular, must use the same protocol software (NetBios, TCP/IP, XNS, NetWare, etc.). However, the nodes may have different hardware and software implementations.

Coexistence on the other hand means only that the nodes can exchange control information without interfering with each other. For coexistence, they require (for example) the same MAC layer, but certainly not the same higher protocol layers. For coexistence, a node must be capable of deciding which packets it must simply let pass and which it should

Table 1.1 Token Ring elements affecting coexistence and communication.

Token Ring element	*Must be the same for:*	
	Coexistence	*Communication*
Physical layer signals	yes	yes
MAC functions and frame formats	yes	yes
Address and network management	yes	yes
Source routing header filter	yes	yes
LLC SAP address filter	yes	yes
LLC type (1, 2 or 3)	no	yes
Protocols, layers 3–7	no	yes
Interface between adaptors and PC	no	no
PC processors (80XXX, 68XXX, ...)	no	no
Computer type	no	no
Manufacturer of computer and adaptor cards	no	no
Adaptor card chip sets	no	no

process. At this level it is most important to have standards for device addressing.

When a node without proper coexistence capabilities is attached to the ring, it may interfere with the operation of the ring or even hinder initialization of the ring.

The extensively documented TI chips should ensure that all Token Ring products are able to coexist, provided that there are no absolute barriers to this (for example, very different transmission speeds). It is up to the manufacturer of the communications software for the higher layers to provide for communications based on coexistence. TI's experience over the last five years has shown that the main problems are associated with protocols and applications and with simpler components such as plugs and cables.

As far as the authorities are concerned, IEEE is responsible for coexistence questions and OTF for coexistence and communication. In the past, much work has gone into ensuring robust communication based on Token Ring. The main starting points for this are flexible protocol stacks with independent device (adaptor) drivers, such as those produced by Microsoft, 3Com and Novell. A universal protocol stack, such as that produced by Schneider and Koch for Ethernet, would not go amiss.

At the moment, the emphasis is on the bridging problem, which has not really been satisfactorily solved. Since IBM stubbornly persists with source routing, there is no alternative other than to look for the coexistence of spanning trees and source routing on Token Rings. Since the standardization authorities are still looking for this (and may only use what they find with reservations, which does not please IBM) all the manufacturers are attempting to come up with their own solutions which they are presenting to the authorities.

Source routing involves routing decisions in the nodes, not in the bridges. Thus, cases in which there is some doubt may require the transmission of a number of search packets which locate the desired node and return to the sender via the intermediate bridges and subnetworks. These packets record where they have been and this information provides the route. Major problems with this include the flooding of the subnetworks with redundant search packets and the inability of the process to cope with changes which occur between the receipt of the relevant routing packet and the transmission of the message itself.

The spanning tree refers to the organization of the network into a tree of subnetworks which are again trees. Each device (terminal) corresponds to a leaf. The bridges adapt to this organization which may be dynamically extended at any time. Here, routing decisions are made in the bridges. The terminals have nothing to do with routing; the bridges are transparent to them and every station in a remote subnetwork appears as if it were in the local segment or subnetwork.

The source routing algorithm is essentially simple and very stable. If we assume the statistical fact that most of the traffic remains in the local subnetwork anyway, we can live with this algorithm. However, IBM, in particular, in the framework of, for example, SAA, envisages a very close cooperation between devices in different networks, namely PSs as workstations and, for example, /370s as hosts, and is essentially basing the SNA hierarchy on a hierarchy of rings. A tree-oriented algorithm could be useful here. The argument for simply retaining the bridges no longer holds water, since even IBM's bridges are at least PS systems. The discussion on routing procedures also involves another dimension, namely the topic of smart and relatively unintelligent adaptor cards.

1.1.2.3 Interoperability problems

In general, interoperability problems may be divided into four classes: problems associated with frame formats; problems associated with protocol stacks and interfaces; problems associated with physical links; and bridging/routing problems.

The Token Ring frame format begins with the MAC header which contains the source and destination addresses. Unlike Ethernet, the 802.5 Token Ring defines a routing information field to support target-directed transmission of data frames over source routing bridges. This is followed by

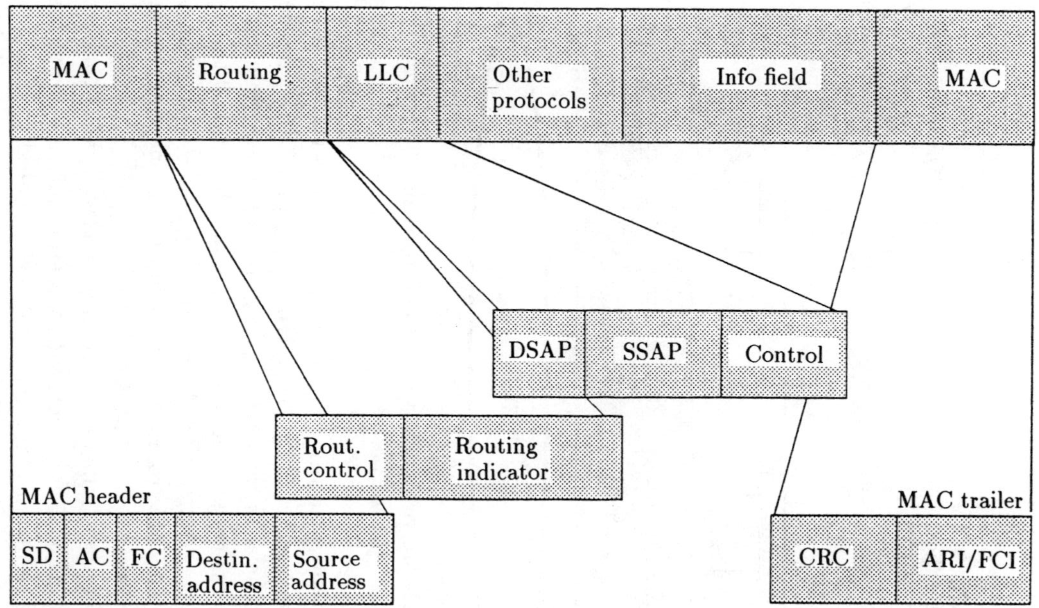

AC	=	Access Control	ARI/FCI	=	Address Recognized Indicator/Frame Copied Indicator
CRC	=	Cyclic Redundancy Check	FC	=	Frame Control
DSAP	=	Destin. Service Access Point	SD	=	Start Delimiter
SSAP	=	Source Service Access Point	MAC	=	Media Access Control

Figure 1.6 Token Ring frame format. IEEE 802.5.

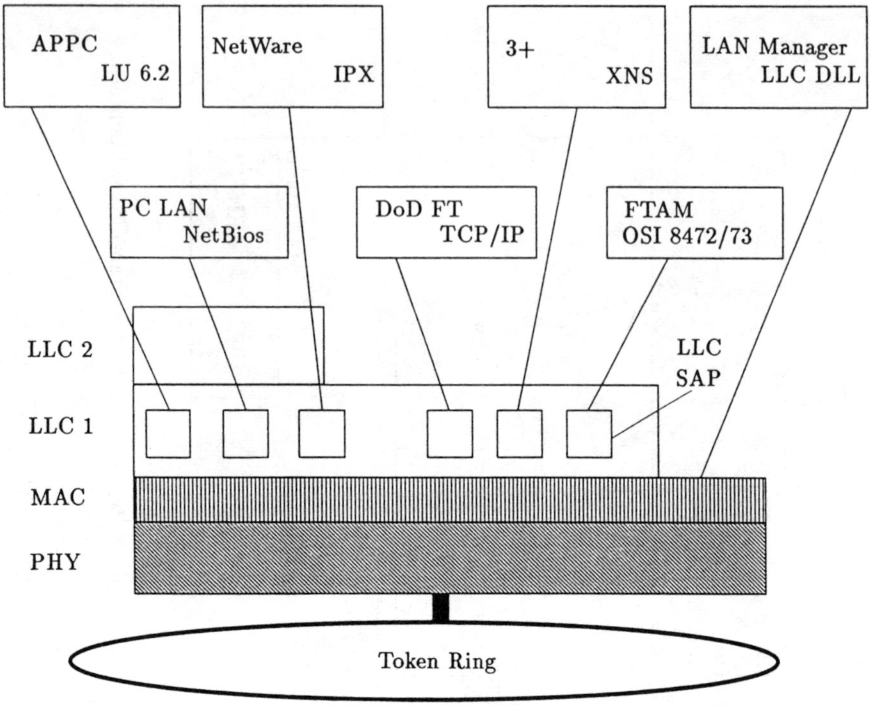

Figure 1.7 LLC service access points. Coexistence of different protocols.

the LLC header for logical link control, as described in the 802.2 standard. Other protocols such as TCP/IP or NetBios may insert their headers after the LLC header. The user data itself (sometimes packed with higher-layer headers and trailers) follows next, while the whole ends with the MAC trailer. For effective coexistence, MAC, routing and LLC fields must be correctly interpreted and processed by all nodes on the ring. In addition, communication requires similar protocol stacks.

Interworking questions arise not only within Token Rings, but also between Token Rings and Ethernet. Since, historically, Ethernet first came into use as a LAN solution, many protocols are oriented to its conventions. Unfortunately, for example, the ordering of address bits in Token Rings differs from that in Ethernet. This leads to a number of problems.

In order to further guarantee the already very stable way in which the Token Ring protocol works, IBM decided to use an LLC based on IEEE 802.2. In so doing, they did not choose one of the simpler alternatives, but went directly for the user-friendly type 2 LLC, with protected logical links, sliding window mechanisms and reception-confirmation signals. The quality of the protected logical links and the algorithm execution is comparable with HDLC or SDLC. Every data frame is given a sequence number, which guarantees the correct sequencing of packets on the logical link and permits a corresponding acknowledgement mechanism. Moreover, should packets be destroyed, new ones are automatically requested without involving higher layers.

When the original Token Ring components came on to the market in 1985, LLC was not very commonly used, in particular, because the old versions of Ethernet (V1 and V2) did not provide for it. Today, with 802.3 networks, things are very different.

According to the guidelines of the ISO/OSI reference model, the LLC is a proper sublayer of layer 2.

Thus, access is provided by a number of *Service Access Points* (SAPs). The existence of SAPs is actually a big advantage. They may be used to provide different protocol stacks with quasi-simultaneous access to an LLC implementation. Thus, completely different message flows may coexist on a single physical medium. A prerequisite for this is the entry of the correct SAP address in the corresponding field of the LLC header. When Token Ring nodes are able to use different protocol software, every node inspects the LLC Destination SAP field (DSAP) to decide whether the packet on hand can be processed by the current protocol stack. If this is not the case, the packet is ignored.

The development of Token Ring shows that the latter is becoming an open, manufacture-independent concept and is on the threshold of a breakthrough. In Chapter 3, we shall discuss hardware and software viewpoints together with criteria for evaluating alternative adaptor cards.

1.1.3 The future of Token Ring: high-speed LANs

At this point, we move away from the further development of the network system architecture (we pick this up again in Section 1.3) and concern ourselves primarily with future technological developments. It has long been clear that the network of the future will be a network of networks. It is also clear that we are not talking about a single network type with a fixed speed, but that there will be relatively low-speed, low-cost networks in the terminal area and that these networks will be connected (if necessary via an intermediate step) to a so-called backbone network.

This backbone network will then implement the links between the distribution points formed by the subLANs. In addition, it will serve very powerful devices such as hosts or special peripheral devices directly. Within the next ten years, comparatively low-cost networks with a rate of 1 Gbps or over will be developed and installed. The technology for this will be fully based on fibre optics. We can expect that, with the latest successes in information processing using purely optical signals, many of the intermediate steps now required for conversion between electrical and optical signals in the context of the forwarding of message streams will become obsolete.

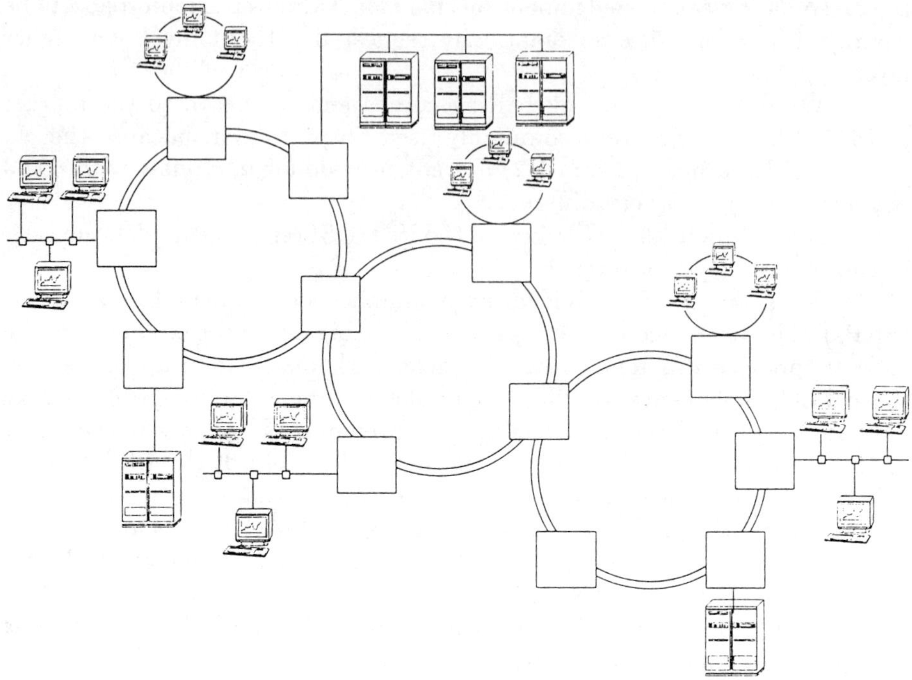

Figure 1.8 FDDI as backbone.

However, we do not need to advertise future developments, since there already exists one concept which clearly characterizes the further development of Token Ring, namely FDDI.

The *Fibre-Distributed Data Interface* (FDDI) is an ANSI standard proposal for a 100-Mbps Token Ring. The FDDI protocol is one of the few access methods which is specially designed for a high bandwidth and the use of a fibre-optic system. At the same time, FDDI is currently the only standard proposal for a fast LAN; thus, it is very interesting.

With a maximum length of 100–200 km, the FDDI ring is designed to serve up to 500–1000 stations at distances up to 2 km apart. Thus, it is offered as a backbone network.

For reliability, twin fibre-optic cables are used; 100/400-, 62.5/125- and 85/125-micron fibres are proposed. The wavelength is specified as around 1300 nm. There are ongoing discussions as to whether it would be expedient to use monomode fibres. When ANSI standardization began, this technology was almost prohibitively expensive; however, nowadays, after considerable improvements and simplifications and since it is preferred by postal administrations worldwide, it has become relatively reasonable.

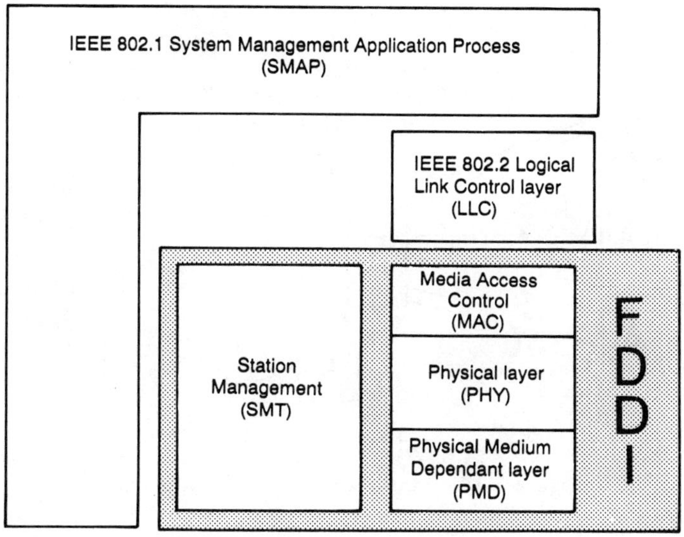

Figure 1.9 FDDI protocol structure.

To overcome line errors, FDDI provides for a network consisting of two rings, a primary ring and a secondary ring, running in opposite directions. The secondary ring will usually be operated purely as a back-up ring. However, ANSI does not rule out using it to increase capacity.

The topology is largely similar to that of Token Ring. There are stations with two or four connections for fibre-optic cables. Stations with four connections are attached directly to the twin fibre-optic ring (class A). For stations with two connections (class B), there is a concentrator (class C) which is attached to the main ring and can undertake back-up functions as a type of multistation access unit.

The A stations and the C concentrators have an intelligent component, the *station manager* (STM). This is able to detect line errors between A and C stations and on the lines to B stations. Errors of the first type are removed using the secondary ring in a self-healing mode. Errors of the second type lead to an outage of the B station and are overcome within the C concentrator.

The FDDI access protocol corresponds largely to the IEEE 802.5 Token Ring protocol. However, there is a basic difference in the way free tokens are generated by the sending station at the end of an emission. In FDDI, a station issues a free token directly to the ring after sending the last data packet within a maximum send duration, while in IEEE 802.5, the free token is only allowed on to the ring once the (single) data packet returns

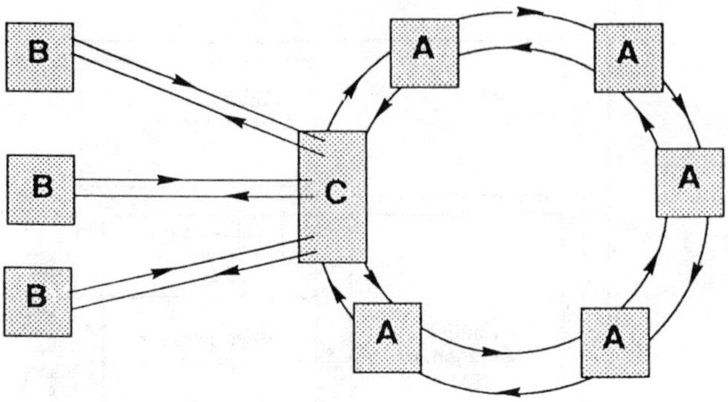

Figure 1.10 Stations of classes A, B and C.

to the sending station. FDDI allows several Token Ring packets to be sent within a single-token possession. IEEE 802.5 only allows a single packet to be sent.

FDDI permits synchronous traffic with higher priorities and asynchronous traffic with lower priorities. Nothing prevents a station from increasing the priority of synchronous traffic. This type of token protocol improves the loading of the medium and to some extent simplifies the electronic control of the interfaces.

The FDDI protocol contains various mechanisms to increase reliability. Unlike other Token Rings, controls and reconfiguration mechanisms are implemented in distributed form. Thus, a monitor becomes superfluous.

Although the standardization is not yet complete, a number of manufacturers already provide FDDI, including Network Systems, Fibronics, Ascom, BICC and Schneider and Koch. Almost all provide connector boxes which permit the connection of Token Ring LANs (for example, Ascom, Fibronics) and Ethernet LANs (for example, Ascom, Fibronics, BICC, etc.) to FDDI.

Thus, FDDI becomes the backbone ring for the attached subLANs. Direct access is primarily reserved for mainframes (IBM /370, CDC, etc.), since class A interfaces are still relatively expensive. Direct FDDI interfaces are also provided for PCs on an individual basis; however, while the price is substantially more than 5000 DM there will not be a great market take-up. Because the standardization is incomplete, the connector boxes for the FDDI ring are not mutually compatible. Moreover, with FDDI, Token Rings can in general only be coupled with other Token Ring networks, since it is not yet possible to access other terminals on others LANs via FDDI (for example, Ethernet).

Thus, FDDI networks will never be a threat to the IBM Token Ring; instead, they provide an ideal supplement as far as high-speed coupling of several LANs and mainframes over large distances using public networks (for example, the VBN network of the German Bundespost) is concerned. In the future, they will have to compete with the 802.6 networks of the postal administrations, which will operate with a different protocol, the *Distributed Queue Double Bus* (DQDB).

A central network management is a *sine qua non* of FDDI networks, since the LAN usually stretches over several buildings, and fast error location and the detection of bottle-necks can only be achieved using management tools. This aspect of FDDI still requires some development. Tying in to well-known network management systems such as IBM's NetView would be desirable.

1.2 Communications technology in distributed data processing

The development of data processing over the last decade has been characterized by a major rethink. With the spread of PCs, the dependence on mainframes as the single source of computing power has decreased. An increasing number of manufacturing tasks could be relocated to these new small systems.

PCs have also, slowly but surely, threatened the so-called office computers. It now takes us some time even to remember which machines were used as office computers.

Fortunately, the onward march of the PC on a broad basis took so long that the, to some extent, unjustified euphoria about total decentralization could give way to an objective discussion of the general problem.

Today, only one thing may be assumed with great certainty, namely that efficient networking of all the components of information-processing processes within a company or a organization, from PCs to mainframes, is the only way of getting to grips with the chaos which is now typical in some subareas.

In this section, we discuss the general problem in further detail and indicate a general route to a solution. This route essentially marks the most important long-term strategic reason for the use of LANs such as Token Rings.

Of course, other high-performance networks may be used, but they are not the main topic of this book. The most important instruments are not the LAN subsystems, but the manufacture-provided network system architectures and the possibilities for their further development.

As a guide to the strategic aspects, we recommend the book by Boell (1989).

1.2.1 Basic problems in modern data processing

At the beginning of the PC craze, many people, including experts, were fully convinced that decentralization could go so far that mainframes or computer centres might be completely dispensed with. This turned out to be a fallacy. On the one hand, there are many applications where a mainframe is still required for the processing; on the other hand, the use of PCs involves completely new problems (for example, relating to data protection, the securing of the processing integrity, the securing of data consistency, etc.), which, with the present state of knowledge, depending on their magnitude, can only be overcome using mainframes.

We have even had to learn that as the capabilities of PCs increase the additional problems do not on the whole decrease but even increase. This is not because of the devices themselves but because of the people who ultimately have to use them. The ability of the user to learn cannot keep pace with the rate of technical development.

Here is an example. The latest processor generation for PCs is the 80486. A computer with this processor has a performance approximating that of a mainframe in the early 1970s. At this point, we are not interested in the performance scale.

The immediate question is whether the owner/user of such a PC 486 has the same knowledge as the operator/planner of the mainframe 15–2 years ago. Statistically speaking, this can scarcely be so, particularly if the 486 follows its predecessors the 8086s, 80286s and 80386s into the masses.

The next question is whether the owner/user actually needs this knowledge to make responsible and sensible use of the 486. This is similar to the question whether one needs to be a car mechanic or a racing driver to drive a car.

Pursuing this analogue brings us nearer to an answer. Clearly, there is a popular belief that one should be able to drive a car without great knowledge. It is assumed firstly that the servicing and maintenance of cars is increasingly simplified (the term foolproof is often used, but this is a term which does not belong in the vocabulary of the PC world) and secondly that there are mandatory road-safety regulations which apply to all traffic. However, the following are immediately clear:

- The ergonomics depends on the vehicle and on its effect on the particular user of the vehicle.
- The regulations are not always conclusive in all situations; there may be misunderstandings.

- The collective accepts a risk in permitting a relatively high individuality. This residual risk leads to regular harm to individual members of the collective, including at times death. Those harmed are not necessarily the same people as those responsible for the harm.
- For various reasons (negligently or deliberately) individuals may choose not to accept the traffic regulations. The expense of monitoring the adherence to the regulations is high and total control cannot be guaranteed.
- The formulation of the regulations is subject to the constraint that the latter should appear just to the collective, since otherwise the acceptance of new regulations will be poor. This leads to regulations which are not based on purely logical or scientific findings.
- Thus, views of regulations are very controversial.

The list could be continued further, and the reader may wish to think up other examples.

The question which follows from this analogy is whether the large-scale introduction of a high technology must necessarily lead to such a list of risks (data protection, data security, processing integrity, hackers, viruses, damage to the information processing due to stupidity, negligence, dissatisfaction, etc.) or whether these can be countered by experience.

Here, the discussion often goes off in a direction which leads one to fear a flare up of so-called neo-Taylorism. In fact, the problems associated with decentralized data processing do not arise when thousands of PCs lie around switched off, but when thousands of individuals work on these PCs.

From experience of regulations in other contexts, and from experience of data-processing rules, most of those currently responsible are aware that regulations (for example, judicial) cannot contribute greatly to ensuring the integrity of large-scale data processing. There are many reasons for this. One serious reason is that the overall development of data processing is far too fast for those who formulate the regulations (whether an international or national legislature or a company-internal system manager who is likely to react more rapidly) to react appropriately.

We must remember one thing. If the car industry had made the same progress as data processing, cars would seat a hundred people, and a tank full of petrol would get one to the moon and back for a cost of around 20 DM. Traffic regulations could never have kept up with such a pace of development.

The focal point of this analogy with cars is the search for a new and sensible balance between individuality and collective necessity.

Such a balance can also be important in data processing. To what extent are collective regulations needed for the achievement of company information-processing targets and to what extent can individuality be supported?

Another question follows immediately. Is individuality in information processing in itself an urgent matter of concern to users or would they prefer a more reliable and more user-friendly system at the price (scarcely visible) of restrictions on their individuality? Even in the 'good life' there must be people who prefer to travel by train rather than leave themselves open to carelessness (their own and that of others) on the motorway.

On the other hand, the alternatives only arise if the technical facilities to balance control and individuality are provided *en masse*.

Thus, another component now comes into play, namely the communications network. Here, the technical aspects are less interesting than the logical ones, since the data processing (whether centralized or decentralized) is based on a set of processes which cooperate to a greater or lesser extent. Thus, from the perspective of use of networks with ever-improved reactions, it is increasingly unimportant whether these processes are implemented on a single computer or on several machines.

The diversity of communications networks corresponds to their possible uses. What happens if the communications network becomes so large and so diverse that an individual person or a small group can no longer obtain an overview of the network and its components? What happens when errors occur which involve combinations of logical and technological elements? How can one master the historically developed heterogeneity? How can the data network be (or be made) secure?

The keyword 'network management' springs immediately to mind. Network management is an example of a subarea of information processing to which little attention was paid until very recently. Only the occurrence of major problems, only the rampant heterogeneous growth of communications networks, only the threat to national security interests from hackers have contributed to forcing the manufacturers of computers, PCs and networks to think about possible solutions beyond a simple monitoring of the technical network and to develop solution strategies, albeit very late. The first half of this book is concerned with these strategies.

The perfidy of the current situation is altogether clear when one thinks of the international standardization of communications networks (keyword: 'ISO/OSI reference model'). Many years after the proposal of a framework for the gradual implementation of application-oriented functions, the authorities realized that network management had been forgotten. Thus, although it is now possible to exchange electronic mail worldwide via X.400 through very different networks involving tens of thousands of stations, the control of the overall system is seen more as a chance favour from God for which we shall have to wait until the mid nineties. This situation will continue until the international standards for OSI management are ready and the first product implementations are ready to go into production. This tendency to relate management to existing application services may be asking for trouble.

The large manufacturers such as IBM and DEC, who are otherwise scarcely lazy in their development of far-reaching strategies, also reacted at a comparatively late stage and, what is more, almost precisely in harmony with the average number of installed devices in their client networks. These manufacturers were primarily concerned about the functioning of their own devices in the network and gave secondary consideration to heterogeneity. Even the OSI-oriented proposals (for example) of DEC and AT&T do not necessarily imply an interworking of the relevant management components.

Two questions now arise. How can I best control my network and where should I be going in the future? As far as control of the existing network is concerned, there will usually be few (if any) alternatives. Thus, the conceptual choice is limited. Questions about the future are more interesting. In this book, we attempt to formulate answers for the small but perspective area of Token Ring LANs.

1.2.2 Distributed data processing

Here, as in the section on the history of Token Rings (Section 1.1), it is clear that we are currently at a point of radical change. We have learnt that purely central data processing is no longer sensible in all cases. We have learnt that we can do a lot with PCs and PC LANs, but not everything. Finally, we have unfortunately had to learn that the uncontrolled use of hosts of PCs in the long term creates more problems than it solves.

The solution currently favoured brings together the worlds of purely central and purely decentralized data processing. This is called *distributed data processing.*

Central data processing (DP) forms the basis. Initially, there was only one computer to which one could allocate jobs. The next steps in the development involved multiuser operation with punched cards (batch) and multiuser time sharing via terminals, for which terminal and data-communication networks were required.

A modern computer centre usually has several computers which may be networked together. In addition, there are communications front-ends and cluster controllers which control local or remote terminals. However, the organizational structure is still central with trained operators.

After more than 30 years of commercial use of central DP facilities a large amount of specialized knowledge of hardware and software questions is available. Normally, computer centres employ staff who help users to solve their problems, assist in troubleshooting and advise users on the choice of the necessary software. Hardware and software interfaces are documented and centrally managed.

A variety of centrally managed software is available, covering a broad spectrum of applications. There is now scarcely any area of industry, commerce or management for which off-the-shelf programs or program packages for use on large DP systems do not exist.

Once generated, thanks to standards for data-recording formats, and data media, data can easily be transferred to other systems. Changes of system do not usually affect user data and programs.

Central data management and storage provides for data integrity and data security both against loss due to hardware or software problems and against theft or malicious destruction. The high processor performance and large memory capacity of today's installations scarcely (if at all) restrict a user's freedom to lay out and dimension the data to which he has access.

A high degree of standardization within a specific system environment ensures that application tools can also be intermixed. New developments may be evaluated and remain usable when one changes to a new model from the same manufacturer. Once made, investments are protected. Expensive conversion work is no longer necessary.

The interfaces for data terminals are well known. The corresponding devices from the manufacturers may be integrated without problems. Terminals may be centrally monitored for errors. Error location and removal may be carried out quickly and specifically by trained staff. The end user does not require a knowledge of data communications.

For cost reasons, the available standard software is aimed at a large user group. In many cases, individual solutions do not exist or are very expensive. It is often very difficult (and sometimes impossible) to adapt the standard software to specific problems. There is a tendency to adapt the problems to the software.

Thus, from the user's point of view the organization is not always flexible enough. Often, only the manufacturer's terminals or compatible devices can be connected. Other devices, if they can be connected at all, require additional hardware and/or software which in many cases makes it uneconomic to connect them.

There are now as many wide-ranging software products available for PCs as for all other DP systems together.

PC user interfaces provide a good example of this. The use of menus and windows has become natural. User-friendly help functions support the user in all situations and provide as much support as requested.

The rapid and, to some extent, uncontrolled development of the PC area means that the user may be faced with large problems when it comes to compatibility and portability.

The main problem of standalone PCs is their lack of integration in various directions. This involves integration into the working process just as much as integration into the overall concept of DP technology.

Often, there are also problems for which the PC can do nothing. For example, pure jealousy may lead a worker to dream up his own improvements to a word-processing system used by a colleague. Of course, he dreams up these improvements over a beer or with the help of his own technically aware offspring whom he also asks for instructions to save photocopying the manual. The fact that he is on shaky ground here is of as much concern to him as speeding in a built-up area.

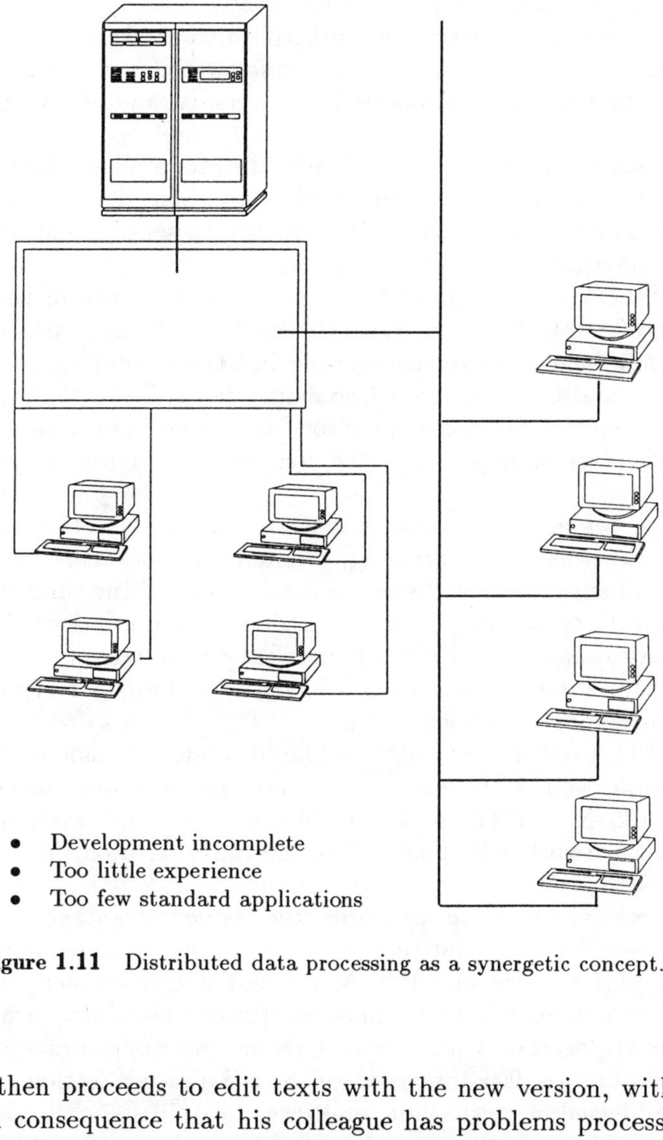

Figure 1.11 Distributed data processing as a synergetic concept.

He then proceeds to edit texts with the new version, with the not unintended consequence that his colleague has problems processing these texts. His colleague either says nothing because he is ashamed of his supposed incompetence or goes straight to the company's DP consultant. The latter is particularly happy to have to explain the manual to yet another simpleton. The idea that a totally different version of the software might be involved does not immediately come to mind, since recently the consultant has, by agreement with the management and without consulting the DP specialists (in that order), authorized use of a particular version.

Finally, after information has been collected from throughout the company, it becomes apparent that a number of documents have been written with an idiosyncratic version. The perpetrator remains undetected and is able to delete the stolen software at any time.

This was just a simplified, slightly fanciful example of a common case of misuse that is facilitated by some software houses which frequently pay scant attention to the compatibility of versions and of standard formats once defined.

In many respects, PC freaks live in the Stone Age of data processing, which equates with data chaos on diskettes and hard disks, lack of software maintenance and in certain circumstances the presence of multiple versions of a single program.

With LANs, networked PCs could remove many of the problems associated with standalone PCs. To the user the PC LAN usually looks at first like a new logical device; for example, in DOS, in addition to his physical drives A:, B: and C:, a user may also define drives E:, ... K:, provided disk space and access rights are defined for him on an appropriate file server. Another standard application is the sharing of a high-quality printer by several users.

Boot servers for remote starts of (diskless) workstations, batch servers for time-deferred processing, communications servers and gateways together with application software packages round off the current spectrum.

Network operating programs supplement the PC operating systems with network capabilities. Unfortunately, they all too often refer to existing bottle-necks in the operating systems and the performance of the PC LAN is thus considerably degraded.

A PC LAN is only worthwhile if there are adequate facilities for communication with other computers; for example, using terminal emulation (327X, VT100) or a general communication system such as a public trunk network with a subscriber interface based on the X.25 CCITT recommendation.

Superminis have in principle the same advantages as PCs. In addition, they have a relatively high computing and memory capacity (usually a performance of 10–40 MIPS and a disk capacity of between 200 Mbytes and 20 Gbytes) and a multiuser capability (usually 16–64 workstations) together with (depending on the operating system used) schemes to improve data integrity and better data protection mechanisms (which are needed because of the multiuser capability).

Everything smaller, covering, for example, 3–16 workstations, is basically a PC with an 80386, 80486 or 68030 processor.

The processors used are almost exclusively 32-bit or 64-bit microprocessors. Above all, the new Intel 80860 (i860) 64-bit RISC chip has good prospects. The best-known systems are based on in-house developments by large DP manufacturers (IBM with the System 6150 and /6000, DEC with the microVAX, Sun and Apollo (Siemens) with workstation concepts, etc.) or on Motorola or Intel processors. These are now a serious alternative to networked PCs, although in 1987, more LANs than minis were sold worldwide.

Here too there is a lack of standardization in the hardware and software areas. UNIX, with massive support from interest groups such as X/Open, POSIX and OSF (Open Software Foundation), has become a *de facto* standard. But who has not heard of the problems with the various different UNIX derivatives? Moreover, UNIX systems do not have the variety of application software which we find on PCs. However, the more one thinks about distributed systems, the more important UNIX and AIX become.

The software costs of compilers and application-program systems are also relatively high. When UNIX is used, one must be clear that it is a 'proper' operating system which makes totally different demands on the user as far as generation, maintenance and extensions are concerned. This is also unreservedly true of OS/2, as experience with this operating system has shown.

The solution of many problems lies in the mixed use of both DP worlds: of decentralized DP with PCs, PC LANs or minis and central DP using a mainframe (for example) in the computer centre.

The more diverse the applications, the greater the possibilities for distributing the computing capacity.

In addition, various DP solutions will coexist in large companies and heterogeneous work environments such as research institutes. The integration of these is a major task.

The network may contain or be linked into a high-performance processor so that the advantages of central DP, as far as the provision of software, and data and program upkeep are concerned, can be used to good effect. Tasks which require so high a performance that decentralized execution is not possible are executed on the central processor. Programs for use on several PCs or minis are developed and tested centrally and then installed simultaneously on all decentralized systems. This is also advantageous and important if changes are required, since only this procedure can guarantee that all central and decentralized systems within a company always use the same software level. The central development of standard and communications software makes for good use of all resources including the facilities of the data network and avoids duplicated development. Individual users are now no longer responsible for the further development of a standard product, which responsibility passes to the centre.

By appropriate development of application software with separate modules on the PC and the host the traffic on the network can be minimized and the performance increased.

The use of many different and expensive terminals, such as high-performance plotters or fast laser printers, which are jointly available to all attached terminals and PCs (device sharing) is simplified. Access to public networks and services is now implemented in a central or decentralized form according to which solution is more economic.

The most important and most advantageous thing about this solution is the improved use of all available data. Shared data is held in the central DP system, while specialized data resides on the corresponding decentralized computers. Data and information requiring protection may be managed and archived centrally while their processing may be decentralized.

A central security mechanism covering decentralized data is possible. The end user no longer needs to worry about his own archives in which his back-up copies are kept, but may now leave this to the computer centre, thus saving himself time and passing on his responsibility.

By relocating PC disk drives and loading software and data remotely, one can effectively counter the most important source of mischief. Wild software versions and the theft of data are ruled out on a large scale. Imagine that you have access to a file which you should not have been permitted to read. If you have access to a PC disk drive, you could simply copy the file and take it home with you. However, if you only have read access, your recall capability will decrease 1000–2000 bytes according to the nature of the information. Technical drawings, for example, can only rarely be removed from the company in this way, since too many details of them become blurred by the memory process.

At present there is very little practical experience of how the common use of PCs, minis and mainframes in large networks with diverse requirements as far as the distribution of tasks is concerned has stood the test of time. For distributed DP to be sensible and effective in the long term, two important basic conditions must be satisfied:

(1) The responsibility for software must be clearly defined. Data security and data transparency can only be guaranteed if this is the case.

(2) There must be a facility for central monitoring and control of the network, including all components. (If such a facility does not exist, it should be striven for as an objective.)

The network system architectures supplied by the manufacturers, together with the associated products, play a particularly important role in the implementation of distributed system solutions. We shall discuss this shortly.

When taking decisions in the information-processing framework, there are two basic points of view which one may adopt:

- **The application-oriented decision** One looks for an application program which optimally covers the needs of the application problem in hand. Then one selects an operating system and hardware on which to run the application program. This includes, if necessary, a network and metasoftware for operation of the network.

- **Decisions oriented to the system infrastructure** One looks for an operating system which determines the future nature of the information technology infrastructure. All machines acquired and all networks must support this system appropriately.

Usually, one is not free to choose one's point of view. This applies not only to the system technology, but also to everything else from the cabling problem upwards.

Nevertheless, one may conceptually come to terms with both points of view. A stubborn adherence to one or the other is highly likely to result in at most the second-best solution.

In shaping the future working environment for information technology, the system infrastructure-oriented approach should not be replaced by the cobbling together of incomplete and emergency solutions.

1.2.3 Program-to-program communication or interprocess communication

Often in discussions of networks and communication, the key words 'program to program' are used. It is almost always clear that scarcely anyone knows exactly what this means. Here, the very quality of the implementation of such communication determines the performance and the reliability of a whole network concept. Accordingly, we would like to draw attention to this point here. However, since this book is not about operating systems as such, the author recommends Deitel and Harvey (1984) or Maekawa, Oldehoeft and Oldehoeft (1987) for more details.

Current applications in computer systems which are not networked to other computer systems for the purposes of cooperation run hidden from the users using a set of so-called processes.

The concept of a process first reaches planners and users intuitively through terms such as 'multitasking'. Multitasking is generally seen as the capability of an operating system to execute several tasks in a quasi-parallel fashion on a single computer. This is the opposite of the sequential processing of several programs one after the other on a single computer. The computer itself usually has only one so-called processor. The operating system accordingly contains a component which ensures that the processing of tasks may be interleaved in time and overlapped. From the outside, each task appears to have exclusive use of the processor.

This virtualization is a normal procedure in the technology of computers, operating systems and networks. Every subscriber to a time-sharing system appears to have the exclusive use of the whole computer. In virtual file systems, the various storage media are so cleverly linked together that one has the impression of an almost infinite memory which can operate at the rate of the main memory; in data transmission, signal currents are multiplexed.

Virtuality is also nothing new; it was used in very different areas some time ago. Indeed, on very large machines pretence is made of the existence of very different (virtual) machines offering full facilities (for example, multitasking). Thus, the capacity of a machine is decomposed into manageable parts.

However, there is a large area of data processing which the concept of virtuality has only penetrated to a small extent: PCs. The original concept of the PC envisaged a user with only one task on a (small) machine. Thus, one process and the DOS operating system were sufficient; however, it was only possible to run one application at a time.

This was long thought to be sufficient. However, the ever-increasing requirements on PC applications and the simultaneously increasing requirements for user-friendliness have led to bottle-necks: programs for user support or for external communication must be able to run virtually simultaneously with application programs. Moreover, when one generates a document, the ability to work almost simultaneously with the word-processing and the graphics program without having to chop and change between programs is practical. Equally, it is very impractical to have only a very small fixed main memory limit. Anyone who wants to run programs which may require more space is left with no choice but to write the programs in such a way that they write to and read from the hard disk – that is in principle a task for the operating system.

The development of OS/2 has, regardless of the final acceptance of this operating system, shown that the days of 'single user – single application – single process – single machine' operating systems are over, at least conceptually.

Windows offer another way of simulating the effect of multitasking.

Instead, there is increasing talk of use of the UNIX operating system, which was originally developed for small mainframes, on PCs. UNIX incorporates the most important concepts of virtuality.

We now return to processes and to multitasking. Why is it not immaterial whether a set of tasks (application programs, requests) is interleaved in a quasi-parallel fashion or executed in a strict consecutive sequence? The capacity of the processor is the same. The use of multitasking is associated with a major characteristic of task implementations, namely the fact that the execution of a program consists of phases. There are at least two classes of such phases, namely phases in which the program actively uses the processor and phases in which the program waits for something to happen (for example, the completion of an input/output operation or the occurrence of an event such as the satisfaction of a condition).

In a sequential execution, the wait phases decrease the effectiveness of the processor, since it is not doing anything useful.

In the wait phases another program could make better use of the processor.

Basically, however, the execution of independent programs at this level must not be allowed to become dependent on the state of each program. This would lead to unfairness.

The control of the use in empty phases must therefore be implemented by a component which is not itself one of the external requests passed to the system for execution.

An operating system is a collection of components which, in the broadest sense, control the use of a computer or make the computer usable in the first place. The component which controls multitasking belongs to this collection.

However, in general, one does not just set a program running and wait for the start of the next empty or wait phase. Instead, the available processor time is divided into static or dynamic time slices, which are generally shorter than the processing time for a very small task.

The requests, represented by program blocks, must enter the queue for the processor. If they are ready in time for a time slice, that's good; if not, they have to wait until they are allocated another time slice. The overall management is usually refined by various program classes and priorities. We shall not go into that further.

Implicit dependencies, such as a general slowing down when a lot of programs place a heavy load on the processor, can never be totally ruled out.

Thus, the execution of large programs is always interrupted. This leads to another aspect: when the execution of a program is interrupted and it is desired to continue it later, it is very impractical to page the whole program (or parts of it) in or out or to represent partial results disproportionately.

During its execution, a program may be permanently described by its so-called overall state. The overall state before the beginning of the program execution is also called the static environment and is described by the individual states (the content) of the memory locations used by this program. These memory cells contain the program data and the program itself. However, the overall state also includes, for example, the memory cell (used by the operating system) which points to the address of the next instruction of the program to be executed (local instruction counter, instruction address register).

Whenever a program instruction is executed, the overall state changes, or at least the local instruction counter changes. However, in relation to the size of the overall state, this change is very small. When now a program is executed in blocks, it is not always necessary to consider the full overall state, since in principle, at the end of a time slice, one only needs to consider that part of the overall state which has actually been affected.

Taken together, these considerations lead to the requirement for a halfway between program and processor to which all these concepts may be anchored: the *process*.

The process is a virtualization of a number of actions in the computer system, which actions are generally associated with changes of state. Firstly, the linking of a program block to a process made available by the operating system leads to an action in the computer system which (we assume) corresponds to the execution of a desired sequence of operations.

In addition, there are a number of operating-system processes which do a great deal for the user and the system without being immediately noticed (for example, memory management, system management, control of units, etc.). However, one would soon notice if these programs were not working.

Communication between application programs and users means, above all, communication between processes. This aspect is almost completely neglected in the literature. A communication link between processes is usually called a session. In the ISO/OSI terminology, this is layer five, far beyond the communications subsystems. In the IBM world, the APPC concept provides a facility for process communication. Misleadingly, APPC is an abbreviation for 'Advanced Program-to-Program Communication'. It sometimes seems as though processes are suppressed like unpleasant shadows of the past.

Thus, all discussions on fast transport subsystems such as Token Ring are hollow words if the interprocess communication is badly implemented, since the latter largely determines what comes through 'end to end'.

In addition to data exchange, another major task of interprocess communication is the synchronization of concurrent processes via shared memory or pipes.

Programming languages, such as the DoD's ADA, already exist in which a problem solution may be directly expressed in terms of parallel tasks, which in the ideal case may be executed concurrently. The increased spread of such concepts will inevitably result in the requirement that a compiler for a distributed applications environment should have appropriate utilities to permit the implementation of these programming language concepts (including the synchronization mechanisms which they contain). Such utilities include powerful interprocess communication.

We shall study these problems further at an appropriate point of the book. At this point it is most useful to place the burning discussions of throughput and overall performance in context.

1.3 The development of network system architectures

This section is intended for readers who do not have access to another book on networks; it summarizes the important aspects of modern network system architectures and their interrelationships.

The development of data communication systems and associated system architectures over the last ten years has followed completely different routes in several areas which at first sight are apparently independent:

- Terminal networks to operate and control less intelligent terminals within the framework of centrally oriented data processing based on mainframes, with the primary goal of optimizing access to these central, relatively homogeneous resources (SNA architecture, TRANSDATA architecture, DECnet).
- Computer networks to further the cooperation of medium-to-large computer installations with a view to network sharing of data, load, services, functions and availability. The goal is to integrate as many heterogeneous systems as possible in order to expand the existing platform of application-oriented services (such as file transfer, remote job entry and electronic mail) within the network (ISO/OSI architecture, TCP/IP suite, networks such as DFN or ARPANET).
- Workstation networks as the communications infrastructure for homogeneous decentralized microprocessor-based systems. Here, the primary goal is the shared use of physical and logical resources, special applications and common system services (LANs for PCs with DOS or workstations with UNIX, such as Ethernet and Token Rings and extended software such as the PC LAN Program, NetWare or the LAN Manager).

However, the evolution of increasingly high-performance workstations with the possible relocation of functional and infrastructural units within distributed applications into workstations has qualified this structural approach to a classification. The inclusion of these devices in a universal application-oriented heterogeneous integrated network of various systems and networks is now favoured, since, in addition to access to basic services such as

- dialogue as an interactive means of access to various local and remote large systems and networks,
- remote job entry to task various local and remote computers,
- file transfer, and
- electronic mail or message handling

access to special shared resources or applications (for example, databases) should also be possible, bringing with it a horizontal and vertical integration.

The horizontal component consists of the system-wide implementation of appropriate services, resources and applications with

ISO/OSI	Standards	DoD family	SAA family	SNA stack
Application	X.400 FTAM	SMTP	DCA/DIA	End user
Presentation	ASN.1	FTP TELNET	SNADS	Presentation
Session	ISO 8326/27	DNS/NSP	APPC interface	Data flow
Transport	ISO 8072/73	TCP	UDP	LU 6.2	Transmission control
Network	X.25 WAN	ICMP	EGP IP ARP RARP	PU 2.1	Path control
Data link	X.25 WAN ISO 8802 LAN	ARPANET ETHERNET TOKEN RING	Token Ring LAN	Data link
Physical	X.25 WAN ISO 8802 LAN	ARCNET X.25 PDN others	or SDLC	Physical

Figure 1.12 Comparison of network architectures.

architectures suitably equipped for the purposes of the integration.

The vertical integration on the other hand must take account of the various classes of devices (workstations, office systems, mainframes) to be linked together and the corresponding operating systems.

The requirements as far as the level of integration, complexity, user-friendliness, performance and costs of a solution are concerned are very different in different application areas. In the scientific area, for instance, particularly important requirements on a solution include, on the one hand, the heterogeneity of existing structures and, on the other hand, maximum flexibility with extensive connectivity and high performance.

Information retrieval, distributed graphics and document processing, integrated network research and the use of supercomputers are but a few key words for possible areas of application.

All functional and procedural specifications for a communications system are specified in a layer-oriented architectural recommendation, in which the lower layers concentrate more on the technical system and the upper layers are concerned more with the linking into the operating system and with the applications. The ISO model for *Open Systems Interconnection*

(OSI) is generally accepted and forms the basis for international standards.

Almost all computer manufacturers have moved towards this model and now implement new elements of their respective network system architectures in as full accordance as possible with the standards (DEC DECnet and DNA, Siemens SINEC, SBA and TRANSDATA). Often, these involve transitional solutions or extensions, since in many cases the standards are incomplete, partially unsuitable or even deficient (network management, data protection). Only IBM, in the framework of its *System Applications Architecture* (SAA) is sticking to its proprietary *Systems Network Architecture* (SNA) as a basic scheme; however, IBM also produces products which permit a transition between OSI and SNA systems. In addition, there are a number of other manufacturer-neutral network architectures, among which the DoD protocol suite has become the most important industry standard.

1.3.1 Open Systems Interconnection

From 1977 the *Open Systems Interconnection* (OSI) reference model of the *International Standardization Organization* (ISO) has been designated as the basis for the formation of standards for communication between communications media and applications. The objective of OSI is to facilitate communication in a heterogeneous environment based on application-supporting basic services. Over a decade later, standards have been released for wide areas of the architecture and are now being used very extensively in the message transport-oriented parts of communications systems (for example, wide area networks based on X.25 and local area networks based on ISO 8802). On the other hand, the breakthrough in the application-oriented layers is still only partial today.

The communication is implemented by a set of elements or entities, each with their own fixed place and task.

In the framework of standardization of communication systems, the following must be defined:

- The division of the architecture into layers.
- The division of the layers into entities.
- The cooperation of the entities within a layer.
- The cooperation of the entities in adjacent layers.

The interface between two layers, seen from the top down, is a client/server interface. An entity in a layer provides a certain service. For this, it may use the assistance available locally or that provided (again in the form of a service) by an entity of the layer below. Lower-lying layers and higher layers cannot be used.

In addition to this interface, the observance of a control mechanism relating peer entities at different physical points in the same layer is also important. Such a control mechanism is called a *protocol.*

The communications architecture is defined to have seven layers. These layers each form a framework for standards, but are not actual communications standards themselves.

The lowest structural layer is the physical layer. This provides the communications-engineering basis for transmission.

The data link layer, which is already an abstraction from the physical connections, combines sequences of binary information into data packets and decomposes larger units arriving from higher layers into smaller packets, where necessary. This layer incorporates elementary error detection and recovery mechanisms. The layer deals mainly with point-to-point connections.

This is not the case in the network layer, the main task of which is routing (the determination of an optimal path through a (possibly branched) network). The optimal route depends not only on the number of intermediate nodes, but also on the load and the susceptibility of the individual stations and links to noise.

The protocols of the next layer, the transport layer, have end-to-end characteristics because they relate directly to logical information sources and sinks. With the functions of this layer, the primary transmission-oriented part is complete.

Thus, the next layer, the session layer, is provided with a universal transport service. A session of the session layer denotes a logical link between two intercommunicating entities of the highest layer. The main task of this layer is to provide assistance to the synchronization of the processes involved in the communication.

The presentation layer lies between layer 5 and the application layer. Its special services provide for a transformation of the data to an agreed standard format and for a uniform interpretation.

The last layer is the application layer which provides the distributed applications with logical communications support in the form of certain services such as file transfer or remote job entry.

The system management is distributed vertically over the layers, since it requires information from each layer and should be able to access each layer.

Examples of stable application-layer standards include X.400 for message handling and FTAM for file transfer. Areas in which much is still open include transaction processing, data protection and network management.

It will be several more years before stable standards are reflected by the availability of reasonably priced product lines. The scientific area has the advantage over commercial users here, as a result of proprietary developments and pilot implementations such as DFN.

1.3.2 SNA and SAA

SNA and its extensions in the framework of the System Applications Architecture (SAA) may be taken as an example of the development of a family of network hardware, software and firmware for terminal control into a basis for the implementation of distributed applications in a multi-faceted environment of machines from workstations to mainframes.

SAA provides uniform applications, user, development and communications support for PS/2 models, /3X and AS/400 systems and mainframes of the /370 series.

The integration aspect is not solely restricted to the communications engineering, but also provides for a common approach to the conception of databases.

In order to achieve this, in the context of communications support, it was necessary to extend the previously exclusively synchronous SNA architecture and to structure the highest SNA functional layer (layer 7) in order to provide for generation, transmission and processing of an electronic document composed of several independent parts at every reachable partner in the network.

In particular, SNA was extended by:

- APPC (Advanced Program-to-Program Communication)
- SNADS (SNA Distribution Services)
- DIA (Document Interchange Architecture)
- DCA (Document Contents Architecture)

Thus, applications may exchange data in large networks with other applications in the network, regardless of whether the application is installed on a central mainframe or a network processor. The necessary prerequisites for a transmission between applications are covered by the APPC interface.

The introduction of the APPC concept, which is also called PU 2.1/LU 6.2 after the SNA components which support it physically and logically (physical unit of type 2.1, logical unit of type 6.2), provides a convenient interface for the communication of transaction programs. So-called 'verbs', which appear similar to a high-level programming language construct, are used as communications objects. Every node in the SNA network which implements this interface may, regardless of its complexity, communicate with another node having this interface, via a logical link (conversation).

The type 2.1 node is also called an SNA low-entry networking (LEN) node and supports a peer-to-peer connection. A network of such nodes permits multiple and parallel connections between the nodes.

The APPC interface is supported not only by IBM but also by many other manufacturers and thus provides an appropriate basis for the communication of transaction-oriented application programs in a heterogeneous networked environment. An ISO working group includes APPC in the OSI standardization as a transaction-processing element.

SNADS specifies the ways in which data and documents are transmitted from one network node to the next until they reach the destination; for this, it uses the services of APPC. DIA is responsible for monitoring the distribution of data or documents. DCA goes a step further and describes the significance, the form and the contents of a document.

The document form and exchange specifications will have to hold their own ground against the ODA/ODIF models defined in the context of the OSI endeavours.

The further development of SNA is characterized by two main streams:

- Construction of the basic architecture with regard to a high transparency in the sense of SAA.
- Opening of the architecture in the interests of heterogeneous communication and international standards.

1.3.3 TCP/IP (the DoD protocol suite)

SAA is restricted to a number of important IBM product lines and compatible systems. Even with convergence to international standards and appropriate facilities for transition to open systems, this approach does not provide an adequate solution in all heterogeneous environments (for example, when an IBM host is not available).

A pragmatic alternative to this communications infrastructure is provided by the elements of the DoD protocol suite (better known as TCP/IP), which have become a conspicuous *de facto* standard over recent years.

The TCP/IP suite consists of a range of protocols for layers 3–7 and was originally developed by the US Department of Defense (DoD) to unify communication in the ARPANET framework.

The TCP/IP suite was not designed for a particular message transport system such as a LAN, but may be used on various transmission media, systems and networks and on various computers. This means that it is naturally suited for a doubly heterogeneous internetworking environment, where the whole network consists of different parts linked by gateways over which various computers from different manufacturers intercommunicate.

The most important boost for the DoD protocol suite was its integration into the UNIX family. From Berkeley UNIX 4.2 the DoD protocol suite has been available to the user for problem-free communication of different UNIX systems. The portability of the operating system has also led to the portability of the communications software. This is a decisive step towards the simplification and unification of communication. TCP/IP is also available under AIX.

Today, the DoD protocol suite realizes the target objectives of the ISO/OSI model; however, it does not correspond to the international standard. Instead, the individual protocols stand out by their relative simplicity. They are thus cost-effective to implement in a PC environment.

Corresponding implementations exist for almost all systems which use UNIX in one of its many different variants and for DEC VMS systems, MS-DOS, OS/2, CP/M and IBM-VM and IBM-MVS. Thus, file transfer, electronic mail and line-oriented dialogue may be executed from a terminal under the various systems. One of the most common applications is the integration of (IBM-)PCs, DEC systems and IBM systems using Ethernet as a communications medium.

The DoD protocol suite has elements in ISO layers 3–7. The *Transmission Control Protocol* (TCP) is used as a secure host-to-host protocol in packet-oriented computer communication networks and in LANs. The *User Datagram Protocol* (UDP) enables application processes to exchange datagrams without establishing a virtual connection. TCP and UDP are based on IP. The Darpa *Internet Protocol* (IP) permits the exchange of data across several networks.

Telnet (dialogue system), SMTP (Simple Mail Transfer Protocol) and FTP (File Transfer Protocol) are applications using both TCP and IP which may be accessed directly by the user.

Telnet Telnet permits a bidirectional byte-oriented communication in the dialogue with other systems. The following links are possible:

- between a terminal on host A and an application on host B,
- between a terminal on host A and a terminal on host B,
- interprocess communication between applications on hosts A and B.

FTP FTP may be used to share files, to copy data and programs between different systems and for indirect access to resources on other computers. Telnet is used to establish the connection and to execute commands.

SMTP SMTP is used to transmit mail to hosts which are attached to the same LAN (network) or which are reachable via a gateway, if the sender and recipient are not in the same network.

In addition to the functionally oriented services there are also the administration-oriented services DNS (Domain Name Service; a directory service for domain management) and NSP (Name Service Protocol; maps host names on to IP addresses). In very large WANs, in addition to the IP network transport service, there are also protocols for monitoring IP services (ICMP), and for management of the IP router (EGP). In mixed installations with Ethernet LANs, mappings from IP addresses to Ethernet addresses are also used (ARP and RARP).

In addition to the wide distribution of the protocols other main advantages of the DoD protocol suite are its 5–8 year lead over ISO solutions as far as implementations are concerned and its relative lack of complexity. Because of the sluggish progress of ISO/OSI standardization late conversion from TCP/IP to OSI may be calmly anticipated.

Despite the DoD internal about-face to OSI protocols over the next years, the wide installation base of TCP/IP means that there are few risks associated with the use of this product.

1.3.4 And the others ...

Other large manufacturers such as DEC and Siemens currently have their own network philosophies. DEC is developing the *Digital Network Architecture* (DNA) and DECnet in a totally OSI direction. DECnet Phase V/OSI will support the OSI stack as far as possible.

In addition to networks based on the TRANSDATA architecture, which are largely terminal oriented, Siemens also has a network philosophy for manufacturing: SINEC AP. Siemens is slowly but surely replacing its own protocol stack by OSI.

In addition to client demand, one reason for the switch to OSI is that the companies have no wish to duplicate development work.

1.4 LAN summary

In this section, we give a brief summary of the most important aspects of LANs. Today, LANs have a wide area of application. There are a number of definitions of a LAN, according to whether it is desired to integrate speech and image traffic in it. Furthermore, LAN is often used as a portmanteau term for data networks such as Ethernet and Token Ring and also for PBXs.

In this book, we shall stick to the following definition (following ECMA/IEEE):

- **LAN** Local area networks are systems for high-performance information transfer which provide a high-quality partnership-oriented message transfer service based on a fast transmission medium to a number of equally authorized users in a spatially restricted area.

The characterizing factors here are spatial restriction and fast data transmission with a low error rate.

One possibility is the implementation of the LAN as a diffusion network, in which a common transmission medium (for example, a bus) supports all subscribers and every transmission is direct from the source to the destination. Another possibility is the implementation of a ring which interlinks the nodes in a store-and-forward technology. In modern cabling technology, these topology differences have been largely relativized so that we also talk of loop-free LANs (bus type, tree type, star type) and LANs with loops (ring type).

A LAN usually has a maximum coverage of around 10 km although there are networks with a far larger coverage. However, this is not a direct restriction, since there is now a tendency to construct LANs from LAN subsystem structures (building blocks) interconnected by bridges, routers or backbone networks, rather than from 'a single piece'.

When a LAN is installed, usually the physical restrictions are less important than the legal usage requirements of the TKO (Telecommunications Office) in Germany, under which a LAN, in the absence of other conditions, may only be operated within a 'postal area'. However, with the reorganization of the TKO at the beginning of 1989, the requirements in respect of the coupling of LANs in different adjacent areas have been relaxed to a certain extent. Thus, for example, a private internetwork based on fibre-optic cables laid by the postal administration is now conceivable.

A LAN achieves transmission rates of around 4–20 Mbps, but may also be able to provide certain systems with rates of 50 Mbps (network systems, HYPERchannel), 100 Mbps (FDDI) or 275 Mbps (network systems data pipe). However, these systems are really intended for the backbone area or for direct coupling of mainframes. The peak of technological development is represented by systems called *High Performance Parallel Interfaces* (HPPIs) which transmit up to 800 Mbps. Backbone systems in the Gbps region will certainly not be long in appearing.

A LAN does not usually stand alone, but is linked (sometimes multiply) with other LANs, classical host networks for terminal control (for example, IBM SNA networks, Siemens TRANSDATA networks) and remote networks.

1.4.1 LAN media and basic LAN types

LANs are transport subsystems within a network architecture. Differences from other network types are only found in the lower layers of the OSI model. Above layer 4 (at the latest) no distinctions can be drawn, since uniformity and the 'end-to-end' argument are mandatory for the higher layers; thus, applications and users do not need to concern themselves with these technical details and differences between the networks.

Users see conventional WANs as a service which can be accessed through a socket. Ultimately, such a perspective is also a desirable objective for LANs. However, this will require a careful planning process.

1.4.1.1 Transmission media and communications technology

The same transmission media are available to LANs as to other message transfer systems in general: twisted pairs of various designs, coaxial cable and optical fibres.

The simplest form of the twisted pair is seen in telephone cables, which are inappropriate for the fast transmission speeds needed in LANs.

There is much misunderstanding amongst people who are led to believe by less than accurate advertising that all the cabling for LANs can be based on telephone cables. There are at least three basic forms of the twisted pair:

- **Star quad**, the normal telephone cable, in which four wires are intertwined and usually have only a low transmission capacity. Strictly, these are not twisted pairs but 'twisted quartets' of wires.
- **Unshielded Twisted Pairs** (UTP) in which two pairs of wires are each twisted.
- **Shielded Twisted Pairs** (STP) are constructed like UTPs but each pair of wires is shielded.

All four-wire cables may be used for true duplex links, even when, as in Token Ring LANs, the second pair of wires provides a back-up function.

Star quad and UTP are, to put it simply, so poor because, as a result of the close proximity of all the wires, the inter-coupling of signals due to inductive interaction is very high. Thus, on duplex links, the inbound and outbound signal currents mutually interfere. This is also true when the return line is used as a back-up.

In addition to the form of the construction itself, the conductor material and the physical structure of the individual wires have an important effect on the transmission capacity. Usually, however, the main problem is not the transmission capacity of a line but the electromagnetic interactions with the surroundings.

In the near future, twisted pairs will principally play a role in terminal areas.

Coaxial cable, as used in HF and antenna technology, is currently the most commonly used medium. Its construction is optimized for high frequencies, which makes it one of the favourite metallic conductors. A transmission capacity of several hundred Mbps may be achieved. In its different forms, it is suitable for almost all LAN schemes. The connector technology should not be based on a cheap technology, since otherwise corrosion and medium errors are inevitable.

The medium of the future, which is already available now, is the fibre-optic cable. In such a cable the information is no longer carried by electric signals but by light. Based on glass fibres, transmission speeds in the Gbps area can be achieved. This medium has advantages even for the standard user. The ease with which it can be laid, its high redundancy capacity, its security against interception together with its insusceptibility to external interference give it particular qualities as far as data protection and data security are concerned. Initially, it is unlikely to penetrate as far as terminals; however, backbone networks and networks with particular requirements in industrial production environments will use fibre optics.

Another variant of the optical fibre is the so-called plastic fibre which now allows transmission speeds of up to around 5 Mbps over several hundred metres. Plastic fibre is in the early stages of development and will certainly blossom into a serious competitor to the twisted pair, since it combines the basic advantages of fibre-optic technology with the cost advantages of the plastic medium. The fibres now used in plastic-fibre systems, unlike glass fibres, lie in the visible area, so that it is easy to see whether or not there is a message flow in a conductor.

In the discussion of LANs, the terms baseband and broadband occur frequently. What do they mean? Most LANs use proven baseband transmission procedures, which take the signal as it leaves the computer, adapt it to the line (for example, convert it into a light pulse) and transmit it over the line. So that this does not lead to confusion, one must impose the requirement that at most one station may send at a given time, otherwise the electrical or optical signals become muddled up. For this, a procedure is required to bring all stations that are ready to send into a sequence or to prevent them from interfering with one another in some other way. For the vast majority of information-processing problems this is a reasonable procedure; the overall bandwidth is easily sufficient for hundreds of stations all of which wish to send almost simultaneously, since the transmissions only contain a few kilobytes on average and the waiting times accruing from this procedure are insignificant as far as the network users and the application programs are concerned.

About 15 years ago, when LANs were still in their infancy, for certain applications and in the framework of a general cabling strategy, consideration was given to whether a so-called broadband system, with the ability to implement a large number of independent channels simultaneously on a single cable, could provide a better solution to the capacity problem. Technically, such a broadband system corresponds to a broadband distribution network, like that used for radio and television cable connections, with the difference that bidirectional and not just single-direction transmission is possible. It was hoped that this solution would lead to the creation of independent logical areas for data transmission, which would provide for a high flexibility of the overall system. The clear disadvantage of such a broadband network is the high cost of connecting terminals, since firstly the distribution network must be carefully planned and laid out itself and secondly every attached station must have its own emitter and receiver appropriate to the channel used. This is still tolerable for hosts, but not for smaller systems such as PCs.

Today, broadband systems are only found in the product lines of a few computer manufacturers who have no wish to carry out their own technical development for networking and in industrial manufacturing environments where their use is mixed (they are used not only for data traffic but also for the transmission of static and moving images, monitoring, control and regulation and even for audio traffic). Broadband networks have only a subordinate importance in conventional information technology, primarily as backbones. Even this position will soon be disputed by fibre-optic systems.

Nowadays, the capacity problem is solved in a different way (if it arises): physically separated networks are laid out and linked by an appropriate backbone.

1.4.1.2 LAN topologies

There are now four established topologies for LANs: stars, buses, rings and trees.

Stars In a star system, all messages flow towards a central converter. In the early days of star networks, the idea was for a switching converter as in PBXs. However, this contradicts the decentralized approach of LAN systems. Nowadays, star structures are most often used in the context of fibre-optic networks, in which a fibre-optic link leads from each attached station to the central point of the network and back again. The central point is an optical or an electro-optical converter, which may be active or passive according to the size and structure of the network. As far as network management is concerned, such a star network poses the same problems as a bus and is managed by similar control procedures.

Buses Buses lead outwards from the body of a medium, which is tapped at certain intervals. The message which a station emits then propagates (as in radio in the air medium) in all directions over the cable. This broadcasting technique is a direct message-oriented solution which has found great acceptance in the market place. The bus is easy to extend by adding an extra tap to those already in existence. Coaxial cable is the standard medium for bus LANs.

Rings The other large LAN group comprises ring LANs in which the stations are connected in series and the first is linked to the last. In the current technology, the messages do not travel as a whole from station to station, but at every station there is a so-called ring interface which has a few memory bits. When consecutively connected, these memory positions form the ring. The lines between the stations are not relevant to the representation of the signals. So as not to increase the orbital time, the individual memories and the number of stations must not be too large.

Trees Tree systems arise from the structure of broadband distribution networks. Because they do not have a wide distribution, a simple mention at this point will suffice.

As previously mentioned, many basic topological considerations are inapplicable in the framework of a reasonable universal cabling strategy. However, the difference between loop-free LANs and LANs with loops still remains.

1.4.2 LAN control procedures

LANs may be classified according to the control algorithms. The following control procedures are widely used:

- CSMA/CD (Carrier Sense Multiple Access/Collision Detection, for buses and trees).
- CSMA/CA (Carrier Sense Multiple Access/Collision Avoidance, for buses).
- Token passing (this involves the handing on of a physical (for rings) or logical (for buses and trees) authorization to send).

From the point of view of security and fairness, deterministic procedures such as token passing or CSMA/CA are clearly preferable, since for heavy loads, in unfavourable circumstances, CSMA/CD cannot provide a reasonable throughput.

In the future, most networks with a transmission speed of up to 20 Mbps will be structured according to the standardization proposal of the IEEE 802 working group.

The ANSI FDDI recommendation for fast LANs (up to 100 Mbps) and the IEEE DQDB standard for Metropolitan Area Networks (MANs) are both structured according to IEEE 802.

The most important elements of the data link layer are the access control methods for shared, sequential, mutually exclusive access to the bus or ring medium.

Both for buses and for rings, for the transmission rates considered in the IEEE 802 standard, the number of bits which may be simultaneously represented in the network is usually smaller than the average number of bits in a data packet. This only changes for very fast networks with rates of over approximately 100 Mbps.

This means that at any time only one station should send, otherwise there will be collisions on the medium.

Another important element is the logical link control, which combines the resources of the access control and transmission facilities into abstract packet transmission resources to which the higher layers can refer.

1.4.2.1 Token-passing control procedure

The token-passing control procedure for implementing mutually exclusive access to a fast communications medium is based on the fact that a station which has just completed an emission passes the authorization to send on to a (physical or logical) successor. If the latter wishes to send, it has a certain time within which to do so and must then pass on the authorization to send. If the recipient of the token has nothing to send, it passes the token directly to its successor. Assuming that the emission time is limited and that no stations are omitted when the token is passed on, the procedure is fair, since every station has a turn after a finite waiting time of predictable maximum duration.

This procedure can be physically implemented on a LAN ring since the successor relation is clear from the ordering of the stations in the ring.

It is also possible to impose a logical control structure on a bus LAN in which there are no conditions on the ordering of the stations, using a memory-based procedure which permits the application of the token control procedure (Token Bus). Examples of this are found above all in the industrial manufacturing environment. One advantage of this is the combination of the merits of token-passing control (freedom from conflicts, determinism) with those of the bus LAN (flexibility, direct transmission from source to destination). However, today's Token Bus LANs are restricted to speeds of up to 10 Mbps. The additional coordination costs of the logical control structure make the Token Bus algorithm unsuitable for higher transmission speeds.

1.4.2.2 CSMA control procedure

CSMA is an abbreviation for Carrier Sense Multiple Access, which means that the stations are synchronized by the fact that a station that is ready to send first listens in to the channel before it sends.

In the CSMA/CD (CD stands for Collision Detection) procedure, a station may only send when the medium is not occupied by another station.

If the medium is occupied, the station waits until the medium is free and it can send. The station finds out about the state of the medium by listening in.

When several stations are waiting to send messages over the LAN, several stations may send their data to the medium simultaneously. In this case, a collision occurs which is detected as a noise signal due to the overlap of the individual messages.

To remove collisions, every station involved in a collision waits for an interval corresponding to a value generated by a random number generator and then reattempts to send the data over the medium. If the medium has in the meantime become occupied, the station must wait again; if the attempt to transmit results in another collision, then the station waits for a new interval determined by twice the old interval.

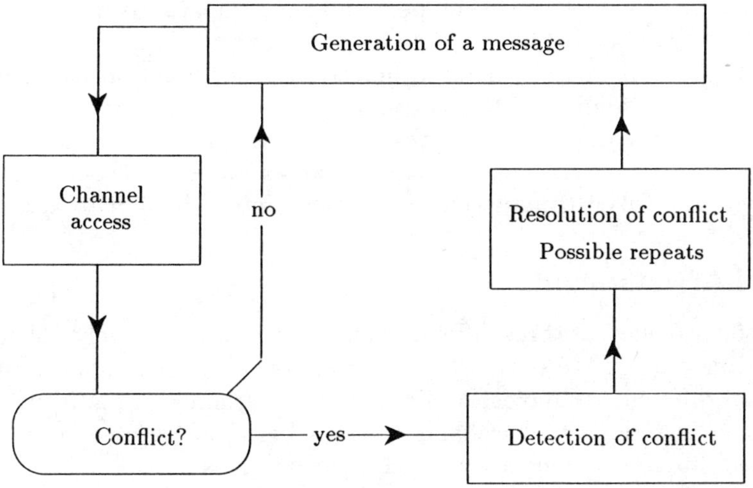

Figure 1.13 Random access methods.

After 15 unsuccessful attempts to access the medium, the procedure is aborted and the application is informed that the medium is unavailable.

This clear disadvantage of the procedure is mitigated by the fact that normally the medium is often free, thus collisions are relatively rare and the data can be transmitted without delay as in the other procedures.

However, one cannot always depend on this favourable behaviour and other procedures should be chosen for applications where high reliability is important.

CSMA/CA (CA stands for Collision Avoidance) avoids unnecessary extra collisions by ensuring that the processing of conflicting requests to send is not random but controlled by priority. This leads to a deterministic behaviour analogous to the Token Ring control procedure.

Priority control also has the advantage that precedential relations between devices may be defined.

Unfortunately, CSMA/CA is only implemented in certain products and is not part of the international standardization.

There are a number of performance comparisons between CSMA/CD and Token Bus or Ring networks. In summary, it can be said that CSMA/CD behaves unfavourably when a large number of stations have a relatively large number of small packets to send, as is the case, for example, for terminal traffic. In this case, the effective useful data rate of the CSMA/CD system sinks according to Suppan (1990) to around 20% of the channel capacity. On the other hand, the token-passing system behaves well even for high loads.

There are very many controversies over the large differences in theoretical performance and very polarized opinions. However, in many cases, the practical value of such performance comparisons has been shown to be very low (Boell, 1989).

In fact, ultimately, many other criteria, including in particular the quality and suitability of the network system architecture, play a much greater and more important role than the overall performance of the access procedure. The authors openly admit that as far as the contest between Ethernet and Token Ring is concerned, they find it difficult to agree

1.4.3 LAN standards

IEEE 802 provides for three different layer 2 procedures, namely Token Ring, Token Bus and CSMA/CD, which are supported by a number of systems based on different technologies. The different technical variants still under discussion include both baseband versions based on twisted pair, coaxial cable and fibre-optic media and broadband versions.

All these various network types are then uniformly bound together under a so-called logical link control, so that a uniform LAN transport system exists above the upper boundary of layer 2. The IEEE 802 and ISO 8802 perspective is restricted to networks with a lower performance (up to 20 Mbps) which provide for the terminal area in a variety of different ways.

The logical link control provides one or more of the following three services, according to the implementation:

- **LLC 0** is an unconfirmed connectionless service. It provides assistance to enable network connections to exchange data units without having to establish a layer 2 logical link. Datagrams may be point to point, point to multipoint or broadcast. Receipt confirmation signals are not expected.
- **LLC 1** is a confirmed connectionless service. It is like the above except that receipt confirmation signals are expected in the data link layer.
- **LLC 2** is a connection-oriented service. This provides assistance for the establishment, use and termination of layer 2 links. For this, there are *Link Service Access Points* (LSAPs) to which the link adapts. The connection establishment service enables a network entity to request a logical link to a remote LSAP. The connection-oriented data transport service enables a network entity to send and receive layer 2 *LLC Protocol Data Units* (LPDUs). This service also provides for sequencing, flow control and restart after error. The RESET facility may be used to reset links to an initial state. The termination service terminates a connection in response to a specific request. There is also a timer for flow control.

The quality of the connection-oriented service corresponds to that of HDLC or SDLC. Thus, a user may decide whether to use a simple protocol procedure (LLC 0) if he is certain that there is little interference in the system and this does not bother him or LLC 2 if he is in a sensitive environment (for example, a process control environment).

1.5 Areas of application of Token Ring networks

As we have seen in the previous sections, Token Ring is based on international standards and is supported by a wide range of products. In the case of IBM, it is an integral component of the System Applications Architecture (SAA). It is also increasingly important outside the IBM world, where the previously Ethernet-oriented area of office communications is a growth market.

Almost all major LAN suppliers support the Token Ring concept. The wide range of transmission speeds from 4 Mbps to 100 Mbps makes Token Ring networks suitable for a large variety of application areas, from simple PC networking to the interlinking of mainframes.

Token Ring LANs are suitable for business use in the following four areas:

- Office communications
- Computer centres and associated areas
- PC networking
- Manufacturing automation

According to predictions of companies such as Diebold or IDC, the German PC LAN market alone will grow so strongly that in 1991, out of an expected turnover of around 500 million DM of LAN components and software, approximately 40–45% will be spent on Token Ring systems.

In the future, LANs will generally increase in importance since they form the basis for integrated information systems, provide an economic alternative in terms of cabling in buildings and are standardized.

Let us stay for a moment in the office communications area. Various devices are currently used in this area. Analogue and digital telephones are used for direct communication and in the future videophones and video-conferencing devices will increasingly be used. As far as general indirect communication is concerned, electronic typewriters and PCs are used for text editing and word processing. In the course of development, new systems will be introduced such as X.400/X.500-based electronic mail, telex, teletext, facsimile, videotex and mailbox and internal electronic messaging systems, which should, where possible, be available from individual workstations or devices. New workstations will be equipped with

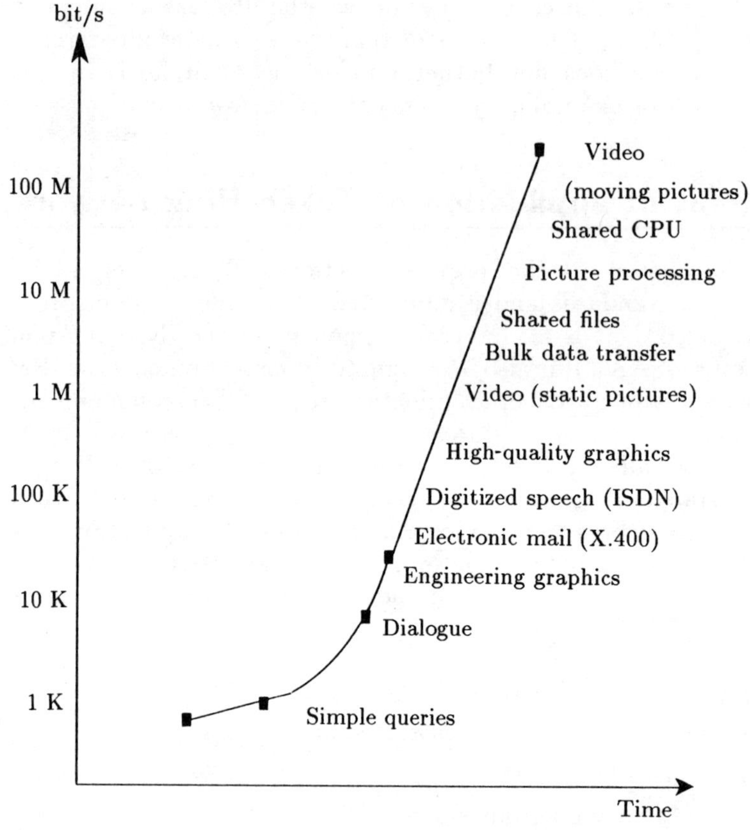

Figure 1.14 Message traffic in modern workstations.

better and better text and image storage systems. Additionally, there is also communication in the context of special applications, such as active and passive database interrogation, generation of text for record devices, software development and maintenance, CAD/CAM systems and data acquisition.

Soon it will be easy to store speech digitally, broadcast it and transmit it over the telephone at cheap-rate periods.

New media will permit the integration of speech, data, text, graphics and images. Transmission is over a medium, the data is usually output via a terminal.

The requirement for corresponding devices and services will increase sharply in the future as will communications requirements with simultaneously increasing demands on speed and quality.

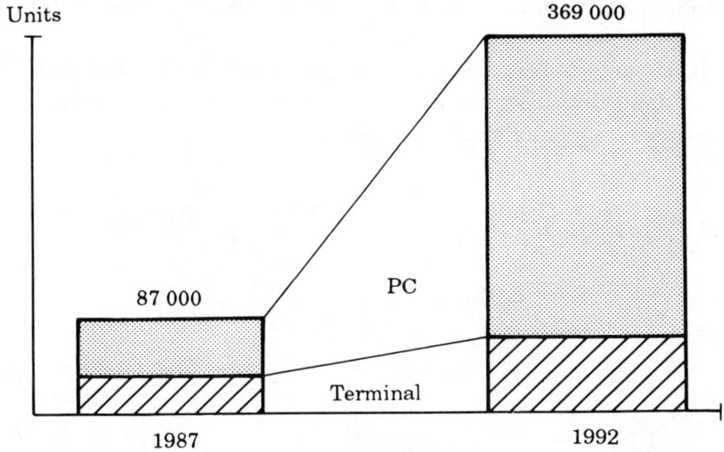

Average annual rate of increase: 35%

	1987	1992
PC	65%	78%
Terminal	35%	22%

Figure 1.15 Development of the German LAN market (network nodes).

It is here that the efficient use of LANs and Token Ring LANs in particular comes in.

Examples of applications of Token Ring LANs in the office communications, manufacturing and scientific and technical areas are legion:

- Relieving of mid-range DP systems using LANs to manage client files, inventories, jobs and journaling.
- Common databases for PCs.
- Common data security for PCs.
- Gateway functions with access to public networks.
- Terminal replacement.
- Process automation (here, there is a requirement for good real-time behaviour of the LAN).
- Computer linking.
- Linking of heterogeneous systems.
- Backbone for speech and information.
- Bus for terminals.
- Backbone for LAN islands.

- Special applications, for example, in medicine, image transmission, patient monitoring, laboratory evaluations, diagnostic support.

The aim is to use Token Ring LANs as the technological basis for the communications infrastructure within a building and a fast communication medium between spatially separated entities.

Chapter 2

Token Ring: foundations

Chapter 1 contained a general introduction to the development of LANs and that of Token Rings in particular. The basic mode of operation and the technical implementation were described. In Chapter 2, we describe the important formats and protocols, algorithms and procedures of Token Ring, essentially independently from their physical implementation.

In Chapter 3, we discuss possible implementations; here, IBM technology naturally takes up a good deal of space.

We begin with another brief summary of the important properties of Token Rings. We use an example to describe the interaction of application programs, protocol stacks, logical links, medium access control and communications technology. We also take the opportunity to situate the most important elements in the ISO/OSI scheme and explain the most important terms from the SNA area. Readers who until now have had only little to do with SNA are recommended to read the appendix on SNA (Chapter 8) in addition to Section 2.2.

Sections 2.3 and 2.4 are devoted to protocols, addressing schemes and formats for the lower layers (physical and data link layers). What about errors? The monitor functions described in Section 2.5 settle most problems. Proper introduction of a station and the so-called NAUN procedure also help to ensure orderly operation. Source routing, which is described in Section 2.8, is the procedure for switching messages between subnetworks via bridges. The final sections of this chapter relate primarily to the work of a Token Ring station in an SNA network, network management and IBM alternatives to Token Ring.

2.1 Overview

Before we discuss the mode of operation of the Token Ring protocol in more detail, we shall use Table 2.1 to give the reader an overview of the most important properties of Token Ring.

As mentioned in Chapter 1, the Token Ring procedure was developed in 1972. The protocol was not invented by IBM; however, IBM has acquired the patent rights and, in common with other companies, has improved and developed the protocol considerably.

Token Ring is a typical representative of ring networks and is standardized by IEEE (802.5) and ISO (8802.5). IBM itself had already gained experience of token protocols, for example, for coupling IBM 8100 systems or IBM series/1 systems. However, these systems did not catch on and with them the corresponding non-standardized procedures (which differed from current token-passing procedures) also disappeared.

Neither was IBM the first supplier of products which differed greatly from the standard. The American manufacturer Proteon, which now produces Token Ring systems operating at 4, 10, 16, 80 and 100 Mbps, first

Table 2.1 Properties of Token Ring.

Property	*Description*
Transmission facility	Fibre-optic, screened and unscreened, 4-wire cable, Coaxial cable
Access procedure	ISO 8802.5 (Token Ring) ISO 8802.2 (LLC) Implementation dependent
Topology	Ring cabled in star shape
Transmission rate Effective user data	Around 500 kbps for 4 kbytes, 1.8 Mbps for 16 kbytes message size (4 Mbps)
Transmission rate on cable	4 or 16 Mbps
Max. distance in Token Ring	800 m without repeater; with repeater around 200 km. Linkable over remote bridge or public network
Max. connections per ring	260, then bridge
Suited for transmission of	Data, text, graphics, speech (sometimes)
Used for:	PC LANs, PC–host coupling, Terminal linkage, Computer linkage
Interfaces, gateways, routers, bridges to	SNA TCP/IP Ethernet X.25 Asynchronous systems ...

marketed corresponding products considerably earlier. These products were only used in small numbers in Germany prior to 1986. The breakthrough came after IBM settled completely on Token Ring as its vehicle for LAN communications. As a consequence of this breakthrough, almost all major manufacturers of LAN components also produce Token Ring products and Proteon has become the leading representative with products which conform to the standards and in part considerably extend upon IBM products.

Some of the first Token Ring installations used 10 Mbps Proteon components for PC internetworking. This type of Token Ring networking was supported by Novell NetWare, which is a network operating system which we shall describe in more detail in Chapter 5. Even before the first IBM products reached the market, Proteon was already supplying products with a better performance.

2.2 Data flow in Token Ring

The IBM Token Ring network is a star-wired ring. For reasons of security, fault tolerance and redundancy, the network is composed of a number of star structures interconnected in a ring shape and logically it behaves like a ring. This facilitates the connection of new terminals and admits simple diagnosis, control and test facilities.

Access to the shared ring is via the procedure described by ISO. Data transmission in the ring is unidirectional. At any given time, there is only one token or frame (single-token procedure, 4 Mbps) in the ring or one token and several frames from different end systems (single-token procedure, early token release, 16 Mbps). Each terminal connected to the ring regenerates the incoming signal (intermediate storage of at least one bit of the data stream in each attached terminal) and forwards the information to the next station. Token Ring interfaces operate in duplex mode (send and receive simultaneously to minimize delays), unlike in FDDI (half duplex) where the high transmission speed of 100 Mbps would make duplex transmission too expensive. Thus, there is no direct link between senders and recipients as in other LAN protocols.

The forwarding of a token from station to station may be compared with a $N \times 100$ m relay race in which the baton (token) is passed from one runner (station) to the next fresh runner (signal repeater). If there is no new runner, in our example, the $N \times 100$ m relay with the given team comes to an end. In the token-passing procedure, outage of a station should not of course lead to interruption of the overall data flow. Here, as we shall see later, the protocol, the mechanics of the IBM multistation access units and the duplicated, redundant cabling in the ring provide appropriate mechanisms. In addition to the stations, passive repeaters also boost the signal flow if large distances are involved. All the usual transmission media may be used (copper cable, coaxial cable, fibre-optic cable) and mixed.

2.2.1 Embedding of Token Ring in the ISO/OSI protocol hierarchy

Although we described the basis of the procedure in the standard protocol stack in Chapter 1, we now consider it again in more detail.

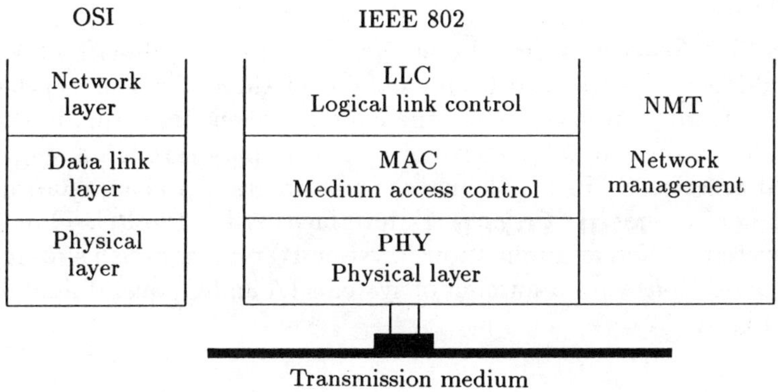

Figure 2.1 The Token Ring protocol elements and their relation to the OSI layers.

The Token Ring protocol is a very simple and very reliable procedure. Unlike Ethernet and the Token Bus it is based on the presence of a monitor and includes procedures for the lowest layer and part of the second layer of the ISO/OSI reference model (see Figure 2.1).

The Logical Link Control (LLC) layer is supported by all three standardized LANs. IBM describes these lowest two layers as the Data Link Control layer.

Token Ring networks may interwork closely with SNA systems. In an SNA network, the otherwise usual data link control layer may be replaced by the Token Ring LAN data link control layer. This permits a secure exchange of data between the LLC layer and the path control layer in an SNA network node.

In the following discussion, several terms from the ISO and SNA worlds are used. For a better understanding, brief explanations of these terms are given below. The reader who even with these explanations is unable to get to grips with SNA for lack of experience, is referred to the SNA summary in Chapter 8.

- **Link** A link is a logical connection between two link stations which is used for data exchange. A link includes end-to-end control mechanisms.
- **Link station** A link station is a protocol machine in an SNA node, which manages procedure elements for the data exchange with the neighbouring link station.
- **LPDU** The message unit which is exchanged between link stations in different nodes is called an LPDU (LLC Protocol Data Unit). It

contains the address of its own service access point and that of the desired destination, together with the control information and the data.

- **SAP** Service Access Points (SAPs) may be described as fixed addresses (ports) which applications of the underlying service layer use to request services. In the case of Token Ring, this is the DLC LAN described below. Several links may pass through a single SAP. In practice, SAPs enable one or more programs to communicate with other systems via the network interface card in the PC. Thus, in any system, different applications (system B) may establish simultaneous connections with a number of systems (A and C) over different SAPs (Figure 2.2).

2.2.2 An example

When does the user need the above facilities? Let us suppose that a user at an OS/2 workstation requires an interactive connection with a mainframe (to call up data there), a connection to the Office Vision Server (to send and receive mail) and a connection to a file server with a database application (to obtain data for report generation from different systems, process it further and forward it to colleagues who require this data). In addition, he maintains a connection to a non-IBM system based on a standardized ISO application (for example, FTAM). This scenario is illustrated in Figure 2.3.

The workstation requires a total of two SAPs, one for the ISO application and one for the NetBios applications. If the 3270

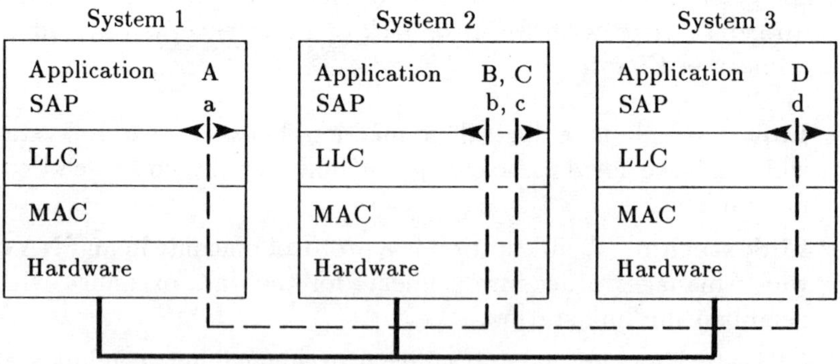

Figure 2.2 Communication between applications via SAPs.

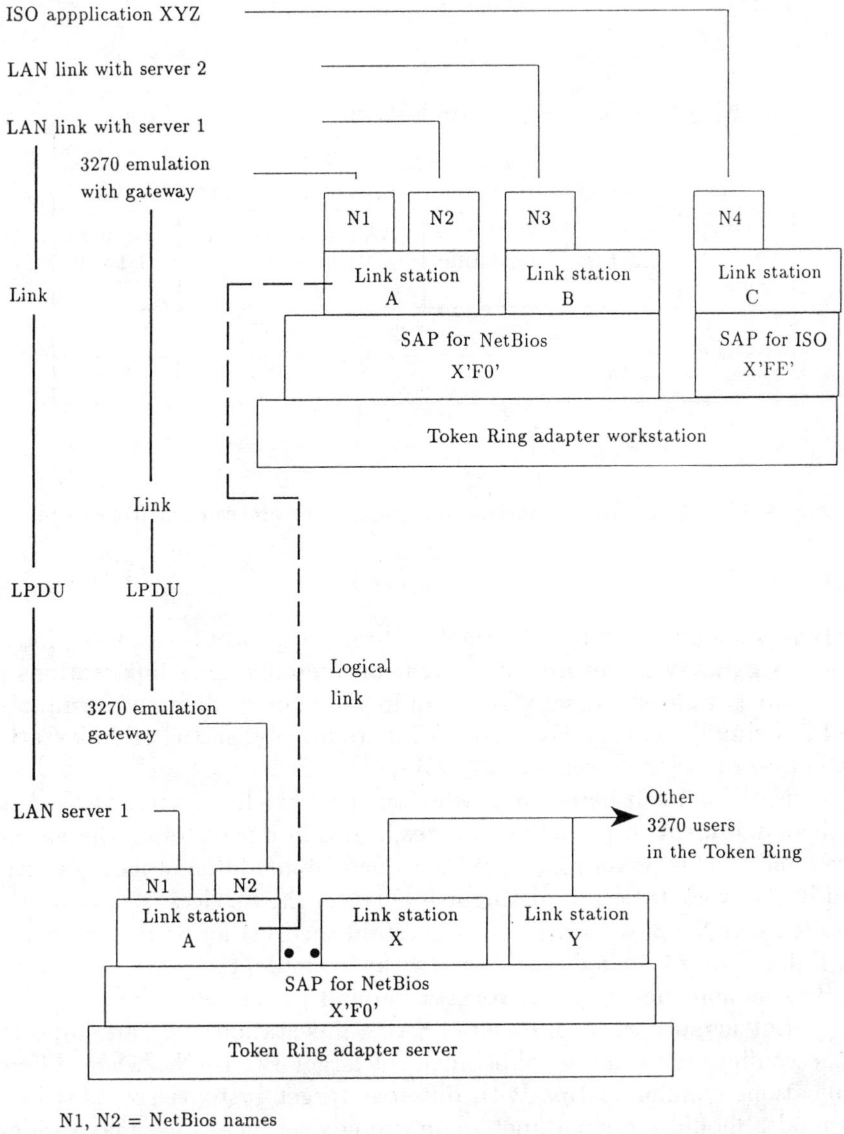

Figure 2.3 Token Ring connections between PCs and mainframes.

application does not go through a gateway server, but, for example, is implemented directly through a local IBM Establishment Controller (3270 controller) a further SAP is needed (address X'04'). We shall discuss the addresses and their meanings in what follows.

For the NetBios SAP with the address X'F0', in our example, there are two link stations in the workstation, since the workstation maintains

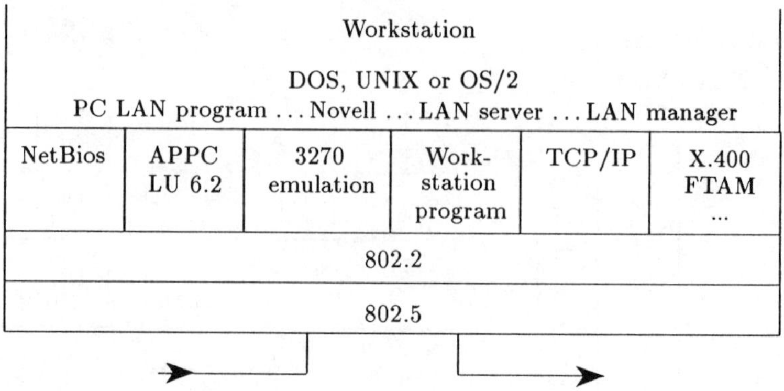

Figure 2.4 Examples of interfaces and application programs on Token Ring.

NetBios connections to two different systems. It is easy to see that, for this reason, a gateway server may maintain considerably more link stations per SAP, namely at least as many as it requires to manage different terminals in the LAN simultaneously. For example, there may be up to 255 link stations in the case of OS/2 servers or gateways.

NetBios itself determines who can use which services, again based on the assignment of predefined names. Since in our example the gateway server and the file server represent the same system, different names must be used in the workstation to distinguish between the services. A link between two identical NetBios names which is established via an SAP and connects two link stations is called a *session*. In our example, there are two different NetBios sessions between the workstation and the server.

Entries such as the number of SAPs, link stations, etc. are important in the configuration and establishment of larger PC LANs, when different applications communicating with different target systems are used in the terminals. Should these parameters be wrongly set, heavy use may suddenly lead to the inability to implement further connections or to a degradation of the network performance, because, for example, the buffer areas for the data areas were chosen to be too small or unnecessary storage in the workstation was allocated when the number of parameters (for example, the number of link stations) was too large. Figure 2.4 shows a hypothetical example of a system with typical practical applications.

Thus, when PCs and workstations are used, correct design and configuration of a LAN is non-trivial and requires detailed knowledge of the system and applications in the LAN. The necessary system parameters are set at different points, depending on the operating system. In DOS

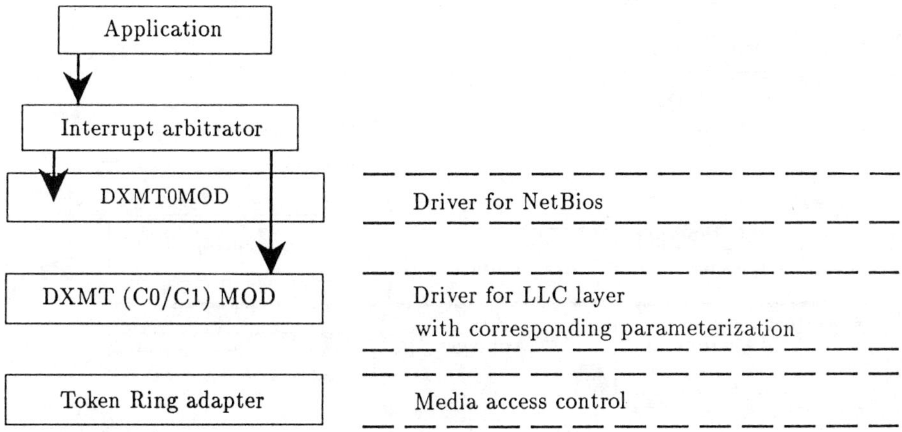

Figure 2.5 LAN drivers for DOS PCs and their interplay.

and OS/2 systems the parameters of the so-called LAN driver in the file CONFIG.SYS are automatically picked up on system start-up and are used to load driver programs and system parameters. The corresponding LAN drivers for Token Ring are called (see Figure 2.5) DXMA0MOD.SYS, DXMCMOD.SYS and DXMT0MOD.SYS.

The interrupt arbitrator (DXMA0MOD.SYS) reloads the DOS interrupt X'5C' and thus permits virtual access to a network device. This means that the user may access the device as if it were directly in or attached to his PC. It is mandatory and requires around 1 kbyte storage.

In the device driver for the LLC layer, the predefined and worldwide unique adaptor address may be altered and another storage area (shared RAM) selected for common use by the adaptor and the PC. The individual parameters, insofar as they are not version dependent, are described in more detail in Chapter 4.

2.3 The protocols of the lowest two layers

After this general description of the data flow between LANs and applications and vice versa, we come to the details of the IBM Token Ring environment.

In an IBM SNA/SAA environment, every node in a Token Ring network must have a Token Ring data link control layer (DLC.LAN for short), otherwise it cannot communicate with other (IBM) systems in the LAN.

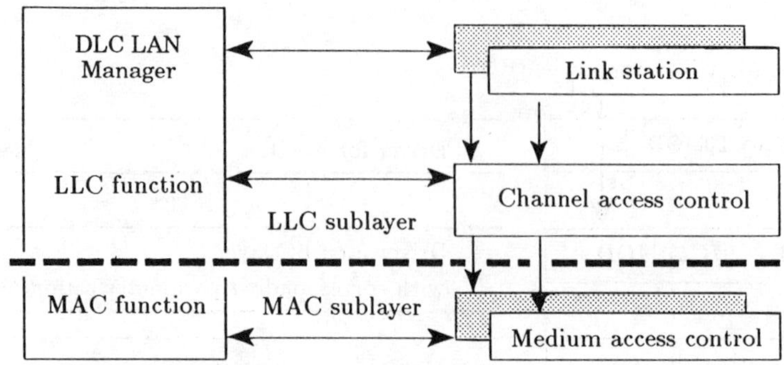

Figure 2.6 Token Ring data link control layer.

2.3.1 DLC.LAN

The DLC.LAN is further subdivided into the DLC LAN manager (DLC.LAN.MGR), the logical link control (LLC) sublayer and the medium access control (MAC) sublayer (see Figure 2.6).

The DLC.LAN.MGR is functionally responsible for both the LLC and the MAC sublayers. It monitors the operations of the DLC.LAN, the data flow between the LLC and the MAC sublayers and connection establishment. It controls access of stations to the ring and their removal from it. As far as the transmission of data or information for other control layers is concerned, the LAN.MGR behaves transparently. It activates or deactivates ring and link stations on request from an application.

In an SNA environment, connection establishment and release are provided for by the physical unit (PU) which is contained in each SNA terminal in various guises (PU 1–PU 5). PCs and workstations in Token Ring normally use PU 2 or PU 2.1 for communication with other systems in the SNA Token Ring. The individual commands and parameters are not discussed here. For a description of these see the IBM Token Ring Network Architecture Reference and the IBM Local Area Network Technical Manual.

2.3.2 Logical link control (LLC) sublayer

Within the LLC, there are three different ways of monitoring a communication between two link stations.

IBM supports connection-oriented data transfer (type 3) and connectionless mode data transfer (user datagram service, type 1). Connectionless mode data transfer with acknowledgement of each individual message unit (type 2) is not supported.

DSAP address	SSAP address	Control field	Information field

Figure 2.7 LPDU format.

Connectionless mode data transfer does not involve the establishment of fixed logical links (link, link station). As soon as an SAP is activated, communications with other SAPs also operating in connectionless mode may be passed through the new SAP. The LLC layer has no involvement with link status information or flow control. In this case, this falls to the layer above.

Connectionless mode data transfer recognizes only three LPDU formats:

- XID Command/response (exchange identifier)
- TEST Command/response
- UI Unnumbered information command

Each command must contain the sender address, the destination addresses and possibly routing information. This procedure does not provide for error detection or removal. Datagram services are based on this form of data transfer.

In its own applications IBM uses connection-oriented data transfer. This form of data transfer is known from HDLC and SDLC in public and IBM networks, respectively. The data transfer approximately corresponds to HDLC ABM for the exchange of LPDUs. Connection-oriented data transfer requires logical links between the partners (link stations). Errors are detected and removed by the protocol.

The so-called LLC frames which are transmitted in Token Ring are of variable length. Figure 2.7 shows the corresponding LPDU format.

The DSAP address (Destination Service Access Point) indicates the destination SAP for which the LPDU is intended (Figure 2.8).

The DSAP address consists of six address bits (A) and a bit which indicates that the address is defined by the user itself (U). When the address is specified by IEEE, the U-bit is set to '1'. The last bit (I/G) indicates whether the destination address is an individual address ('0') or a group address ('1').

Bit 0							Bit 7
A	A	A	A	A	A	U	I/G

Figure 2.8 Structure of the DSAP address.

The most important SAPs specified to date are:

- Zero SAP (X'00'). This is used when no SAP has been activated. The SAP only supports connectionless mode data transfer (TEST, XID LPDUs).
- DoD Internet protocol SAP (X'06'). This SAP is reserved for TCP/IP as defined by the US DoD.
- ISO network layer SAP (X'FE'). This is reserved for use by the ISO network layer.
- Global SAP (X'FF'). Every SAP contains a copy of this LPDU.
- SNA path control SAP (X'04'). This is a standard SAP address for SNA nodes (for example, local cluster controllers). When several links between two SNA nodes are established via the same adaptor, only one link on each side (SNA nodes) may use this address (X'04'), since links are uniquely defined by their destination and source addresses. Thus, in an SNA node, another SAP may have to be chosen (for example, 3270 workstation program with SAP X'08' in the PC. Other possible SAPs would be various X'04's).
- LAN management SAP (X'F4'). This is reserved for LAN management functions occurring at the LLC level.
- NetBios SAP (X'F0'). This SAP is used by all LLC links which use NetBios emulation.
- Application-specific SAPs (X'8y'–X'9C' with y not equal to B'xx1x'). These are reserved for original applications.

Other SAPs have also been defined; however, these are of a lesser importance as far as an understanding of the mode of operation of Token Ring is concerned and thus we shall not describe them further here.

The source address (Figure 2.9) has a similar structure to the destination address.

It again consists of the six source address bits (S) and the U-bit. The seventh bit (C/R) indicates whether the LPDU is a command ('0') or a response ('1').

The control field contains the commands which are required for connection-oriented data transfer.

Bit 0							Bit 7
S	S	S	S	S	S	U	C/R

Figure 2.9 Structure of the source SAP address.

As in SDLC/HDLC, the following formats are used:

- Information transfer format (I format) for the transmission of data and information, monitored by send and receive counters. The maximum window size is 128 (in other words, up to 127 frames may be transmitted without acknowledgement).
- Supervisory format for the transmission of control and monitoring information such as
  - REJ (Reject)
  - RNR (Receive not ready)
  - RR (Receive ready)
- Unnumbered formats for additional control information, with no facility for transmitting accompanying acknowledgement information:
  - **SABME** (set asynchronous balanced mode extended) is used for connection establishment. A link station which receives a SABME replies with a
  - **UA** (unnumbered acknowledgement) when the connection can be established.
  - **DISC** (disconnect) indicates that a station wishes to clear a connection previously established using SABME. It is confirmed by a UA.
  - **DM** (disconnect mode response) is used to clear a connection established by the other station. It can also be used to prevent a SABME (and with it, a connection establishment).
  - **FRMR** (frame reject) is used by a link station if it receives an incorrect or unidentifiable LPDU format.
  - **XID** (exchange identification) is used to establish a connection. The sending (link) station tells the recipient its characteristics and waits for an XID response to the XID from the remote link station. IEEE 802.2 prescribes the layout of the first three bytes in the information field of an XID LPDU (Figure 2.10).

Byte 0								Byte 1								Byte 2							
1	0	0	0	0	0	0	1	0	0	0	C	C	C	C	C	W	W	W	W	W	W	W	0

Figure 2.10 Structure of an XID LPDU.

The value X'81' in byte 1 indicates that it is a standard IEEE XID information field. XID LPDUs may also be exchanged with an SNA-specific format. Byte 1 specifies whether the transmission is connectionless B'00001' or connection oriented B'00011'. Byte 2 specifies the maximum window size which may be used between the two link stations.

— **TEST** The test command is used to exchange test information with other link stations. It contains an optional message field with information which is normally confirmed by the responding station. TEST and XID are used to establish a connection between link stations operating on different Token Ring LANs linked via bridges.

Figure 2.11 gives a summary of the most important LLC commands.

2.3.3 Medium access control (MAC) sublayer

The MAC sublayer monitors the transmission of information between the physical and the LLC layers. A control field in the frame to be transmitted indicates in each case whether the frame is a MAC frame or an LLC frame. This enables each protocol layer to determine whether or not it should interpret the frame. Within the MAC protocol layer, functions such as

- token management,
- timing,
- address recognition,
- frame copying,
- frame status generation and verification,
- routing, and
- priority management

are executed. We shall describe these functions in detail later. The token protocol itself is executed in this layer.

Commands	Commands/Responses	Responses
SABME	REJ	UA
DISC	RNR	DM
TEST	RR	TEST
XID		XID
		FRMR

Figure 2.11 LLC commands.

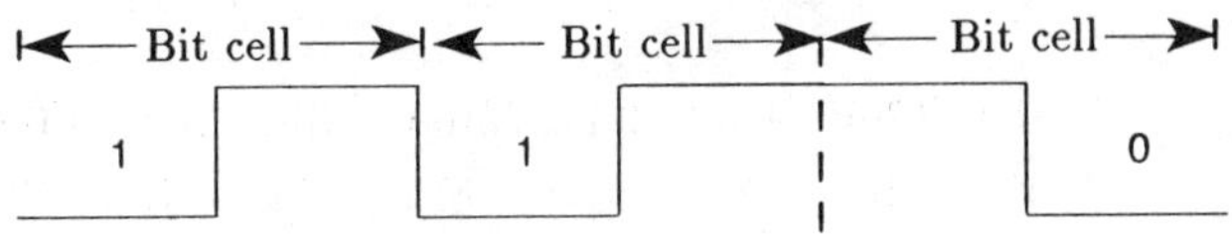

Figure 2.12 Manchester coding procedure.

2.3.4 Physical layer

Finally, the physical transmission and bit detection take place in the physical layer. Connection of the stations to the ring involves the generation of a so-called phantom voltage in the terminal which ensures that, if faults arise, stations are automatically removed from the ring since this voltage drops immediately. The phantom voltage is in the range 3.9–5.2 volts with a maximum delay of 50 ms in the case of faults.

Other functions of the physical layer include the generation of the master clock, the bit detection itself, detection of signal losses and code violations and the provision of an equalization buffer to compensate for small time differences between two stations.

2.3.4.1 Coding in Token Ring

Before the data is transmitted on the cable, the binary data must be converted into signal elements. In Token Ring, the so-called Manchester encoding procedure is used.

This is a derivative of the Manchester coding procedure (Figure 2.12) which is used, for example, in Ethernet LANs.

These procedures have a number of advantages in the case of the LAN implementation. They are relatively easy to implement, self-synchronizing, do not require a separate clock source and are DC free.

In the Manchester encoding procedure, the first half of the bit value contains the complemented value, while the second half contains the actual bit value. This ensures that even when binary data which may contain a consecutive sequence of several logical B'0' or B'1' is transmitted, DC signals cannot be formed (this would mean that clock synchronization could not be guaranteed).

Differential Manchester coding in Token Ring is based on the Manchester code. Unlike the Manchester code, it uses the code violation error condition for certain signal sequences, such as the start and end byte of a frame or token. Here, code violation means that if there is no polarity change in the middle of a bit, an artificial error condition arises which is used to detect a frame or a token. As before, no code violations should

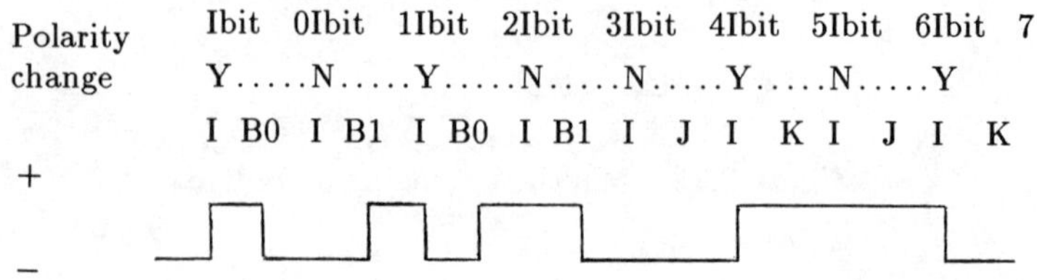

Figure 2.13 Differential Manchester code. Generally for normal bits, there is a polarity change in the middle of the bit.

occur within a frame or token. The special bit patterns which are used, for example, in HDLC or Ethernet to detect a frame or a token are now dropped.

Unlike the Manchester code, it is not the second half of the bit which determines the information content (B'0' or B'1') but whether or not a polarity change occurs at the beginning of the bit. The following rules may be identified from Figure 2.13:

- Transmission of a 0: polarity change
- Transmission of a 1: no polarity change
- Transmission of J (positive code violation): no polarity change
- Transmission of K (negative code violation): polarity change

According to the previous bit state, the information unit shown symbolically in Figure 2.13 may also be represented by its mirror image (Figure 2.14).

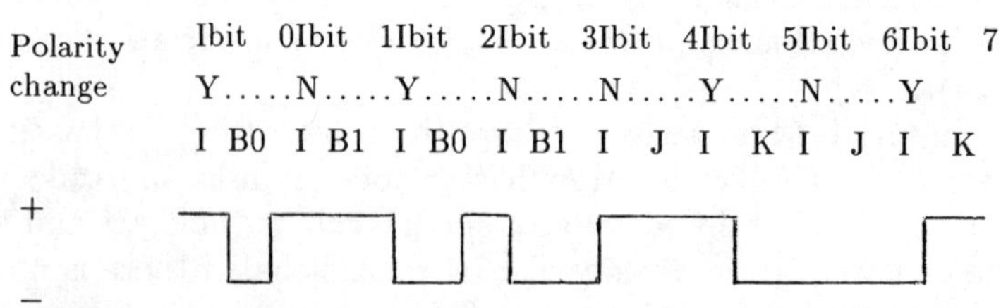

Figure 2.14 Differential Manchester coding (alternative representation).

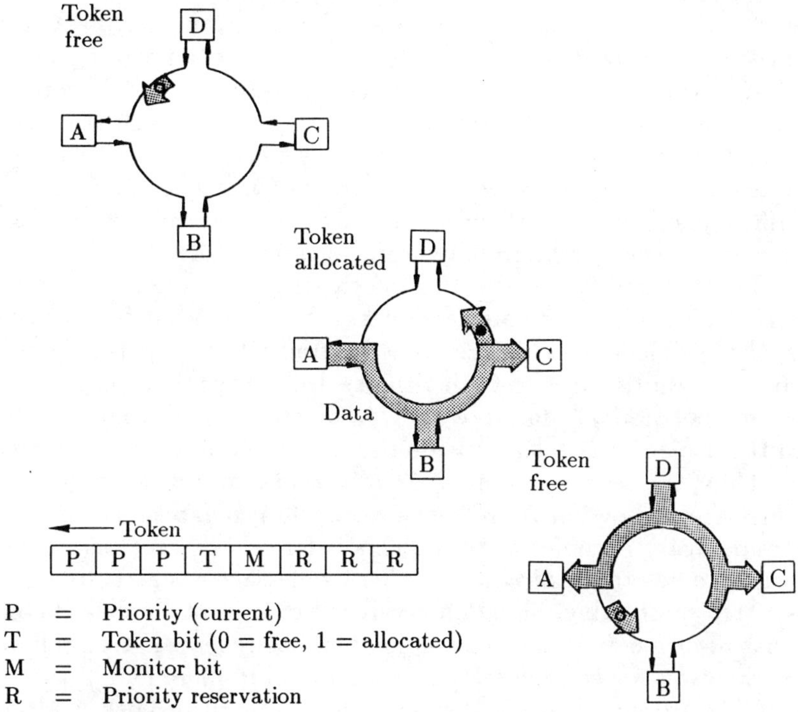

Figure 2.15 Token Ring – the token-passing procedure.

2.4 Token passing, addressing and formats

Before we go into the details of Token Ring and components of it which are available on the market, in the following, we provide the reader with further details of the mode of operation of the Token Ring protocol.

2.4.1 The token-passing principle

Whenever a station wishes to send information over the ring, it must wait until it receives a free token, the send authorization (Figure 2.15).

This token is generated and monitored by the active monitor in the ring. The monitor is usually (according to the procedure described in Section 2.5.3) automatically the first station to be actively connected to the ring. All other stations are introduced to the ring as stand-by monitors, so that if necessary, should the actual monitor fail, these stations can take on its control functions immediately.

As soon as a station receives a free token (a specific 3-byte bit pattern), it adds its own address, the address of the recipient and the information to be transmitted (the length of this is limited) to the token. The frame thus formed from the token is received and automatically forwarded by all subsequent stations in the ring even though these stations may themselves have data to transmit. They must wait until they receive a free token. Since each station may only transmit a single frame with a prescribed maximum length, it is very easy to determine the maximum waiting time before a station may begin to transmit data.

The station for which the information was intended copies the information into its storage area and marks the frame as having been copied. Thus, the recipient does not remove the frame from the ring, but again forwards it onwards. Amongst other things, this means that the transmission checksum (polynomial) does not have to be recalculated, since the field in which the copier bit is set is outside the area controlled by the checksum.

Thus, the sender of a message receives its own message back as the next message, removes it from the network and generates a new free token. The frame again becomes a token. This is for security reasons. It enables the sender to determine directly whether its message has actually been fully transmitted by the ring. Should it receive a message other than its own, an error has occurred and the transmission must be repeated. We shall explain the mechanisms for error detection and removal in more detail later.

This procedure, using a single token, is used in both 4 Mbps and 16 Mbps Token Rings. The difference between the two procedures is determined by the time at which a new token may be generated and whether or not more than one frame may circulate in the ring at the same time.

In the case of the 16 Mbps Token Ring, one speaks of the early token release procedure.

Why are there different procedures for the 4 Mbps and the 16 Mbps Token Rings? What are the advantages of this and when is this procedure sensible? Let us look at Figure 2.16 to understand this.

In our example, four stations are attached in one case to a 4 Mbps ring and in another case to a 16 Mbps ring. The message to be transmitted has the same length in both cases. The ring length is also the same in both cases. In the first case of the 4 Mbps ring, the message occupies almost the entire ring. The sending station only has to generate a few so-called idle characters, until it receives its own message back. As a rule it will even manage without idle characters and receive the same message back whilst it is still being sent. At first sight, this seems improbable, so we shall explain this below.

The storage capacity of a ring comprises the number of bits in the ring itself together with the number of bits of intermediate storage used in each active station to boost the signal. The number of bits in the ring at a

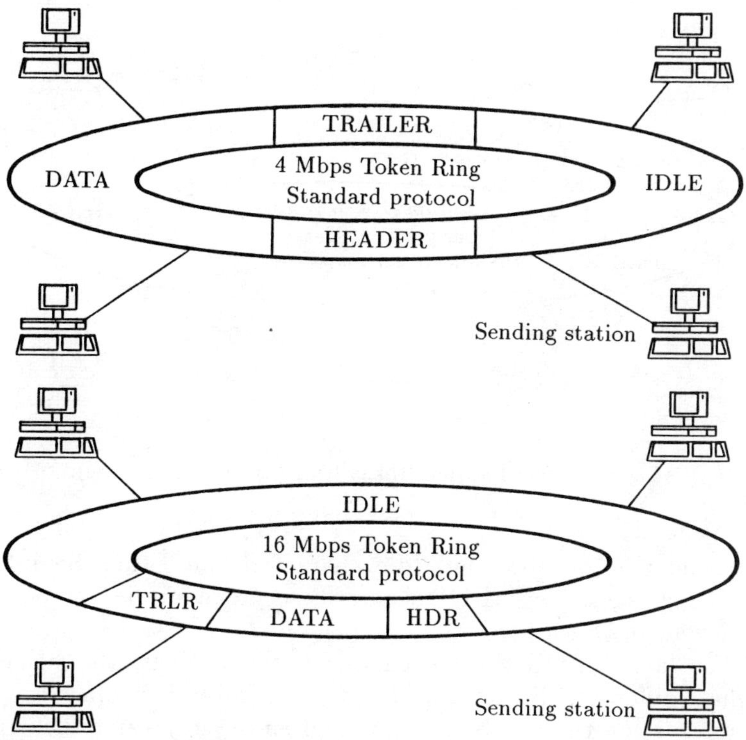

Figure 2.16 Token Ring standard protocol for 4 Mbps and 16 Mbps.

given time N may be calculated using the following simplified formula

$$N = (D \times L)/V$$

where D is the data rate of the ring protocol (bps), L is the length of the ring in metres, and V is the signal propagation rate in metres per second.

It is easy to see from hand calculations that

- bit length for 4 Mbps : 50 m
- bit length for 16 Mbps : 12.5 m.

Assuming the values $D = 4$ Mbps and $L = 2000$ m, we obtain a storage capacity N of approximately 7 bytes, provided we also assume that only one bit of intermediate storage per station is needed for signal boosting. Thus, every message that is longer than 8 bytes fills the ring completely.

For small installations, there is no drastic change in this if the ring speed is multiplied by a factor of 4 to 16 Mbps. Instead of 8 bytes,

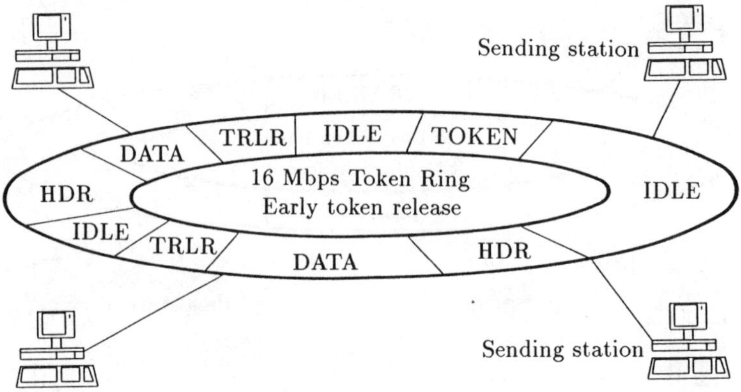

Figure 2.17 16 Mbps Token Ring (early token release).

32 bytes now fit on the ring. Idle characters must thus be introduced for small messages. The early token release procedure is not particularly advantageous in this case.

For large installations such as backbone rings, the behaviour is somewhat different. Here, ring lengths of several kilometres are not uncommon. Even the number of attached end systems may be very high. Thus, such a ring may have enough storage capacity for several frames.

The early token release procedure is sensible in this case. This procedure admits several frames on to the ring, but operates, as before, with a single token. In Figure 2.17 the first send station (bottom right) has transmitted a frame consisting of a header, a data part and a trailer. After a short waiting time (Idle 1) it generates a new free token. This free token is used immediately by the second send station (top right) to generate and transmit its own frame. Here too the station generates a free token after a brief waiting time. An instantaneous snapshot of this is given in Figure 2.17. Next, station 1 removes its message from the ring and regenerates the message from station 2 which is then removed from the network by station 2. Note that at any one time, there is at most one token in the ring and every send station receives its own message back in the next frame (provided no errors occur) for removal from the network.

2.4.2 Addressing in Token Ring

What is addressing in Token Ring like? What exactly is a token? How is a frame structured? We shall now answer these questions in detail.

A total of 6 bytes or 2 bytes are reserved for addressing at the MAC layer level. IBM uses 6-byte addressing in all applications. The addressing takes place in the frame and not in the token since the token has no knowledge of a particular destination. In Token Rings, distinction is drawn between:

- individual addresses, and
- group addresses,

and between

- unique addresses managed by the manufacturer (for example, IEEE globally unique addresses), and
- locally managed addresses (4000 ...) corresponding to local schemes and adapted to the company structure.
  Caution: when two Token Rings are joined together, the occurrence of two identical addresses in the different LANs may give rise to errors which are not immediately identifiable. It is not possible to introduce the second station with the same address into the ring. Generally, there is no error message.

In addition to these general addresses, there are also addresses with special functions. These are as follows:

- Zero address X'0000 0000 0000' or test address. This is 6 (IBM) bytes or 2 bytes long. A frame with this address may be sent but not received. The frame is removed from the ring by the send station when a free token is again generated.

- Broadcast addresses X'FFFF FFFF FFFF' and X'C000 FFFF FFFF'. A frame with such an address is intended for all active stations in the ring. It is used, amongst other things, for all datagram communications. The extent to which a broadcast message may be forwarded over bridges to other subrings is determined in a special field in the frame (routing information).

2.4.2.1 Function-dependent addresses

In IBM Token Rings, function-dependent addresses are used for particularly common applications. The addressing involves bit masks, where each bit of a mask is assigned to a particular function or application. A total of 31 different bit masks may be defined.

Destination addresses, source addresses and function-dependent addresses have different structures.

The destination address identifies the station which is intended to receive (copy) the frame. The destination address (Figure 2.18) is always

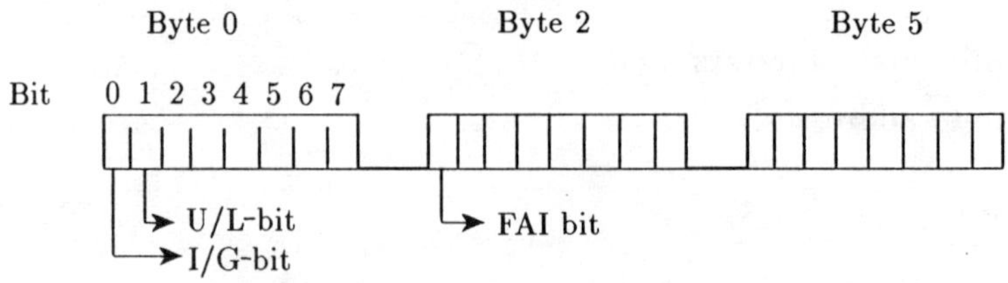

Figure 2.18 Structure of destination addresses in Token Ring.

6 bytes long in IBM LANs.

Bit 0 (I/G bit) in byte 0 is used to distinguish between an individual or a single address (B'0') and a so-called group destination address (B'1') as used for broadcast messages.

Bit 1 (U/L bit) in byte 0 may be used to determine whether the destination address is universal (B'0') or local (B'1'). Universal addresses are predefined by the factory and are unique worldwide (provided the factory adheres to the standard).

If bit 0 in byte 2 (FAI bit) is set to B'0' the address is a function-dependent address. All function-dependent addresses must be locally defined group addresses in accordance with the previous definitions (in byte 0, bit 0,1=B'11'). In certain circumstances, they may denote several destinations (group) and do not correspond to addresses specified by the manufacturer of the interface card.

A function-dependent address mask may be specified using the remaining 7 bits in byte 2 and the bits of the address bytes three, four and five. Thus, there is a total of 31 possible function-dependent addresses.

Function-dependent addresses include the following:

Active monitor	X'C000 0000 0001'	(byte 5, bit 7)
Ring parameter server	X'C000 0000 0002'	(byte 5, bit 6)
Ring error monitor	X'C000 0000 0008'	(byte 5, bit 4)
Configuration report server	X'C000 0000 0010'	(byte 5, bit 3)
NetBios	X'C000 0000 0080'	(byte 5, bit 0)
Bridge	X'C000 0000 0100'	(byte 4, bit 7)
Free for applications	X'C000 0008 0000'	(byte 3, bits 0–4)
	up to	
	X'C000 4000 0000'	(byte 2, bits 1–7)

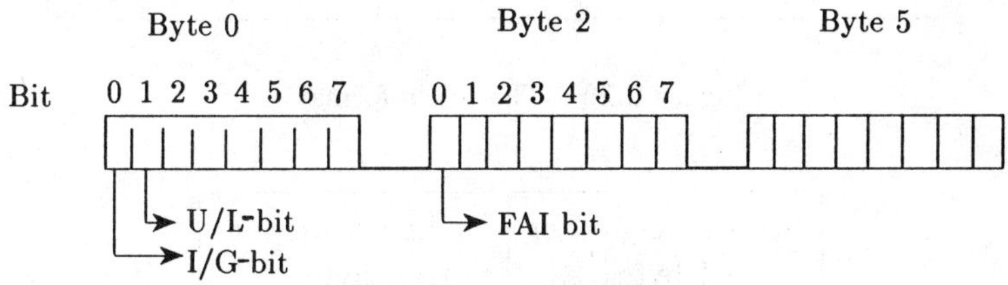

Figure 2.19 Structure of source addresses.

Stations in the ring may incorporate several of these functions at the same time. If, for example, a certain user function has the mask X'C000 0008 0000' and another has the mask X'C000 4000 0000' then the station in the ring which incorporates both these functions has the mask X'C000 4008 0000'.

2.4.2.2 Structure of the source address

The source address (Figure 2.19) is only slightly different from the destination address.

Since a source address cannot be a group address, bit 0 of byte 0 is used for another purpose. If this bit is set to B'1' then this frame contains routing information. The destination address refers to a station in another ring, which is linked to the subring of the send station via at least one bridge.

This addressing may be used to define globally unique addresses. The addressing permits 12-character hexadecimal addresses. Local addresses may be recognized immediately, since they all begin with 4....

Where the addresses of users are inserted, and how these may be read or altered is described in detail in the sections on the corresponding hardware and software components.

2.4.3 Tokens, abort delimiters and frames

We now return to the Token Ring protocol itself and its most important components, the token and the frame.

The token (Figure 2.20) consists of two particular fields which identify the token (or frame) as far as a station is concerned, namely the starting delimiter field and the ending delimiter field, together with the access control field. We shall describe the individual fields in more detail in our description of the frame.

Starting delimiter 1 byte	Access control 1 byte	Ending delimiter 1 byte

Figure 2.20 The token format.

Starting delimiter 1 byte	Ending delimiter 1 byte

Figure 2.21 The abort delimiter.

The abort delimiter (Figure 2.21) is of particular importance. This is generated by a station in the ring when it detects a faulty token or a removable or irremovable error in its own functioning. If the error is not removable, the station deactivates itself.

The frame format (Figure 2.22) is used to transfer information in Token Ring. Like the token, the frame contains a starting and an ending delimiter field, the access control field (AC) and the address fields as described previously together with additional control and information fields which we shall describe in detail later.

2.4.3.1 Starting delimiter and ending delimiter

The starting and the ending delimiter fields (Figures 2.23 and 2.24) contain the non-coded information bits J and K (code violation) for the differential

SD	AC	FC	Destin. address	Start address	Routing information (optional)	Data (optional)	Frame check sequence	ED	FS
1	1	1	6	6	— variable length —		4	1	1

Length in bytes

SD	=	Starting Delimiter	AC	=	Access Control
SFS	=	SD + AC; Start of Frame Sequence	FC	=	Frame Control
DA	=	Destination Address (2 or 6 bytes)	ED	=	Ending Delimiter
FCS	=	Frame Check Sequence	FS	=	Frame Status
EFS	=	ED + FS; End of Frame Sequence			

Figure 2.22 The frame format.

Bit 0							Bit 7
J	K	0	J	K	0	0	0

J = Code violation
K = Code violation

Figure 2.23 Starting delimiter.

Bit 0							Bit 7
J	K	1	J	K	1	I	E

Figure 2.24 Ending delimiter.

Manchester code. These bits only occur in these two fields and thus permit unique identification of a token or frame without the need for a special procedure (for example, bit stuffing in HDLC) to introduce artificial bits into the information to be transmitted in order to prevent the accidental occurrence of delimiter fields in the data part.

The ending delimiter field contains two additional information fields. Setting the I-bit to B'1' (intermediate frame bit) indicates that a frame is the first or *n*th frame of a logically connected group of several frames which are to be transmitted consecutively. Setting the bit to B'0' indicates that this is the last of the frames to be transmitted or a single frame.

The error-detected bit (E-bit) is always set to B'0' when a frame or a token is generated by a station. The first station to detect that the frame is faulty sets this bit to B'1'. Errors such as the occurrence of code violations (J, K bits) in the middle of a frame or outside the starting and ending delimiters are detected in this way.

2.4.3.2 Access control field

The access control field (Figure 2.25) occurs both in a token and in a frame.

Each station uses the token bit to determine whether it is dealing with a token (T=B'0') or a frame (T=B'1').

This field is also used for control purposes by the ring monitor. According to the token-passing procedure, each frame or token with

Bit 0 … Bit 7

P	P	P	T	M	R	R	R

P = Bits for access priority
T = Token bit
M = Monitor bit
R = Reservation bits

Figure 2.25 Access control field.

additional priority information may only pass each station once since the sender of the message (or priority information) removes it from the network. To prevent a message from going round the ring several times or even blocking the ring, when, due to an error in the send station, it cannot be removed from the ring, the monitor marks every message which passes with the monitor bit (M=B'1'). Should it now receive a frame in which the monitor bit is already set, the message has not been removed from the ring. The monitor then deletes all the information in the ring and generates a new token.

In the Token Ring protocol, access priorities may be allocated to control the access of each station to the ring. Generally, a station may only access the ring and turn a token into an information frame if the priority allocated to it is greater than or equal to that of the token. The station can also allocate priorities to the individual applications. A total of eight priority levels may be defined. The details of the operation of the priority algorithm are given in the section on the MAC layer.

Stations with high priority may use the reservation bits of tokens or frames which they have generated to specify that the next free token should be allocated the same high priority.

2.4.3.3 Frame control field

Just as the token bit in the access control field is used to distinguish between frames (occupied) and tokens (free), the F-bit in the frame control field (Figure 2.26) is used to distinguish between an LLC frame (data frame) and a MAC frame (level 2 control information).

At present the Z-bits only have a meaning for MAC frames. When these bits are set to B'0' the MAC frame is treated normally (in other words, it is placed in intermediate storage and is processed in order or passed to the next higher protocol level). If the buffer areas are full, the next MAC frame cannot be copied. Some of these frames must be processed as soon as

Bit 0 Bit 7

F	F	r	r	Z	Z	Z	Z

F = Frame-type bit
B'00' = MAC frame
B'01' = LLC frame
B'10' and B'11' not currently defined
r = Reserved
Z = Control bit

Figure 2.26 Frame control field.

possible. An express buffer is used for this. When this is used other frames are detected but not copied, while the processing of the precedential MAC frame continues. MAC frames of this type include:

- Remove ring station. The station must remove itself from the ring, for example, by command of the LAN manager.
- Claim token. This is a procedure to determine the ring monitor.
- Beacon. Here, a timer for the period in which a token should have reached a station has elapsed.
- Active monitor present. This involves a functional test of the ring, the initiation of the NAUN procedure and a signal that an active monitor is present.
- Stand-by monitor present. This is cleared by an active monitor present MAC frame.
- Duplicate address test. This test involves introducing another station with the same address into the ring.
- Ring purge. This is activated by the monitor in the case of token error and at the end of the token-claiming process.

These frames are described in detail below.

2.4.3.4 Frame check sequence

This 4-byte field may be used in conjunction with the CRC procedure to determine whether or not the message to be transmitted is altered during the transmission itself. The procedure corresponds to the HDLC and SDLC CRC procedures. However, a different check polynomial is used; we shall not discuss this further here. The CRC procedure covers all fields except the frame status field and the ending delimiter.

Bit 0							Bit 7
A	C	r	r	A	C	r	r

A = Address recognized bit
C = Frame copied bit
r = Reserved, function not currently defined

Figure 2.27 Frame status field.

2.4.3.5 Frame status field

Since the frame status field (Figure 2.27) is not covered by the normal CRC checksum, the two information fields A and C are each duplicated. They must also be identical, otherwise transmission errors may occur. It lies outside the coverage of the CRC checksum to prevent unnecessary delays in the copying procedure. Were this field to be covered by the CRC checksum, it would be necessary to recalculate the CRC field in each copy process.

Using the A-bits, the sender of a message can determine whether the destination station it addressed is present in the network. When the destination detects a frame addressed to it, it sets the A-bit to B'1'.

This enables a station being introduced to a ring to determine whether there is already an active station in the ring with the same address. The new station sends a MAC frame with its own address as destination address to the ring. If the A-bit is set, there must be another station with the same address in the ring.

If the C-bit remains unset (B'0') the destination station has not copied the data into its input buffer area. When this bit is set to B'1', the sender knows that the information has reached the recipient.

The following are valid bit combinations:

- AC=B'00'. There is no station present in the ring with the given destination address or no bridge which has forwarded this information.
- AC=B'11'. A station in the ring has copied the frame intended for it or a bridge has transmitted the frame to a neighbouring ring.
- AC=B'10'. The station detected the message intended for it but was unable to copy it (for example, because the bridge was overloaded).
- AC=B'01'. This combination is invalid.

2.5 The Token Ring monitor

What does the monitoring of the protocol execution involve?

Every Token Ring is composed of active interconnected stations, which intercommunicate via a transmission medium which may also operate in sections with differing transmission media. Every ring station may serve one or more terminals. Typical representatives of these include the PC, the screen controller, the front-end processor, the AS/400, the IBM 93xx or the IBM UNIX systems. Most recently, systems from other manufacturers (for example, Sun, Apple, Apollo) may now be directly attached to Token Ring. Normally, the token procedure operates without further intervention. However, when tokens are lost, missing or duplicated, intervention by a particular functional module, the monitor, is required.

2.5.1 A basic description of the monitor

Every ring has exactly one station which takes on the functions of an active monitor. All other active stations in the ring take on the functions of the stand-by monitor. Any station may become the active monitor in the ring at any time. A ring always has a monitor.

Every ring interface has two modes: listen (copy) and send. In the listening mode, the token or frame is always regenerated. In the send mode, the interface interrupts the link between input and output and the station data comes off or goes on to the ring. To facilitate rapid switching, the send data is held in a special buffer area (duplex mode). This means that delays to the data flow in the ring at the individual stations are made small. Only 1 or 2 bits are placed in intermediate storage at any one station.

If no station wishes to send the token circulates in the ring. Thus, the storage capacity of the ring must be at least as large as the token itself (24 bits). That this statement is non-trivial has already been discussed by means of an example. We recall that for 4 Mbps and 10 stations, ring lengths of 400 to 700 m are required to achieve a ring storage capacity of 3 bytes. If the storage capacity is insufficient the monitor artificially increases the capacity by providing buffer areas. In addition to the 24-bit buffer area of the monitor the monitor also needs equalization buffer areas (for example, to compensate phase shifts) when, for example, all 260 possible stations in the ring are active. 27 bits of the buffer area are initialized and this is expanded or decreased according to signal speed and ring size.

The station converts the free token into a frame by adding further check and control information and data as described in the last section. Each individual station may hold on to a token for a maximum of 10 ms for this purpose. At the same time, the maximum possible frame size is predefined. Only one frame may be transmitted. The actual maximum fragment size is predefined by the application or the interface (NetBios, APPC, etc.) according to the size of the available buffer area on the interface card.

It generally depends on the choice of transmission speed and is around 4000 bytes for 4 Mbps and 18 000 bytes for 16 Mbps. Some applications reduce the frame size even further. For example, the PC 3270 emulation program works with a frame size of only 256 bytes.

2.5.2 The monitor functions

The monitor monitors the timers and ensures that a valid token or frame is always present in the ring.

It detects ring errors such as:

- faulty or incomplete tokens,
- frames and priority tokens passing round the ring several times, and
- more than one active monitor in the ring.

The monitor also

- ensures that the ring has a minimum storage capacity of 3 bytes,
- monitors the ring master clock,
- controls the timing,
- synchronizes all timers in the ring,
- initiates the NAUN procedure T(neighbour_notification) 7s,
- monitors the NAUN procedure,
- monitors the transmission of tokens and frames,
- detects lost tokens or frames T(any_token)=10 ms, and
- clears the ring when faults occur and generates a new token.

What are the monitor's individual reactions in the case of faults?

2.5.3 Monitor reactions in the case of faults

In general, when faults arise the ring is cleared (the MAC frame 'ring purge' is sent as a broadcast frame to all active stations in the ring). What faults may occur?

(1) Loss of a token or a frame. The monitor waits for the starting delimiter field of a token or frame for a fixed time interval (T(any_token)). If this field does not arrive, the token is cleared and a free token generated. This timer is activated when a station takes on the monitor function and generates the first token.

(2) Infinitely circulating priority token or frame. Normally, the message is removed from the network by the original sender. Thus, each frame

must pass the monitor exactly once. In passing the monitor, a marker is set in the frame or priority token (monitor bit in the access control field). If a frame or a priority token in which this bit is already set reaches the monitor, a transmission error must have occurred, since after removing its frame or token from the ring, the sender always generates a new token in which this bit is set to B'0'. In this case the ring is cleared and a new token is generated.

(3) Duplication of a token or a frame. Every sending station checks the source address of the next incoming frame. According to the transmission procedure, this address must be its own address. If this is not the case then a previous message has not been removed from the ring and there is an error.

(4) Monitor outage. When a monitor fails (see Section 2.5.4) another station (chosen according to a fixed algorithm) takes on the monitor function. Every station may be or become a monitor.

2.5.4 Functions of the stand-by monitor

Every stand-by monitor (all other active stations in the ring) monitors the active monitor for error functions. Two timers are used for this, namely the timer T(good_token) and the timer T(receive_notification). The timer T(good_token) is set at 2.6 s in an IBM Token Ring network which is greater than the monitor's timer T(any_token) which monitors the network for error functions. Thus, it takes effect only when the active monitor fails. The timer is reset whenever a token or a frame passes the station.

Which station becomes the new monitor when the Token Ring monitor fails? This is decided by the token-claiming procedure.

This procedure determines which station next takes on the monitor function. The algorithm only applies to stations for which the corresponding option is set. The default value is 'non-participant'. However, the station which detects the error state must always take part in the token-claiming procedure, regardless of whether the option is set or not. If several stations participate in the token-claiming procedure, the monitor is chosen based on the individual addresses of each participating station. The station with the highest address wins the procedure.

The 'receive notification timer' is used in a special monitor procedure, to notify the stations of the address of the current (monitor) station at regular intervals. Normally, this procedure is executed approximately every 7 seconds by the monitor. In this case, the timer in the station is reset. If more than 15 seconds pass without the monitor initiating this procedure, there must be an error. After the token-claiming procedure, the address of the new ring monitor is notified.

2.5.5 The NAUN procedure

The NAUN (Next Addressable Upstream Neighbour) procedure is initiated by the active monitor and is primarily used for fast error detection and isolation (beaconing). The procedure is cleared by the timer T(neighbour_notification) which is set to 7 s. Should this expire, the monitor generates an active monitor present MAC frame with the broadcast address X'C000 FFFF FFFF'. The frame itself is given the highest priority (access control field=X'F0') to ensure that timers do not expire prematurely.

The first station to receive the active monitor present frame copies this frame and sets the address recognized and frame copied bits in the frame status field to B'1'. The source address in the frame is its NAUN address which it stores. After it has waited for the notification response timer to expire (20 ms) it itself generates a 'stand-by monitor present' MAC frame with frame status bits A and C set to B'0'.

The next station in the ring lets the active monitor present MAC frame pass since both bits in the frame status field have already been set to B'1'. However, it copies the address of the following stand-by monitor present MAC frame as its NAUN address and resets A and C to B'1'. It also waits for the notification response timer to expire (20 ms) whereupon it generates its own stand-by monitor present MAC frame with A and C set to B'0'.

This procedure continues until the monitor receives a stand-by monitor present MAC frame with the address recognized and frame copied bits set to B'0'. The station which sent this frame must be the station immediately before the monitor. Thus, the NAUN procedure is complete.

Should the monitor receive its own frame back with A and C set to B'0', it is the only active station in the network. If the NAUN procedure does not terminate within a predefined time, at least one station in the ring is defective. One possible cause of error is continual transmission of data over the ring without forwarding of the token (streaming).

2.6 Connecting a station to the ring

Anyone who has worked on a PC attached to a Token Ring will certainly have wondered why it sometimes takes so long for the PC to be actively switched into the ring. In certain circumstances, this process takes several seconds, and some impatient users find this so long a time that they restart their PCs using CTRL_ALT_DEL, assuming the PC to be defective. To calm the jumpy PC user this procedure is usually accompanied by beeping. Thereafter, the PC is able to access the server or gateway functions it requires in the ring. If there are more than four beeps or none at all, caution is advisable. This is usually symptomatic of a protocol or hardware error.

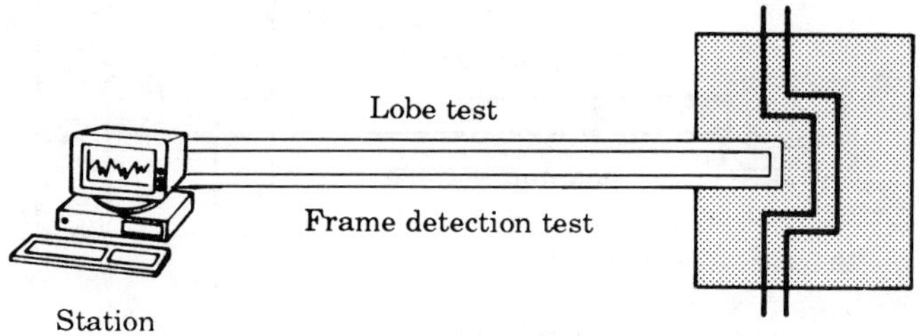

Figure 2.28 Process of connecting a station to the ring. Phase 1.

The procedure of connecting a station to the ring is subdivided into six separate phases.

(1) Firstly the functioning of the connecting cable (often also called the lobe cable) between the terminal and the ring (or MSAU) is tested. A special MAC frame, the 'lobe test MAC', is generated for this purpose. The destination address is the zero address. If the station receives its own frame back over the bridged lobe cable, the connecting cable is assumed to be fault free (see Figure 2.28).

Next, the new station tests its own receiver logic by generating a duplicate address MAC frame and checking whether it can detect frames which are intended for it.

This is followed by the actual connection to the ring via the MSAU, when a phantom voltage is transmitted over the lobe cable. This phantom voltage picks up a relay in the MSAU so that the data flow is now led through the station.

(2) The station checks whether there is already an active monitor present in the ring. For this it sets off the T(attach) timer and waits for an active monitor present, a stand-by monitor present or a ring purge MAC frame. If the timer expires after 18 seconds in IBM networks without an appropriate MAC frame having been received the station assumes either that it is the first active station in the ring or that the monitor has been deactivated by the interruption of the ring. It starts up the token-claiming procedure and becomes the monitor, provided it is the first active station in the ring. If a monitor is detected, the station becomes a stand-by monitor and phase 3 begins (Figure 2.29).

This is the only phase which may make a recognizable contribution to the long waiting time before the station is taken into the ring. If a monitor in the LAN is detected immediately, the waiting time is reduced by the above 18 seconds.

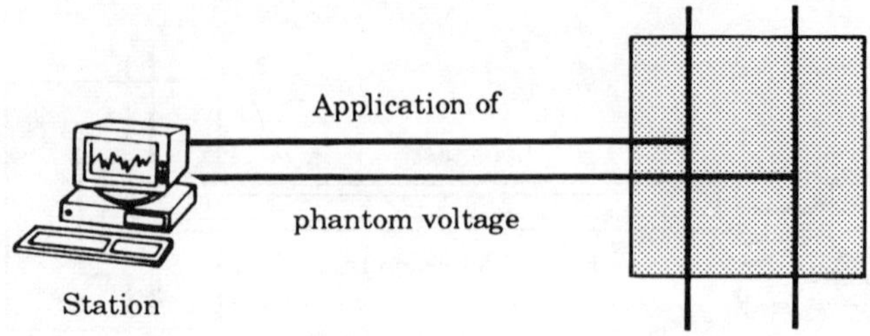

Figure 2.29 Process of connecting a station to the ring. Phase 2.

(3) In phase 3, as in phase 1, a duplicate address MAC frame is generated. This time however it is used to determine whether there is already another station in the ring with the same address. If this is the case, the station is immediately removed from the ring (the phantom voltage is dropped).

(4) The station participates in the NAUN procedure (see Section 2.5.5).

(5) Special ring parameters are requested from the ring parameter server (ring number, soft error report timer, etc.). If there is no ring parameter server, standard values are used. The functional address provided for this purpose (X'C000 0000 0002') is used for addressing.

(6) The station may now be operated normally in the LAN. The application required by the user may now be started.

2.7 Source routing

Source routing is necessary when two or more Token Ring LANs are to be linked together. As with other LAN technologies, so-called bridges between the individual Token Ring LANs must be installed for this purpose. A bridge may only be implemented with the assistance of a dedicated PC. Likewise, it is normal to use 'real' bridges, the hardware and software of which has been specifically developed to implement bridge functions.

Source routing is a procedure which, unlike the usual Ethernet spanning tree procedure, does not involve routing tables. The route describes the exact path information must follow so that it may be received by the destination station. The necessary information about the Token Ring LAN to which the destination station is attached and the bridges over which the information must be transmitted is sent within the frame in an optional field, the routing information field. It is possible to determine whether or not this field is present from the first bit of byte 0 of the source address. If this bit is set to B'1', the frame contains source routing information; if it is set to B'0', the frame does not contain source routing information. Not all stations in Token Ring support source routing. For example, source routing is not supported by older versions of Novell's network operating system. However, two stations may intercommunicate as long as they are located in the same Token Ring.

2.7.1 Source routing: mode of operation

The necessary routing information is obtained by the sender of a message using a TEST or XID command LLC PDU (LPDU). First an attempt is made to reach the destination station without an additional source information field. If no station replies, the destination must be located in another Token Ring and a source routing field is added to the message. The message itself is sent as a broadcast communication over all reachable subnetworks. Whenever a destination station in one of the networks is reached with this address, it replies with a TEST or XID response LPDU. The zero SAP X'00' is used as destination SAP, since this allows a station to reply even when no connection exists. Thus, this is a connectionless-mode service of level 2. Since the broadcast communication may reach the receiving station over various paths, several replies may be generated (response LPDUs), only one of which will be used by the sender for the subsequent logical link. Normally, the first response LPDU to return with the desired routing information is used for connection establishment, since it is assumed that this route represents the fastest connection at that time. All other response LPDUs are ignored.

Source routing is particularly effective for very interlaced LANs (many ways of reaching the destination over bridges). It ensures that when there are several alternative paths to a destination station, the most favourable route is selected as far as connection establishment is concerned. Should this route fail, another route is automatically sought using the protocol and the logical link between the sender and the recipient is re-established. The rings themselves may be interconnected in every conceivable way. Particular intelligence in the bridges (as in Ethernet) is not required for route determination. Two examples are shown in Figures 2.30 and 2.31.

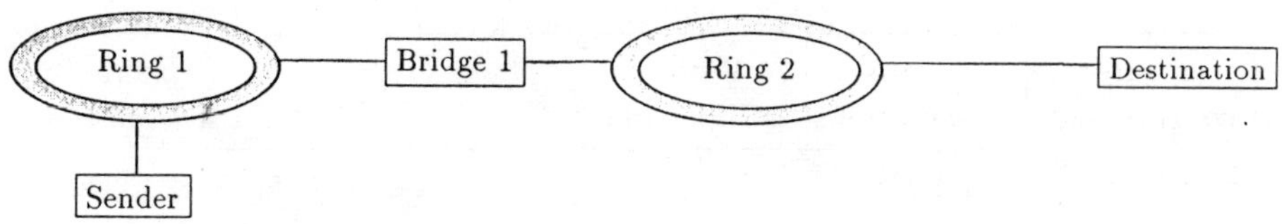

Figure 2.30 Example 1: simple coupling of two tokens.

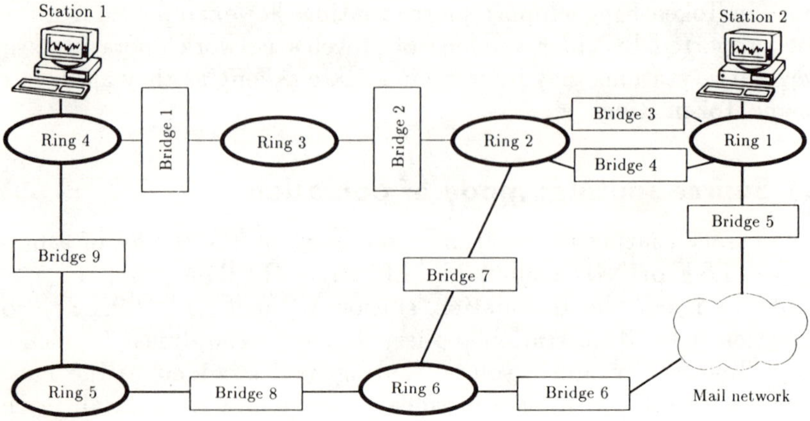

Figure 2.31 Example 2: more complex ring structure with several bridges.

In the second example, which has a total of 6 rings and 9 bridges, including two bridges which are connected by a public network (remote bridge function), there are several possible routes which a logical link between a station in ring 4 and a station in ring 1 may follow. At least four routes are considered. Two of these routes are almost equivalent. In this case, the instantaneous load will determine which route is chosen:

$$\text{Ring}\,4 \leftrightarrow B1 \leftrightarrow \text{Ring}\,3 \leftrightarrow B2 \leftrightarrow \text{Ring}\,2 \leftrightarrow B3 \leftrightarrow \text{Ring}\,1 \quad \text{and}$$
$$\text{Ring}\,4 \leftrightarrow B1 \leftrightarrow \text{Ring}\,3 \leftrightarrow B2 \leftrightarrow \text{Ring}\,2 \leftrightarrow B4 \leftrightarrow \text{Ring}\,1.$$

2.7.2 The routing information field

The information needed for connection establishment and data transfer over bridges is contained in the frame routing information field (Figure 2.32).

Route control field	Route designation	Route designation	...	Route designation
2 bytes	2 bytes	2 bytes	$n \times 2$ bytes ($n \leq 4$)	2 bytes

Figure 2.32 Routing information field (RI field).

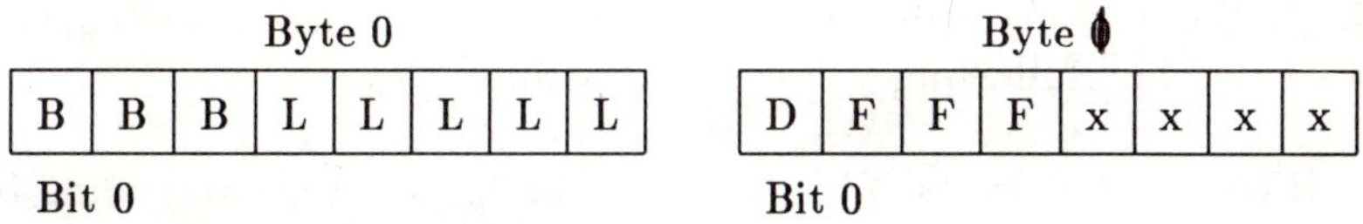

Figure 2.33 Routing control field.

There may be a maximum of eight 2-byte routing information fields, one field for control information and up to seven fields for specification of the logical link. This also means that the number of bridges which may be crossed consecutively is limited to seven.

2.7.2.1 The routing control field

Figure 2.33 shows the structure of the routing control field. The B-bits (broadcast indicators) indicate whether a logical link already exists or whether one must be established. If the first bit is set to B'0' (B'0xx'=Non broadcast) a route for the frame to be transmitted already exists. If this bit is set to B'1', the second bit indicates whether the frame is a true broadcast frame (B'10x'=All routes broadcast) or whether the frame should only be transmitted over a few selected bridges (B'11x'=Single-route broadcast). The third bit has no meaning.

The length of the routing information field is given in the next five L-bits. In the case of a broadcast frame, this value is set to two, corresponding exactly to the length of the routing control field. The second bridge increases this value by four (2 bytes for the first Token Ring segment and 2 bytes for the next segment) and each further station increases the value by two.

For existing routes, this field contains the total length of the routing information field and is not modified during the transmission of the frame. Every bridge checks this length field. If its value is less than two, odd or larger than 18, the frame is not forwarded by a bridge. The number Z of bridges to be crossed is calculated from the formula $Z = ((L-2)/2) - 1$.

The D-bit (direction bit) enables the bridge to interpret a transmission frame correctly. If the bit is set to B'0' the routing information field is evaluated from left to right; if it is set to B'1', the field is evaluated from right to left.

Why is this implemented in this way? For example, in the case of a TEST response frame, in reply to a TEST command frame, it is not necessary to reconstruct the whole of the routing information field since simply resetting the direction bit ensures that the reply to the command is also transmitted over the correct bridges (in reverse order).

The three F-bits (largest frame bits) indicate the maximum frame length (without control information) which may be transmitted between two stations. The following values are possible:

- B'000' = 516 bytes. This is the smallest frame size according to ISO 8802/2 LLC and ISO 8473 (connectionless mode).
- B'001' = 1500 bytes corresponds to ISO 8802/3.
- B'010' = 2052 bytes. This corresponds to the full screen data 3270 mode.
- B'011' = 4472 bytes. This is the maximum frame size for FDDI and ISO 8802/5 for THT = 9 ms.
- B'100' = 8191 bytes corresponds to ISO 8802/4.
- B'111' is used in broadcast frames.

2.7.2.2 The route designator field

The actual specification of the route which a frame should take for transmission to the destination station is given in the route designator field.

Every ring in a network consisting of several rings (segments) is allocated a unique ring number. In addition, every bridge is allocated a bridge number, which is not necessarily unique. If several bridges are attached to a ring, it is advisable to enter several bridge numbers; if not otherwise specified, a redundant bridge should be provided.

The route designator field consists of bridge and ring numbers. In the case of a broadcast frame, every bridge adds its ring and bridge number (Figure 2.34).

Since the end of a route is always in a ring and is not a bridge, the bridge specification in the last component of the route designator field is always X'0'.

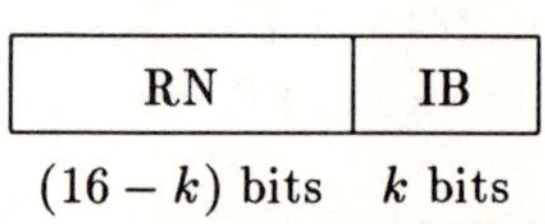

RN = Ring number
IB = Individual bridge number
RN + IB = Segment address

Figure 2.34 Routing designator field.

2.7.3 Mode of operation of a bridge

In this context, the most important aspect of the mode of operation of a bridge is the question as to when a frame is transmitted by the bridge.

The decision depends on the configuration parameters of the bridge. These include:

- Ring numbers.
- Limited broadcast transmission.
- Maximum number of bridges which may be crossed (hop count).

On the other hand, the decision depends on the values in the routing information field, and on the segment address in particular.

(1) In the case of a general broadcast frame (for example, when a new link between two stations is to be established) when the bridge is not the first to transmit this frame, the bridge checks the segment numbers which have already been entered:
   - If one of these segment addresses agrees with the destination segment address, the bridge does not copy the frame (the frame has already been in the other ring; this prevents a broadcast message from circulating in an endless loop).
   - If one of the segment addresses agrees with the bridge's own segment address, the bridge deletes the frame (the frame has already been forwarded).
   - If the ring number in the last entry of the routing information field does not agree with the bridge's own ring number, the frame is also deleted (stray frame or defective information field).
   - If none of the above cases apply, the bridge adds to the routing information field and transmits the frame to the next ring.

(2) In the case of an information frame, the bridge checks the segment numbers:
   - If the source and destination of the segment numbers agree with the bridge's own entries, the bridge transmits the frame to the next ring.
   - If the source address agrees but the destination address does not, the frame is deleted.

In general, frames are transmitted in temporal order. If a bridge is overloaded, it may no longer accept the frame (frame status field with 'address recognized', 'frame not copied' bits). If a LAN manager is installed, such situations will be logged. In this case, it is advisable to use two parallel bridges between the two rings to be linked.

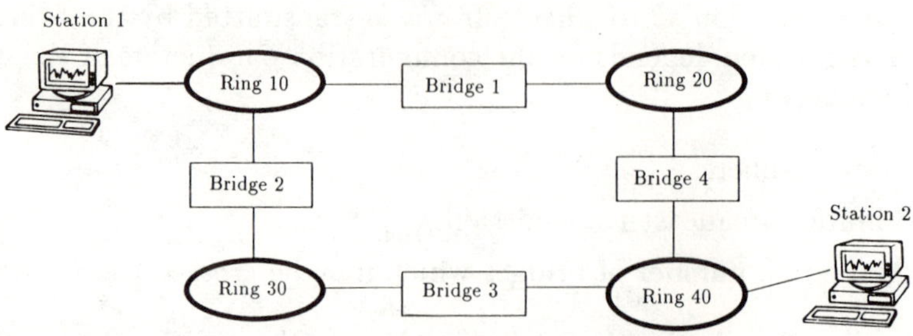

Figure 2.35 Example of the transmission of a frame.

2.7.4 Example of the transmission of a frame over bridges

We shall use the example of Figure 2.35 to explain the way in which a connection is established between two stations in different rings.

In Figure 2.35, station 1 sends a TEST request LPDU with the address of station 2 as a broadcast message. This is because it has determined that this command will not be answered without a source routing information field and the destination station must be in a different ring (segment) (see Figure 2.36).

This procedure ensures that on connection establishment the fastest link at the time will be chosen. Since only frames with routing information, and of those, only frames which involve the bridge in question, are transmitted, the bridge guarantees a decoupling of the load.

The bridge control mechanism described above means that the transmission of broadcast frames is always controlled and that uncontrolled multiplication of broadcast messages is impossible.

These techniques for linking several rings over bridges are thus used not only to increase the number of attachable terminals but also (primarily) to provide a decoupling of the load in the individual ring segments. A typical example is the backbone ring (Figure 2.37), which we shall describe in detail later.

2.8 Prioritization in Token Ring

Contrary to popular opinion, Token Ring does have facilities for assigning priorities to frames in the ring. The protocol provides for at most seven different priority levels. Two of these may be used by applications, the rest are used as network management functions.

(1) The routing control field is set.

B=1, D=0, L=2

(2) The first bridge receives this frame, extends the routing information field and transmits the frame to the next ring.

B=1, D=0, L=6	10 | 1	20 |

The second bridge also extends the routing information field and transmits the frame to the next ring.

B=1, D=0, L=6	10 | 2	30 |

(3) Similarly, bridges 3 and 4 transmit the message to the next ring.

B=1, D=0, L=8	10 | 2	30 | 3	40 |

B=1, D=0, L=8	10 | 1	20 | 4	40 |

(4) In our example, station 2 receives two broadcast frames, which reach it via different routes. The receiving station answers both frames in the time order in which they arrive with a TEST response LPDU. In these frames the broadcast bit is set to B'0' (not a broadcast message) and the direction bit is set to B'1' indicating that the bridge should interpret the information field from right to left.

B=1, D=1, L=8	10 | 2	30 | 3	40 |

B=1, D=1, L=8	10 | 1	20 | 4	40 |

(5) Station 1 receives the two TEST response LPDUs one after the other. It assumes that the first frame to arrive represents the most favourable route between the two stations. The other frame is discarded.

Figure 2.36 Example of the construction of the source routing information field.

The following priorities are available:

- B'000' to B'001' are user priorities.
- B'010' denotes a high user priority or MAC frames which require a token.
- B'100' applies to bridges.
- B'111' is used for station management.

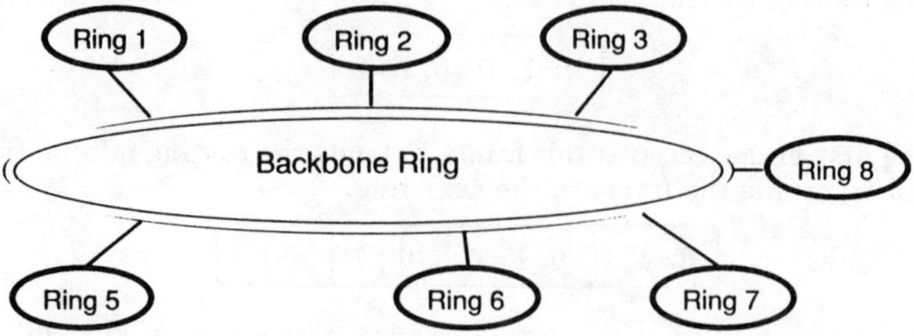

Figure 2.37 Backbone ring for large installations.

Figure 2.38 illustrates the way in which the prioritization facility may be used in Token Ring.

---

(1) Normal state. Station 1 sends a frame to a destination station, after it receives a free token.

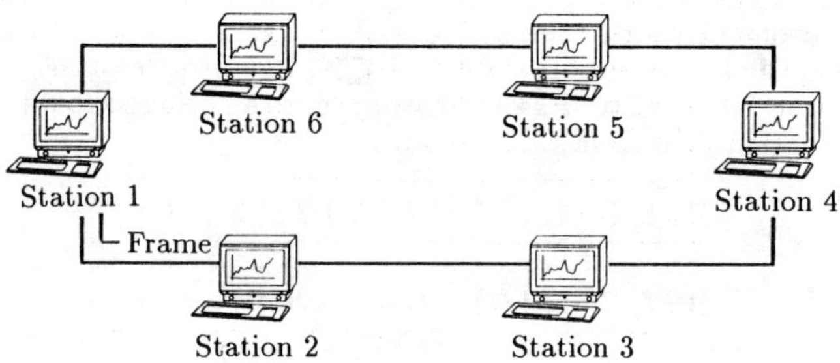

(2) Station 4 which receives the frame, enters a high-priority reservation in the access control field (for example, 7).

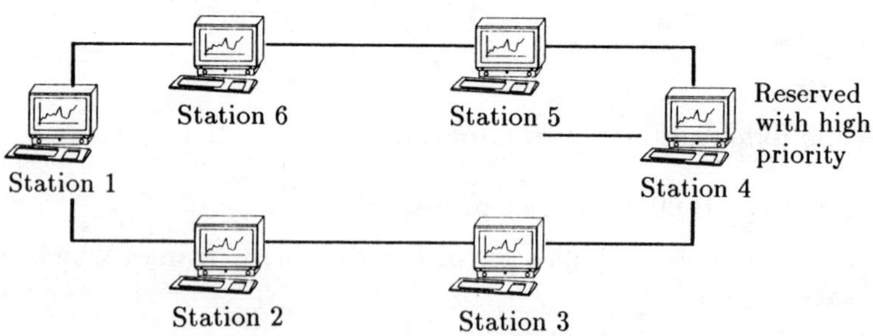

Figure 2.38 Prioritization in Token Ring.

(3) Station 1 receives the original frame, detects the priority reservation and generates a priority token. It itself remains in the so-called priority mode.

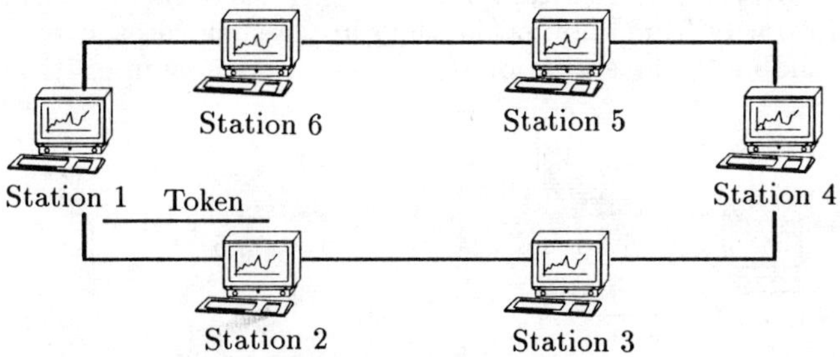

Station 1 switches to priority mode (notes the priority reservation). Station 2 wishes to send with normal priority. Station 2, which would normally be the next to transmit a frame, determines that the access control field contains a priority reservation. Since it can only transmit with normal priority (0) it must pass the token on.

(4) By virtue of the priority entry and since it itself wishes to transmit with identical or higher priority, station 4 may now start to transmit the frame.

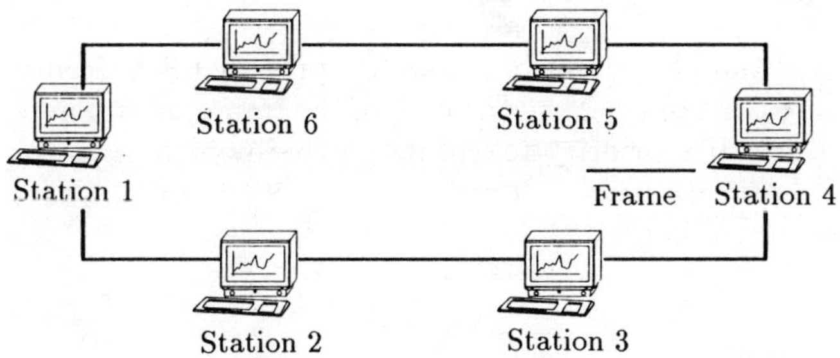

Station 4 transmits by virtue of the priority reservation.

(5) After successful transmission of the frame, station 4 generates another free token with high priority.

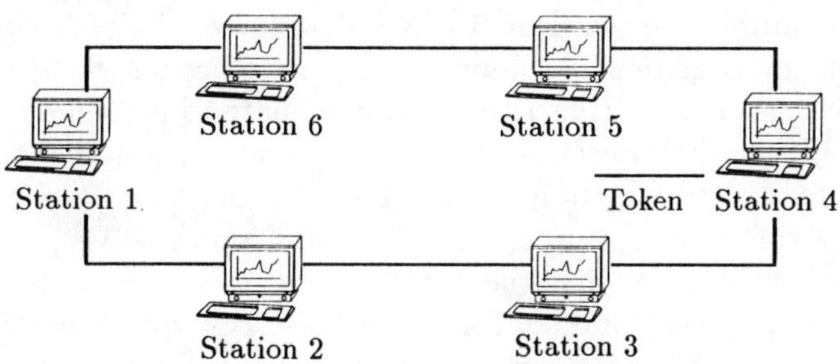

Station 4 generates a free token with high priority.

Figure 2.38 (continued).

(6) Station 1, which is still in the priority mode, receives the token and detects the priority set by itself in the token. It resets the priority to 0. Station 2 may then begin to transmit immediately. This automatic resetting of the token prevents the station which wishes to transmit continuously with high priority from dominating the ring. In such cases, every second token is available to the successor station for transmission of its information.

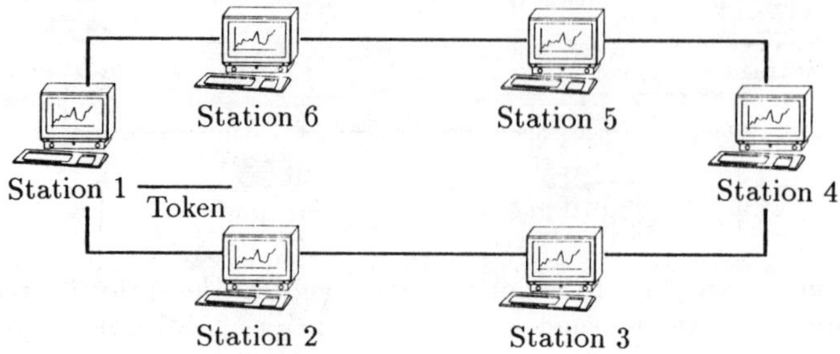

Station 1 resets the priority to the normal value. Station 2 may now send.

Figure 2.38 (continued).

In addition, the monitor prevents a priority token from passing round the ring more than once. As in the case of the frame, so too here, the monitor bit may be set. If a priority token passes the monitor again (with monitor bit set), the priority has not been correctly reset. In this case the monitor generates a new token.

2.9 Network management: functions of the lower layers

In Token Ring networks it is also possible to collect management information and, for example, forward it to NetView. We shall discuss the area of network management in more detail in Chapter 6. However, since management in Token Ring may be implemented independently of a host environment, we shall describe its most important components here.

Prerequisites include management servers (LAN reporting mechanism, ring error monitor, configuration support server, ring parameter server, LAN bridge server), the LAN Manager (add-on software product under DOS or OS/2) and at least one SNA control point (for example, NetView/PC) for communication with the SNA environment. Management information LPDUs are used to transmit information from the server to the LAN Manager. The management information LPDUs contain their own

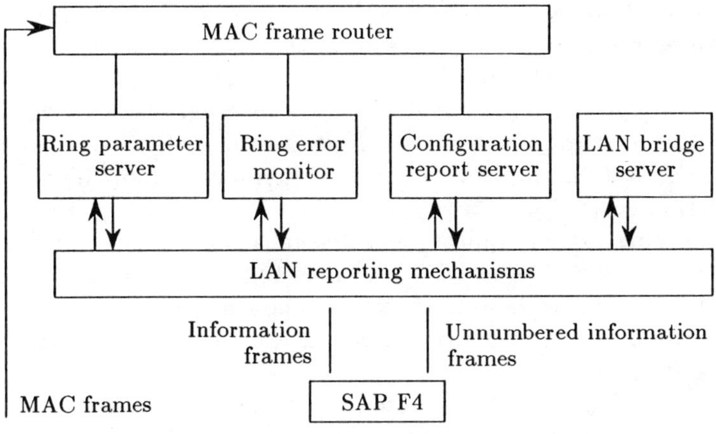

Figure 2.39 Network management in Token Ring.

check and control information and also permit the transmission of complex control information (see Figure 2.39).

MAC frames which have a functional management address as destination address are forwarded by the DLC.LAN.MGR local management service to the appropriate management server. The bridge server does not process MAC frames. It only receives information in LLC LPDUs via the relevant SAP X'F4'.

What are the most important functions of management servers?

The ring parameter server sends initialization information to stations which are newly introduced to the ring. It ensures that all stations are using the same operational parameters and forwards information about active stations which have been introduced to the ring to the LAN Manager. This information contains the address of the ring station, the ring station microcode level, the NAUN address, the number of the ring to which the ring parameter server is attached and the current availability of the station.

The ring error monitor collects and analyzes all hardware and software errors which may occur within a Token Ring. The ring error monitor function is usually undertaken by the IBM LAN Manager.

Hardware errors are indicated by beacon MAC frames. Each station in the ring may generate such a frame if it detects an error condition in the ring. The frame goes to all the stations in the ring. Even normal connection and disconnection of stations in the ring may lead to hardware errors.

The ring error monitor is responsible for evaluating the information in the frame (address of the sender of the beacon frame, its NAUN address, the reason for the beacon frame). As soon as it detects an error condition, it sets off a timer. If this timer expires before the error condition has been removed, the error is permanent or irremovable and a message is sent to the LAN Manager. Even when the error is removed before the timer expires an appropriate message is sent to the LAN Manager. The ring error monitor checks beforehand whether either of the two stations involved in the beaconing procedure are still active in the ring. If both stations are in the ring, the error may be removed. If at most one of the stations is still in the ring, the stations have disconnected themselves from the ring because of an internal error.

The ring error monitor operates in a similar way in the case of software errors. Software errors are notified to the LAN Manager as soon as a predefined error threshold is exceeded. The ring may contain several ring error monitors, or it may contain none. In the latter case, errors cannot be located or flagged.

In what follows, we shall use the example of the ring error monitor to show which frames may be exchanged with the LAN Manager and what the data content of these frames is.

When necessary, the configuration support server notifies the LAN Manager of all changes to the configuration (NAUN change). It executes status queries initiated by the LAN Manager and, on request, removes stations logically from the ring. For this, for example, a remove ring station frame including the ring number and the address of the ring station is sent by the LAN Manager to the configuration support server. The latter then generates a remove station MAC frame for the given station and confirms the removal of the station from the ring.

We shall not discuss the server functions operating on the MAC frames any further here. Detailed descriptions may be found in the Token Ring Network Architecture Reference.

Finally, the LAN bridge server collects primarily statistical information about bridge load and usage and sends this information to the LAN Manager. The LAN Manager may also be used to configure bridges and to carry out changes to the configuration from a central point. Thus, the bridge PCs may be operated without a monitor or keyboard. In the bridge itself, the frames (bytes) are counted. The counts cover not only frames which are transmitted but also frames which for various reasons (defective frame, wrong routing field, bridge overload) could not be transmitted. These messages are automatically transmitted to the LAN Manager at predefined time intervals.

The LAN Manager interprets and analyzes all the messages it receives. If the LAN Manager is linked to the NetView of a central DP system, error messages and advice for removing errors may be forwarded to the operating centre for the whole system using so-called alarms.

2.9.1 Details of the data structure

- Correlator (2 bytes).
- Ring number(s) of the ring(s) to be monitored (2 bytes).
- Indicator field, indicates the errors which must be notified to the LAN Manager and the accompanying description.
- Frame defect counters.
    - Errors on copying frames.
    - Token errors.
    - Error masks for: line errors, internal errors, burst errors, A/C errors, aborted transmissions, lost frames, token errors, receiver blockages.
    - Description of areas of faults in the ring, for each sender and recipient with the following entries: station address, NAUN address, destination address, etc.
    - Ring status: normal; temporary error, no analysis; temporary error, both stations still active; temporary error, one station no longer in the ring; temporary error, both stations no longer in the ring; permanent error.

2.10 IBM alternatives

Before the announcement of Token Ring two other networks were introduced and marketed by IBM as stopgaps. However, it was clear from the start that IBM's support for these networks would decrease noticeably as soon as Token Ring components became commercially available in larger quantities. Neither of the two networks corresponded to any international standard.

The PC Cluster network was designed for low-cost applications and for the networking of a small number of PCs. It has now disappeared from the market place, at least in Europe.

PC Network on the other hand is still on sale and has even been functionally extended. The network is based on the PC DOS operating system (> 3.0). PC Network is available in a broadband version (original version with Sytek's Know How) and in an inexpensive newer baseband version. The following list shows the most important details (the baseband details are shown in brackets):

- Transmission medium: coaxial cable, 75 ohms.
- Baseband: ICS.
- Access method: CSMA/CD.
- Topology: Bus/tree (bus).

- Signal transmission: broadband (baseband).
- Frequency scheme in broadband case: receive – 219.00 MHz; send – 50.75 MHz.
- Maximum distance. 300 m from frequency converter (120 m from the extension unit, for baseband).
- Maximum coverage. Around 600 m for broadband; up to 3 km with other frequency converters (around 240 m for baseband).
- Maximum transmission speeds: network 2 Mbps; terminals 500 kbps.
- Maximum number of connections. 72 or 500 if tailored to the client by Sytek (80 for broadband).
- Possible forms of communication: data, text, graphics.
- Connection via PC interface card.
- Connection types. Virtual logical link datagram, broadcast.
- System extension. With interruption, if no connection in the access unit is free.

The topology of the broadband network corresponds to a tree with the frequency converter at its root (or a bus structure in the baseband version with a total of ten connections to the extension unit and daisy chaining for at most eight PCs).

The broadband network consists of the following components: IBM PC network adaptor; network frequency converter (broadband); and network cabling components.

In an IBM broadband network standard RG 11 coaxial cables of length 7.5 m, 15 m, 30 m and 60 m are used. Expensive surveying of the network, which is otherwise usual for broadband networks, may be dropped in this case. For the baseband network all cables of types 1, 2, 3, 6, 8 and 9 in the IBM cable system may be used. For small installations with at most eight terminals the individual stations are linked together in a chain. Depending on the number of stations, the total length of such a bus may be up to 91 m. For plugs, a (US standard) telephone plug is used for the interface cards. Using a so-called extension unit, the baseband network may be considerably extended, both in terms of the number of attachable stations and in terms of the maximum length between two stations (245 m) (Figure 2.40).

This network is very cost-effective and is especially suitable for smaller PC LAN networks. Unfortunately, in Germany, it is as good as unknown.

IBM has until now guaranteed that all applications generated for Token Ring may also be used in the PC Network. The necessary device drivers are already contained in the PC LAN Support Program (DOS) and in OS/2 Extended Edition.

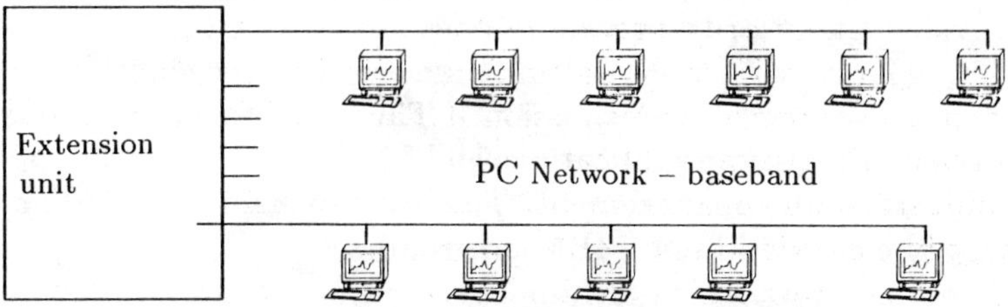

Figure 2.40 IBM PC Network broadband.

PC Network broadband is often used where broadband networks are already used for other purposes (machine control, sound and image processing, etc.). In this case, the broadband network may also be used to link Token Ring networks over the existing broadband medium (Figure 2.41).

2.11 Evaluation of the ISO 8802.5 token procedure

The most important conclusion about the behaviour of the Token Ring protocol described above is contained in the following statement: *the token procedure is a fair procedure.*

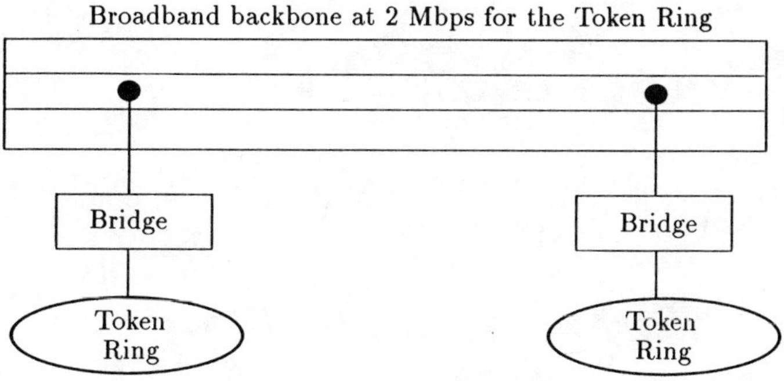

Figure 2.41 IBM PC Network bridge program.

When there is little traffic, a free token is usually available for data transmission.

When there is a lot of traffic, stations are sequentially authorized to send, provided the priority procedure does not change this.

This guarantees a finite waiting time provided the length of a message is bounded above (packet transmission!). Thus, the Token Ring protocol is suited for real or real-time applications and for almost all current application areas in industry and management. This may explain why Token Ring is increasingly being used in non-IBM environments.

The token protocol is also independent of the transmission medium and the transmission speed. If technology permits, rates of several hundred Mbps are conceivable. Moreover, the Token Ring protocol is relatively independent of the LAN coverage. Timers allow for ring sizes of several kilometres, with signal regeneration and variable-length frames. The higher the load in the LAN, the smaller the control information component. Thus, this is an ideal protocol for standard LAN applications with their strongly oscillating load patterns and varying information lengths.

Chapter 3

Basic Token Ring hardware

The protocols described in Chapter 2 may theoretically be implemented in any manufacturer's system architecture which is currently on the market and on practically any sufficiently powerful hardware base. The best example of this is Ethernet, which has been on the market for more than five years and is now supported by all major manufacturers. Token Rings will also soon achieve the same level of acceptance. More and more manufacturers are including Token Ring products in their sales range, developing their own products for their system-specific buses (AT bus, microchannel, EISA bus, VME, etc.) or supplying diskless workstations for Token Rings.

Not all the products described here conform completely to the ISO 8802.5 standard. However, these products are increasingly helping to reduce costs or permitting existing infrastructures or systems to be used for Token Ring. We shall indicate any incompatibilities with the ISO standard or with IBM products which we know of. Since many of these products are continually subject to improvement, we recommend that you check whether such incompatibility still exists before making a purchase.

Token Ring products may be divided into various categories (Figure 3.1).

In principle, for the sake of simplicity, we may distinguish between:

- general Token Ring hardware for connection and for transmission of the data from diverse end systems,
- the interface cards in the individual systems,
- the system-oriented software and programmer interfaces used,
- (where appropriate) the network operating system, and
- the actual application software in Token Ring.

In what follows, we shall concern ourselves firstly with general Token Ring hardware which is largely independent of the end system.

3.1 General system-independent hardware and associated software

The basic hardware components of Token Ring, which are used to construct a terminal-independent network are:

- transmission cables,
- repeaters and fibre-optic converters,
- multistation access units, and
- bridges and/or routers.

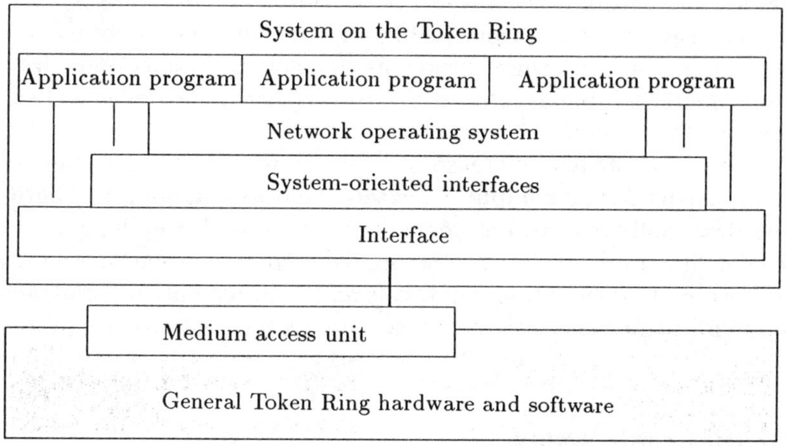

Figure 3.1 Token Ring components.

These are designed for transmission speeds of 4 or 16 Mbps (also for 10 and 80 Mbps) and are produced by a number of manufacturers. In what follows, we describe the specific properties of these components and compare them.

3.1.1 Transmission cables

Layer 1 (physical layer) of Token Ring uses various, line-related transmission media. We are not aware of any solutions (at least in Germany) for line-independent media (infrared, directional radio).

Here is a quotation which is certainly a good cable-oriented description of the state of many large installations:

Am Kabel fehlt's
zum Kabel drängt's
am Kabel hängt's
am Kabel klemmt's.[1]

Firstly, a basic infrastructure is created in order to connect various particularly important terminals to the network. Naturally, this has scarcely happened before all the other users want to connect to the network in order to access the extra information and services. Thus, the cabling and the connection go on until the false ceilings or the cable ducts overflow. With the increasing number of terminals, line faults are increasingly difficult to detect

[1] There isn't enough cable, we need some more cable, everything depends on the cable, we're stuck with the cable.

and remove and finally the point is reached where nothing works any more! The cable won't go into the cable shafts and cable faults are irremovable. Thus, there isn't enough proper cable and the foregoing quotation begins all over again. Initially, these problems did not arise since networks were relatively small and manageable and the destination system was always the mainframe in the computer centre.

With the steady increase in the numbers of PCs, information providers, departmental computers, external databases, etc., this picture has changed drastically over recent years. The foreground is no longer occupied by the central mainframe but by the unified communications network which enables terminals with various protocols and requirements to be attached to the communications services of several destination systems simultaneously.

3.1.1.1 IBM cable system

The IBM cable system (ICS) forms the basis for IBM to meet these requirements. It includes several types of data cable and a uniform data plug.

Data cable The new IBM data-cable types are intended to replace all previous mutually incompatible cables such as the RG62 A/U coaxial cables for the IBM 1370 world, twinax cables for the S/36 world, twisted cables (IBM 4700) and multiply-twisted cables (IBM 8100). As far as possible and where sensible, IBM uses a copper twisted pair with double screening. The double screening adds to the ground potential. This symmetric transmission medium is characterized by low electromagnetic interference and a relatively high transmission capacity of up to 20 Mbps. The two-wire pair also transmits an accompanying DC component which Token Ring uses when introducing terminals dynamically into the ring (phantom voltage). If this voltage falls off, the station is automatically removed from the ring, as provided for in the protocol. In ring networks such as Token Ring, senders and recipients are permanently active. When they are close together, with symmetric media such as the IBM cable, little energy can reach the recipient side from the send side (crosstalk), unlike what might happen with coaxial cables. Thus, the cable is particularly suitable for use in Token Ring. It is also suitable for the networking of almost all other IBM systems (IBM 3600, IBM 4700, IBM 5250, IBM 8100, IBM systems /34, /36, /38, /1, AS/400, etc.).

In order to bridge large distances or in areas of very strong electrical interference, IBM recommends the use of fibre-optic cables. This also provides for a considerable increase in data security since fibre-optic cables cannot be intercepted and are relatively safe against tapping.

In the USA, unscreened twisted pairs are the norm in the telephone network. This cable may also be used (with restrictions) in Token Rings

Table 3.1 Comparison of performance: screened – unscreened.

Parameter	*Data cable type 1*	*Data cable type 2*
Conductor diameter	0.4/0.64 mm	0.5/0.6/0.8 mm
Tested data rate (IBM) (Manchester coding)	16 Mbps	4 Mbps
Line distance at 4 Mbps from terminal to distributor	max. 375 m	max. 100 m
For type 1 cable between distributors: Terminal – distributor room Distributor room – distributor room	 max. 100 m max. 200 m	 max. 45 m max. 120 m
No. connectable devices	260	72
Type 3 cable filter Type 3 connecting cable	Not applicable Not applicable	Required Required

with the IBM cable system. It is primarily used to connect terminals to the multistation access units in the distributor room (lobe cable); however, in the ICS, it is not suitable for transmission in the 16 Mbps ring. A type 3 medium filter is required for connection to the terminal. It also converts the 9-pin plug to the Western plug which is the norm in the USA. This type of plug is also known as an RJ11 or RJ45 plug and is used in Europe as a connector in ISDN networks. However, one should be wary about equating this cable type with the telephone cables used in Germany and other countries. The cables used in Germany are often not twisted pairs, but quadruply-stranded cables. They may only be used (if at all) under certain conditions in Token Ring networks with the IBM cable system.

In addition to the cables listed in Table 3.1, the IBM ICS includes several other cable types. At the moment, it covers seven different data-cable types:

(1) Two double-screened twisted pairs, in which each twisted pair is screened and the whole is screened. This is the standard ICS cable for connecting MSAUs.

(2) Like type 1 plus four simple telephone wire pairs outside the screening.

(3) Four unscreened twisted pairs of telephone wires corresponding to the US norm.

(5) Fibre-optic cable with two fibre-optic conductors (100/140-micron multimode fibres) for cabling between distributor rooms.

(6) Flexible implementation of type 1, for connecting terminals to the Token Ring socket (lobe cable).

(8) Flat cable used for extending links and laying under carpets, etc. Like type 6 only suitable for connection of terminals.

(9) The simplest implementation of IBM type 1 cable.

It is noticeable that IBM itself does not produce cables or plugs and only sells them off-the-shelf on a small scale. Instead, the cable manufacturers must have their cables checked by IBM before they can be sold with an IBM type number. Of course, this procedure is not free as far as the cable manufacturers are concerned. Thus, many manufacturers are beginning to produce cable types similar to those of IBM which are not subject to checking by IBM and therefore more cost-effective. In this case, the user accepts the risk of deciding whether to believe the cable manufacturer's view that his cables are at least as good as if not better than the ICS cable types.

Data plugs Even more important than a uniform cable is a standard plug for the cabling system, to provide for uniform connection of all IBM products including Token Ring. This new data plug was introduced by IBM with its Token Ring products. It has the interesting property that it is a plug and a socket at the same time. This is termed a hermaphrodite construction method (Figure 3.2). The one problem in the case of V.24/RS232C or Centronics interfaces, as to the sides on which male or female connectors are required, is inapplicable when choosing connection cables (Figure 3.3). This greatly simplifies installation and storekeeping.

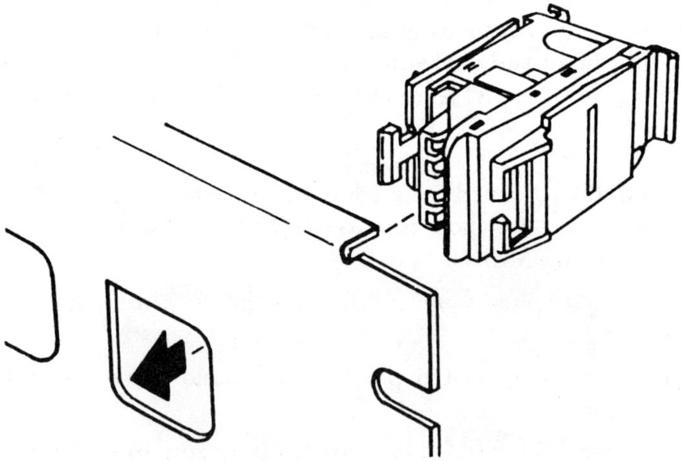

Figure 3.2 IBM data plug.

Figure 3.3 Connection cable.

The plug is delivered unassembled. Other elements delivered with it allow one to feed in the cable from any desired side. The plug is inserted using a clamp fastener. A catch which comes with the plug is used to prevent the data plug from being unintentionally pulled out. The contacts for the ICS cable are colour coded, so that miswiring is essentially ruled out. No soldering is required. The wires are only clamped to the contacts. The data plug may be converted from a standard built-in socket into a wall socket (surface or concealed), without a great deal of extra knowledge on the part of the electrician. Special tools, as for example in Ethernet, or special training, as for example in broadband networks, are not required. A loop short occurs automatically whenever a plug connection is undone.

Terminals are connected directly to Token Ring using the hermaphrodite plug. PCs and controllers generally have a connection cable with the IBM data plug on one end and a 9-pin male connector on the other.

IBM data stations which are still designed for other transmission media are for the present adapted using so-called baluns (balanced–unbalanced) (Figure 3.4).

Figure 3.4 Data plugs with (integrated or external) baluns.

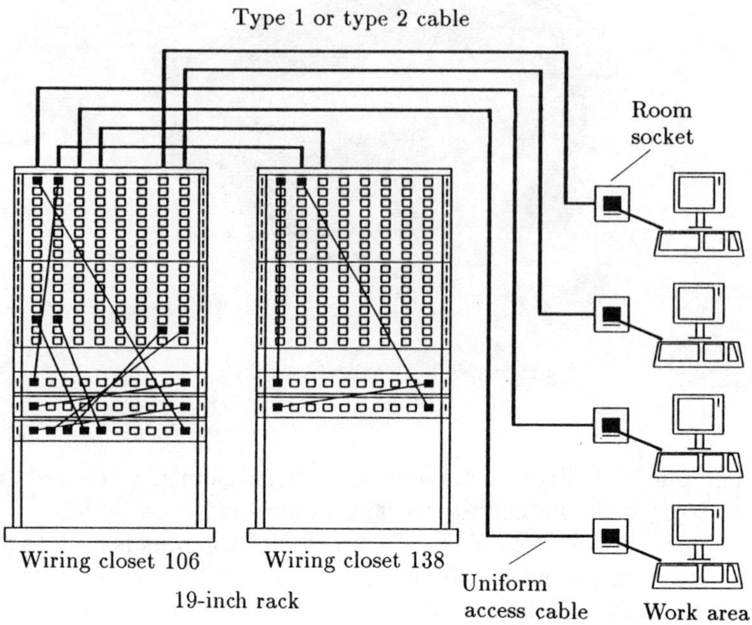

Figure 3.5 Wiring closets and distributor rooms.

These usually contain small transformers which permit a conversion from symmetric to non-symmetric cables. The baluns are colour coded. Thus, the red balun converts to IBM 3270 terminals and the green balun converts to 5520 terminals (Figure 3.4) There are baluns for almost all IBM terminals. Not all baluns are made by IBM. More recent IBM devices have an integrated balun.

Wiring closets and distributor rooms Terminals are connected in a star shape around one or more wiring closets. 19-inch rack cabinets incorporate the necessary wiring closets, the MSAUs, 3299 multiplexers, etc. Several such distributor rooms will be needed in larger buildings; the cables go out in a star shape from these to the individual rooms (lobe cable).

The advantage of this type of cabling with decentralized distribution panels is that the cabling may not only be used in IBM terminals and for Token Ring but is also suitable for other systems with synchronous or asynchronous RS232C interfaces and for Ethernet or ISO 8802.3 components. The disadvantage is that sufficient room must be provided for the rack cabinets and the wiring closets. Figure 3.6 shows one effect which may result in large Token Ring installations.

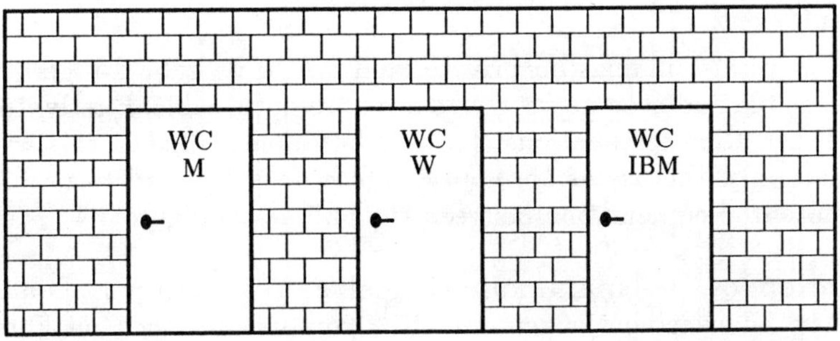

Figure 3.6 The new storey philosophy.

This new storey philosophy may be planned into new buildings, but leads to difficulties when older buildings are recabled. There is not always a quiet unused corner which can be used for the new tasks in a way for which it was not intended. The quotation at the beginning of the chapter then results in the transfer of the cabling mess from the computer centre to the individual storeys. If room cannot be provided a small central space must be divided off as close to the climbing shafts as possible (often near the lifts). This space should be secured so as to prevent undesirable misuse by unauthorized users.

Cabling strategy In large installations, this leads to a multi-step cabling strategy with a total of four subareas.

(1) The individual devices are connected to the system in the device-connection area. Type 6 cables are generally used for this, although type 3 cables are an option.

(2) Cables go out in a star shape from the socket in the room to the distributors for each storey. ICS type 1 or sometimes type 3 cables are suitable for this. The number of storey distributors provided for depends on the size of the planned installation. If a large number of terminals are to be connected (more than 50 in a storey), we would advise several smaller storey distributors, which may be located in wall cupboards, etc. Thus, the cable lengths between the distributors will be greater, but the lengths of the connection cables to the terminals will be considerably shorter. Neither will the dreaded thick cable trees be needed for each storey and cable conduit. 50 IBM type 1 cables scarcely fit into a normal standard cable conduit.

(3) The individual storey distributors are linked to one or more central-building distributors. For large buildings or 16 Mbps Token Rings,

fibre-optic cables should be used here. For smaller installations with 4 Mbps Token Rings or Ethernet installations, type 1 cables are sufficient.

(4) If several buildings on private land are to be cabled together, it is sensible and even necessary to use fibre-optic cable. Firstly, 16 Mbps Token Ring installations can only be implemented in this way and, secondly, the use of fibre-optic cables does not lead to problems of potential equalization between the buildings (Figure 3.7).

Calculation of the maximum ring size The decision about which cable may be used and whether active components such as fibre-optic converters or line repeaters must also be installed ultimately depends on the coverage of the Token Ring and on its transmission speed (4 or 16 Mbps). In the following examples, it is assumed that no repeaters or fibre-optic converters are used. Should these be required, the following examples are valid as before for the separate logical subrings formed for each repeater section. If all the ring sections consist of fibre-optic cable, ring lengths of over 200 km are possible. In practice, such lengths are very rare, either because of the extremely high charges imposed by the postal administration on fibre-optic networks or because the maximum number of connectable terminals on Token Ring would be exceeded. For large installations, it is more sensible, as in the case of Ethernet, to work with bridges which are available both for local and wide areas. More details of this are given later.

The following are examples of calculations of the coverage of a ring without active repeaters:

In the following calculations, we distinguish between two ring types: rings with only one distributor room and rings with at most 12 distributor rooms.

In the case of rings with only one distributor room, the cable lengths between the individual MSAUs should be as short as possible (≤ 2.4 m). If the MSAUs do not fit in a single wiring rack the cable length between the wiring racks should be less than 9 m. The maximum lobe length may be derived from Figure 3.8.

Here is a general recommendation. For 4 Mbps Token Ring installations, the lobe lengths should if possible be under 100 m. A subsequent extension of the ring will then not affect the lobe lengths. The maximum lobe length in the case of a single MSAU is approximately 390 m. This corresponds to a maximum ring length of around 780 m, if no repeaters or additional stations in the ring are used. Thus, a Token Ring interface card must be able to transmit a token over approximately 800 m, in such a way that it itself can identify the token again when there is no active station in between.

In the case of rings with several distributor rooms, the lobe length depends on the so-called adjusted ring length (ARL). The adjusted ring

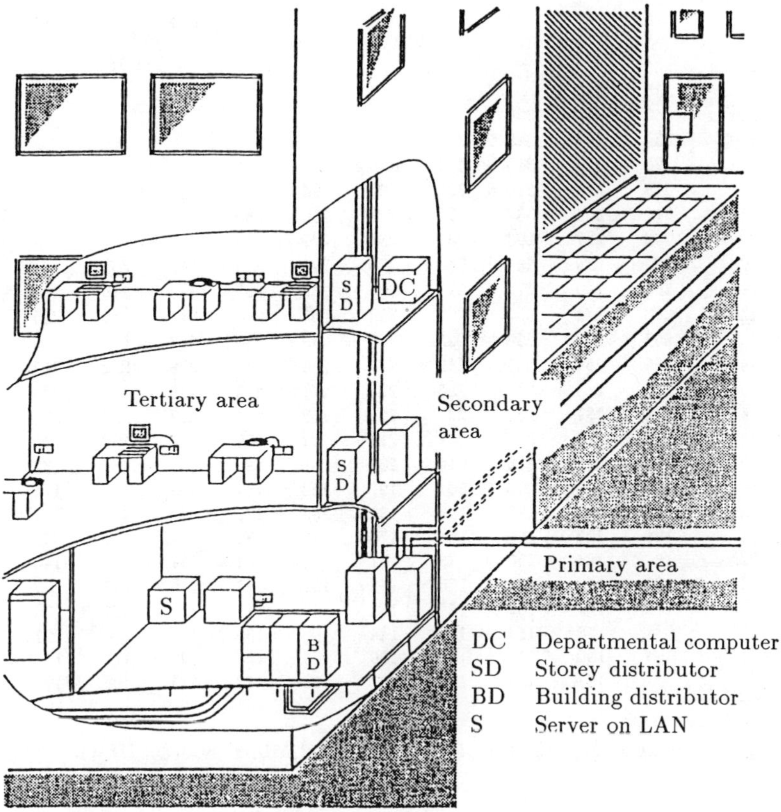

Figure 3.7 Multi-step cabling strategy.

length is given by:

$$\text{ARL} = (a + b + c) - a$$

In our example (Figure 3.9), this amounts to 150 m.

This situation takes into account the worst possible case of a fault in which the shortest link section between two MSAUs fails. In this case, the ring will be diverted over the Token Ring secondary line between the MSAUs. Thus, the shortest cable length must be subtracted from the overall ring in order to calculate the maximum possible overall length of a ring which must then be traversed by a token or a frame, namely twice $(b + c)$.

Let us now calculate the maximum lobe length for our example, taking into account the MSAUs and the number of distributor rooms.

NUMBER OF IBM 8228s \ NUMBER OF WIRING CLOSETS	2	3	4	5	6	7	8	9	10	11	12
2	363										
3	354	350									
4	346	341	336								
5	337	332	328	323							
6	328	324	319	314	310						
7	319	315	310	306	301	296					
8	311	306	302	297	292	288	283				
9	302	297	293	288	284	279	274	270			
10	293	289	284	280	275	270	266	261	257		
11	285	280	275	271	266	262	257	252	248	243	
12	276	271	267	262	258	253	248	244	239	235	230
13	267	263	258	253	249	244	240	235	230	226	221
14	259	254	249	245	240	236	231	226	222	217	213
15	250	245	241	236	231	227	222	218	213	208	204
16	241	237	232	227	223	218	214	209	204	200	195
17	232	228	223	219	214	209	205	200	196	191	186
18	224	219	215	210	205	201	196	192	187	182	178
19	215	210	206	201	197	192	187	183	178	174	169
20	206	202	197	193	188	183	179	174	170	165	160
21	198	193	188	184	179	175	170	165	161	156	152
22	189	184	180	175	171	166	161	157	152	148	143
23	180	176	171	166	162	157	153	148	143	139	134
24	172	167	162	158	153	149	144	139	135	130	126
25		158	154	149	144	140	135	131	126	121	117
26		150	145	140	136	131	127	122	117	113	108
27		141	136	132	127	122	118	113	109	104	99

Figure 3.8 Table of distances for 4 Mbps (Source: IBM).

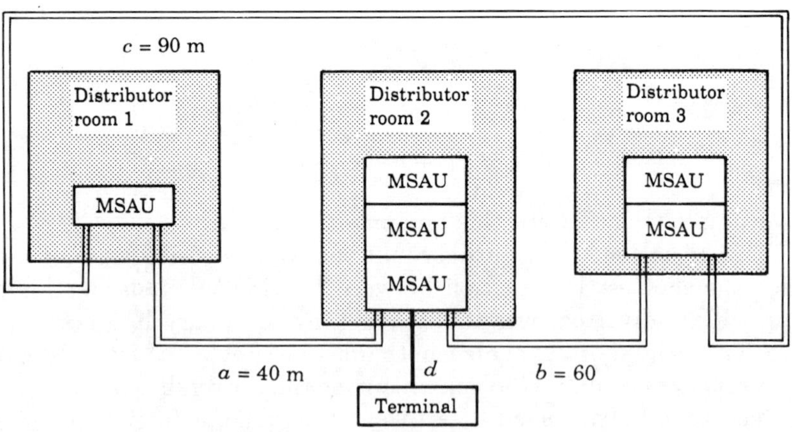

Figure 3.9 Calculation of lobe lengths.

4 Mbps example:
6 MSAUs, 3 distributor rooms
Table value: 324 m
$\Rightarrow$ *Lobe:* 324 − ARL = 332 − 150 = 182 m

The maximum possible connection cable length of 182 m is considerably more than the 100 m recommended by us.

The table values are different for 16 Mbps (Figure 3.10).

If we again calculate the maximum lobe length in our example, but now based on a ring with a transmission speed of 16 Mbps, we obtain:

$$\begin{aligned}&\textit{Lobe}:\\ &\text{ARL} - 150\,\text{m} = 130\,\text{m} - 150\,\text{m} = ???\end{aligned}$$

In this case, use of a repeater section (for example, a fibre-optic section) between two distributor rooms is already advisable. If now the longest section is replaced by a fibre-optic section, the calculation then becomes:

$$\begin{aligned}&\textit{Lobe}:\\ &\text{ARL} - (a+b) - a = 130\,\text{m} - 60\,\text{m} = 70\,\text{m}\end{aligned}$$

As a rule of thumb we have the following. For 16 Mbps the maximum possible separation is approximately one-third of that for 4 Mbps and the average lobe cable length is around 50 m. IBM does not provide support for unscreened 4-wire cable for the 16 Mbps Token Ring.

NUMBER OF WIRING CLOSETS

		1	2	3	4	5	6	7	8	9	10
	1	173									
	2	167	162								
8	3	160	155	150							
	4	153	148	143	138						
2	5	147	142	137	132	127					
	6	140	135	130	125	120	115				
2	7	133	128	123	118	113	108	103			
	8	127	122	117	112	107	102	97	92		
8	9	120	115	110	105	100	95	90	85	80	
	10	114	109	104	99	94	89	84	79	74	69
S	11	107	102	97	92	87	82	77	72	67	62
	12	100	95	90	85	80	75	70	65	60	55
	13	77	82	77	72	67	62	57	52	47	42
	14	64	69	64	59	54	49	44	39	34	29
	15	51	56	51	46	41	36	31	26	21	16
	16	38	43	38	33	28	23	18	13	8	3
	17	25	30	25	20	15	10	5	-	-	-
	18	12	17	12	7	2	-	-	-	-	-

Figure 3.10 Maximum permitted distances for 16 Mbps (Source: IBM).

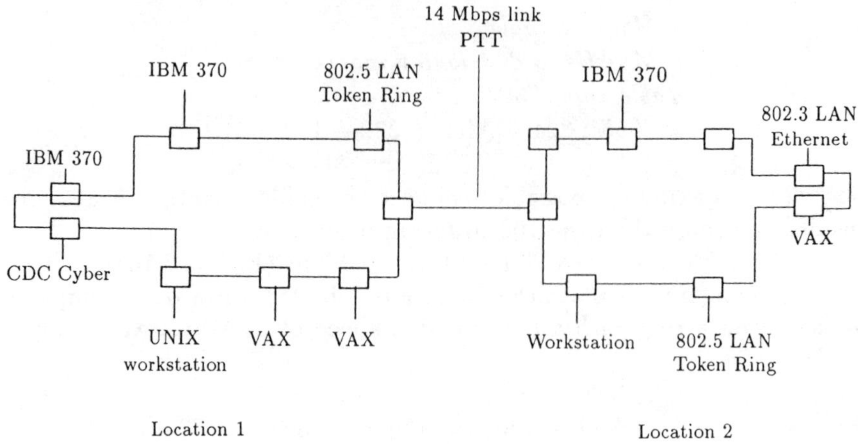

Figure 3.11 Fibronics Finex.

3.1.1.2 Alternatives to the IBM cable system

As an alternative to IBM, many firms produce their own cabling systems. These systems are based in part on other cable types, use other connection components or provide facilities for monitoring and controlling the ring and the cabling system from a central point. These cabling systems are not simply restricted to IBM DP systems but were designed from the start for the networking of other DP systems and LANs. We shall use examples of cable systems which are currently available to describe the facilities offered by these systems and the uses to which they may be put.

Examples of other cabling technologies

(1) **Fibronics** Fibronics offers a complete cabling system based primarily on fibre-optic components, but also incorporating other media such as coaxial and unscreened 2- and 4-wire cables. It ranges from the connection of 3270 terminals via multiplexers to channel coupling of IBM mainframes and supports both Ethernet and Token Ring networks. Fibronics focuses mainly on the provision of components for large fibre-optic backbone networks connecting various components. The IBM world with its multiplexers, channel interfaces, etc. is supported as a matter of priority together with the complete FDDI world. Fibronics was one of the first suppliers to market FDDI components. In the meantime, both Ethernet and Token Ring networks may now be linked using FDDI. A protocol-transparent gateway from terminals on the Ethernet to terminals on Token Ring is not yet possible (Figure 3.11).

(2) **SNI** SNI's TWIST (Twisted Wiring Infrastructure Star Topology) cabling system is based on 4-wire topology (fibre optic) and/or a broadband backbone network. It supports Nixdorf products, Ethernet and Token Ring. The cable cabinets in this system provide for a maximum of 100 connections. Special media converters allow connection to the Nixdorf broadband network (NBN backbone).

(3) **Siemens** Unlike SNI, the Siemens system is based on fibre optics and not on broadband networks. Siemens is also attempting to integrate its PBXs (HICOM, ISDN equipment) into the cabling system. For economic and control engineering reasons, this is of great importance, as far as future developments in the area of high-speed communications are concerned.

It remains to be seen to what extent the integration of data, speech and image communication will succeed and a central network management be created. The approaches to this are already recognizable.

(4) **Nokia–Ericsson** This cabling system is based exclusively on the use of fibre-optic cables. The fibre-optics communications system (fibre optic only) ZAT 128 may be constructed using various types of fibre-optic cables. The following may be connected: IBM 3270 terminals, IBM 3299 multiplexers, Token Ring, Ethernet and terminals with V.24 asynchronous/synchronous or V.35 interfaces. It is principally used in areas with high data-protection requirements (military areas, etc.) or in areas with high interference (reactors, blast furnaces, etc.). In addition, IBM channel extensions and video and audio transmission (6 MHz) up to 3 km are possible with this system.

As a standard, Nokia–Ericsson supplies components which may be used to take fibre optics right up to the terminal. With IBM, the lobe cable is typically of type 1 or type 6 (screened 4-wire cable) with Nokia–Ericsson, the components are designed in such a way that optical fibres may also be used on these sections. For this, a fibre-optic converter is installed in the PC, quasi on the Token Ring card. Thanks to this technology, Token Ring networks may also be installed in environments with very high interference (for example, in accelerators). As required, Ericsson also supports existing (already laid) RG62 A/U coaxial cable to connect terminals to the MSAU.

(5) **SEL (Alcatel)** SEL also produces a manufacturer-independent communications structure. In the local area (steps 1 and 2) it uses 2-wire, 4-wire or fibre-optic cable and in the global area (steps 3 and 4) only fibre-optic cable. As for other networks, both Ethernet and Token Ring are similarly supported on the same medium. 3270 terminals are directly linked in, as with Fibronics, via fibre-optic multiplexers. Both monomode and graded index cables are supported (9/125, 50/125, 62.5/125, 85/125) (Figure 3.12).

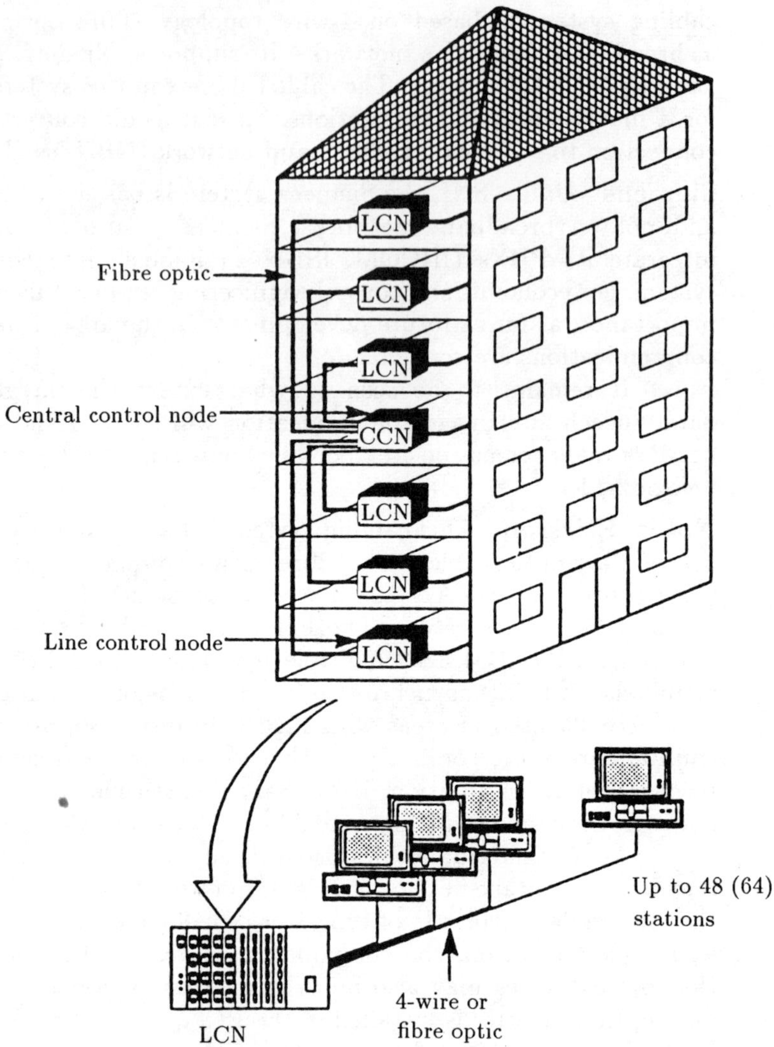

Figure 3.12 SEL cabling system.

SEL's cabling strategy uses components from Lattisnet (Ethernet) and various other suppliers for its communications infrastructure. SEL itself recommends, at least for new buildings, not a four-step cabling strategy like IBM, but a three-step technology without storey distributors. These are replaced by fibre-optic cable up to the room socket (FOLAN). The additional costs for the fibre-optic cables and plugs and for the fibre-optic converters are balanced by lower structural costs (extra space for the storey distributors is no longer required), lower costs for the cable conduits, an improved technology which is not sensitive to interference and the almost complete absence of limitations on the maximum distance between individual terminals in the ring.

The core of this system comprises the fibre-optic converters which are installed in a fixed position in the cable shaft in the room of the end user. As required, special plug modules are attached to these fibre-optic converters which permit the connection of 3270 terminals and terminals with V.24 interfaces or provide LAN interfaces for Ethernet or Token Ring (Figure 3.13).

(6) **Ungermann Bass** Ungermann Bass's ACCESS/ONE is a standalone universal network architecture which permits support for and monitoring of almost all current systems. Terminals are usually connected by a 4-wire cable (IBM ICS or AT&T UTP). Token Ring, Ethernet, the 3270 world, asynchronous terminals and the Apple world with its Macintosh PCs are supported.

ACCESS/ONE permits the coupling of Ethernet and Token Ring (TCP/IP or XNS) terminals provided Ungermann Bass products are involved.

ACCESS/ONE permits the coupling of Token Ring networks with the aid of an intermediate Ethernet installation. Ethernet becomes a transparent backbone for Token Ring. However, terminals on Token Ring cannot communicate with terminals on Ethernet.

ACCESS/ONE has its own network management centre for central monitoring of all attached components.

ACCESS/ONE also supports IBM's NetView via NetView PC. It contains a module which permits control of the network from NetView PC and provides for remote diagnosis through the central IBM operating system.

Ungermann Bass also produces its own bridges and MSAUs, together with facilities to connect 3270 terminals (NIU 74/78 Token Ring), asynchronous terminals (NIU 180 Token Ring) and PCs (PC NIU) directly to Token Ring.

The Ungermann Bass cabling system (Figure 3.14) is a completely self-contained concept which provides an extension/substitute for IBM Token Ring products.

3.1.1.3 Trends in cabling systems

There is currently a demand for standalone multi-functional cabling which is suitable for use with various terminals and networks. At the present time, with the extreme growth rate of increasingly fast communications networks, particularly in the connection area, the choice of a sensible cabling system

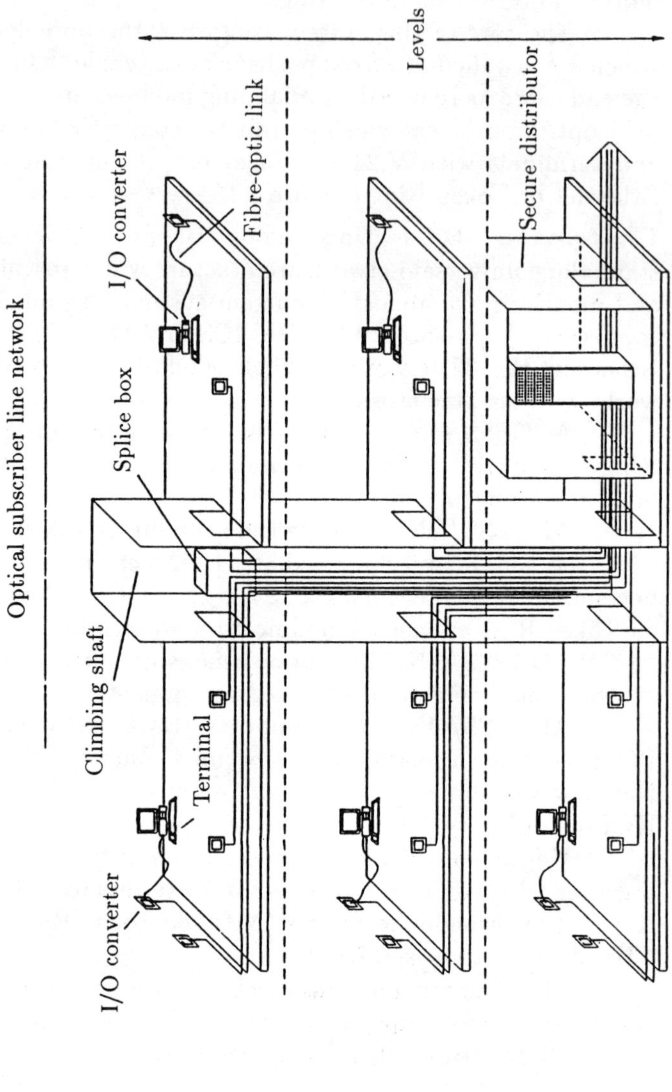

Figure 3.13 SEL cabling strategy.

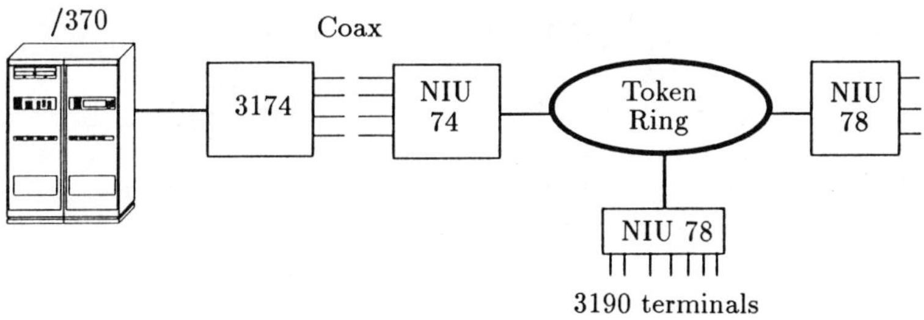

Figure 3.14 Ungermann Bass components for connecting terminals to Token Ring.

is one of the most important decisions when designing new buildings. New cabling at a later stage is labour and cost intensive and should be avoided. In the USA, there is a clear trend towards the use of existing telephone cables, both for Token Rings and for Ethernet. Fibre optics is seen as an alternative which is primarily suitable for future applications and for bridging large distances.

In Germany, the security requirements in the office communications area appear to be considerably higher than those in the USA. Unscreened 4-wire cable is only used with great hesitation, even though, with the advent of ISDN technology with its S_0 interface (4-wires) and the RJ45 plug (this so-called Western plug is also the plug for some Token Ring MSAUs and interface cards), the conditions for this would be ideal. However, companies are increasingly tending towards the screened 4-wire cable recommended by IBM.

We cannot support this general trend in Germany. Firstly, other manufacturers (for example, Ackermann) produce thin screened cables which are easier to lay. Secondly, we find it more sensible when introducing new technology to use the best technology (fibre optics) straightaway and otherwise to carry on working with the telephone cable which the installers trust. Because of the large external diameter, IBM's ICS cable takes up a lot of space in the cable shafts.

Within a building, we also recommend the use of fibre-optic cables to implement large rings. Other cable types should only be used in the terminal connection area. These cables may be screened or even unscreened 4-wire cables, or, if it is already present, the tried-and-tested IBM coaxial cable. Between individual buildings it is only sensible to lay graded index or monomode fibre-optic cables. Nationwide the use of public networks (which in the high-speed area also use monomode fibre-optic cables) is advised.

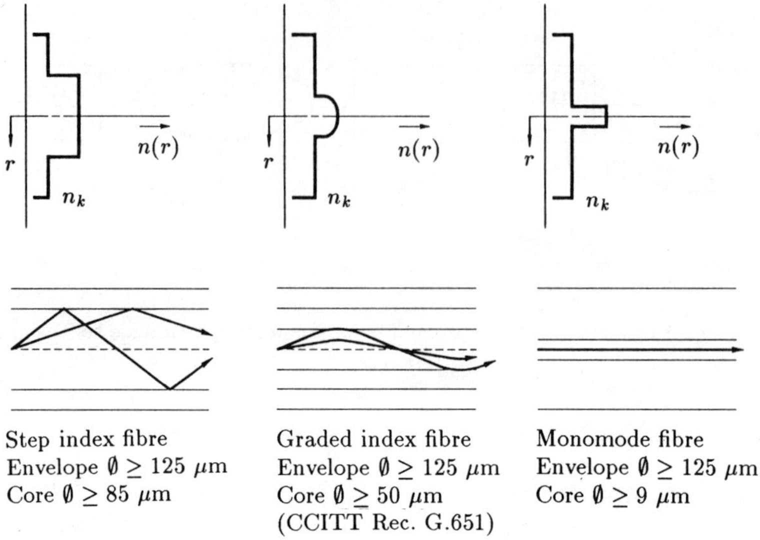

Figure 3.15 Path of rays as a function of the refractive index.

3.1.1.4 Fibre-optic cables

The most important medium of the future is clearly optical fibre. Why is this?

(1) Fast networks such as FDDI are based exclusively on fibre optics.

(2) The post office already has a large fibre-optic network (VBN).

(3) Fibre-optic cables are relatively difficult to tap.

(4) There is no problem with the equalization of potential between buildings.

(5) As far as future developments are concerned, transmission speeds up to the order of Tbps are possible, even though greater distances may have to be bridged.

The basis for the transmission of data using fibre optics is the principle of total reflection (Figure 3.15).

When light leaves a vacuum and enters an optically thicker medium, or more generally leaves an optically thinner medium for an optically thicker medium, its speed decreases by a medium-independent factor, which is a constant called the refractive index. Light which is incident on a joint face at an oblique angle is refracted according to the ratio of the refractive indices of the media on either side of the joint face. If the angle of incidence exceeds a certain value the light is no longer able to enter the optically thicker medium.

This property is used in fibre optics. Here, we have a casing with a low refractive index and a core with a higher refractive index. It follows that all light which enters the fibre-optic waveguide within a certain range of angles will be subject to continuous total reflection.

Light which is incident on the waveguide with an angle close to the maximum angle of incidence and subsequently passes through the waveguide in a marked zigzag pattern is called high mode light. Correspondingly, light which enters the waveguide at an angle relatively close to the optical axis of the waveguide is called low mode light.

When we view reflection in this way, we see that high mode light takes longer than low mode light to pass from one end to the other. This means that a light pulse which simultaneously contains light of both modes enters the waveguide with near-vertical edges and leaves it with relatively flat edges. This procedure is called mode dispersion.

This flattening occurs in particular for fibres with a step profile, as discussed above. In order to avoid this flattening to some extent, the casing/core and core/casing transitions are made less abrupt and the refractive index of the core is steadily increased towards that of the casing. The result of this is that higher-mode waves stay longer in areas where they travel faster and lower-mode waves are slowed. Thus, if the waveguide is sufficiently long the effects cancel out and the differences in the times taken to pass through the waveguide disappear. Such an optical waveguide is called a graded index profile fibre.

Monomode fibres result in even less dispersion. Here, the core has such a small diameter that almost only the mode along the optical axis may propagate.

Losses of intensity may have other causes apart from mode dispersion:

- Scattering due to impurities in the fibres.
- Absorption losses due to excitement of individual oscillations of the molecules of the medium.
- Coupling faults. The linking together, ramification or collection of optical waveguides is non-trivial. This problem area also covers switches.

However, these problems have now been solved, so that a broad spectrum of really powerful systems is available and represents a serious alternative to cable-linked technologies with metallic conductors. Optical waveguides have an attenuation which is largely independent of frequency; thus, they are superior to the best coaxial cables.

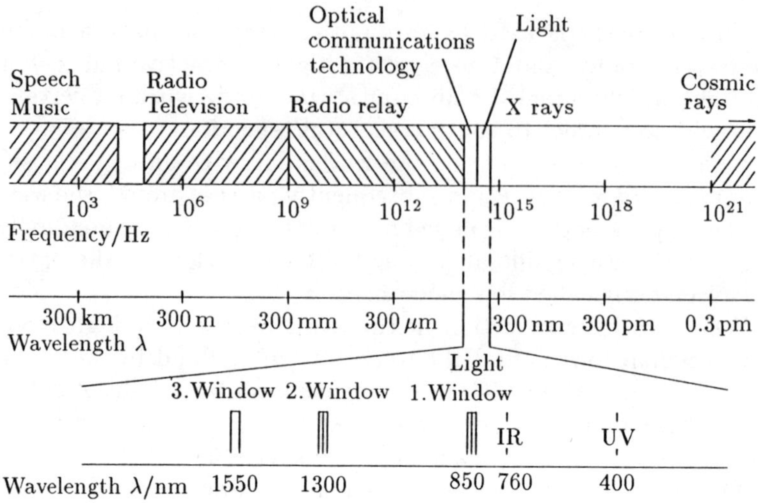

Figure 3.16 The electromagnetic spectrum.

There are various categories of optical signal emitters and receivers. Using light-emitting diodes (LEDs) and photo-conductive cells, it is possible to build relatively cheap transmission systems which achieve transmission rates of 10–20 Mbps over a distance of several hundred metres, without intermediate repeaters.

For higher requirements, laser diodes must be used for the emitter and PI photodiodes or avalanche diodes for the receiver. To date, transmission speeds of up to 400 Mbps have been achieved over sections of several hundred metres. For longer stretches, repeaters must be inserted otherwise the transmission speed falls. The control electronics are currently still the weak point of high-performance transmission systems, since the electro-optical structural elements could be used to achieve transmission bandwidths of several hundred GHz.

From the overall electromagnetic spectrum, the infrared area is chosen to transmit the data. Within this area, so-called local windows are used (Figure 3.16).

The reason for this lies in the signal attenuation of optical waveguides, which, depending on the fibre type (graded index fibre or monomode fibre), exhibit the least attenuation at wavelengths of 850 nm, 1300 nm and 1550 nm (Figure 3.17).

Fibre-optic cables are now available in many forms for practically all types of applications. In communications engineering, monomode and

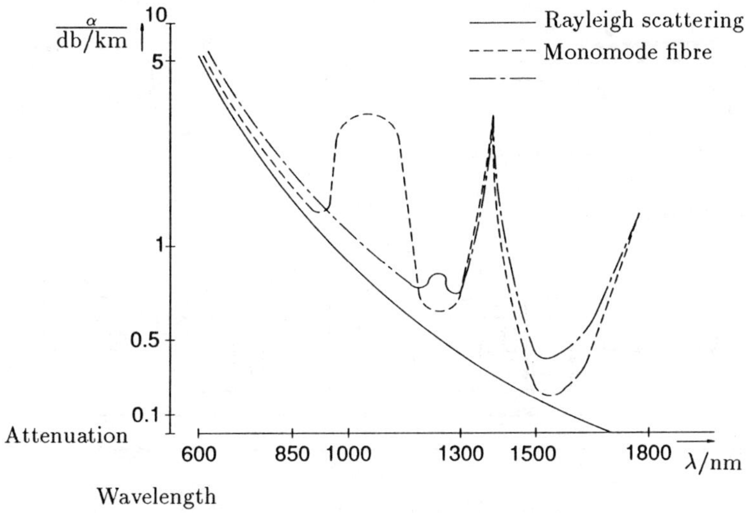

Figure 3.17 Signal attenuation for fibre-optic cables.

graded index fibres (aerial cables, underground cables, underwater cables) are used, sometimes with signal repeaters built into the cable. The first trans-oceanic cables are now being used and are indirectly becoming a competitor to satellite transmission. However, for conventional Token Rings, it is not yet sensible to use this form of fast data transmission.

3.1.2 Active repeaters and converters from different manufacturers

Whenever one nears the maximum distance limits in a Token Ring network, signal repeaters or signal converters must be installed to boost and regenerate the data signal. When fibre-optic cables are used in a Token Ring network, converters convert the electrical signals into light pulses. When screened or unscreened copper cables are used line repeaters help to increase the coverage of the network.

3.1.2.1 Active components in the IBM Token Ring network

IBM 8218 line repeater IBM provides the 8218 line repeater for IBM cable type 1. This permits an increase in the distance between two MSAUs to

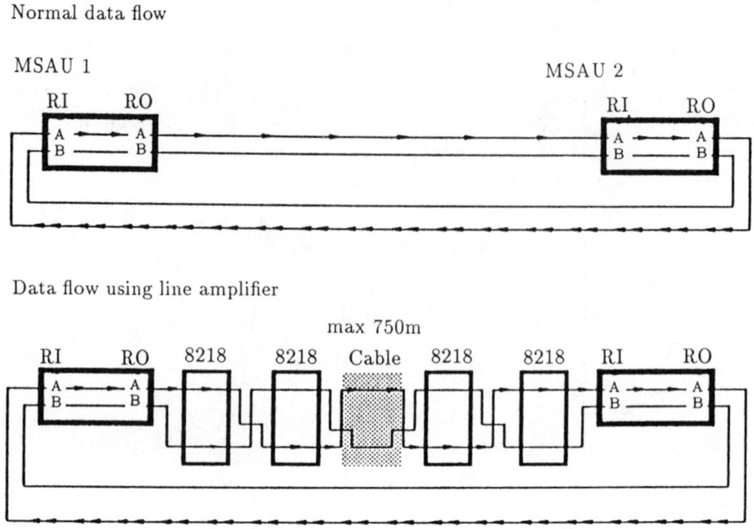

Figure 3.18 Data flow in Token Ring.

a maximum of 750 m, although at present this only applies for a transmission speed of 4 Mbps. The line repeater only boosts one line route between two MSAUs. An extra pair of repeaters is needed for the secondary route which is used in case of faults or also when the ring is not closed (Figure 3.18).

Several companies produce similar products which are alternatives to the IBM line repeater. Here too the maximum distance is 750 m. However, with some products, signals in screened 4-wire lines may also be regenerated and boosted, in which case the maximum distance between two MSAUs reduces to around 350 m. Some of the repeaters produced by these companies are built into the MSAUs.

IBM fibre-optic converters 8219 and 8220 IBM provides two different fibre-optic converters. The cheaper IBM 8219 is suitable for the 4 Mbps Token Ring. It only converts signals which are encoded according to the Token Ring encoding rules (differential Manchester coding). It uses LED technology, operates at a wavelength of 850 nm and is suitable for IBM cable type 5 (100/140 micron) and for the cable types 50/125, 62.5/125 and 85/125 micron which are preferred by industry. The 8219 may be used to bridge a maximum of 2 km without further signal amplification. If this range is insufficient the fibre-optic cables may also be cascaded (in theory, arbitrarily often). Both data routes are boosted so that only one pair of fibre-optic converters is needed between two MSAUs (Figure 3.19).

In its fibre-optic converters, IBM uses so-called mini BNC plugs for the fibre-optic cables. The connection lines between the patch panels

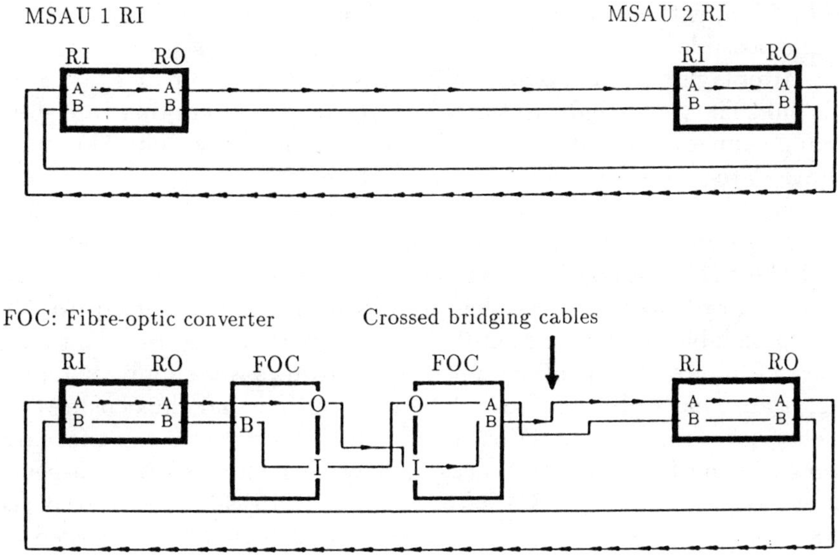

Figure 3.19 Use of fibre-optic converters.

and the fibre-optic converters (also called pigtails) must be fitted with these same plugs, which are otherwise rarely found in Germany. This is most annoying when FDDI links, public lines or fibre-optic Ethernet connections exist in the same data network, since these use other types of plugs which are not mutually compatible. Most other suppliers of fibre-optic converters also use other plug types, namely either the FSMA plug which is widely used in Germany or the ST plug which is used by the post office.

The MSAUs are again connected in a uniform way using the IBM's hermaphrodite data plugs.

IBM states that the maximum bridgeable distance using its fibre-optic converters is around 2 km. In practice, the actual distance which may be bridged is considerably higher. This depends on a number of factors. Firstly, the quality of the fibre is important. Only high-quality fibres with low attenuation, which correspond to the DIN norm, should be used. Secondly, the number of splices (points at which two fibre-optic cables are joined) and the way in which these splices are made are important in the calculation of the maximum possible distance between two MSAUs. If the splices are made using adhesives, the attenuation at these points is relatively high (around 0.4–2 db). When the optical fibre ends are arc welded together using special devices, the splice has an attenuation of around 0.1–0.4 db. Moreover, every plug connection and thus also every patch panel means an additional loss of power. For an average power of around 18 db, with a good fibre-optic converter for graded index fibres, it is possible to bridge distances of up to 4 km, without having to cascade fibre-optic converters (which is in principle possible).

After laying a line it is generally advisable to draw up an exact profile of this link. The profile indicates how long the link is, where there are splices and plug connections and the overall attenuation of the link. This profile facilitates later error location in the case of line failure.

Unlike the 8219, the IBM 8220 fibre-optic converter is suitable for both 4 Mbps and 16 Mbps. The functional description is comparable with that of the 8219 fibre-optic converter. It is also only suitable for graded index fibres, operates at a wavelength of 850 nm, can bridge up to 2 km and is cascadable. Unlike the 8219, the 8220 is an active ring station. In the case of failure of a trunk circuit or of its own power supply or internal errors, it automatically switches to the back-up line and thus ensures that the network continues to function. Even more important, at least for larger networks, is the fact that its functions may be monitored from a central point (for example, by the IBM LAN Manager) (critical network resource). Errors such as a defective line are thus directly detected and analyzed at a central point. Since it is an active ring station in the LAN, the 8220 also occupies one of the 260 possible connection positions in a Token Ring LAN. For large networks with several fibre-optic sections, this may lead to bottlenecks and force the division of a Token Ring into two subrings linked by a bridge.

When several fibre-optic converters are installed in a distributor room it is best to use the 19-inch rack cabinet with its own power supply, which is available for this purpose.

3.1.2.2 Alternative fibre-optic converters

As an alternative to IBM, very many manufacturers now supply their own fibre-optic converters for use in Token Ring.

We shall describe two representative examples of these products, namely SIECOR from Siemens and SEL from Alcatel.

Example: SIECOR (Siemens) Like IBM, Siemens supplies fibre-optic converters for 4 or 16 Mbps. They have a range up to 2.5 km and are cascadable. Unlike the IBM fibre-optic converters these converters may also be used to connect terminals to the MSAUs (substitute for IBM's type 6 lobe cable) and thus enable individual terminals to connect to the ring from distances of up to 2.5 km from the MSAU. As with the IBM 8220, there is an automatic switchover to the back-up path in the case of cable faults. However, these fibre-optic converters do not generate error messages which can be evaluated by NetView. They also occupy positions in the ring as active stations in the network.

A maximum of 34 fibre-optic converters may be interconnected in a star shape using universal concentrators (Figure 3.20).

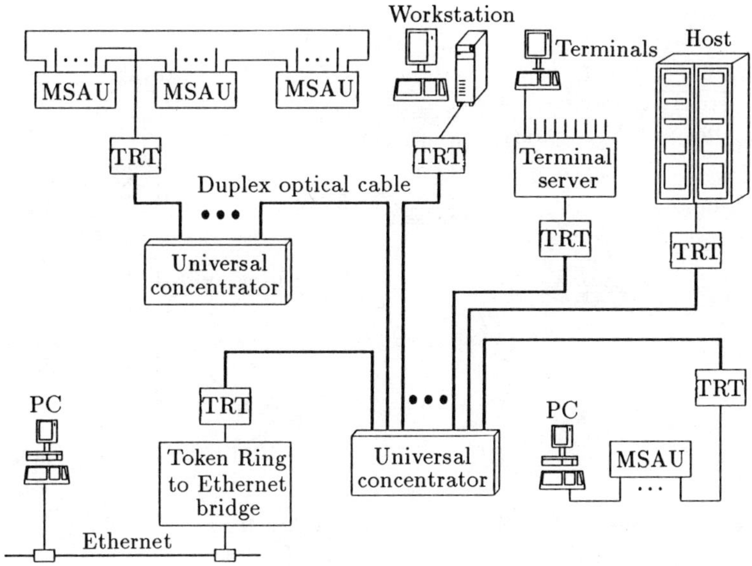

Figure 3.20 Siemens fibre-optic converters.

The concentrators may also be used with Ethernet fibre-optic converters, so that Ethernet fibre-optic LANs and Token Ring fibre-optic LANs may be operated together.

Example: SEL (Alcatel) Alcatel is one of the two largest manufacturers of fibre-optic products in Germany; thus, it produces a large range of fibre-optic converters for Token Ring and Ethernet and also for other cabling systems. The choice ranges from fibre-optic converters built into the MSAUs (4 Mbps, maximum range 2 km before boosting, graded index fibres), through switchable fibre-optic converters (4 or 16 Mbps, maximum range 4 or even 12 km, graded index fibres, wavelength 850 nm) in LED technology, which may also be used for lobe cables, to fibre-optic converters (4 or 16 Mbps, maximum range 18 km, wavelength 1300 nm) which may use the monomode 9/125 monomode cables still used by the post office. The latter fibre-optic converters have an FTZ[2] authorization and thus may also be used in public networks.

Apart from these classical forms of Token Ring signal boosters for IBM cable types 1/6 and fibre-optic cables, there are also many other hybrid forms on the market which permit the use of other cable types and networks.

[2]FTZ = (German) Federal Bureau for Telecommunications.

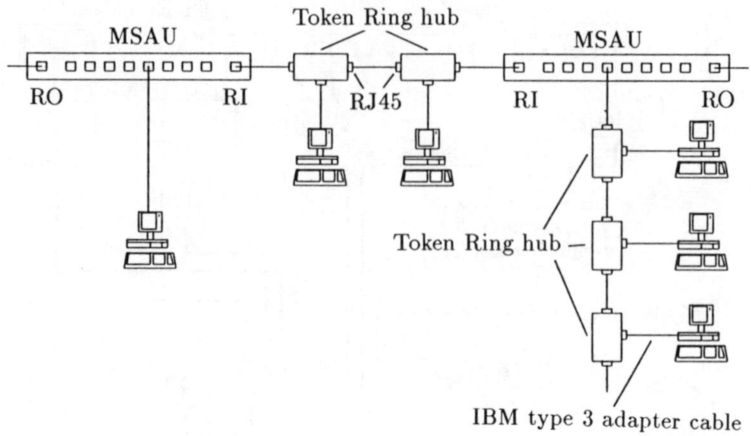

Figure 3.21 Example: RAD – Token Ring mono hub.

Here are two examples. Both products are manufactured by the company RAD and are sold by several suppliers in Germany.

The so-called Token Ring mono hub (Figure 3.21) provides for the use of unscreened twisted 4-wire cable between MSAUs and thus permits the connection of additional terminals without the introduction of further MSAUs. In this example (Figure 3.22) remote terminals may be connected to Token Ring via the public network, as though they were directly on the ring.

Here, the Token Ring extender (TRE) converts the Token Ring interface, as required, to a V.24 (RS232C) interface (max. 19200 bps), a V.35 interface (max. 48000 bps) or an X.21 interface (max. 64 000 bps). A special protocol is executed between the two TREs to permit distance-independent connection of the terminals. In the ring, use of the TRE does not lead to time delays for the other attached stations. As far as a terminal which is connected over the public network or via a dedicated line is concerned, the transmission speed used on this link becomes a criterion for the throughput. In pure interactive applications, the response time as far as the end user is concerned is only slightly worse than that for a subscriber attached directly to Token Ring, since the information units transmitted are usually smaller than 512 bytes (the delay at 64 000 bps is around 1/8 seconds).

In the future there will be similar systems for Ethernet. It is notable that, with the various booster components currently available for Token Ring, more flexibility is now being obtained than with Ethernet LANs.

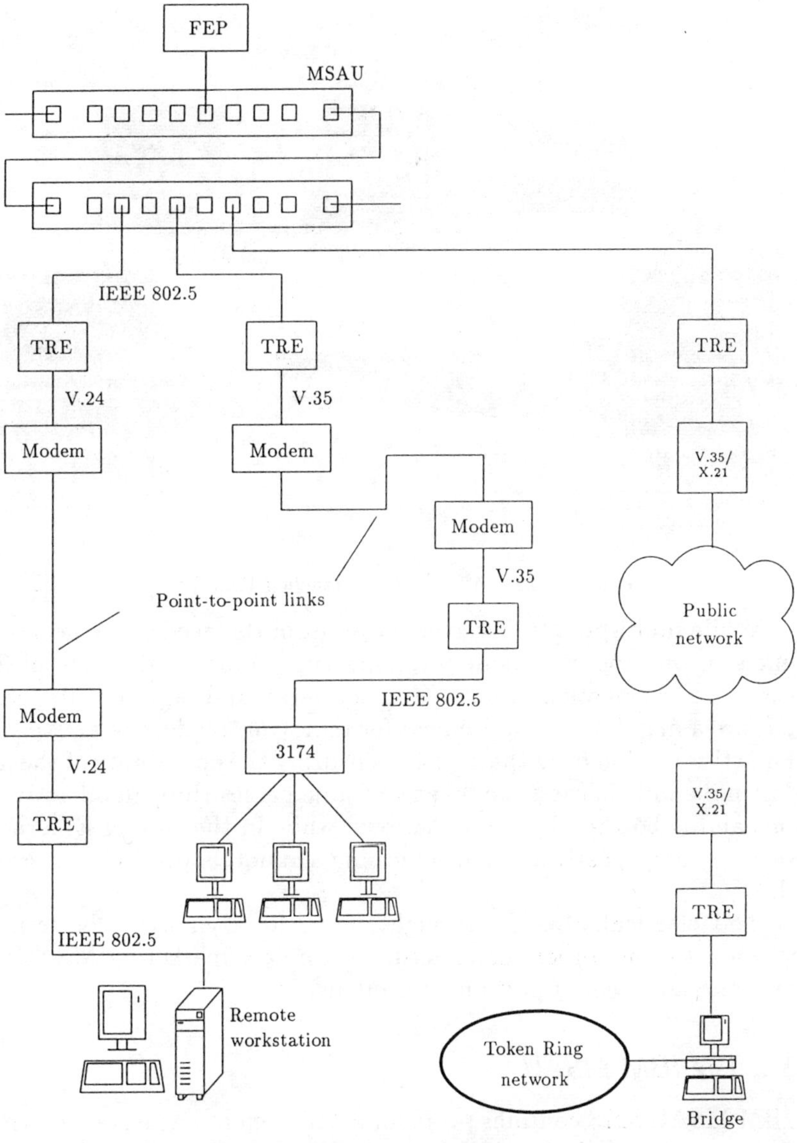

Figure 3.22 Token Ring extender (TRE).

3.1.3 Multistation access units

After cables, cabling systems, plug connectors and boosters, we now come to the actual point at which terminals are attached to Token Ring, namely the multistation access unit (MSAU). MSAUs are comparable with Ethernet multi-port transceivers. An MSAU or a multi-port transceiver may be used to construct a star-shaped mini-LAN (Figure 3.23).

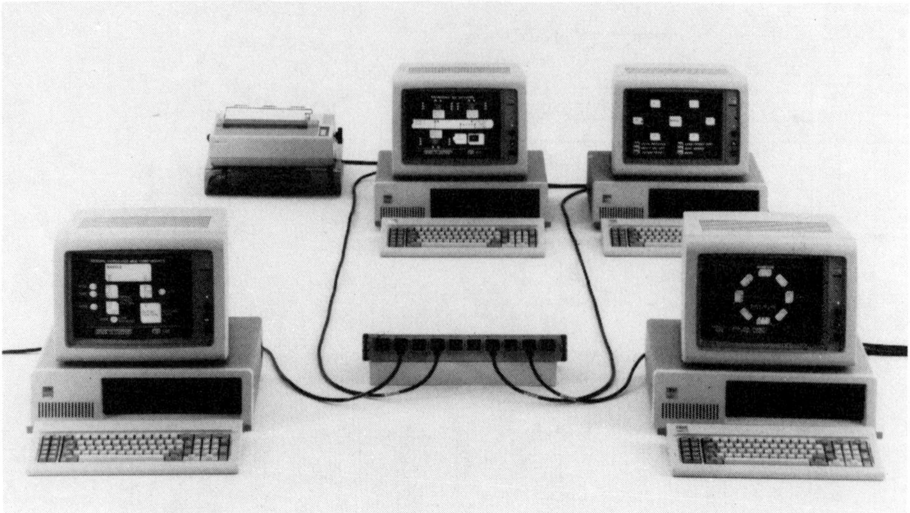

Figure 3.23 MSAU with attached IBM PCs.

While multi-port transceivers arose from the need to connect several terminals in one room without retaining the minimum distance of 2.5 m between two connection points (transceivers) and are not imperative, MSAUs are a mandatory requirement for removing a defective active station or an inactive station from the ring and ensuring the operability of the latter.

Unlike in Ethernet, the token or frame passes through all active data stations and is boosted by these stations, while in the case of Ethernet the stations are only passively connected and cannot boost the transmission signals.

The classical MSAU has eight ports for connection of terminals. As opposed to this, other manufacturers are now marketing MSAUs with between one and twenty ports for terminals.

3.1.3.1 The IBM MSAU

The IBM MSAU 8228 contains ports for at most eight connectable terminals and forms an internal ring for these eight terminals. It operates without current using mechanical relays and thus may be installed anywhere, even in false floors or ceilings. The cables connecting the terminals to the MSAU are generally called lobes. Up to 33 MSAUs may be attached to a ring. The ports for connection of terminals and the ring input/output ports are treated in different ways. Relays are only found in the terminal connection sockets (IBM hermaphrodite plug connection) and not in the RI (ring input) and RO (ring output) interfaces to the next MSAU. If the RI and RO interfaces are not busy the associated relay is closed and the internal return circuit is used to close the ring. Thus, faults on the cable between two MSAUs

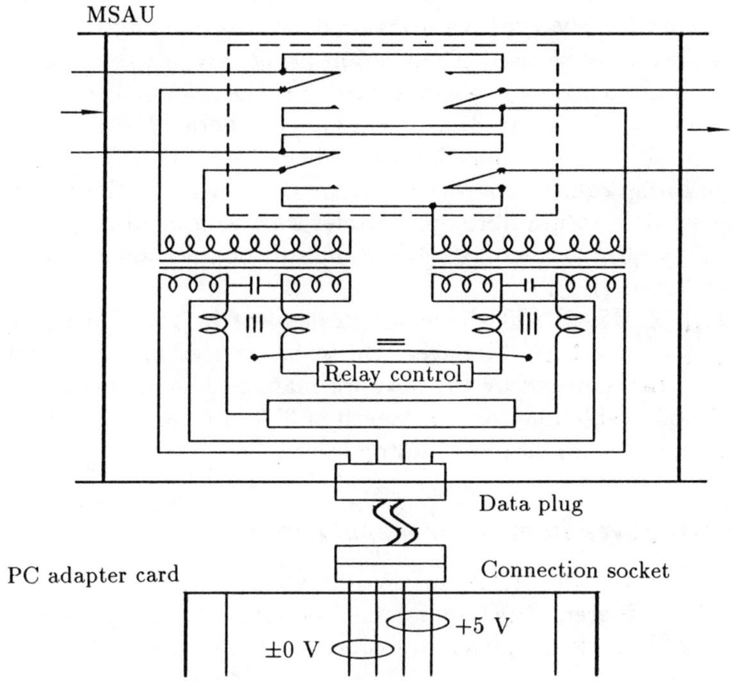

Figure 3.24 MSAU (Source: IBM).

can only be removed manually or by introducing active components such as intelligent repeaters or fibre-optic converters as previously discussed.

The IBM MSAU 8228 may be delivered in a 19-inch rack version or with an additional housing for the wall or ceiling assembly including a bracket for the connection cable. There are no particular room temperature or relative humidity requirements (from +5 to +50 °C). Normal electromagnetic fields do not affect the MSAU.

Mode of operation of the IBM MSAU A station is only connected to the active ring once the protocol mechanism described in the previous chapter has been executed (Figure 3.24). Only then does it generate the modulated phantom voltage which is needed to pick up the relay and thus lead the data flow through the station. When a station is introduced a voltage of between 4.1 and 7 volts is needed on one line pair and 0 volts on the other. If the voltage difference falls below 1 volt the MSAU relay automatically returns to its ground state and the station becomes inactive.

This process of mechanical closure of the relay should not take longer than about 5 ms.

With IBM, terminals are in principle connected using IBM cables types 1/6. Alternatively, type 3 (unshielded twisted pair) and type 6 (fibre optic) data lines may be used. Connection using type 3 cable requires the use of filters (baluns). Here, we again note that the telephone cable used in Germany is not usually a type 3 cable and has considerably worse properties. Thus, type 3 cables should only be used when, for structural reasons, it is not possible to lay cables of a different type belatedly. On the other hand, it is always sensible to use fibre-optic cables such as graded index cables of size 62.5/125 or 50/125 microns (DIN standard) or the monomode cable of size 9/125 microns (PTT).

The IBM MSAU 8203 is an active element in Token Ring and can be monitored by the LAN Manager. Up to 80 devices may be connected. Each port can be managed by the network manager. Since this is an active device, each lobe cable may have a length of 375 m (4 Mbps) or 145 m (16 Mbps). Cable faults are corrected automatically.

3.1.3.2 Alternatives from other manufacturers

Based on the motto: what IBM can do others can do (more cheaply) better (or at least in a different way), many manufacturers of cabling systems and accessories for Token Ring have now introduced their own MSAUs. Here are some examples.

Proteon MSAU Proteon was the first manufacturer to provide 10 Mbps and 80 Mbps components worldwide. It was thus sensible that this manufacturer should also produce MSAUs for the 4 and 16 Mbps Token Rings. These MSAUs extend upon the functions and facilities provided by IBM 8828 MSAUs. In Germany, they are supplied by SEL, Fuba, Racal Milgo and Telemation, amongst others. Because of their extra functions they need their own power supply. An integrated display provides information about the function and the state of individual MSAU connections. Every port may be individually monitored and controlled from a central monitoring PC. Proteon also has its own network management system. The control information is transmitted via its own cable network (asynchronous, telephone cable). If a link section between two MSAUs fails, unlike for IBM MSAUs, there is an automatic switchover to the secondary path and the operation continues uninterrupted.

MSAUs of this type may have either one or two built-in fibre-optic converters for the link sections to the next MSAU (Figure 3.25). This saves space and money as far as wiring cabinets are concerned. Proteon also produces a series of MSAUs which are exclusively designed for the use of unshielded twisted pair cables (UTPs). Instead of the hermaphrodite plug connections, these MSAUs use the Western plug as a plug connection,

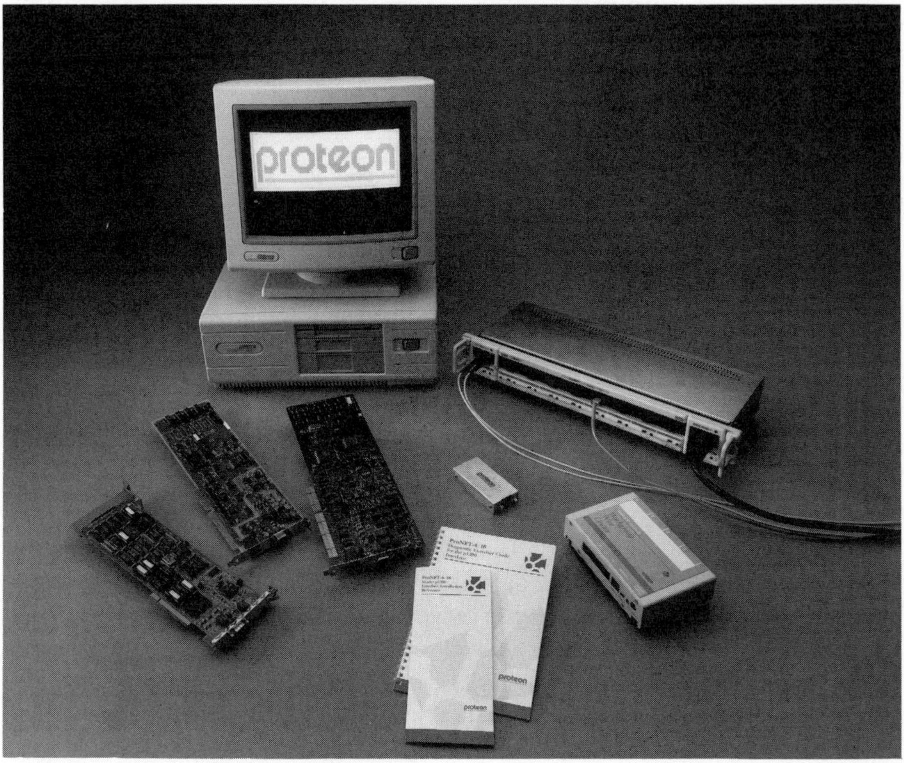

Figure 3.25 Proteon MSAU.

which requires considerably less space. This technology supports both the 4 Mbps and the 16 Mbps Token Ring.

Nokia–Ericsson Nokia–Ericsson builds MSAUs for security-related and safety-critical areas. Here both the connection cables between the MSAUs and the ports for the lobe cables are constructed completely in fibre-optic technology. Thus, distances of up to 2.5 km between terminals and MSAUs and between pairs of MSAUs may be bridged. To round off the programme and to increase the data security and data protection, Nokia–Ericsson also produces a fibre-optic connection card for PCs.

Ericsson also produces MSAUs which support existing RG62 A/U cables from the IBM 3270 world as terminal connection cables.

Ungermann Bass This cabling system (ACCESS/ONE) includes MSAUs with 10 and 20 ports. They also have an LED functional display and the ports may be individually monitored and controlled. Protocol expressions permit a precise overview of the use of the individual ports over time. To improve access protection, every individual port of an MSAU may be protected with a password.

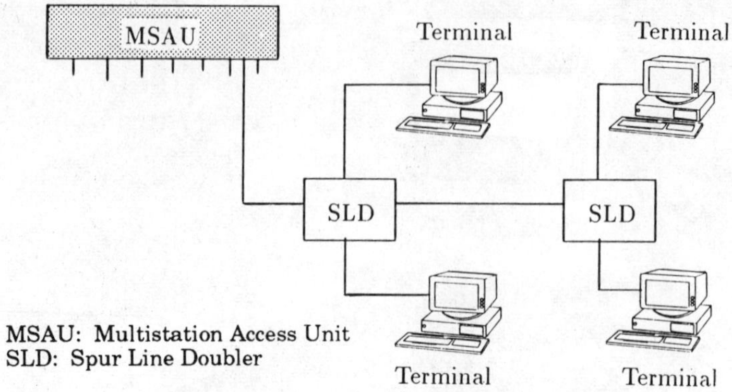

Figure 3.26 Cascaded 2-spur line doubler.

Local Data This company provides MSAUs with 4 or 8 ports for the 4 Mbps Token Ring. An unshielded twisted pair cable is used for connection. The RJ11 terminal plug is used. Two versions are available:

- LD 82xx for maximum distances of around 170 m between two MSAUs and between MSAUs and terminals.
- LD 92xx for maximum distances of around 300 m between two MSAUs and between MSAUs and terminals.

Other alternatives Other manufacturers produce MSAUs with 8 or 16 ports which may be equipped according to the requirements of the end user. Possible options include:

- Built-in fibre-optic converters (max. 4000 m, automatic switchover if cable breaks).
- Built-in copper cable boosters (750 m).
- Automatic switchover to the secondary line on cable faults between two MSAUs.
- SLD 2-spur line doubler (doubly cascadable, see Figure 3.26).

So-called Token Ring mono hubs (Figure 3.27) emulate MSAUs with a single connection. At most seven terminals may be operated in series. This considerably reduces the cabling costs and fewer MSAUs are needed for smaller networks.

A typical Token Ring configuration might then look like that shown in Figure 3.28.

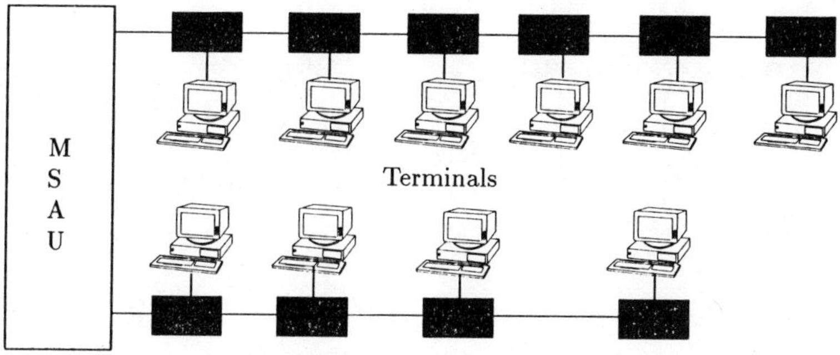

Figure 3.27 Token Ring mono hubs.

3.1.4 Bridges and routers

In Token Ring networks, bridges are the means by which individual Token Ring installations are linked into a complicated, homogeneous network. They should always be used when:

- The number of stations per ring could be greater than 260.
- The number of distributor rooms per installation is greater than 12.
- Interworking of 4 Mbps and 16 Mbps Token Ring stations is required.
- For reasons of security, redundant rings must be constructed.
- The distances between the individual stations are too large and the public network has to be used.
- A backbone network for the overall communication is required.
- The overall throughput has to be increased.
- For organizational and security-related reasons partitions are required.
- Only terminals with (one or more) special protocols may communicate with terminals in another ring.

In principle, several parallel bridges may be installed between two Token Ring networks. This helps to spread the load and results in a marked increase in availability. Unlike in Ethernet, as described in the last chapter, the link information is not held in the bridge but is transmitted with each data packet (source routing). The optimal route for a connection is sought on establishment of the logical link. Thus, the bridges do not need to hold and manage (possibly expensive) tables. Therefore, the throughput of a Token Ring bridge is largely independent of the number of intercommunicating

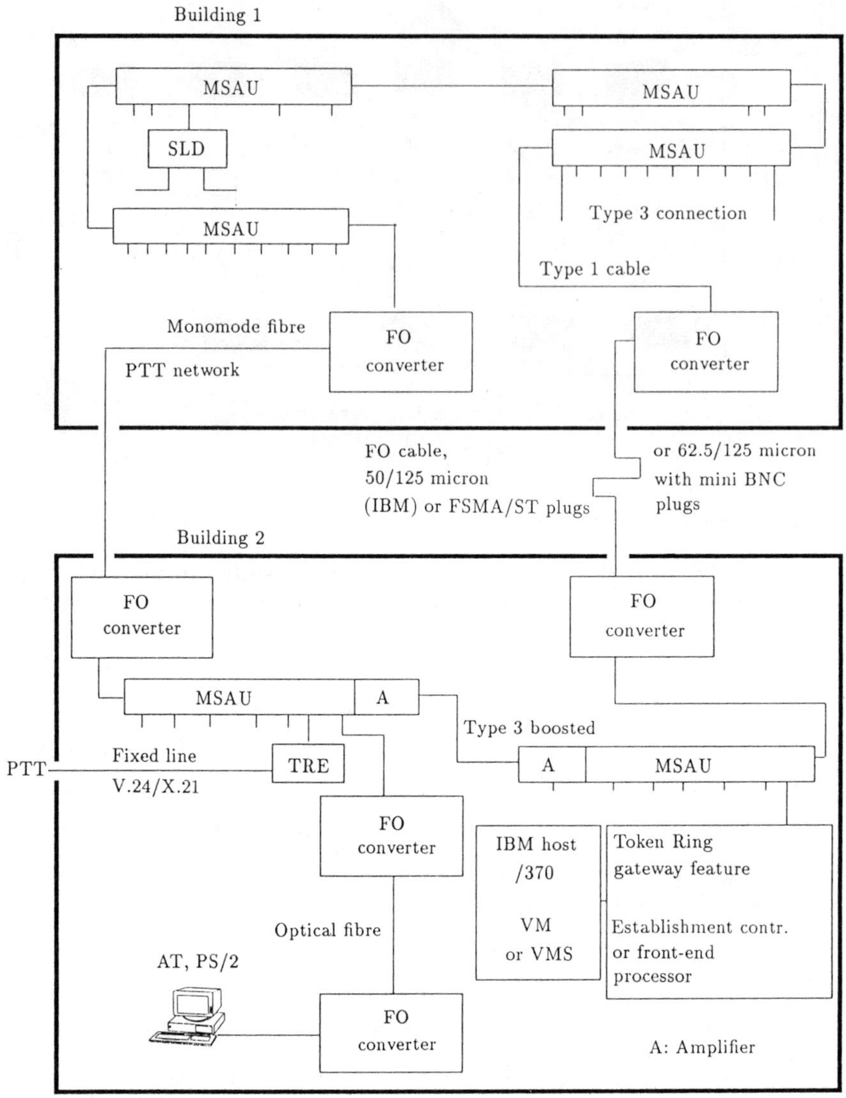

Figure 3.28 Typical Ethernet configuration.

devices in the LAN. On the other hand, the length of the routing information field, which is transmitted with every data field, is necessarily limited so as to avoid the need to transmit too much control information in each packet. Thus, IBM limits the number of consecutive bridges which may be crossed between two terminals to seven. If the destination on a route is only reachable after the eighth bridge, this connection is no longer recognized. The number of bridges in a network may of course be considerably greater. It

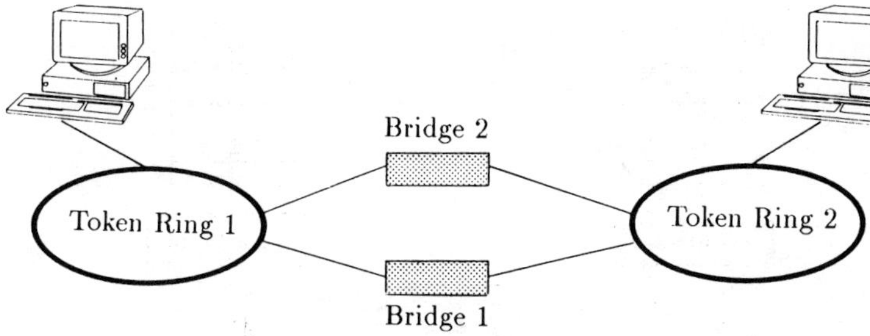

Figure 3.29 Simple duplicated bridges.

is only important that on connection establishment there should be at least one route between two end systems in which the number of consecutive bridges is less than or equal to seven.

Figures 3.29 to 3.32 show examples of the construction of networks using bridges. In the first example (Figure 3.29) two networks are interlinked via two parallel bridges. This provides the link with increased protection against failure and improves (doubles) the data throughput between the Token Ring subnetworks.

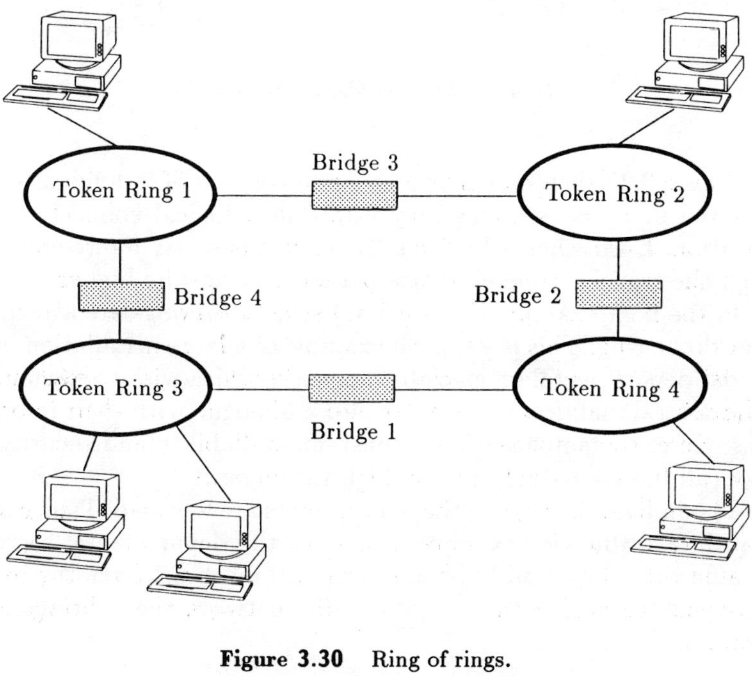

Figure 3.30 Ring of rings.

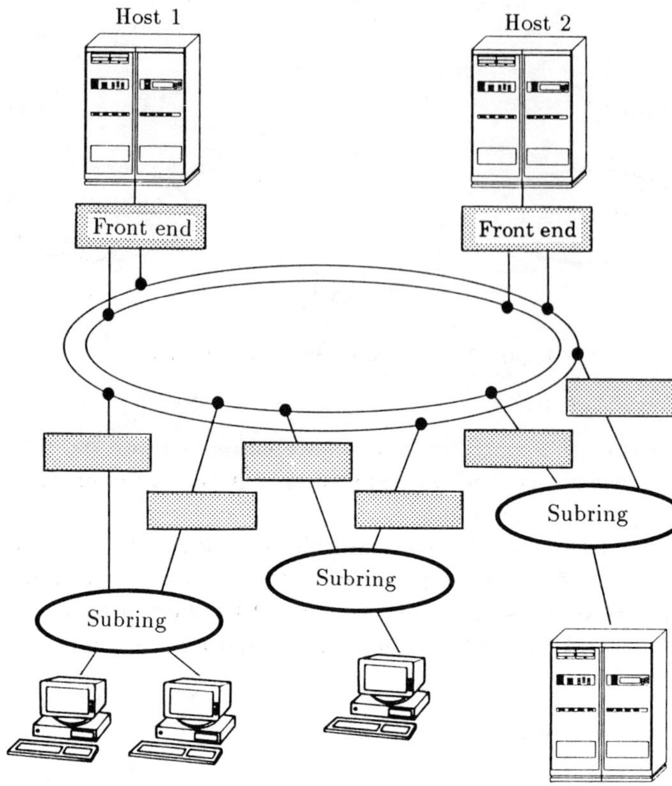

Figure 3.31 Backbone ring, dual.

Figure 3.30 shows a ring which again consists of individual subrings. Each of the attached stations may establish a logical connection to any other station. Even when a bridge fails, all stations may intercommunicate, although the transfer time of a data packet may now be higher.

In the next example (Figure 3.31) several subrings are attached to a dual backbone ring. This is a typical example of a large installation in which there exist departmental or specialist networks which wish to exchange data with the central mainframes or enter into a dialogue with their information systems. Here, the emphasis is on constant availability and security of the network (all links are dual) and on high throughput.

The individual rings in the departments are less loaded since only the internal data traffic (for example, access to the departmental server) and data traffic with the central systems is carried by these. Even the backbone ring only has to deal with the data traffic between the subrings and the mainframes.

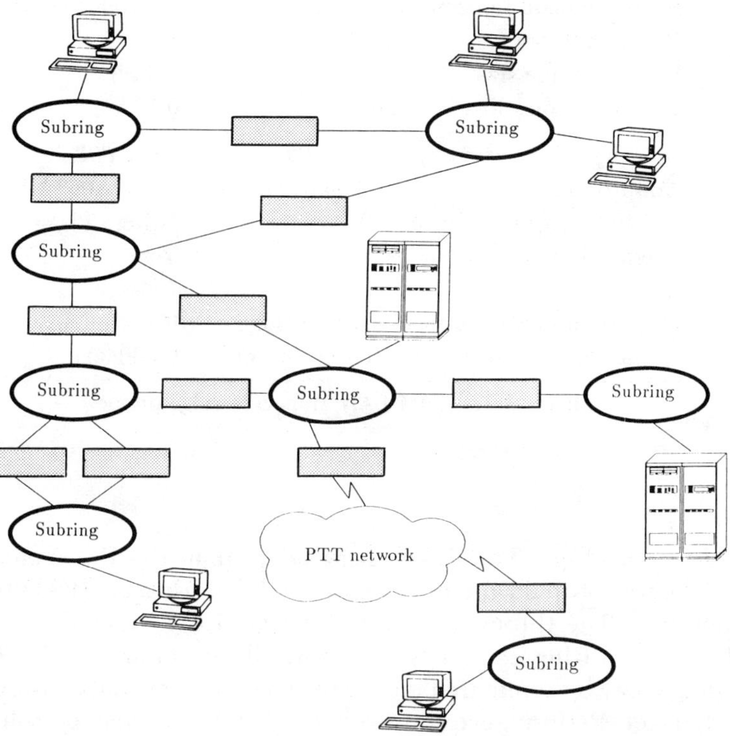

Figure 3.32 Complicated ring structure.

Finally, Figure 3.32 shows a complicated, multiply-intermeshed network which also involves the public network.

What does a bridge in Token Ring look like? What products exist and what requirements or constraints must be satisfied? Here are some examples.

3.1.4.1 IBM Token Ring network bridge program

IBM buries the bridges which it supplies on the PC and only delivers the bridge program which must be installed on a PC dedicated to that purpose. For reasons of throughput, it is advisable to use at least an 80286-compatible PC. Neither a screen nor a keyboard are needed to operate the system, above all when the IBM LAN Manager is also available in Token Ring.

The bridge software is transparent to applications which are based on the 802.2 standard and use source routing (NetBios, APPC). It may be used to interconnect Token Ring LANs operating at different transmission rates, provided that the bridge PC contains one adaptor for 4 Mbps and

Bridge name		BRING 13
Bridge version information		0101006403831
Bridge number		1
Largest frame size		2052
Percent frames lost threshold		0.10%
Routing information	*Ring 001*	*Ring 002*
Adaptor address	10005A061D93	10005A062AA8
Symbolic name	Bridge 11	Bridge 12
Single routing broadcast	Yes	Yes
Hop count	7	7
Date counter values reported by bridge		01-04-89
Time counter values reported by bridge		09:30:33

Figure 3.33 IBM LAN Manager bridge profile.

another for 16 Mbps. The Token Ring adaptor in the PC should have at least 16 kbytes of main memory for the 4 Mbps ring or 64 kbytes for the 16 Mbps ring. The throughput of each bridge PC is around 1–2 Mbps for a 4 Mbps Token Ring and leads to message delays of around 10–20 ms. An IBM bridge may be configured locally or remotely (centrally) using the IBM LAN Manager. Performance statements and statistics may be collected and evaluated. If desired, the IBM LAN Manager may also be used to transmit status information, configuration data and performance data.

Filter functions, which may be used to monitor and control the network, may be defined using a programmer interface.

Figures 3.33 and 3.34 show an example of the configuration of an IBM bridge and the instantaneous performance data (respectively).

Frames forwarded values for:	Ring 001	Ring 002
Broadcast frames	60315	14030
Broadcast bytes	4021327	909255
Non-broadcast frames	31191	61169
Non-broadcast bytes	1886177	8571896
Frames not forwarded because:		
Target ring inoperable	0	0
Adaptor congestion	0	0
Other reasons	0	0

Figure 3.34 Performance counters.

When IBM bridge software is used in public networks (remote bridges) two PCs with the bridge program are required for each link. Each PC must have a Token Ring adaptor card and an IBM X.25 interface coprocessor/2 or a real-time interface coprocessor. Transmission in the public network is synchronous with a rate of 9600 or 19 200 bps (V.24 or X.21) and 64 kbps up to 2 Mbps (V.35, X.21).

When the bridge is installed, the ring number and the individual bridge number are entered. The so-called hop count limit parameter gives the user the facility to reduce the limit on the number of consecutive bridges which may be crossed from 7 to a number between 1 and 7. This may be used to exclude excessively long routes.

Initialization of a bridge takes some two to three minutes. Once the Token Ring adaptor card has been successfully initialized, it executes a number of tests which ensure that the connection is properly established.

First it generates a TEST request frame with the address of the other adaptor, but without routing information in the frame. If it receives a TEST response frame both adaptors must be attached to the same ring. In this case an error message is generated and the connection establishment is aborted. Otherwise, it generates a new TEST request frame with the necessary routing information field, for direct transmission by one adaptor across the bridge to the other adaptor. If no reply to this is received there is a hardware or software fault in the bridge. If several replies are received, at least one link already exists and the connection establishment is again aborted. The tests are always carried out in both directions until it is certain that the bridge has been properly generated.

3.1.4.2 Alternatives to IBM

Ungermann Bass Unlike IBM, Ungermann Bass uses the black-box solution known from Ethernet LANs. Thus, one buys not only the software, but software and hardware as a unit. This has the advantage that this dedicated bridge has a higher performance than the IBM solution. The Ungermann Bass bridge is also suitable for linking Token Rings to Ethernet; however, it is not protocol transparent.

Proteon Proteon produces routers which may also be used to link Ethernet and Token Ring networks, if, for example, TCP/IP is used. Proteon naturally also supports its 10 and 80 Mbps Token Ring.

Similar solutions based on TCP/IP are also produced by CISCO. Bridge/routers (brouters) are now available which carry out protocol-dependent router functions and switch to the transparent mode when they do not recognize the protocol.

RAD RAD's Token Ring bridge is an example of what is now possible with remote Token Ring bridges (RTBs) (Figure 3.35).

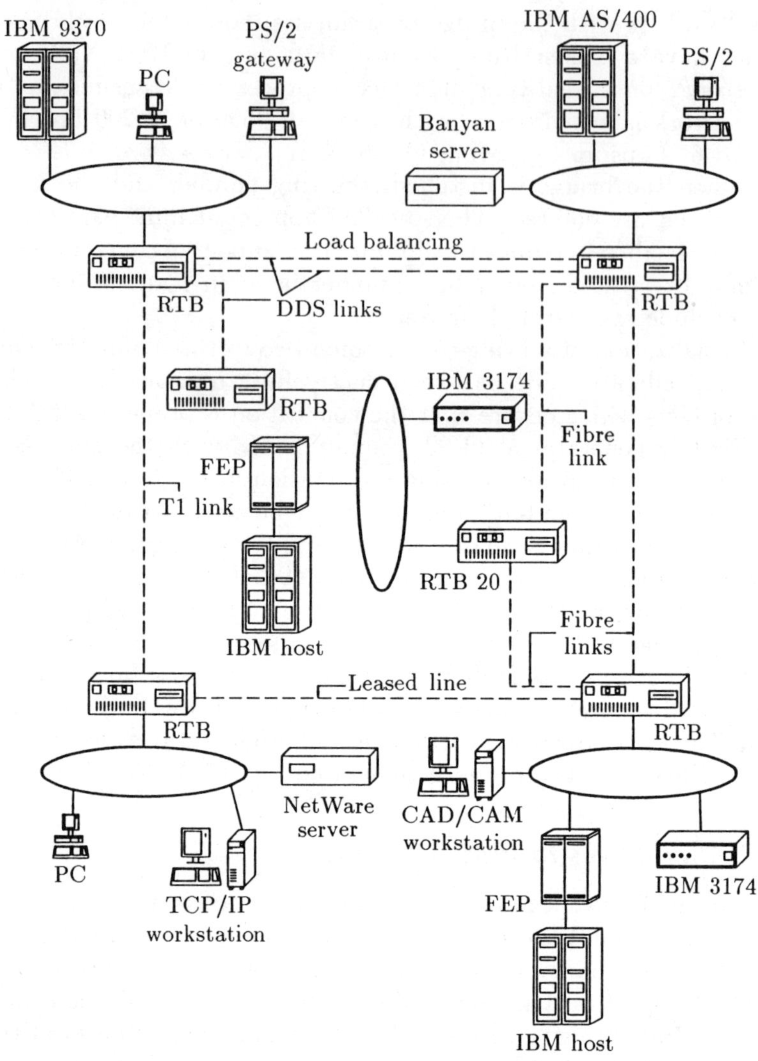

Figure 3.35 Token Ring wide area network (Source: Telemation).

The bridges may be connected by fibre-optic links, X.21 interfaces, X.25 interfaces or T1 and S2 links (1.5 Mbps and 2 Mbps). Worldwide Token Ring installations may be constructed in this way.

Other manufacturers such as CISCO or Crosscom produce bridges which are partially protocol transparent and which, for example, enable one to use Token Ring as a backbone in order to interlink Ethernet LANs or

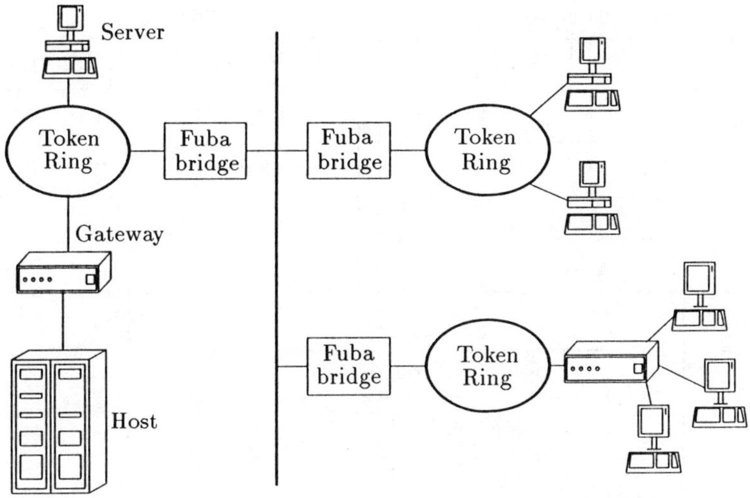

Figure 3.36 Token Rings on a broadband backbone.

to support different protocol stacks. Vitalink optimizes the linking of two Token Ring installations via public networks by implementing remote Token Ring bridges with data compression, which increases the bridge throughput by a factor of 2 to 4.

Care is advised when products from different manufacturers are used. The protocols between the bridges are not standardized. When you have chosen a manufacturer, you should stick with its products.

A special function is carried out by bridges which facilitate the coupling of Token Ring networks over existing broadband networks. IBM uses its own PC Network broadband network for this. The disadvantage of this solution is the resulting decrease in throughput, since the transmission rate in the PC Network broadband network is only 2 Mbps. Fuba has a considerably better solution (Figure 3.36).

The Fuba bridge is transparent to the attached end systems. Existing broadband networks may undertake the backbone function for Token Ring networks.

3.1.4.3 Bridges between Token Ring and Ethernet

In many installations there exist both Ethernet and Token Ring installations. There has been a long-standing desire to interlink these two worlds in as protocol transparent a way as possible. Even IBM has recognized this need and now provides a relatively cheap facility for coupling

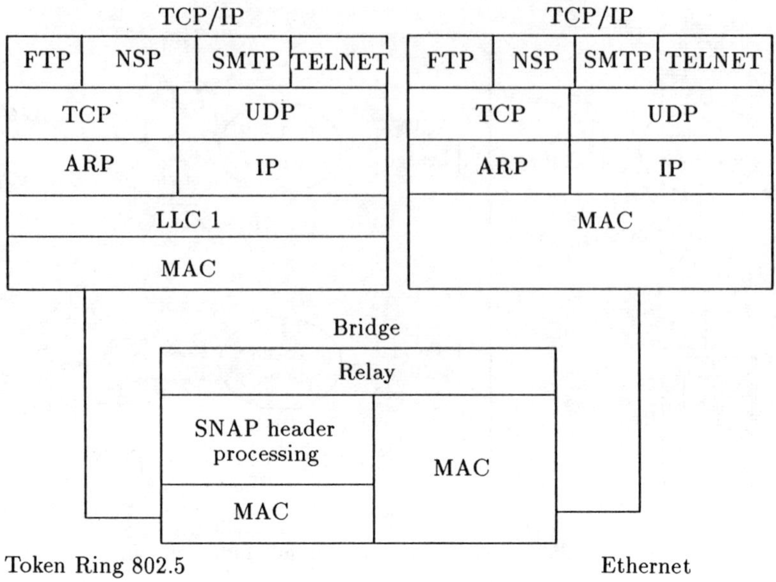

Figure 3.37 Mode 1: Token Ring ↔ Ethernet version 2.

the two LAN architectures in the form of the IBM 8209.

The bridge supports the 4 Mbps and the 16 Mbps Token Ring (with and without early token release) and Ethernet version 2 or 802.3-compatible LANs. Compatible protocols such as NetBios, TCP/IP, OSI, SNA and ISO 8802.2 are used. A hybrid of both variants Ethernet V.2 and ISO 8802.3 is possible, if the bridge is set up in such a way that it automatically analyzes the type involved. The bridge can also link two Token Ring LANs.

The bridge operates in the Ethernet V.2 mode mainly when TCP/IP is to be supported. In this mode, Token Ring operates with both connection-oriented and connectionless communications services while Ethernet only operates with the latter (datagrams). Thus, Token Ring connection-oriented LLC frames are picked up by the 8209 and converted into Ethernet frames (Figure 3.37).

The reverse conversion is expensive. The 8209 generates routing information for this link and adds an SNA network access protocol header.

In the ISO 8802.3 mode, OSI protocols, and SNA and NetBios protocols are transmitted (Figures 3.38 and 3.39).

The protocol layers above the MAC level are transmitted transparently. For terminals on Token Ring, the IBM 8209 looks like a bridge to another Token Ring. Conversely, the IBM 8209 is transparent to

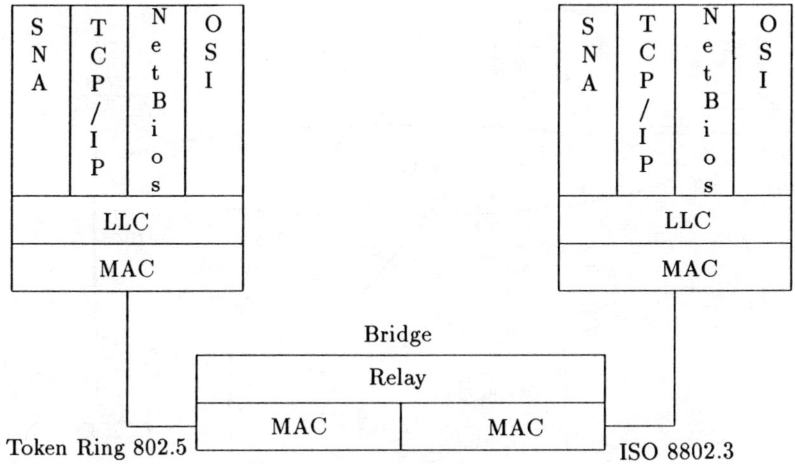

Figure 3.38 Mode 2: Token Ring ↔ ISO 8802.3.

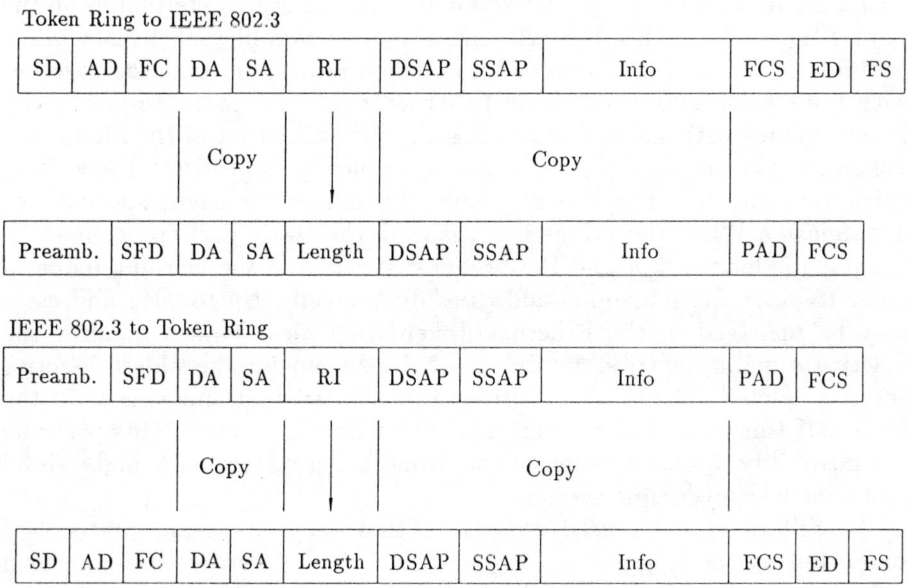

Figure 3.39 Frame transformation (Source: IBM).

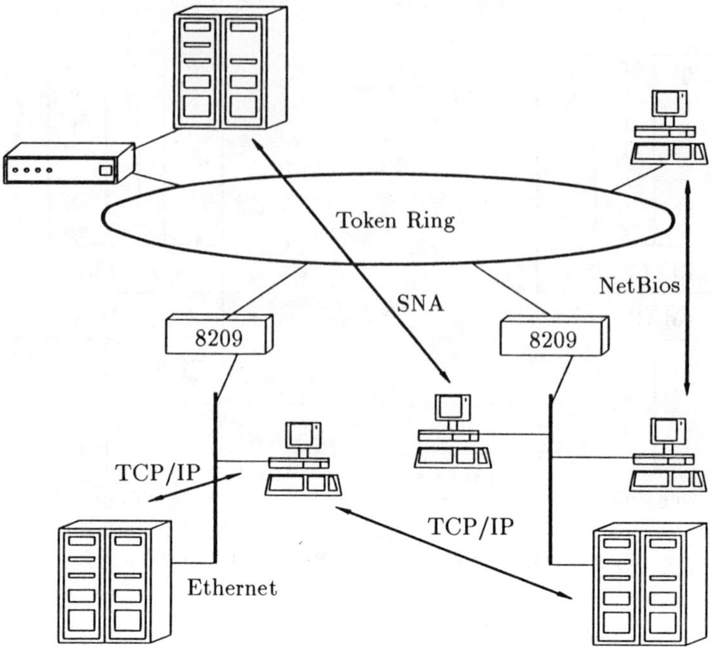

Figure 3.40 The IBM 8209.

terminals on the Ethernet/802.3 and looks like one or more terminals on the same Ethernet. For this, the 8209 must manage two files (in RAM) which contain the Token Ring station addresses and routing information together with the station addresses of the Ethernet/802.3 terminals (respectively). In accordance with the source routing algorithm the part of the file for the Token Ring entries is always managed dynamically. Up to 1024 Token Ring entries are possible. The Ethernet/802.3 file may be managed statically or dynamically. When the bridge is initialized, the static part (predefined by the user) is loaded first and the bridge switches into the learning mode in order to enter the remaining addresses dynamically. Up to 2048 addresses may be managed in the Ethernet/Token Ring files. Timers monitor the inactive dynamic entries. In the case of new entries the oldest inactive entry is deleted. The bridge also monitors the time a frame spends in the bridge. If this exceeds a certain value the frame is deleted. This prevents the possibility of transmission of the frame being restarted by higher-level protocols whenever timers expire.

Filters may be used to ensure that only a certain protocol is supported by the bridge (for example, TCP/IP). This decreases the load in the subnetworks and increases the bridge throughput.

Figure 3.40 gives an overview of the possible uses of the IBM 8209.

All stations may intercommunicate provided they use the same protocol. If the bridge has to be specially configured by the user (for example, to set filters and static file entries, spanning tree parameters, ring and bridge numbers) a special control program for a DOS or OS/2 PC must be used. The bridge is configured via the Token Ring connection.

We stress that these bridges, like the normal Token Ring bridges, may also be monitored and controlled by the IBM LAN Manager. Thus, it is possible to obtain information about the load in the Ethernet segment and statistics about the data traffic.

Similar bridges are now available from several manufacturers. They differ in their performance and in the protocols that are supported. Unlike the IBM 8209, Crosscom also supports (for example) Novell and Banyan Vines.

At the moment, IBM is trying to get a generalized version of its 8209 bridge into the IEEE 802.1D standard. The so-called SRT (source routing transparent) bridge in that standard uses an information field to determine whether a packet should have source routing or transparent bridging.

This avoids the need for a division into control domains in which only one or other type of routing exists. Crosscom already produces bridges like this.

3.1.5 Help in the planning of Token Ring installations

Let us now summarize the functions and facilities of the terminal-independent part of a Token Ring LAN under the ten commandments for the planning of Token Ring LANs.

Particular attention should be paid to the following:

(1) In general, plans for new buildings should provide for distributor rooms for cabling and cable shafts should be sufficiently large. The larger the building, the more fibre-optic cable will be used. It may possibly be advantageous to lay fibre-optic cable up to the room socket, if this means that fewer distributor rooms have to be planned.

(2) In almost all cases, the existing normal 4-wire telephone cabling does not correspond to IBM type 3 cabling! Such telephone cables are only recommended for the lobe cables and where RJ45 plugs and sockets are already in use (for example, ISDN).

(3) If possible, fibre-optic cable should always be laid between buildings (very low susceptibility to interference, no problems with potential equalization between buildings, etc.).

(4) Note when moving up to the 16 Mbps Token Ring that there are considerable distance restrictions for IBM type 1/6 cables.

(5) There are always problems with loose plug contacts or cable that is badly laid out. Avoid these as much as possible, since faults like this

are sometimes very difficult to locate

(6) As always, there are no standards for fibre-optic plugs in sight. You must decide! We recommend the ST plug.

(7) Problems with incompatible MSAUs may arise with certain applications and when the maximum possible distances or maximum numbers of connections to a ring are used.

(8) Always check the distance dependencies precisely. Errors between MSAUs should be automatically detectable and removable. Appropriate tools are available from a number of suppliers.

(9) Plan in central monitoring of critical resources.

(10) Experience shows that it is better to lay two cables too many than one too few at first and another one later.

3.2 Hardware for connecting terminals to Token Ring networks

In Section 3.1 we described possible ways of constructing Token Ring network infrastructures. This section is concerned with interface cards and Token Ring adaptors, which are used to attach terminals to Token Ring. Here, IBM systems are in the foreground.

Initially, we consider the connection of PCs, PS/2s and compatibles; later we consider the direct connection of other IBM devices.

3.2.1 Connection of IBM PCs, PS/2s and compatible systems

The most important terminal on Token Ring today is the PC-AT or the PS/2. Whether for an AT bus, a PC bus, microchannel or an EISA bus, there is now a Token Ring interface card (4 Mbps or 16 Mbps) for every bus. These cards differ (often greatly) in their user-friendliness, speed and price. There are also already Token Ring cards for other systems (Apple, IEC-, Unibus systems, etc.).

3.2.1.1 IBM Token Ring adaptor cards for PCs

Up to now, IBM itself has already brought a number of different cards to the market. They differ in their size, mode of application (trace, bridge, etc.) and on-board buffer memory.

(1) IBM Token Ring network adaptor (4 kbytes memory, IBM's first adaptor card, not recommended).

(2) IBM Token Ring network adaptor II (16 kbytes memory).

(3) IBM Token Ring network adaptor/A (16 kbytes memory).

(4) IBM Token Ring trace and performance adaptor (AT + PS/2).

(5) IBM Token Ring network 16/4 adaptor (64 kbytes cache memory).

(6) IBM Token Ring network 16/4 adaptor/A (64 kbytes cache memory, RIPL).

(7) IBM Token Ring network busmaster adaptor (currently IBM's best performing adaptor card).

According to the card type, the IBM PC adaptor card occupies a short or long slot in the PC. On the card, the following are hardware or software adjustable by the user:

- the ROM address area occupied by the card,
- the interrupt level at which the card communicates,
- whether this is the first or second network adaptor card in the PC.

According to the bus, the installation is by DIP switch or by software (microchannel). The adaptor implements logical control according to IEEE 802.2 and supports the physical interface according to IEEE 802.5 with a speed of 4 or 16 Mbps.

According to the card, there are 4, 16 or 64 kbytes of main memory on each card for fast data exchange (RAM paging or shared memory with 16–64 kbytes) (Figure 3.41).

The maximum number of possible link stations varies according to the available memory between 32 and 254.

The maximum frame size for these cards is 4501 bytes for the 4 Mbps Token Ring and 17 997 bytes for the 16 Mbps ring. By default the 16 Mbps cards are set to support the early token release procedure.

The PC adaptor address is set by the factory. Its format is shown in Figure 3.42.

User addresses always begin with X'4000'. The address area available to the user then ranges from 1 to 7FFFFFFF. This should be sufficient except for the very largest installations.

When the PC is switched on the adaptor for the IBM Token Ring network runs through the usual test and diagnostic functions. The adaptor is only automatically connected to the ring after the tests have been executed. First the adaptor is initialized and the connection to the MSAU is activated. This is followed by tests of the adaptor to see whether it is able to send and receive MAC frames and whether it is able to send and receive data (DLC level test). According to the state of the Token Ring, the adaptor takes on the functions of a monitor or a stand-by monitor for all the stations connected to the ring and in critical situations generates error messages

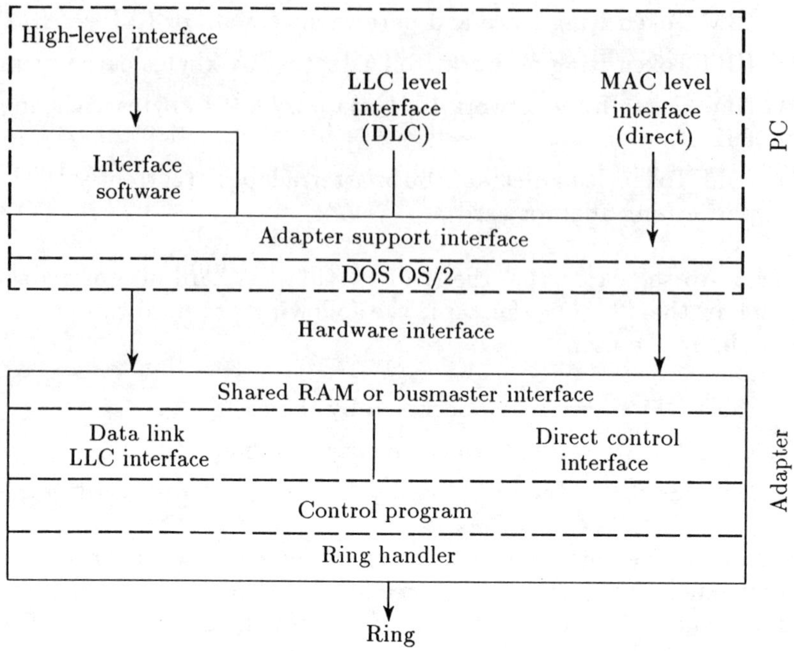

Figure 3.41 Adaptor structure.

00 <-------------> MFID <------------> | Generally specified (IEEE)

Byte 0 1 2 3 4 5

This address may be altered by the user. In IBM networks the first two bytes and the first bit of the third byte are already specified.

01000000 00000000 0 <------------ User-specified

Byte 0 1 2 3 4 5

Thus, user addresses always begin with X'4000'. The address range 1 to 79999999 is available to users. This should be more than adequate, even for large installations.

Figure 3.42 PC adaptor addresses.

about temporary (for example, lost token) or permanent errors with advice on how to locate and remove them.

3.2.1.2 Alternatives from other suppliers

Other manufacturers of LAN adaptor cards have also gone over to producing Token Ring Boards, since almost every other PC adaptor card sold is intended for connecting terminals to Token Ring. The variety of adaptors is only limited by the fact that at present only three companies produce chip sets for the Token Ring protocol. IBM and Ungermann Bass only produce for their own needs. As of writing, the Texas Instruments chip set is built into every other adaptor.

What is the difference between these adaptors? Why should a user not buy an adaptor directly from IBM? What are the advantages and disadvantages of the other adaptors?

One of the main recurring arguments is price. According to whether it is an 8-bit, 16-bit or 32-bit adaptor, the current price varies between around 500 DM and 3000 DM.

There are other reasons for using other products.

Firstly the cards in part have their own intelligence through additional processors on the card and also their own associated additional on-card memory of up to 512 kbytes. In addition to the MAC level protocol, these smart cards can support other on-board protocols and thus take the load away from the PC's processor and, more importantly, from the PC's main memory. The SMART interface cards from the English manufacturer Madge Networks, for example, may be used to provide direct support on the card for Novell NetWare protocols such as LLC or IPX (internetwork packet exchange).

Another difference is the number of network operating systems for which there exist drivers from the card manufacturer or the network operating system manufacturer. Almost all support the IBM PC LAN Program or Novell NetWare. Relatively few provide support for Banyan Vines or 3Com 3+. The number of suppliers supporting the OS/2 LAN Manager and UNIX is steadily increasing.

A further difference is the method used to exchange the data between the adaptor and the PC. The most popular method is to map part of the PC memory quasi as a window into the Token Ring adaptor memory. This method is known as shared memory or memory mapped I/O; it is used by IBM, Western Digital and Ungermann Bass. Data from the network is stored temporarily in the adaptor memory area provided for this purpose. The PC processor can read out this data directly from the Token Ring adaptor as though it were stored in its own main memory. This method is relatively independent of the bus structure of a PC and of the processor type. Thus, cards of this type can be used (almost) everywhere without problems. However, one disadvantage is the maximum window size. The

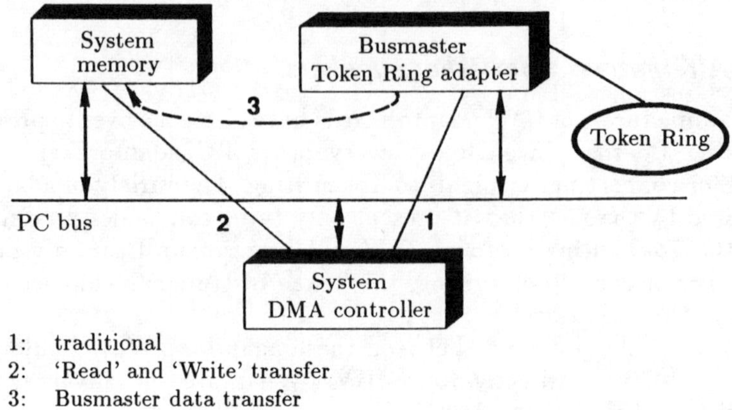

Figure 3.43 Busmaster DMA.

larger the window reserved for the shared memory area, the more memory is lost to other applications. Thus, one has to try to find an optimum between fast data transfer and space for other I/O drivers, etc. Window sizes of 16 kbytes are usual at present.

Another method of exchanging data between the adaptor and the PC is DMA (direct memory access). This does not require a virtual memory window. Access to the PC memory is direct. One disadvantage of this method is that the PC processor must first be interrupted and initialized before the transfer can take place. For small data sets, this takes a relatively long time and the data transfer is ineffective. This procedure can be optimized if the Token Ring adaptor card has its own bus controller chip; this avoids the time overheads of PC DMA. This is called busmaster DMA and permits very high data throughput rates; however, it is also dependent on the bus used in the PC (Figure 3.43). Thus, the cards cannot be used or installed in all systems. Token Ring cards using the busmaster principle are available for the AT bus (16 bit), microchannel and the EISA bus (32 bit).

The third data standard transfer method uses the PC's I/O port. This is the standard method for the data transfer between the various I/O cards of a PC (printer interfaces, RS232 interfaces, etc.). However, this procedure is not particularly suitable for large data blocks or high transmission speeds and is only supported in older Token Ring cards.

Which manufacturers produce Token Ring cards? Table 3.2 gives a brief overview. This table is only a snapshot of the currently available Token Ring adaptor cards and does not claim to be complete. A full market analysis should always precede any decision in favour of a specific type of adaptor

Table 3.2 Some suppliers of Token Ring adaptor cards.

Company	*Name*	*Data transfer*	*Bus*	*Interrupts/ Speed*	*Intell.*	*Memory kbytes*	*Other*
3Com	Token Link Token Link Plus	DMA, I/O DMA, I/O	AT AT	9/4 Mbps 12/4 Mbps	No Yes	16 256	 Own network
Gateway C	G/TR AT G/TR PC	Busmaster DMA I/O port	AT PC	8/4 Mbps 4/4 Mbps	No No	2 128	
IBM (e.g.)	16/4 /A	Shared memory	MCA	4/16 Mbps	No	64	
Madge	PC R.N AT R.N MC R.N EISA 16/4	Busmaster DMA Busmaster DMA Busmaster DMA	PC AT MCA EISA	4/4 Mbps 8/4 Mbps 3/4 Mbps 12/16 Mbps	No Yes No Yes	16 128 16 128	
NCR	T.R. 16	Shared memory	PC/AT	8/16 Mbps	No	16	
OLICOM	TRA	Busmaster	PC/AT MC	6/4 Mbps	Yes	128	
Proteon	P1990 P1347 P1840 P1346 P1390	I/O port Busmaster DMA Busmaster DMA Busmaster DMA Busmaster DMA	EISA AT MCA AT AT	6/16 Mbps 9/4 Mbps 6/4 Mbps 6/4 Mbps 6/16 Mbps	No No No No 	18 18 18 18 18	UTP UTP
Philips	EISA	32 bit	EISA	5/16 Mbps	Yes	128	
Racore	M8110 M8111 M8112	Busmaster DMA Shared memory Shared memory	AT MCA PC	2/4 Mbps 4/4 Mbps 4/4 Mbps	No No No	18 18 18	
Schneider and Koch		Busmaster DMA	MCA AT		No		
Ungermann Bass	NIUPS/TR PC-NIU/TR	Shared memory Shared memory	MCA AT	2/4 Mbps 4/4 Mbps	No No	512 256	
Western Digital	Token Card	Shared memory	XT	6/4 Mbps	No	128	NetBios on card

card. We recommend sticking to a single manufacturer if possible since the adaptors are not always 100% compatible with each other and mixing them could lead to errors in certain network programs.

The manufacturers will certainly continue to develop adaptor technology further. The trend is towards storing more and more communications program sections on the adaptor. This relieves the PC memory and the processor. Thus, the main memory requirement for NetBios, LLC and MAC programs with the Microsoft LAN Manager Program decreases from around 100 kbytes to around 20 kbytes when a smart PC adaptor card (for example, OLICOM) is used instead of a normal PC-AT adaptor card (IBM). The throughput of the cards is also being continually improved. While simple Token Ring cards (4 Mbps), for example, in Novell NetWare networks, achieve a throughput of around 250 kbytes/s, fast cards reach over 1.5 Mbytes/s. Cards for the EISA bus reach up to 2 Mbytes/s.

Not all cards work only with the IBM cable system. 3Com uses some of its own cabling and does not require MSAUs. Cabeltron, Proteon, Thomas Conrad and Western Digital produce cards which also have an interface (Western plug or RJ11/45) to the unscreened cabling networks which are very common in the USA. Proteon produces a complete system for this, including an MSAU which also supports the 16 Mbps Token Ring. The use of the pluggable Token Ring adaptors (for example, SMART) is interesting, particularly as far as the short-term use of portable PCs is concerned. These are not built in to the PC, but plugged into the printer interface externally. Thus, they are ideal for short-term access to resources in Token Ring without requiring a card slot in the PC. Diagnostic and LAN support programs are delivered with these. These cards are easy to use.

However, some of the adaptors are not 100% compatible with the IBM software. In many cases, the manufacturers produce adaptors with their own drivers which are not compatible with all IBM software (and communications software in particular). One example of this is the 3Com Token Link Plus adaptor which has its own processor (80186) with 256 kbytes RAM and is mainly suitable for 3Com network software and the Novell software. The Ungermann Bass PC-NIU/TR adaptor also has an 80186 processor with 256 kbytes RAM, which also allows parts of the communications software to be loaded on to the card. The Net/One Extended Adaptor Support Interface permits communication with IBM and UB applications.

An interesting test of adaptor cards is given in Data Communications 4/90. Here, a number of cards were subjected to practical tests by the independent National Software Test Laboratory (NSTL). The winner by a long way was the IBM 16/4 card, ahead of Madge (Figure 3.44).

Here are some details of the NSTL Token Ring adaptor test.

NSTL is an independent test institute. Most of the test results are published in NSTL reports or (as here) in the journal *Data Communications*. The NetBios test shows the differences between the adaptor cards most clearly since it is independent of, for example, disk access.

The following cards were tested:

(a) Gateway – G/TR AT
(b) IBM – 16/4 adaptor switched to 4 Mbps
(c) IBM – adaptor II
(d) IBM – 16/4 adaptor switched to 16 Mbps
(e) Madge – Smart AT

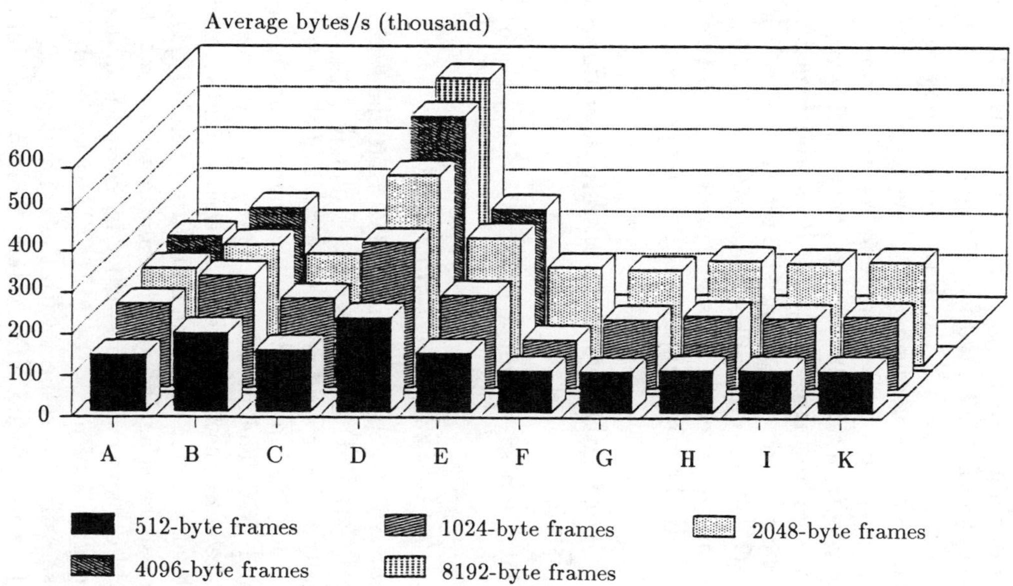

Figure 3.44 NSTL Token Ring adapter test.

(f) Proteon – Pronet 4
(g) Racore – M8112
(h) Racore - M8110
(i) Western Digital – Token Card
(k) Thomas Conrad

The throughput was tested. The systems used for testing comprised two Compaq Deskpro 386S and two Compaq 386/25. The four computers were all attached to an MSAU. Each system was loaded with the NetBios program files recommended by the card manufacturer. Conventional NetBios programs for sending and receiving were optimized so that they did not access background devices, thereby slowing down the transmission. Data was sent using 64-kbyte NetBios send requests so as to minimize the NetBios overheads. The frame size for the transmission was specified in the CONFIG.SYS set-up file. For the 4 Mbps Token Ring, 4096 bytes was the maximum permitted frame size. However, even this was not supported by many cards. The throughput was then determined over a number of trials.

3.2.2 Other IBM systems which may connected to Token Ring

Nowadays, almost every new IBM system may be connected to Token Ring.

3.2.2.1 IBM 6150 and system R6000

The above is true of both the IBM 6150 and the IBM R6000 which are atypical (for IBM) UNIX systems. The older system 6150 uses an AT bus internally to incorporate extension cards. Ethernet (Ungermann Bass) and Token Ring are supported. The communications protocols include TCP/IP, NFS and TCF. The more recent IBM /6000 systems use a high-performance RISC (reduced instruction set) processor and the AT bus is replaced by the considerably faster microchannel with extended I/O functions. The virtual address space is again extended and now amounts to 4 Tbytes (232); the real address space amounts to 4 Gbytes and is divided into 4 kbyte pages. A throughput of up to 13 MFLOPS is achieved. IBM first indicated its seriousness in this respect with the announcement that it was to market a powerful concurrent UNIX system. Here again, Token Ring and Ethernet cards may be fitted.

The new operating system AIX, from version 3, provides additional communications facilities based on TCP/IP and other communications protocols which permit the connection of both IBM mainframes and smaller OS/2 systems to Token Ring. The SAA/AIX interoperability is extended by common functions in the two environments and by additional bridges for exchanging information. This is increasingly based on the LU 6.2

protocols. The operating system supports the most important standards in the UNIX area, such as IEEE Posix 1003.1 and X/Open from XPG3 (X/Open Portability Guide Version 3). The TCP/IP subsystem contains protocols such as Telnet for dialogue (including VT100 and 3270 emulation), FTP for file transfer and SMTP for electronic mail. Add-on products are available for the X.400 standard, the Network File System and the Network Computing System which is used to distribute the functions and the load of NCS computers in Token Ring. As far as the SNA world is concerned, the LU 0, 1, 2, 3 and 6.2. are supported. The LU 6.2 is, for example, the basis for the VIADUCT program which permits AIX systems to access the AS/400 relational database. AIX error messages (alerts) may be sent directly to a central NetView. NetView/DM may be used to exchange files with the mainframe which may again send commands to the System /6000 using HCF (Host Command Facility). This permits a central network management. In addition, SNMP (Simple Network Management Protocol), the *de facto* standard in the TCP/IP area, is supported.

The integration of DOS systems over Token Ring also involves the use of a special DOS server function in AIX. DOS systems may use the AIX file system like an extra virtual disk and may also use the System /6000 printer. Direct operation under AIX is also possible using terminal emulation.

3.2.2.2 IBM 937x or IBM 1390 small systems

Even the IBM 93xx systems, specified for area and departmental computers, use their own built-in Token Ring interface for 4 and/or 16 Mbps. Several 9370 systems which use the VM (Virtual Machine) operating system may be connected together into a homogeneous network using Token Ring (TSAF=Transparent Service Access Facilities). In this type of linkage, the users no longer need to know which machine their application is located on. Token Ring provides them with transparent, system-independent access to all the resources of the attached systems. PCs in Token Ring with 3270 emulation also have direct access to 937xs attached to Token Ring. According to their construction, the 93xx systems also support the MVS and AIX operating systems. In this case, Token Ring hardware and software is linked-in in a different way.

3.2.2.3 AS/400 and S/36

Like 937x systems, mid-range IBM /36 systems and AS/400s may now be directly attached to Token Ring. For the older /36 systems, connection is indirect via a PC. The newer systems (IBM 5363) and AS/400s are connected directly (Figure 3.45).

The /36 only has a direct Token Ring connection to the 4 Mbps

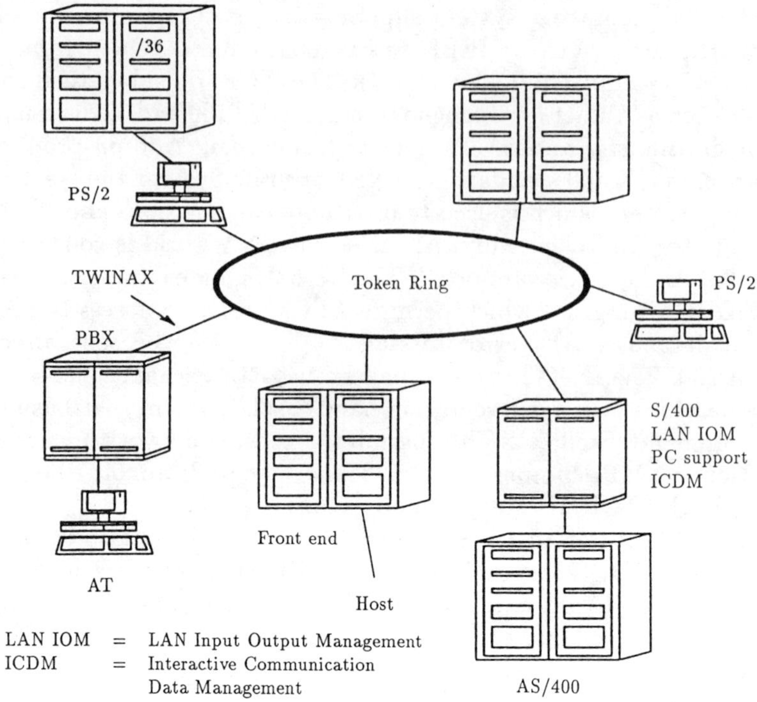

Figure 3.45 AS/400 in Token Ring.

Token Ring. When a system /36 is available for use, the system makes server functions available to PCs attached to the ring. Examples of this include virtual disks and printer functions. File transfer functions are also supported. The AS/400 PC Support also provides other functions. Communication between an AS/400 and a PC is controlled by the router program on the PC. Here too file transfer between the PC and AS/400 is supported. Several file types are supported (8-bit ASCII, BASIC, Data Interchange Format, transparent mode) and file transfer may be initiated from both sides. The printers in Token Ring may be used both by AS/400 systems and PC systems. Each PC may be simultaneously connected to up to five AS/400 systems (sessions). To improve the use of the storage, parts of the AS/400 support program may be relocated to the extended memory area of the PC. Naturally, it is also possible to access /370 mainframes and emulate a 5250 terminal in the PC.

3.2.2.4 IBM series /1

IBM's most universal system (and also most unknown), the IBM S/1, may also be connected directly to Token Ring. If necessary, the S/1 may be

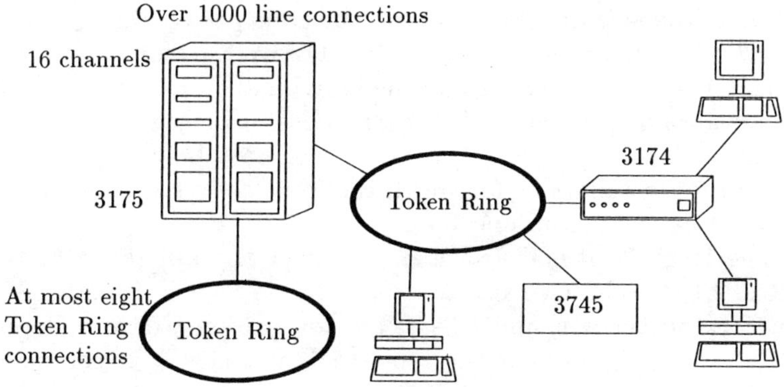

Figure 3.46 The IBM 3745 controller.

used as a server for PCs attached to the LAN. Its main function is to adapt emulations as a front-end processor and to preprocess time-critical applications.

3.2.2.5 IBM /390 systems with front-end controllers

IBM produces a number of controllers and front-end processors for linking terminals attached to Token Ring to mainframes (see also the appendix on SNA in Chapter 8).

IBM 37xx The classical system for connecting all forms of communications systems and terminals in the IBM world is the front-end processor. IBM supports various types, which, according to their size, permit the connection of more than 1000 physical terminals over public networks, in-house networks and LANs. Here, two software components are needed to support the communications network, namely ACF VTAM (Advanced Communication Facilities Virtual Telecommunications Access Method) in the mainframe and ACF NCP (ACF Network Control Program) in the front end. NCP also supports direct access of Token Ring to the front-end processors (Figure 3.46). The new software versions of VTAM and NCP even permit the coupling of mainframes over Token Ring, using front-end processors of type 37xx for LAN interconnection.

The smaller 3720 11/12 models support at most two Token Ring adaptors, while the older IBM 3725 support up to eight Token Ring adaptors but only with a transmission speed of 4 Mbps. The maximum throughput for these controllers is around 300 kbps.

The IBM 3745, which is currently the largest model in the front-end family, supports up to eight Token Ring installations with transmission speeds of 4 or 16 Mbps (TRA2). In theory, up to 9999 terminals may be connected to Token Ring networks, with the ability to communicate with the attached /370 systems via this controller. The overall throughput is around 500 kbps, but is very dependent on the individual applications so that such statements are not generally valid. It is advisable to carry out application-dependent performance measurement in each case before deciding on the number of ring installations for which the front-end processor may be used as a gateway to the mainframe.

The large front-end processors support the full range of IBM PU types 1, 2, 2.1, 4 and 5 (see also the appendix on SNA in Chapter 8). While support for the types 4 and 5 is taken for granted (front-end processor and mainframe), support for the type 2.1 is not nearly as common. Until now, PU 2.1 sessions have been used in AS/400, S/36 and OS/2 EE applications and permit direct coupling over the network without needing the mainframe for connection establishment. The hardware and software of the large front-end processors also support a number of elegant solutions, so that processing may continue when errors occur. Thus, if a front end has two Token Ring interface cards (TICs) to a ring, it can automatically switch to the second should the first fail. Should the front end fail, under the control of the IBM network management system (NetView), it is possible to switch automatically to a second front end without the need for manual intervention.

Front-end processors may be linked to mainframes over channel interfaces or over the public network. In the second case, at least one attached front end is required. Any currently available network may be used to link remote front-end processors to local ones. Transmission speeds of between 9600 bps and 2 Mbps may be achieved. Unlike in the case of remote 3170 controllers (establishment controllers), links to front ends are not loaded with polling (which is otherwise usual with IBM) (Figure 3.47). Thus, the overall throughput on such a link is considerably higher.

For the control of Token Ring, the NCP Token Ring interconnection software is loaded into the front end. Only one channel address is needed for a VTAM↔NCP link. Every end system attached to Token Ring is supported transparently by the front-end gateway as a so-called DSPU (downstream physical unit). VTAM in the mainframe manages the necessary systems on Token Ring exactly as though they were real SNA terminals connected to the front end by a switched connection. Mainframes do not distinguish between SNA and Token Ring terminals.

For VTAM, only two parameters are important when establishing a connection from a terminal to Token Ring, namely IDBLK and IDNUM. These parameters uniquely identify the terminal in Token Ring. If the parameters in the terminal do not agree with an NCP generation entry (the SDLC command XID described in Chapter 2 is used for this), the

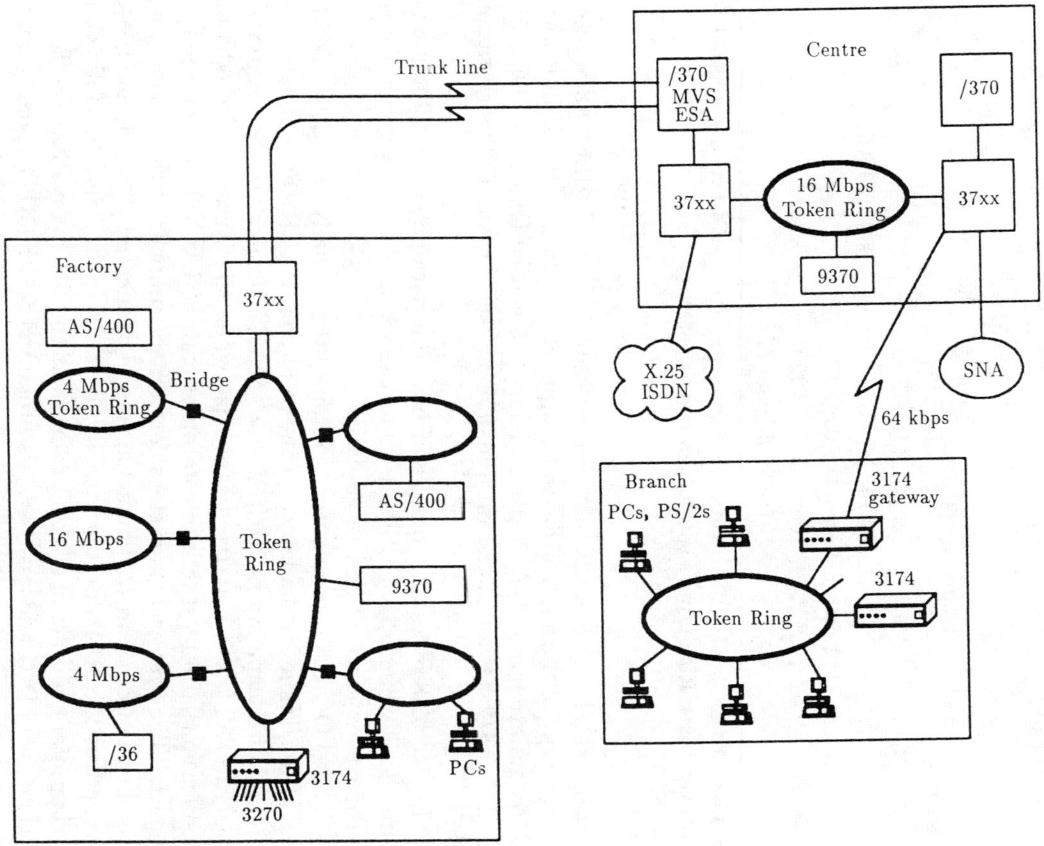

Figure 3.47 A large IBM Token Ring installation in IBM surroundings.

```
NCP: Line macro  LINE  ADDRESS = (0777, FULL),
                       PORTADD = 0,
                       LOCADD = 400001000077,
                       RECBUFC = 4095,
                       MAXTSL = 2044,
                 LU ISTATUS = INACTIVE,
VTAM             PU    PUTYPE = 2,
                       IDBLK = 017,
                       IDNUM = C0007,
                       MAXPATH = 1,
                       MODETAB = ...
                 PATH DIALNO = 0004400031740001
In the 3174 establishment controller:
                 106: 400031740001
                 107: 400001000077
```

Figure 3.48 Example of VTAM and NCP parameters for a 3174 DSPU connected to the host over Token Ring using a single front end as gateway.

connection establishment cannot be executed. The IDBLK parameter defines the type of the application to be supported. IDBLK=017 stands for a PC 3270 emulation or a 3174 in Token Ring, 050 is used for APPC/PC, 05D is used for OS/2 EE and, for example, 05E is used for the PC workstation program.

Figure 3.48 gives an example of how the parameters in VTAM and NCP may look when a 3174 DSPU is to be connected to the host over Token Ring using a single front end as gateway.

The LOCADD parameter contains the 'locally assigned' MAC address of the Token Ring adaptor in the front end. RECBUFC indicates the maximum buffer capacity in the front end. MAXTSL specifies the maximum PIU size. ISTATUS = inactive means that when the system is brought up the connection is not established automatically. DIALNO is composed of three parts. The first two characters contain the number of the Token Ring adaptor in the front end to which the ring is connected (00), the next two bytes contain the SAP for the station (here SNA=04) and the following eight characters contain the MAC address of the 3174 controller on Token Ring. The two MAC addresses are also required for the 3174 generation.

IBM 8232 The IBM 8232 supports workstations which communicate with the mainframe using TCP/IP (Figure 3.49).

Up to two 7532 industrial computers may be used as controllers in the IBM 8232. However, other systems may also be used, and may increase the throughput if they incorporate the more powerful Intel 80386

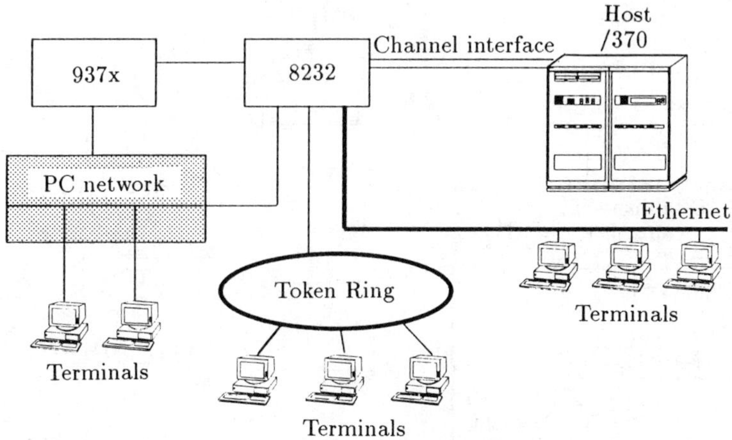

Figure 3.49 TCP/IP as a vehicle for communications, based on the example of the 8232.

processors. TCP/IP components (which are available both for VM and for MVS) in the mainframe are a prerequisite for operation. When AIX/370 is used in the mainframe, the TCP/IP support is already contained in the operating system. Connection to the mainframe is via the IBM block multiplex channel.

IBM 3172 Unlike the IBM 8232 the IBM 3172 supports up to four local area networks simultaneously and may also be attached to up to two mainframes. It supports both the 4 Mbps and the 16 Mbps Token Ring together with Ethernet or 802.3 LANs. TCP/IP is again the communications protocol for connection with the mainframe. Thus, both controllers are ideally suited for linking IBM and non-IBM systems, since nowadays almost every system supports TCP/IP. For example, the UNIX and DEC worlds (ULTRIX and VMS) may be elegantly linked with the IBM world. The variety of the protocols installed then determines the user-friendliness of such an interconnection. Standard features now include line-oriented dialogue (Telnet), secure file transfer and simple mailing. Add-on features include the direct linking of existing mail systems (for example, IBM PROFS and DEC All-in-One), screen-oriented dialogue (3270 emulation with or without colour support and VT100/220 mode) and the Network File System (NFS) (which permits each system to access the disks of other multiuser systems transparently; server mode).

In addition, if required, 802.4-based LANs operating at 5 or 10 Mbps are also supported. These LANs use the MAP 3.0 protocol for communication.

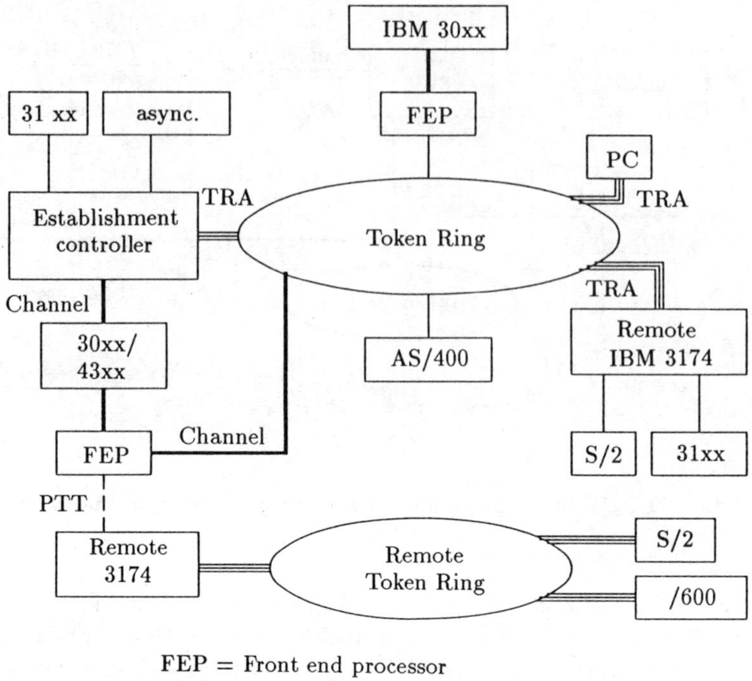

Figure 3.50 Establishment controllers in Token Ring.

IBM 3174 (establishment controller) Establishment controllers which represent the new generation of the IBM 3174 controllers (Figure 3.50) are cheaper alternatives to the front-end processor with restrictions on the throughput and the support for terminals.

These controllers currently support PU type 2 terminals and may be used as network nodes in an APPN network. Establishment controllers are available with a direct channel or with RS232C, X.21 or X.25 interfaces. The maximum transmission speed is 64 kbps in the latter case, when a local front end is also required. A remote controller attached to Token Ring can provide the attached terminals (PCs, terminals) with simultaneous access to up to eight IBM mainframes, when up to five links to any attached terminal may exist at a given time. The user may use hot keys (special key combinations) to switch sessions without having to log off and log on again.

When the 3174 is implemented as a local controller and used in its Token Ring gateway function, all the terminals attached to Token Ring are used in the so-called pass through mode. As far as the mainframe VTAM is concerned, the end systems in Token Ring behave like DSPUs of type 2 as though they were directly attached to the IBM channel. Here, the local 3174 translates the computer addresses into MAC addresses in the Token Ring. Each 3174 gateway supports up to 250 DSPUs. Each DSPU has its own channel address in the mainframe. This also exhausts the address capacity of an IBM channel, which can control a maximum of 255 subaddresses. One should not be irritated by this limitation to at most 250 DSPUs, in relation to the 9999 for front-end processors. Each of these 250 PUs may have up to 255 LUs, so that theoretically the gateway may support up to 63 000 terminals. This theoretical number is nowhere near reached in practice, since the gateway throughput capacity is exhausted first. The only annoying thing is that in the extreme case every supported PC in Token Ring needs its own PU and thus its own address on the channel. For large installations this may rapidly lead to bottle-necks. In this case it is advisable, for example, to use a gateway PC with OS/2 EE (from version 1.2) as a gateway/concentrator, thereby saving addresses on the channel.

The 4 Mbps and the 16 Mbps Token Ring are both supported. The 16 Mbps adaptor may optionally be operated at 4 or 16 Mbps (optional early token release protocol). The maximum frame size at 16 Mbps is 4105 bytes, an SNA RU may only have up to 4096 bytes. Only one channel interface per 3174 may be incorporated.

Bottle-necks and throughput problems arise very rapidly when the 3174 is used as a remote gateway. Above all, polling lists, which have been standard until now, led to a considerable deterioration of throughput for DSPUs. So-called group polling, which must be installed both in the NCP and in the microcode of the IBM 3174, brings a considerable improvement. However, experience shows that, despite these features, not more than 15–25 DSPUs should be supported per remote 3174 so as not to impair the response times. The number of DSPUs depends on the nature of the application. For example, dialogue loads the controller less than file transfer, the transmission of print lists or LU 6.2 applications.

By way of example, Figure 3.51 shows the typical calls which might be used in generation for a 3174 gateway with a DSPU (3174).

For each controller or individual station attached to the 3174 gateway the corresponding MAC address must be a fixed entry in the gateway. In order to retain a somewhat limited flexibility here, it is advisable not to use the addresses predefined by the factory, but to allocate MAC addresses to the terminals oneself, according to a company-specific scheme. Firstly, use of the MAC address makes it easier to generate a reference to the location of any possible errors and, secondly, addresses in the gateway may be pregenerated so that new terminals can use the gateway as part of the ongoing operation. In this case, if a Token Ring adaptor fails, it is sufficient to plug in a new adaptor and overwrite the factory-defined addresses in it with the reserved addresses using software before bringing the terminal immediately into operation again. Had one used the factory addresses, it would have been necessary to regenerate the software for the 3174 gateway. This may

```
Macros in the VM operating system:
  RDEVICE   ADDRESS = 350, (channel address for 3174 gateway)
            DEVTYPE = 3705,
            ADAPTOR = TYPE4,
            MODEL = E8,
            CPTYPE = NCP
  RDEVICE   ADDRESS = 351, (channel address for DSPU)
  ...
VTAM:
  PU        CUADDR = 050,
            ISTATUS = ACTIVE,
            PUTYPE = 2,
            MODETAB = ...
  LU        LOCADDR = 2
            ...
  PU        CUADDR = 051,
            ISTATUS = ACTIVE, (address is activated on start-up)
            PUTYPE = 2,
            SECNET = YES (indicates that it is a DSPU)
  LU        LOCADDR = 2
3174 gateway controller:
  104:50 (lowest channel address)
  105:51 (highest channel address)
  900: 400031740007 (own MAC address)
  940: Ring@400031740008 (address of the DSPU)
  941: F=3  Frame size is 2042 bytes. This size would be
            smaller for PC emulation; for example,
            256 bytes for 3270 emulation V 3.
Remote 3174:
  106: 400031740008 (address of this DSPU)
  107: 400031740007 (address of the 3174 gateway)
  380: 2048 (maximum frame size)
```

Figure 3.51 Typical calls used in generation for a 3174 gateway with a DSPU.

take up to 15 minutes, during which time the unit cannot be used by any of the terminals attached to it.

The 3174 may also be used as a protocol converter. Up to 24 asynchronous terminals may be connected to it, with access to the attached IBM mainframe (3270 terminal emulation) and/or to an ASCII computer (for example, DEC or UNIX host) (transparent mode). Conversely, a 3270 interactive terminal may also access the ASCII computer. In general,

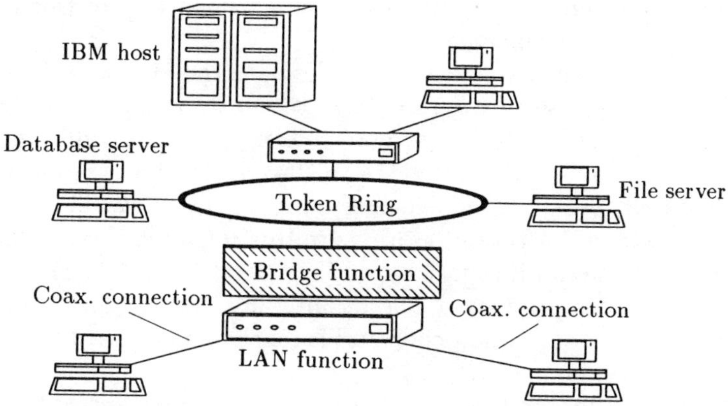

Figure 3.52 Virtual Token Ring for PCs with coaxial interface cards.

wherever both these worlds exist, only one interactive terminal is required.

Another very interesting variant for large existing installations is the use of the IBM 3174 as a bridge for all PCs attached via coaxial interface cards.

Until now, this classical PC-coaxial world was separated from the services and applications in a LAN. Expensive conversion of PCs was

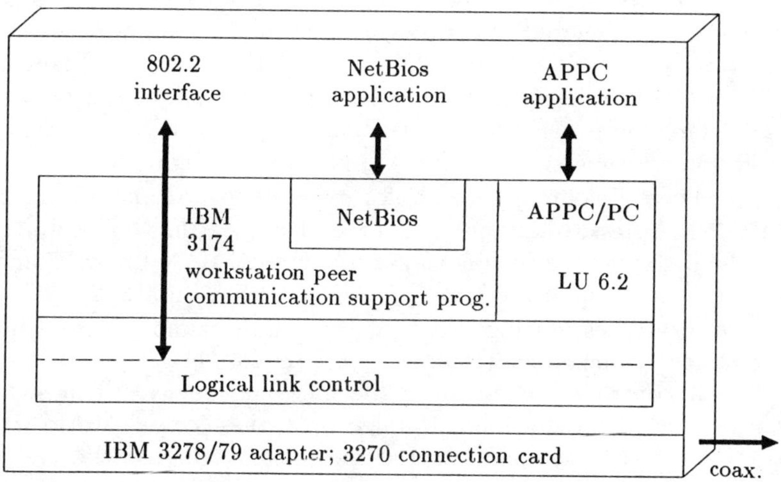

Figure 3.53 PC software for virtual 3174 Token Ring.

necessary (the 3278 interface card exchanged for a Token Ring card) before they could access services such as servers or gateways in the LAN. For large installations with hundreds or thousands of attached PCs of this type, the cost factor was not unimportant.

This conversion is no longer needed if both the 3174 and the DOS PC are fitted with add-on software from IBM (the software has been announced for OS/2). In the IBM 3174 the microcode is extended, while in the PC part of the LAN support program (DXMC0MOD.SYS) it is replaced by the 3174 workstation peer communications support program. Thus, the 3174 becomes a standalone LAN and a bridge to this controller for all PCs which are attached via coaxial interface cards (Figures 3.52 and 3.53).

Every PC attached by a coaxial interface card is allocated its own MAC address in the 3174 microcode and is reachable by the other terminals in Token Ring via this address.

However, the pseudo Token Ring LAN operates at the typical transmission speeds for coaxial interface cards of around 1 Mbps and behaves like a star-shaped ring with a maximum of 32 attachable PCs. This LAN is controlled centrally using the microcode extension in the IBM 3174. This also supports source routing and thus permits access to all resources which are available on the true Token Ring. The 3174 does not behave completely like a true IBM Token Ring bridge. In the area of central network management and monitoring (see Chapter 2), the microcode extension only supports the error monitor function.

The replacement of parts of the PC LAN support program in the PC opens up very different (even software-related) possibilities for the PC. While until now PCs attached to the host could only behave as LU 2s in the DFT mode (distribution function mode; five simultaneous sessions possible) or in the CUT mode (control unit terminal mode; simple 3270 terminal), attached PCs may now behave, in a software sense, like a DSPU and support the complete SNA protocol stack in the same way as stations directly attached to Token Ring. The usual 3270 software for Token Ring, which sits directly above the LLC level (see Chapter 4), may be used for this. APPC/PC links over the coaxial interface cards may now be established to destination systems such as the AS/400, the System /36 or the /370 mainframe. These links may also be, for example, peer-to-peer links based on the PU 2.1. Access to the server in Token Ring via the NetBios interface may also be implemented in this way. Both the PC LAN Program and the DOS Requester are supported if an OS/2 EE PC with the OS/2 LAN server is used as a server.

This extension does complete justice to the IBM 3174 name establishment controller. It becomes the universal device which supports the ASCII world, provides ideal links with the coaxial world and is a cost-effective gateway solution for the Token Ring world. With its protocol converter functions (ASCII passthrough, ASCII ↔ 3270), its bridge function, its simulation of a Token Ring for PCs attached via coaxial interface cards and its enormously improved performance it is becoming an all round star turn.

3.2.3 Advantages and disadvantages of hardware from other manufacturers

Many companies now include Token Ring interfaces among their products. Here, Token Ring is not always the IBM 4 Mbps or 16 Mbps Token Ring but may include other variants at 10, 80 or even 100 (FDDI) Mbps. In Germany, many companies produce connection boxes, adaptors, etc. for Token Ring. These range from adaptors for individual computer worlds (NCR, Apple) through connection boxes for asynchronous terminals (Ungermann Bass) to facilities for connecting 3270 interactive terminals directly (HOB, Ungermann Bass). Most notable here is the American manufacturer Proteon, which markets its own product range for 4, 10 and 80 Mbps Token Ring LANs.

The disadvantage of this range is that the 10 Mbps and 80 Mbps products do not conform to the standard.

The advantage of this range is that connection facilities are available for systems based on the Multibus, VMEbus, Q bus or UNIBUS.

Proteon is represented by a number of suppliers in Germany. The number of suppliers is steadily increasing. Shortly, the users will have as great a choice as that now available for Ethernet. Many people believe that because of the advantages of Token Ring protocols, Ethernet's position in the market place will come under increasing threat in the future.

Chapter 4

PC–host communication over Token Ring networks

Communication via LANs is often compared with the communication between PCs in their role as intelligent workstations and servers. So-called client–server applications which are intended to distribute tasks and loads between the PCs in the LAN and to provide many systems with access to shared information bases are steadily gaining ground. Currently, PC LANs overwhelmingly dominate the PC world. PC LANs are increasingly used as a replacement for the earlier so-called office computers. Companies such as Nixdorf, Wang, etc., which dominate this area have recently been stretched to the full limit of their capabilities and have sometimes had to accept considerable losses. Other companies too have not remained exempt from these developments.

Originally, the first LANs on the market were designed for other purposes. They were intended to form a fast vehicle for communications for access to other larger systems and helped to minimize the otherwise considerable cabling costs. LANs are still preferred for this function in mainframe environments. In IBM environments in particular, the Token Ring LAN is currently the medium with which to link terminals to the mainframe. Token Ring is becoming a super-fast highway to the mainframe for all terminals. It is possible to connect hundreds of 3270 terminals to the mainframe using a single interface to the mainframe. Emulation is used on PCs, which emulate the classical IBM 3270 terminal and provide additional user-friendly facilities for PC–host communication. Recently, Token Ring has increasingly been used for local linking of computers. Expensive interfaces for channel coupling were required in this area until now.

In the meantime, Token Ring is no longer just a fast vehicle for communications in an IBM area, but may also be used to link asynchronous terminals to ASCII hosts (for example, UNIX systems). The first Token Ring adaptors for the VME world, the Apple world and the increasingly popular UNIX world are now on the market.

Thus, we next consider the various possibilities for communication over Token Ring in order to access a mainframe. Figure 4.1 gives an overview of the various possible ways of implementing such a link. These range from simple asynchronous connection of a terminal attached to Token Ring to channel coupling with direct program-to-program communication between the attached systems. The connection to the mainframe may be implemented via the universal V.24 (RS232), X.21, S0 or X.25 interfaces or via IBM-specific coaxial interfaces (3270, 5250) right up to the channel adaptor. We shall describe the various possibilities in greater detail later. Figure 4.1 brings together a number of examples.

Since here too the PC has taken on a dominant role as a replacement for a classical terminal, we shall concentrate on the ways in which it may be connected. Here, we must distinguish between two very distinct possibilities, namely the use of existing or add-on software interfaces to Token Ring to generate individual application programs or the use of existing emulation

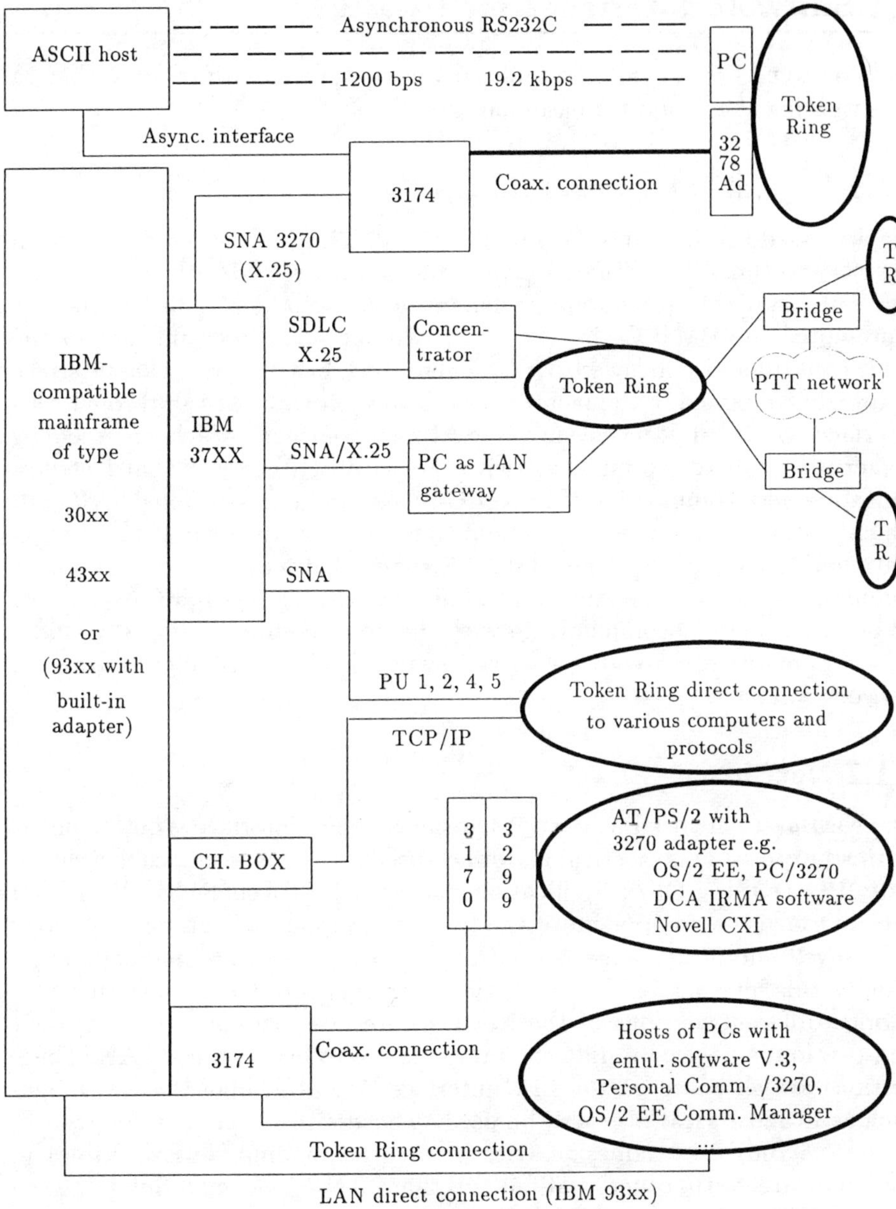

Figure 4.1 Token Ring – connection possibilities.

or gateway software as the basis for developing applications software. Even this software almost always uses the available software interfaces in Token Ring. In this case, the user often no longer has a means of modifying the protocols for his own purposes.

4.1 Software interfaces for PCs

We consider firstly the available software interfaces for PCs, before investigating the programs based on these.

4.1.1 Logical link control (LLC)

We discussed the LLC interface in Chapter 3. This is the interface between the PC and the Token Ring adaptor, and requires very detailed knowledge. The only available programming language is assembler. This interface is represented in IBM PCs by the PC LAN Support Program, and in the DTE controllers by firmware, or by microcode. In OS/2 EE, this interface is already contained in the factory area of the software. Access through this interface to Token Ring is via the SAPs (see earlier) which are used by higher protocols to communicate with the adaptor. We recall that NetBios, which is a very common interface in PC LANs, has a specific fixed SAP (F0) which a station may use to communicate with several other stations (link stations). Each station in the IBM LAN requires at least one link station to communicate with every other DTE. For example, a gateway PC over which 32 other PCs are to communicate with the host requires 32 link stations.

In practice, scarcely any users now use this interface to generate their network software.

4.1.2 NetBios

The NetBios (Network Basic Input Output System) interface is better suited to this purpose. This classical and much-used PC LAN interface is used for most PC DOS or OS/2 application packages in Token Ring. With IBM this interface is a component of the PC LAN Support Program or of OS/2 EE. Novell and 3Com, together with many other hardware manufacturers, provide this interface as a client option with their products. Unfortunately, various different versions of the NetBios interface are now on the market and caution is advised if different products are to be used in a LAN. These versions are all based on the LLC interface. In OS/2, high-level languages such as C and Pascal may also be used to access the NetBios interface.

NetBios uses names (entries in a corresponding NetBios table) to communicate with other stations in the LAN. A formal link between two NetBios names is called a session. A station may maintain several simultaneous sessions to other names via a single name (example: a gateway). The NetBios commands CALL, LISTEN and HANG.UP control session establishment and clear down.

NetBios covers layers 1 to 5 of the ISO reference model. Every command to be executed is described by a Message Command Block (MCB). This MCB has the same structure as the Network Control Block (NCB) in PC Network. The MCB describes the command, defines parameters, displays data, returns error messages, etc. The first field of the MCB indicates which interface should be used. If the content of this field is greater than X'03', this is a NetBios interface, otherwise the LLC interface should be accessed directly. As part of the first command to the NetBios interface, the adaptor is automatically initialized, if this does not happen when the PC is started up.

There are two different ways of processing commands. The first way uses the WAIT option. The calling program waits until the command is executed by the interface. Using the return code in the MCB, the calling program is able to determine whether the command was correctly executed (X'00' = command correctly executed, X'40'–X'4F' = user error, X'50'–X'FE' = PC or adaptor error). When the NO WAIT option is used, the calling program continues its operation in parallel with the NetBios call. Either the calling program is interrupted by a routine as soon as the NetBios call terminates or the program continues its operation until a specific point when it checks whether the result has reached the MCB.

The NetBios interface to Token Ring recognizes five types of commands:

- General control commands
- Name support
- Session support
- Datagram support
- Debugging support

The general control commands are:

RESET ends all sessions and cancels the corresponding table entries.

CANCEL stops all MCB commands which have already started. Some commands cannot be interrupted.

STATUS returns the adaptor status (local or remote) to the calling program.

LAN_STATUS_ALERT enables the application program to detect temporary ring errors.

UNLINK is used only for PC Network and not for Token Ring.

Communication in the network is only possible provided names, between which the sessions may be established, are agreed beforehand. NetBios uses a names table which may vary in size according to the adaptor type (16–255 entries). The calling program may manage the names using the Name Support Service.

ADD NAME adds a new name to the names table.

ADD GROUP NAME In the case of group names, several stations have the same name in the ring.

DELETE NAME deletes a name entry from the resident names table.

FIND NAME enables the calling program to determine whether the name is already being used by another station in the LAN.

A session is the logical link between two names. A PC may have several simultaneous sessions. Statistics are always recorded on a session basis.

CALL opens a session with another station in the ring.

LISTEN waits for a session to be opened (CALL).

HANG UP ends a session.

SEND sends data which may be up to 64 kbytes long.

CHAIN SEND chains send buffers together. Here too the maximum message length is 64 kbytes.

RECEIVE receives data from a session.

RECEIVE ANY receives data from any sending station.

SESSION STATUS returns the status of all existing sessions corresponding to the given name.

SEND_NO_ACK provides for data transfer without a NetBios acknowledgement.

In the case of datagrams, the message is not acknowledged. The length of a datagram is limited to 512 bytes. The sender and the recipient must look after the security protocol themselves, when this is desired.

SEND DATAGRAM is used by an application program to send a datagram to a specific name, a group of names or all stations (broadcast). The RECEIVE DATAGRAM command is used to receive datagrams.

The TRACE command is used for error analysis. It provides the user with a precise description of the state of the adaptor, should errors occur.

LAN header	DLC Header	NetBios header	User data

NETBIOS SAP: X'F0'
Functional address: X'00000080'

NetBios header	X'EFFF'	Command	Opt. data 1	Opt. data 2	Xmit/ resp corr	Dest. ID num	Source ID num

Commands:
X'00' –'13' UI frames (e.g. X'01' = ADD_NAME_QUERY,
X'0D' = ADD_NAME_RESPONSE)
X'14' –'1F' I frames (e.g. X'15' = DATA_FIRST_MIDDLE)

UI frame:
Dest/Source ID: 16 bytes
I frame:
Dest/Source num: 16 bytes

Figure 4.2 The NetBios frame format.

The NetBios frame format is shown in Figure 4.2.

Figure 4.3 shows a small example. A station wishes to enter a name which is unique in the network, but the name already exists in another network station.

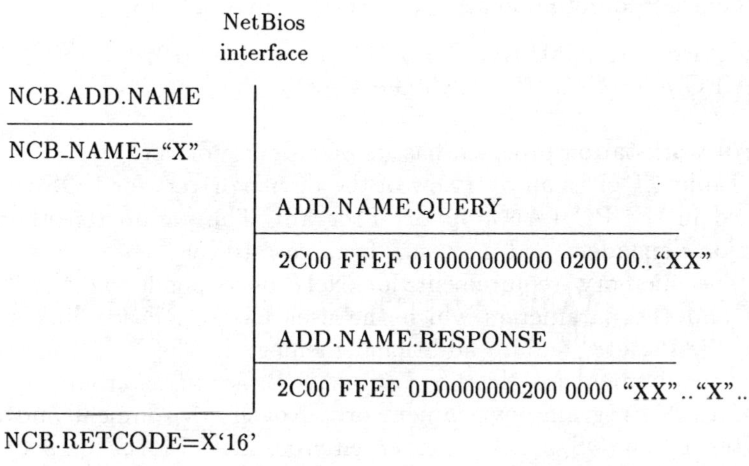

Figure 4.3 NetBios – connection establishment.

Table 4.1 Device drivers for DOS (overview).

Device driver	*Parameter*	*Bytes*	*Use*
DEVICE = DXMA0MOD.SYS	1	≈ 2K	Interrupt arbitrator
DEVICE = DXMC0=MOD:SYS or DXMC1MOD.SYS (instead of ..COM, if 3270 workst. progr. running)	Adaptor address Shared RAM	≈ 11K	Token Ring network adaptor support
DEVICE = DXMT0MOD.SYS	ST,S,C,N,O,DG,CR, DS,DN,R,TT,TC, MO,MI,RA,ES,EST	≈ 25K Min	NetBios interface

The application generates a network control block by means of the ADD.NAME command. NetBios then uses this to generate an ADD_NAME_QUERY frame. The corresponding frame structure is shown in the figure. The station which already possesses this name answers with an ADD.NAME.RESPONSE. The return code X'16' is then entered in the control block. For the application, this means that the name is already being used by another station. The link is not established unless a different name is chosen.

NetBios is either a component of the operating system used (OS/2 and OS/2 LAN Server for DOS PCs) or must be installed as an add-on (PC LAN Support Program). The device driver is loaded in the initialization file of the system:

```
device = dxmt0mod.sys        (NetBios driver DOS)

device = C:\CMLIB\NETBDD.SYS        (OS/2)
CFG = c:\CMLIB\xyz.CFG
```

The 3270 workstation program has its own device driver.

Table 4.1 gives an overview of the device drivers for DOS which are contained in the PC LAN Support Program. The parameters themselves are version dependent and may vary from case to case.

The memory requirement for NetBios depends on the NetBios version and the parameters which the user has set. Extra link stations, sessions, SAPs, etc. require additional memory in the PC. The standard memory requirement for NetBios (PC LAN Program) is around 23 kbytes in a PC LAN Program environment or a Novell environment and around 30 kbytes in an OS/2 LAN Server environment. In the case of server and gateway functions in the LAN, the memory requirement may increase sharply: 40 to 70 kbytes main memory is not uncommon. A PC with DOS 4.0 plus PC LAN Support Program and driver (mouse, printer, etc.) requires approximately 160–180 kbytes main memory. Thus, there is an understandable desire to relocate program sections into the extended memory area of a DOS PC with an 80x86 CPU (x > 1). If in addition a windows interface is included, DOS PCs should themselves have around 2–4 Mbytes main memory if they are to be operated in the network with a user-friendly interface.

NetBios is a platform for PC applications. It is the PC protocol for LANs. All current products, such as the OS/2 LAN Server, the DOS Requester for Office Vision or Remote Data Services, Word and Word Perfect, use NetBios as a communications interface.

4.1.3 Advanced program-to-program communication

Why is the apparently universal APPC interface not used everywhere? The answer to this is not simple. Both APPC and NetBios have their advantages and disadvantages. APPC is the interface for communication with different families of systems over all of today's customary communications media. NetBios is the LAN interface for PC applications and is thus not universally applicable. In comparison with APPC, NetBios requires considerably less memory and is simple to use. However, NetBios cannot be used in S/370 or AS/400 environments or for communication with other systems such as DEC, Siemens or Unisys. This is the province of the APPC interface which is manufacturer, system and network independent.

The APPC interface (see Chapter 8) is based on SNA LU 6.2 rules. It permits communication between distributed processes and programs. Application programs which use the APPC interface are called transaction programs. Transaction programs access the services of the APPC interface using verbs, which may be viewed as an extension of a programming language and are used to implement so-called conversations. The term conversation refers to the actual link between two transaction programs.

There are two types of conversations, namely basic conversations and mapped conversations. Basic conversations are used for direct device control (for example, of a 3820 laser printer) or for system applications (for example, SNA/DS). Mapped conversations are designed to enable the application programmer to generate his applications. They provide for data exchange in any desired format and, unlike basic conversations, contain no system-specific parameters.

The LU controls the access itself. Several transaction programs may share an LU. Transaction programs communicate with the local LU using the APPC verbs. The data flow with the partner LU in the destination system is implemented according to these verbs. The controlled data flow is termed a session or an LU–LU session (Figure 4.4).

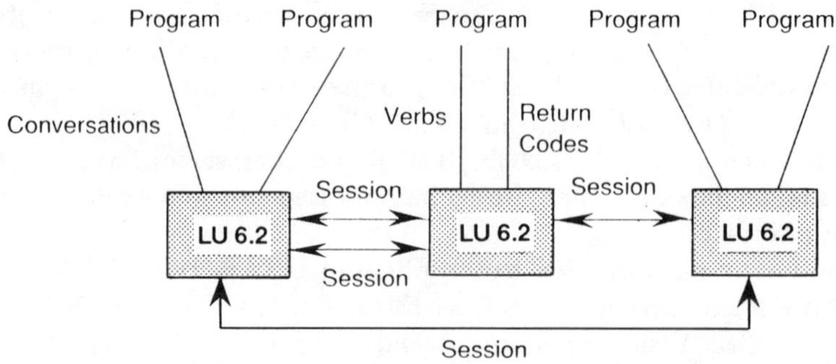

Figure 4.4 APPC.

There may be several parallel sessions between two partner LUs. The session management and the data flow control falls not to the transaction program, but to the LU. Unlike NetBios the APPC interfaces may be used from almost all programming languages. For example, interfaces to C, COBOL and Pascal are available under OS/2. Naturally, macro-assembler may also be used here.

We now give an overview of the most important verbs. Verbs may be divided into two categories: control operator verbs and conversation verbs. Control operator verbs are only used by privileged programs which execute the LU control functions. Conversation verbs may be subdivided again into the familiar basic, mapped or type-independent verbs.

The following control verbs may be used to set up a transaction:

TP_STARTED uses APPC to reserve the corresponding local resources in the LU, in order to generate a new link.

TP_ENDED terminates a link and releases the resources.

RECEIVE_ALLOCATE generates a link between the local and the remote transaction programs, as soon as the latter has executed an MC_ALLOCATE verb.

Mapped conversation verbs control the data flow.

MC_ALLOCATE initiates a link with a remote transaction program which is in the wait state.

MC_CONFIRM permits synchronization of local and remote programs.

MC_CONFIRMED is the corresponding response from a remote station after synchronization.

MC_DEALLOCATE establishes a conversation.

MC_FLUSH results in the direct transmission to the remote LU of all the information in intermediate storage in the transmission buffer of the local LU.

MC_PREPARE_TO_RECEIVE indicates a change from send mode to receive mode and includes the emptying of the transmission buffer.

MC_RECEIVE_AND_POST returns control to the local transaction program which continues its operation until data from the remote transaction program is received.

MC_RECEIVE_AND_WAIT makes the local transaction program wait for data.

MC_RECEIVE_IMMEDIATE has the effect that all currently available data is received from the remote transaction program, which does not need to wait for further information.

MC_REQUEST_TO_SEND forwards the local transaction program's request to send data to the remote program.

MC_SEND_DATA transmits a data record to the remote transaction program.

MC_SEND_ERROR notifies the remote transaction program that an error has occurred.

MC_TEST_RTS checks whether the local LU has received an MC_REQUEST_TO_SEND from the remote transaction program.

MC_GET_ATTRIBUTES determines the attributes of a conversation.

The mode of operation of the interface is best explained by means of examples.

Example 1 This example (Figure 4.5) concerns the transmission of a single data record between two transaction programs.

It is immediately clear in this example that the data record is not transmitted immediately but only after the link has been established. The reason for this has to do with the send and receive buffer areas which each

Local transaction program		*Remote transaction program*
TC_STARTED		
MC_ALLOCATE		RECEIVE_ALLOCATE
MC_SEND_DATA		
MC_DEALLOCATE		
	⟶	
		MC_RECEIVE_AND_WAIT (receives data)
		MC_RECEIVE_AND_WAIT (receives connection request)
TP_ENDED		
		TP_ENDED

Figure 4.5 Transmission of a data record between two transaction programs.

LU uses for transmission. The physical transmission of the data only takes place when such a buffer area is full. Firstly this optimizes the transmission itself and secondly it reduces the protocol costs to the bare minimum.

Of course, a sender may force the transmission of the data even when the buffer area is not full. This is shown in Example 2.

Example 2 In this example (Figure 4.6), the two transaction programs send each other data consecutively.

Let us consider the individual phases of the transmission in more detail. In (1), the conditions for the establishment of a link are generated using TP_STARTED. Normally, this procedure takes place when the system is started. The resources for the local transaction program are made available. In (2), the actual link to the partner LU in the destination system is established. All the specific characteristics of the link are exchanged as parameters between the participants in the link. If the link is successfully established, the local transaction program switches from reset status to send status. From now on the transaction program uses a conversation identifier which is used in all subsequent verbs. The data transmission itself begins in (3). Normally, the data is transferred to the send buffer and the transmission itself only takes place when this buffer is full. However, parameters may be used to alter the send type so that the data is sent directly (mc_send_and_flush), possibly with a request for direct confirmation (mc_send_and_confirm). In our example, the transmission is carried out using the confirm verb (4). The local program must then wait until the opposite party confirms receipt of the data (5). Both parties

	Local transaction program		*Remote transaction program*
1	TP_STARTED		
2	MC_ALLOCATE		RECEIVE_ALLOCATE
3	MC_SEND_DATA		
4	MC_CONFIRM	⟶	MC_RECEIVE_AND_WAIT
			MC_REQUEST_TO_SEND
5		⟵	MC_CONFIRMED
6	MC_RECEIVE_AND_WAIT		
7			MC_RECEIVE_AND_WAIT
8			MC_SEND_DATA
9			MC_DEALLOCATE
	MC_RECEIVE_AND_WAIT		
10	TP_ENDED		TP_ENDED

Figure 4.6 Transaction programs send data consecutively.

then transfer to the wait status (6,7) so as to receive and process data, status information and requests for confirmation.

The remote station transmits data again (8) and clears down the conversation between the two transaction programs (9). TP_ENDED (10) terminates the transaction programs involved. The resources reserved for them are released.

We note that, normally, the session between the stations is not cleared down when a conversation ends. Thus, the existing link may be immediately used by other transaction programs.

An application program may be involved in several conversations with different transaction programs on various mutually incompatible DP systems (for example, in order to implement complicated search procedures in several databases on OS/2, UNIX and /370 systems).

Thus, APPC may be used as a basis for the management and control of decentralized processes. The best implementation of the APPC interface to date is that in OS/2 (Figure 4.7).

Unfortunately, because of its complexity, its high memory requirements and its sometimes poor software support, APPC has not achieved the sales originally expected of it. This has changed only recently. Firstly, direct interfaces including a built-in APPC interface in mainframes (VTAM) are now available and, secondly, IBM's OS/2 is available as standard and is now used for various applications. In OS/2 the routines are dynamically loaded. This saves storage space. APPC interfaces are now also available in most UNIX systems. Only Novell still supplies APPC as an add-on interface in its network operating system.

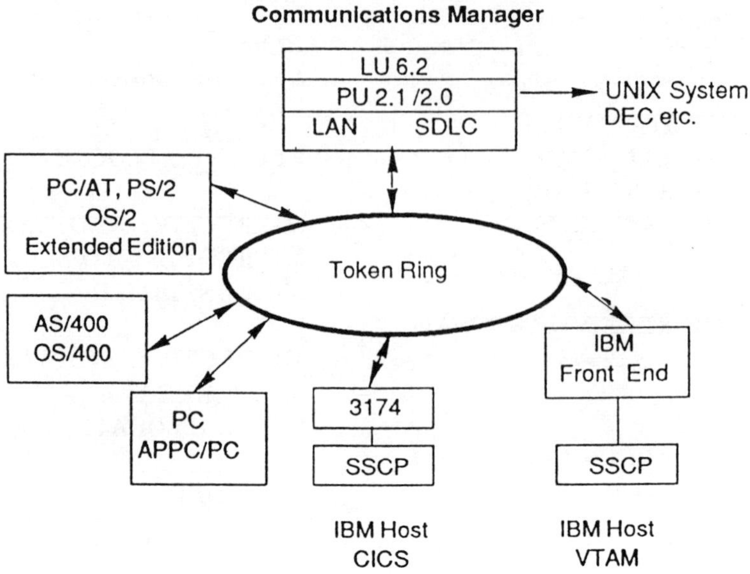

Figure 4.7 Connectivity with SNA LU 6.2.

4.1.4 IBM's server requester programming interface (SRPI)

SRPI is IBM's interface for communication between IBM hosts (VM or MVS/XA) and IBM PCs. Like APPC, it is a very user-friendly interface for pure PC–host communication. Unlike APPC, SRP interfaces only exist in pure IBM environments. For DOS, VM and MVS, IBM supplies its own applications which are based on this interface and which enable the mainframe to be used as server in a PC network. Although from the interface to user applications SRPI is more user-friendly than APPC, it does not use the LU 6.2 rules but is (still) based on the LU 2. SRPI is usually based on a master–slave principle. The server functions are on the mainframe and the requester functions are on the PC; thus, there is no peer-to-peer communication as with the APPC interface. SRPI uses a single verb (SEND_REQUEST) for communication, which provides for synchronous communication with the server. SRPI is available for DOS, OS/2, VM and MVS2 (Figure 4.8).

The parameter area for data transmission between PCs and hosts is also called the CPRB (connectivity programming request block). Under OS/2, a number of applications may use the SRPI simultaneously. A prerequisite for this is the establishment of a 3270 link in each case. In the case of active SRPI applications, no 3270 functions are available to the user. Thus, SRPI is the most user-friendly programmer interface between hosts and PCs (Figure 4.9).

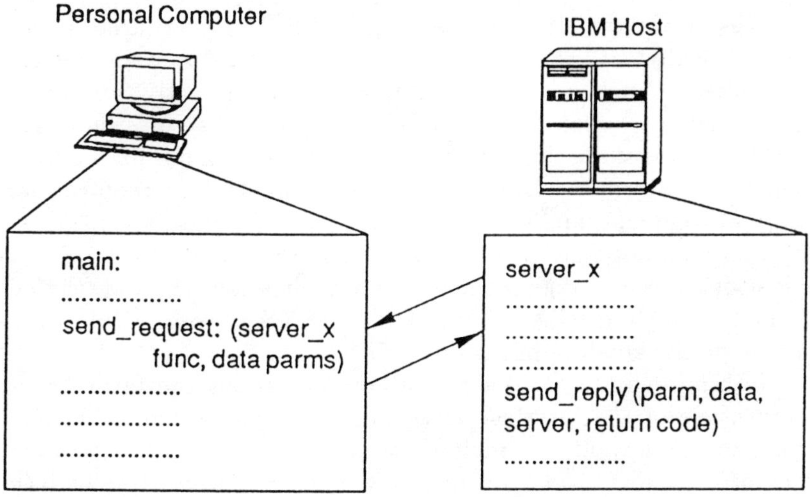

Figure 4.8 Server/requester relation.

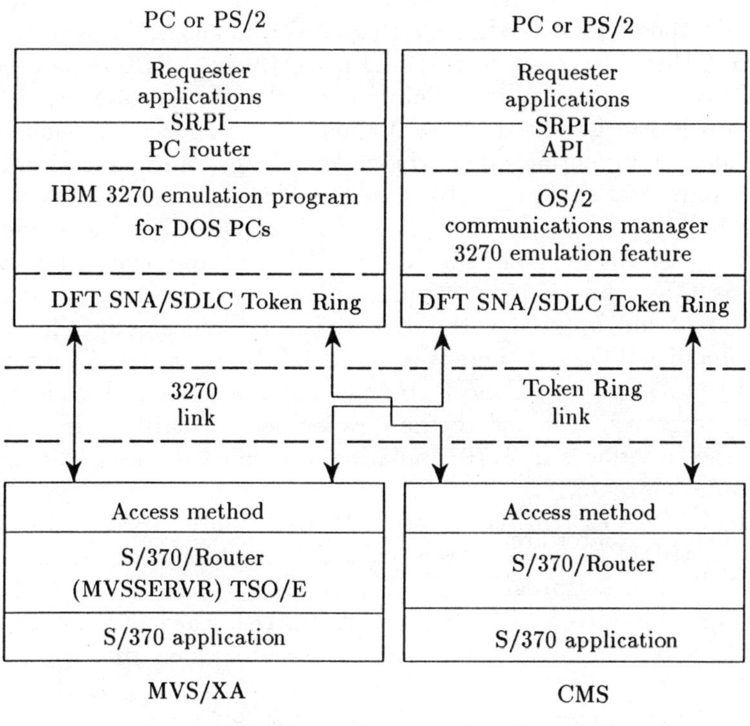

Figure 4.9 Server/requester.

The maximum size of the request/reply buffer area is around 32 kbytes (64 kbytes). The same storage area may be used for request and reply parameters and for data. SRPI may be called directly from high-level languages such as Pascal, C and COBOL and from macro-assembler.

The storage requirement under DOS is around 30 kbytes plus the application itself. An additional 180–210 kbytes are required for the necessary 3270 emulation. Thus, DOS systems often have too little storage available for exacting functions. The situation is different under OS/2. Here, there is enough free storage for individual applications. In VM, the add-on programmer interface REXX is available. REXX is very simple to use to test and generate small applications.

Nothing definite can be said at present about the future of SRPI. One advantage of the interface is that it is simple to handle in an IBM environment. Disadvantages include its poor acceptance by the user and the lack of implementations on non-IBM systems. Were IBM to base the interface on the LU 6.2 instead of the LU 2, its future as a user-friendly programmer interface for individual PC–host applications would be secured. SRPI-based applications are now available from IBM under OS/2.

4.1.5 Application programming interfaces

The various 3270 APIs currently available are very different to SRPI and APPC. Of these, IBM's HLLAPI (high-level language API) is the most common. Other APIs include EHLLAPI, IRMA API, PCOX API, etc.

These interfaces were originally developed out of necessity. The IBM world is still governed by 3270 emulation. Hundreds of thousands of applications, representing an enormous knowledge and financial potential, use 3270 terminals as input/output media. Thus, it was natural to develop a 3270 emulation for the PC. In this way, IRMA cards became a trademark for a new function of the PC in the IBM environment, namely as a replacement for the classical terminal. The many existing programs on mainframes could be used without modification and existing investments were protected. However, there was a natural desire to use the intelligence of the PC to improve PC–host communications without having to alter the host programs. This led to the development of 3270 APIs. These are programmer interfaces in 3270 emulation via which the user can influence the 3270 data stream.

HLLAPI, EEHLLAPI and EHLLAPI are IBM's best-known interfaces. HLLAPI incorporates a total of 44 functions and is contained in the 3270 workstation program. EEHLLAPI is a subset of HLLAPI with a total of 31 of the 44 HLLAPI functions. EHLLAPI, which is compatible with EEHLLAPI, is contained in the OS/2 communications manager and has 16 additional commands. HLLAPI is also available on many UNIX systems.

All programmer interfaces use only the 3270 data stream. All aim to support the PC user in his daily tasks, to decrease his load and thus to increase productivity and user-friendliness. This also leads to a decrease in the data throughput between the PC (or gateway) and the host. As with APPC and SRPI, APIs also permit the generation of new distributed applications on PCs with the DOS, OS/2 or UNIX operating systems. Simultaneous access to several systems for the purposes of data extraction is also possible.

The mode of operation of APIs is easy to describe. In order to emulate a 3270 terminal, the individual key assignments of the original must be converted to the PC keyboard and the 3270 data stream for screen display must be edited so that it may be represented in the same way on the PC screen. This requires a presentation area in the PC's memory, which is used to convert to the PC screen and keyboard. Since the 3270 functions have a precise description, the software manufacturers have each generated subroutines to implement the conversion between the PC and host worlds. In this way, the desired result should be obtained every time a simulated PF key is pressed on the PC. Once this protocol mechanism was implemented, it was natural to extend it so that PC programs could also access these functions directly. It is now possible to derive complicated, user-friendly applications by pure terminal emulation (still completely controlled by the user).

- It is now possible to implement user-friendly dialogue-driven menus in support of users.
- Automatic database interrogation of the host with direct post-processing in PC applications is now possible.
- Frequently used functions may now be automated. For example, it is possible to implement an automatic Logon directly even into host applications. For simple applications the complete service procedure may be automated (automatic operator).
- In HLLAPI, user entries may be filtered and replaced by complicated sequences of characters (so-called keyboard macros).
- In HLLAPI, the user may obtain a unified screen display, the contents of which are in reality composed from relevant information from several host connections and various applications.
- HLLAPI allows the user to verify entries directly and immediately on the spot. The data does not have to be transmitted to the host first. Errors in entries may be detected as they are typed in and clarified using error and help menus. This reduces the line load and decreases the load on the host.

Figure 4.10 shows the mode of operation of HLLAPI.

HLLAPI contains programmer interfaces to various languages including C, Pascal, Basic, COBOL and (naturally) macro-assembler.

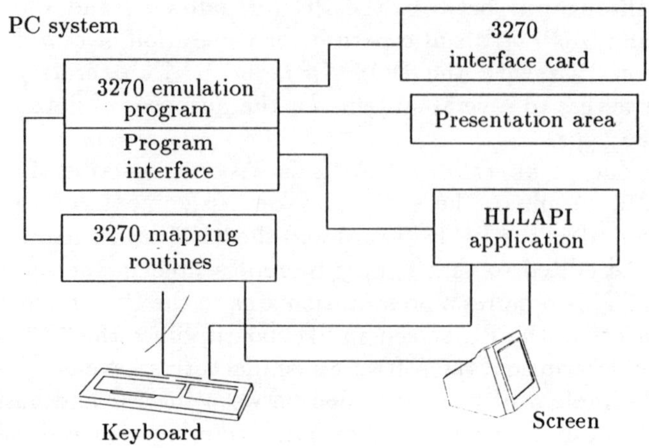

Figure 4.10 HLLAPI.

The HLLAPI functions are subject to constant extension and updating. They may be subdivided into a number of classes. Each function is activated using a number assigned to it.

- User support
  - SEND KEY (3)
  - WAIT (4)
  - SET SESSION PARAMETERS (9)
  - QUERY SESSIONS (10)
  - PAUSE (18)
  - QUERY SYSTEM (20)
  - RESET SYSTEM (21)
  - QUERY SESSION STATUS (22)
  - START HOST NOTIFICATION (23)
  - QUERY HOST UPDATE (24)
  - STOP HOST NOTIFICATION (25)
- Presentation support
  - CONNECT PRESENTATION SPACE (1) (links the HLLAPI application with a predefined presentation area (host session))
  - DISCONNECT PRESENTATION SPACE (2)
  - COPY PRESENTATION SPACE (5)

- SEARCH PRESENTATION SPACE (6)
- QUERY CURSOR LOCATION (7)
- COPY PRESENTATION SPACE TO STRING (8)
- QUERY FIELD ATTRIBUTE (14)
- COPY STRING TO PRESENTATION SPACE (15)
- SEARCH FIELD (30)
- FIND FIELD POSITION (31)
- FIND FIELD LENGTH (32)
- COPY STRING TO FIELD (34)
- SET CURSOR (40)

- Device support
  - RESERVE (11)
  - RELEASE (12)
  - START KEYSTROKE INTERCEPT (50) (all keyboard entries go directly to the HLLAPI application)
  - GET KEY (51)
  - POST INTERCEPT STATUS (52)
  - STOP KEYSTROKE INTERCEPT (53)
- Communications support
  - SEND FILE (90)
  - RECEIVE FILE (91)
- Miscellaneous
  - STORAGE MANAGER (17)
  - CONVERT POSITION OR ROW COLUMN (99)
- Only in OS/2 from version 1.2 (PM = Presentation Manager)
  - CONNECT PM WINDOW SERVICES (101)
  - DISCONNECT PM WINDOW SERVICES (102)
  - QUERY PM WINDOW COORDINATES (103)
  - PM WINDOW STATUS (104)

In OS/2, a call to HLLAPI may look as follows

```
Basis: IBM PASCAL/2
Declaration part:
  type str_type = array[1..1920]
  procedure HLLAPI(vars api_func:integer;
           vars api_string:str_type;
```

```
                vars api_len, api_retc:integer); EXTERN;
    Call:
      HLLAPI(api_func, api_string, api_len, api_retc);
      ...
```

Thus, HLLAPI is the ideal interface for the careful person, who wishes to modify as little as possible (and, if possible, nothing) on the mainframe and who nonetheless does not wish to dispense with the facilities of his PC in the PC–host communication. HLLAPI is particularly suitable for Token Ring when the linkage to the mainframe is implemented via a single gateway.

A number of software houses have developed and now market complete application packages based on these APIs. URUS, Corporate Tie and Telon are examples of such applications using APIs which have also generated additional applications for the host. They provide for user-related integration of the PC into the mainframe environment and contribute decisively to decreasing the load of the mainframe.

4.1.6 TCP/IP

Some 15 years ago the US DoD developed and implemented its own protocols for its various systems: TCP/IP (Transmission Control Protocol/Internet Protocol). These protocols have now become the *de facto* industry standard. All manufacturers have implemented at least the most important TCP/IP-based protocols in their products! The DoD's aim was to facilitate communication between the various systems in its own area. In addition, it was intended to link together the various systems over public networks in as secure a way as possible. This led to the development of the ARPA (Advanced Research Project Agency) network and the CS (Computer Science) network in the scientific area.

Nowadays, these protocols are primarily supported in LANs. TCP/IP has become known in the UNIX area and in Ethernet LANs. In the meantime, these protocols are now common in Token Ring LANs and are available for operating systems such as DOS, OS/2, Novell, VM (IBM), VMS (DEC) and MVS (IBM).

They are used as secure protocols between different systems and are already and will continue to be the industry standard for networking systems in LANs.

What is so special about these protocols?

For some time TCP/IP has been the only basis for other protocols which provide mutual access to different computers linked over a network. The publication of almost all the associated protocols, including the source code, in the form of public domain software has meant that they are cheap to port to a variety of systems. TCP/IP is also contained as standard in many UNIX variants.

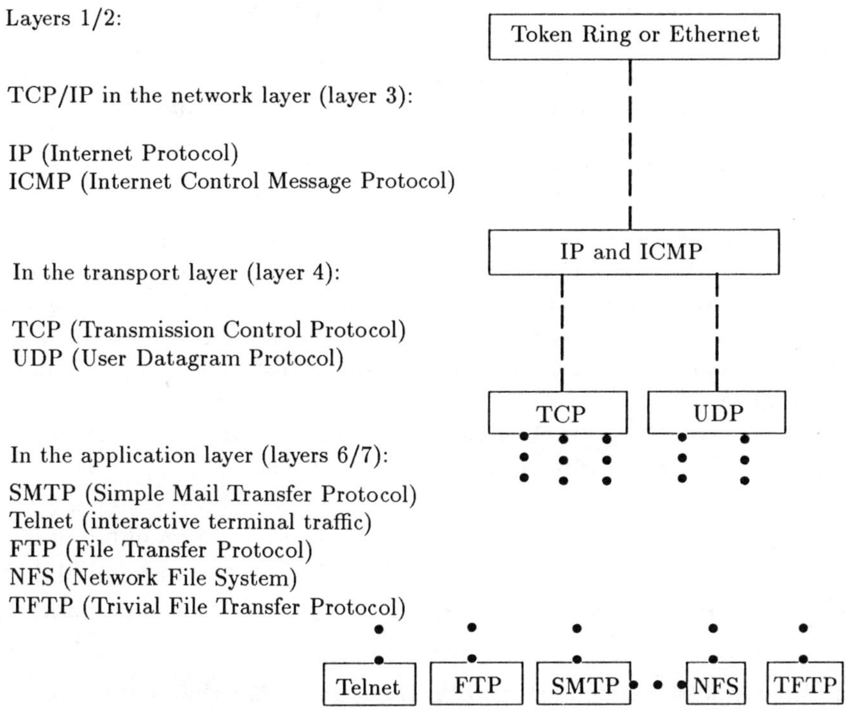

Figure 4.11 Overview of the structure and interrelationships of the TCP/IP suite.

The replacement of TCP/IP by ISO/OSI protocols is only now slowly beginning. In the LAN area, it is clear that this conversion is very sluggish, since TCP/IP provides all the conditions for fast communications in the LAN. Thus, the interfaces to the user (levels 6/7) are only being replaced by ISO/OSI applications when necessary, and often work still continues with TCP/IP. TCP/IP software may be downloaded on to intelligent LAN adaptors and does not require extra storage space in the system. Similar solutions for level 4 OSI protocols are almost unheard of.

The structure and the interrelationships of the TCP/IP suite are shown in Figure 4.11.

4.1.6.1 General description of TCP/IP

TCP/IP defines a server/client model for network services. A server is a system which makes certain services available to other participants in the network. A client is another system which uses these services.

The Internet Protocol (IP) provides for data packets to be

transported from the sender over various networks to the recipient. The IP data packets are called datagrams. There is no acknowledgement mechanism in IP. Thus, IP guarantees neither the datagram sequence nor the secure delivery of the datagram to the recipient. However, IP does have a facility for fragmentation, which enables it to transport large datagrams over networks in which the maximum permitted length of a datagram is smaller.

4.1.6.2 Addressing

Senders and recipients in TCP/IP networks may be uniquely identified using 32-bit addresses. A central point allocates an address area free of charge to an installation, to ensure that end systems are always uniquely identifiable. Anyone who maintains a private network and does not permit communication with other networks may tailor the addressing according to his own needs.

Since the sizes of networks and installations may vary, IP provides for division of the addresses into three different classes

Class A: (large networks)	0–126	nnn.hhh.hhh.hhh
Class B: (medium networks)	128.1–191.254	nnn.nnn.hhh.hhh
Class C: (small networks)	192.1.1–223.254.254	nnn.nnn.nnn.hhh

Here 'n' denotes the network and 'h' the host within the network. Certain addresses are reserved for special functions such as test and diagnostic facilities. A destination computer may be addressed not only via these addresses but also using predetermined names. The conversion of the names to the individual destination addresses is controlled by the Name Server Protocol.

The SEND and RECV commands are used to transfer data to the next highest layer. Parameters such as the address, the protocol type, the service type, etc. are transferred with the data. The header information in the IP datagram has a minimum length of 20 characters.

Figure 4.12 shows an example of addressing from CSNET.

The Transmission Control Protocol (TCP) lies directly above IP and guarantees a reliable transport (end-to-end) connection between two systems. If the command OPEN is used to establish a virtual link using TCP/IP, data may be securely exchanged with the partner program. Here, every data byte (segment) to be transmitted is given a segment number. A transmission window is then opened as in HDLC. The size of this transmission window may be dynamically determined and modified by each partner and depends on the amount of buffer space available in the system. The confirmation of a given segment number provides an automatic acknowledgement of all previous data packets. Should no acknowledgement be received from the recipient within a given time (which depends on the

```
The format for entries is:

NET : NET-ADDR : NETNAME :
GATEWAY : ADDR, ADDR : NAME : CPUTYPE : OPSYS : PROTOCOLS :
HOST : ADDR, ALTERNATE-ADDR (if any): HOSTNAME, NICKNAME: CPUTYPE OPSYS : PROTOCOLS :
  Where:
    ADDR = internet address in decimal, e.g. 26.0.0.73
    CPUTYPE = machine type (PDP-11/70, VAX-11/780, FOONLY-F3, C/30, etc.)
    OPSYS = operating system (UNIX, TOPS20, TENEX, ITS, etc.)
    PROTOCOLS = transport/service (TCP/TELNET, TCP/FTP, etc.)
NET : 4.0.0.0 : SATNET :
GATEWAY : 4.0.0.38, 128.39.0.1, 192.5.46.4 : NTARE-GATEWAY, NTA-GATEWAY
GATEWAY : 128.10.0.4, 192.5.40.5 : PUCC-NET-A-GW : VAX-11/780: UNIX : IP/GW
GATEWAY : 192.5.2.55, 192.12.12.1 : WISC-ETHER-GW : VAX-11/750 : UNIX
HOST : 4.0.0.0 : SATNET.ARPA, SATNET ::: IP :
HOST : 192.5.17.153 : NRL-OSTC.ARPA, NRL-OSTC : PDP-11/45 : UNIX
```

Figure 4.12 Example of addressing from CSNET.

underlying network), the transmission is repeated. The frequency with which this occurs is again implementation dependent. TCP also has a minimum header length of 20 bytes. Thus, TCP/IP is unsuitable for particularly short information units, since in this case the proportion of control and check information far outweighs the data part.

4.1.6.3 Other protocols of the TCP/IP suite

UDP The User Datagram Protocol (UDP) is suitable for sending smaller data sets, above all in the Token Ring LAN with its secure transmission protocol. No virtual links are established. Datagrams are used to exchange the information. UDP operates like TCP. A header, containing the source and destination address together with length entries and a checksum, is added to the data. UDP does not guarantee delivery and no precautions are taken against duplication of datagrams. UDP is used, for example, by the Name Server Protocol when determining a network address for a user name.

ICMP The Internet Control Message Protocol (ICMP) is used to transmit error and signalling messages over the network within the TCP/IP software. The protocol structure is simpler than that of UDP.

The traditional TCP/IP services are file transfer, simple mailing and line-oriented dialogue.

FTP The File Transfer Protocol (FTP) enables the user to exchange files with another computer. FTP uses TCP as a transport vehicle. Access to the other computer is secured using a user name and a password. The file transfer between two systems cannot be interfered with from the outside (in other words, by a third party not involved in the file transfer). Arrangements for the nature and mode of operation of the file transfer are made over a separate Telnet link. FTP supports character-based and binary-coded data transfer. The protocol provides utilities to ensure that the data is correctly converted for the desired destination system.

Files may also be transferred more easily and more rapidly without the above security mechanisms using TFTP, which uses UDP and not TCP as its underlying protocol.

Telnet The network terminal protocol (Telnet) allows a user to login on another computer in the network. The standard operation is line oriented. Anyone may login to another system provided he is authorized to do so. There are now several variants of this simple terminal emulation protocol on the market. These emulate, for example, a VT100, VT 220/320 or a 3270 terminal. Now it is even possible to emulate a 3270 colour terminal via TCP/IP with the IBM host.

SNMP SNMP enables a user to send messages to another network user. Integration of the SMTP into the local mail system (for example, that of the manufacturers DEC or IBM) is currently popular.

NFS Sun is one of the largest manufacturers of workstations in the USA and the spiritual father of the Network File System (NFS). Sun has always set great store by the fact that the disclosure of its interfaces has led to their being taken up by other manufacturers. NFS implementations are now produced by all major computer manufacturers. NFS is available not only for UNIX systems but also for 'foreign' systems such as DOS, VM and VMS. NFS, together with the above protocols, can, with certain restrictions, provide the same functionality as current network operating systems for DOS and OS/2, except that NFS, as noted, does not depend on the manufacturer or the operating system. NFS uses the underlying Remote Procedure Call (RPC) and External Data Representation (XDR) protocols for secure communication over Token Ring.

XDR corresponds approximately to the ISO layer 6. XDR specifies the data format for transmission in the network. Complicated data structures may be constructed based on primitive data types (conversion routines). XDR is the basis for the exchange of RPCs, which represent an extension of the procedure call mechanism of popular programming languages, based on a network transport link. Function calls are transmitted to the server over the network and executed there.

NFS is based on the RPCs. It is stateless: the parameters of each procedure contain all the information needed to execute the procedure. NFS also uses UDP and IP (not TCP) and it is only sensible to install it in the LAN, although other applications (for example, in ISDN networks) might be conceivable. If necessary, these transport protocols may be exchanged (for example, via ISO transport class 4).

NFS provides direct transparent access to remote data on disks or devices of other computers corresponding to the classical PC server concept. Systems from different manufacturers may be combined into a unified network. However, it is not a network operating system as in the case of PC LANs, since NFS is composed of independent network services!

Another aid for the network manager is the name server function. Large networks contain different numbers of resources and different amounts of information, such as:

- the number of users,
- their names and passwords,
- network addresses for computers and their names,

which should be accessible to all users. Because of the volume of this data (database) it is only installed in a few computers. Other systems may, if necessary, access these systems over the network. This leads to a central uniform network-wide management of all resources, which is highly significant in a heterogeneous network. The otherwise customary equalization of all data on the different systems may be largely dropped.

4.1.7 Summary

Which interface should be used for what purpose? If we had a famous all-round star for PC communications in Token Ring, this chapter would have been very short and limited to the description of a single interface. Unfortunately, as the previous descriptions and examples have shown, this is not the case. However, this variety of interfaces provides for the implementation of bespoke solutions for all applications. In this case, we are really spoilt for choice. However, this choice rapidly becomes limited.

NetBios is the industry standard in the LAN area. Many (so far failed) attempts have been made to replace NetBios by other interfaces in the LAN. Even Novell, which believes that its own interface is better and faster, offers NetBios as an optional interface. NetBios is less suitable for PC–host communication and is used almost exclusively for communication between PCs from different manufacturers in the LAN.

The 3270 APIs were originally designed as transitional solutions and aids to PC–host communication, until better interfaces such as APPC and SRPI could be implemented. As is so often the case, this emergency solution led to the currently most common interface for PC–host communication. The functions became increasingly user-friendly and the acceptance grew, if only because no modifications to the somewhat expensive and sensitive host applications were required. Thus, 3270 APIs are always used when a PC application needs to access data in a standard host application. This interface is primarily used in the conventional area (PC linked to the 3170 controller via 3270 interface card). In the LAN area mainly gateway solutions are used.

The APPC interface is the most variable and is primarily used in heterogeneous environments. APPC places high demands on the programmer and is independent from the network, from the operating system used and from the hardware manufacturer. At the same time, APPC is also very complicated and, possibly because of that, not very common at present, since the development costs are still very high. Standard applications have rarely been available until now. However, APPC will in the future be the interface for communication between peer systems, although it also requires the rewriting or adjustment of programs in the host.

This universality was never provided for in the case of SRPI. However, in the special case of IBM host–PC interconnection, this interface could replace APPC, since it is nearer to the user's application and thus more user-friendly. Until now SRPI has used the LU 2. The success of this interface would be guaranteed if it were to be based on the LU 6.2. IBM itself provides application programs (the ECF programs) which permit use of the host as server for PCs in the LAN.

TCP/IP is the interface for products from all manufacturers in all networks and is the interim solution on the road to ISO/OSI.

4.2 Current PC emulation programs in Token Ring

After the theory of interfaces, we now discuss the practical aspects. We shall use a number of Token Ring products to illustrate the possibilities for PC–host communication. It is appropriate to begin with IBM products and then to compare these with others.

4.2.1 3270 emulation programs

For several years to come, terminals operating in the 3270 mode in a /370 environment will remain the most important input/output media.

There are three main products for DOS PCs in Token Ring:

- The IBM 3270 emulation program, from version III.
- The IBM 3270 workstation program from version 1.1.
- The IBM personal communication/3270 program.

All three products may also be used outside Token Ring with the 3270 adaptor for PCs. The personal communication/3270 program is the most universal product and may be used as a gateway program in Token Ring. The other two products are only suitable under certain conditions when, for example, special demands are imposed.

Version III of the 3270 emulation program may be thought of as a forerunner of the personal communication/3270 program. It supports:

- the multi-protocol adaptor (SNA/SDLC or X.25).
- the IBM 3270 adaptor (coaxial direct connection to the controller).
- direct communication with the IBM 3720/25/45 or IBM 3174 with the Token Ring gateway feature.
- cluster functions in Token Ring for connections via 9370/3174.

The following are supported:

- menu-driven file transfer, with a maximum buffer size of 7 kbytes.
- variable national character sets.
- hot key function.

- 3287 printer support.

EHLLAPI and SRPI are available as interfaces. The PC LAN program (NetBios) is a prerequisite for use in Token Ring. If this version is used to link individual PCs to the mainframe, the restrictions on controllers regarding the maximum number of connectable terminals must be observed.

Even when the actual communication with the mainframe is conducted via an IBM 317x or an IBM 37xx controller, it may be sensible to use this emulation to define a PC in the ring as a gateway for other PCs in the ring. To the mainframe this PC looks like a remote controller attached to Token Ring with up to 32 attached terminals. Firstly this saves channel addresses and secondly this clustering permits simplified dynamic management and control of the terminals using the VTAM/NCP operator. It is then also easier for the network manager to alter the allocation of PCs to the gateway. This allocation is based on NetBios names and not understood in the controller of the mainframe (Figure 4.13).

Version III of the 3270 emulation program requires up to 390 kbytes, according to the configuration. Variable printers are supported (thus

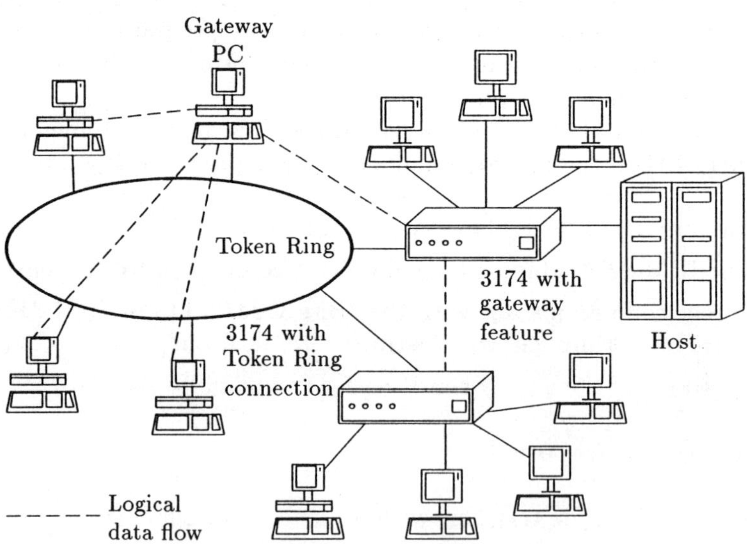

Figure 4.13 IBM 3174 and PC in Token Ring with host connection.

allowing the possibility of virtual printing on floppy disks). The software automatically recognizes LU types 1 or 3 (see Chapter 8). However, only IBM printers are supported and adaptation to printers from other manufacturers is unfortunately not planned. The printing process is menu driven and may be controlled from the emulation. This version does not support graphics applications or APL programs.

File transfer with or without conversion is possible. A blocking factor of from 256 bytes to 7 kbytes may be set in the emulation. A prerequisite in the host is that the corresponding file transfer program (IND$FILE module) should be procured first.

Programmable or application-driven access to the mainframe is possible using:

- Presentation Space Application Programming Interface Support (subset of the API for the 3270 PC)
- Personal Services/PC (DISOSS in the System /370)
- PROFS Personal Computer Support (for PROFS from version 2)
- Server Requester Programming Interface (SRPI)
- High Level Language Application Programming Interface (HLLAPI)

When a 3270 adaptor card is available as an interface to the host, at most five links may be simultaneously implemented. Normally, the gateway PC itself is also available as a 3270 workstation so that a further four PCs may interwork in the ring with the host.

When a multi-protocol adaptor is used for connection purposes, up to 32 simultaneous sessions may be established. In the case of 12 or more links, it is advisable to dedicate the PC to the gateway function (Figure 4.14).

4.2.2 Personal Communications/3270

Personal Communications is the base software for all future IBM emulation programs for DOS PCs and is the medium-term replacement for all other IBM products now on the market. Unfortunately, this program is partial to storage space and its 300 kbytes or more (above all in the gateway function) do not leave much room for other applications. Indeed, additional existing memory is also supported (extended memory support) in order to provide more space for the applications themselves. As with the 3270 software version III, the SNA SDLC adaptor, the DFT mode and Token Ring are directly supported via NetBios. However, if, for example, the emulation is used on a PC attached to Token Ring, up to eight links (screen or printer) to one or more hosts may be generated at the same time. A maximum of 32 kbytes of buffer memory may be made available for file transfer. This is advisable if large files frequently have to be transmitted.

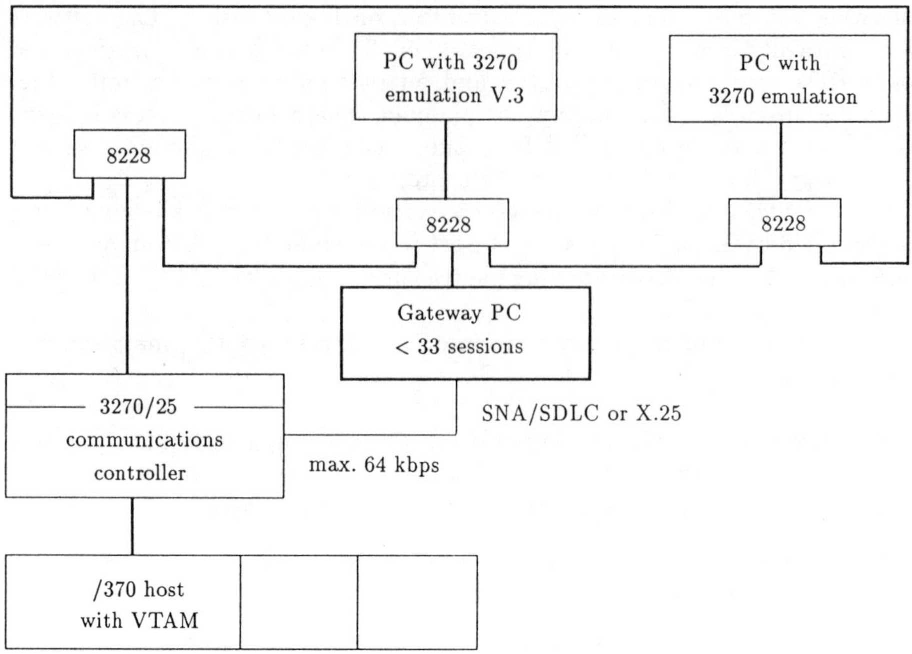

Figure 4.14 3270 emulation in the Token Ring environment.

As in version III, DOS applications may be executed at the same time. Hot keys are used to switch between one or more host sessions and DOS. The emulation resides in the PC memory.

The HLLAPI interface has again been extended. Above all, this version now also contains subroutines for the programming languages Pascal, COBOL and C and the Basic interpreter. The same is naturally true for SRPI. Another new feature not included in version III is the linkage into the central IBM network management when the LAN Manager is installed in Token Ring and NetView is installed in the host. Using the IBM program GDDM PCLK and the corresponding host program, it is now possible to represent, print and plot IBM GDDM graphic functions on the PC. Thus, almost the same user-friendly functions are now available in DOS as under OS/2 EE in the communications manager. Features still lacking include the support for Ethernet together with the facilities to execute several applications simultaneously and to link in the Presentation Manager which permits the use of window techniques to subdivide optionally the screen display for various functions. Here, Windows 3.0 is a reasonable, user-friendly and cost-effective alternative and thus the differences from OS/2 are increasingly smaller.

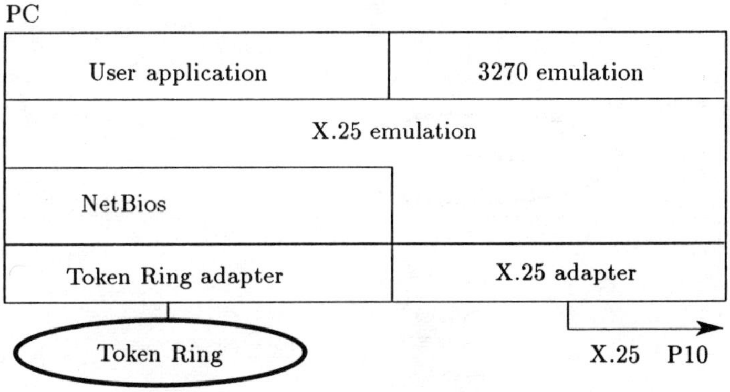

Figure 4.15 3270/X.25 gateway in Token Ring.

4.2.3 IBM 3270 workstation program

This program may also be used to represent between one and four 3270 sessions simultaneously and up to six DOS sessions. Graphics support for GDDM and GDDM PCLK is available.

Up to two notepad sessions make it easier to transmit information from one window to the next in sections. It is only sensible to install this program when at least 2 Mbytes of main memory is available on the PC. Then a maximum of 480 kbytes of main memory are available per DOS session. Unfortunately, there is no APL support here and the software cannot be used as a gateway for other stations on the ring. Moreover, the software also requires other drivers in the PC CONFIG.SYS file and uses a different SAP to other SNA applications. It is not sensible to install this program with its 640 kbytes. However, it does have a pseudo-multitasking operating system and the facility for data transfer between the individual windows.

4.2.4 PC SNA emulation/X.25

IBM also supplies this variant, for the case in which Token Ring connection is implemented over the Datex P network (Figure 4.15).

The software, which is not IBM's own, supports (possibly because of this) not only IBM printers but also most other popular printer types. Naturally, this software is available in a single-user version and in a gateway version. The QLLC (qualified LLC) and the PSH protocols are used. File transfer is just as standard as the so-called PAD (packet assembly disassembly) functions which permit access to non-SNA systems via the

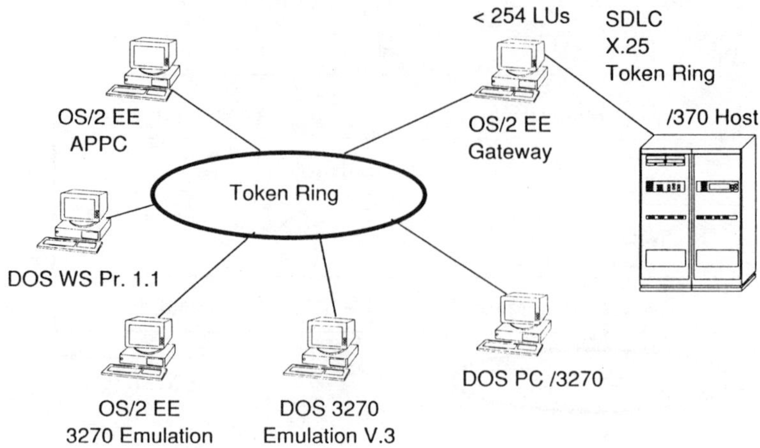

Figure 4.16 Token Ring gateway in OS/2 EE from version 1.2.

same hardware. On the subject of hardware, both the multi-protocol adaptor and the real-time interface coprocessor board may be used. The latter may be used to implement links at up to 64 kbps. If it is necessary to access other DP systems, other emulation programs such as the Siemens 9750 software are also available for these cards.

4.2.5 IBM OS/2 EE Communications Manager (extended services for OS/2 V 2.x)

In OS/2 up to ten simultaneous 3270 sessions are possible per workstation. The gateway version supports a maximum of 254 simultaneous links (Figure 4.16).

From version 1.2, Ethernet support (2.0) and IEEE 802.3 support together with support for LU 2, LU 6.2 and NetBios are standard features as is Datex P support. Of course, support for SRPI, API and APPC is available as standard. File transfer has been further optimized. Measurements have shown transfer rates of up to 24 kbytes/s (gateway: local 3174) in contrast to 14 kbytes/s under DOS. In the gateway mode, both the OS/2 Communications Manager and the Personal Communications Software for DOS support various other IBM emulations (Figure 4.16). As far as the mainframe front-end processor is concerned, the emulation behaves like a PU 2 with up to 64 LUs. As far as workstations attached to Token Ring are concerned it behaves like a PU 4 (front-end processor) to which several PU 2 workstations with several LU 2 sessions are (transparently) attached.

The gateway prevents too many channel addresses from being lost and looks to the host like an SNA gateway which maps several independent

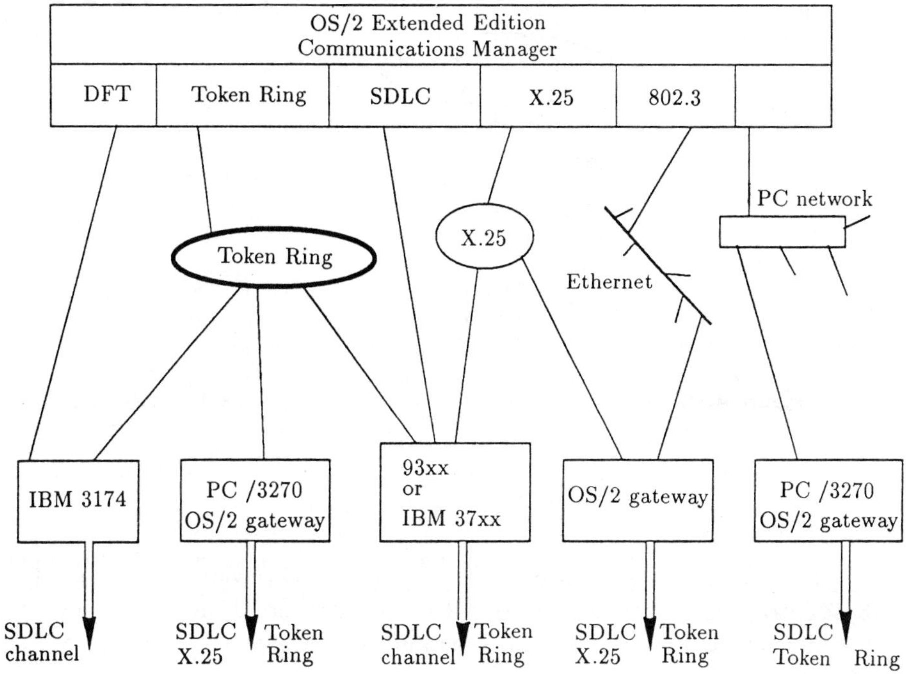

Figure 4.17 Connectivity in OS/2.

LUs on to a PU 2. Thus, almost as a side effect, different emulation programs for DOS and/or OS/2 may use the same gateway to the host. Figure 4.17 shows the communications facilities provided by OS/2.

4.2.6 Alternatives

There are numerous other manufacturers and suppliers in the market place. Companies such as CXI (Novell), DCA, EICON, MICADO, NCP and Stollman, to name but a few, supply their own hardware and software solutions. These have the advantage that they are easy to implement on other LAN installations; they often have a number of other advantages (unfortunately they also sometimes have disadvantages) as far as the user is concerned. Many of these products have a considerably lower storage requirement and many support other emulations such as Siemens or even Wang. In some cases, sessions may be simultaneously established with different hosts. Up to 128 LUs (even under DOS) is no rarity.

Figure 4.18 shows an example of Novell 3270 Token Ring gateway software.

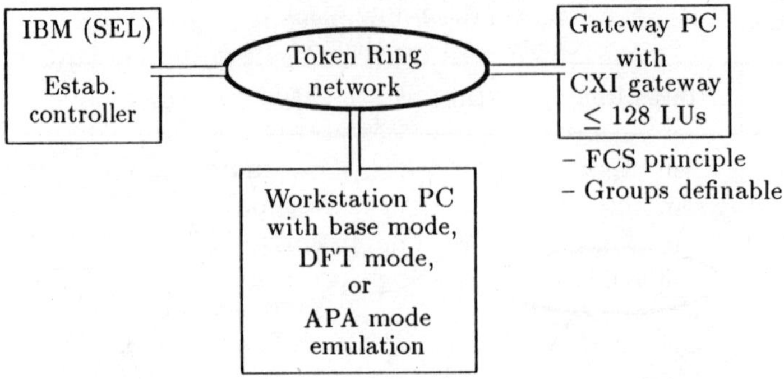

Figure 4.18 Novell's solution for Token Ring with direct linkage.

This hardware/software solution provides gateway support for the 3278 adaptor card and also for Novell's own 3299 emulation adaptor card with which up to 40 sessions may be simultaneously established.

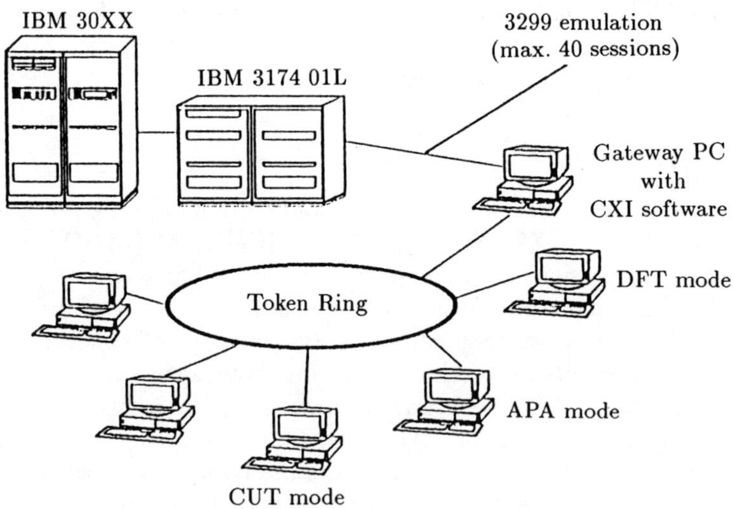

Figure 4.19 Token host linkage with Novell (CX) software.

The software provides interfaces to NetBios and to Novell (IPX) in order to permit the implementation of the most efficient form of transmission. Graphics applications are possible. Access may be given to a larger number of terminals than that specified in the host system by defining user groups. The user groups are assigned fixed LU positions. The first-come-first-served principle operates within a group. The LU positions are allocated their tasks in time order; if no more are free the next user must wait until an active user clears down its connection. This provides for effective use of the existing connections. In the so-called CUT mode (simple mode without graphics) this emulation occupies only 80 kbytes in the PC.

We shall only describe the following programs in brief, for sake of completeness, since they are rarely used in Germany.

(1) The IBM Token Ring Network IBM PC Network Interconnect Program. This provides for data exchange between PCs in the PC network and PCs attached to Token Ring. A dedicated PC is required as a gateway.

(2) The IBM series/1 Token Ring Network Connect Program. This enables the series/1 to be used as:

- a file server (at most 26 virtual disks of 32 Mbytes each),
- a print server,
- a gateway server (between LANs and to SNA).

(3) The IBM Asynchronous Communications Server Program. This provides access to the ring via the communications server to computers and databases which are reachable over switched networks.

- The gateway PC need not be dedicated to this function.
- Two connections may be simultaneously established per gateway PC.
- There may be several gateway PCs to a LAN.
- Both incoming and outgoing connections are established.
- Connections are established by entering the telephone number or a logical name. Connection requests are queued if all lines are occupied.
- The transmission of data between LAN terminals and partners in public networks is transparent.

(4) The IBM LAN Asynchronous Connection Server Program (Figure 4.20). This enables PCs outside Token Ring to access services in the ring or services which are reachable via the ring over dedicated lines.

- The gateway PC must be dedicated to this task.

- 32 links per gateway PC may be simultaneously established using the IBM Real-time Interface Coprocessor Multiport Adaptor. There may be several gateway PCs to each LAN.
- Both incoming and outgoing connections are possible (maximum 19 200 bps).
- Two programmer interfaces are supported, namely the IBM Asynchronous Communications Server Program Protocol interface and the enhanced Bios interface.
- Gateways in the LAN may be used (YTERM).
- The transmission of data between LAN terminals and partners in public networks is transparent.

Alternatives to this are available from Ungermann Bass (its own boxes, NIU TR 180) and from Novell (ACS).

(5) Direct linkage of 3278 terminals to Token Ring. Two available solutions are relatively well known in the market place.

By interposing boxes, normal 3270 terminals may be directly connected to Token Ring.

(6) HOB. The company HOB Elektronik markets IBM 3270-compatible displays and controllers. These displays may be directly attached to Token Ring and operated without additional converters, etc.

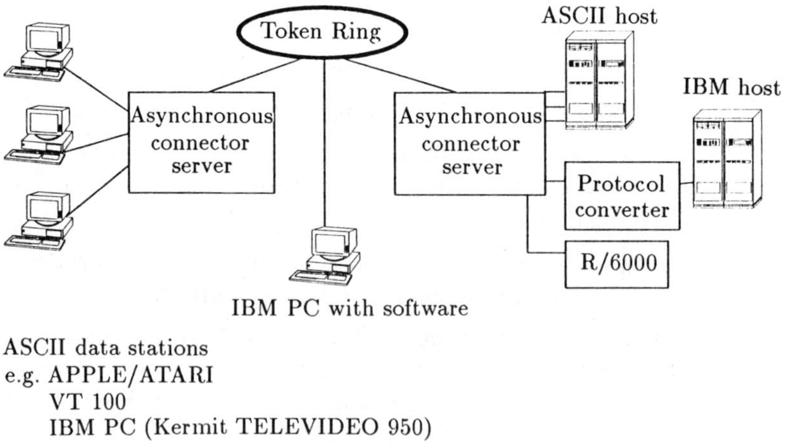

Figure 4.20 Asynchronous communication in Token Ring.

4.2.6.1 General advantages of non-IBM products

The following list summarizes the most important advantages of a number of products for Token Ring–host interconnection.

- Cards are also suitable for other LANs.
- Storage requirement may be low.
- Products contain on-board processors with their own memory.
- Optimized file transfer.
- Printer definitions are variable and adjustable.
- More simultaneous LU sessions.
- Better printer support (manufacturer independent).
- Graphics.
- APL.
- User interfaces.
- Specially adapted software.

The market for these products is growing exponentially. The 3270 emulation with its various features and APIs will dominate the market for some years to come before it is replaced by ISO applications or by old distributed applications (for example, based on APPC).

4.3 Token Rings for linking computers

With PC and terminal networking, Token Ring is increasingly being brought into an SNA environment. This is certainly the right thing and also corresponds to most applications in a Token Ring network. On the other hand, the facility for linking mainframes over Token Ring is relatively unknown. Some of the first systems for which this was possible were the IBM 9370 systems with the VM operating system and the TSAF (Transparent Services Access Facility) software component. IBM 9370 systems may be interconnected using Token Ring into a network which is transparent and homogeneous from the user's point of view. The system on which his application runs or in which his data is located is no longer important to the user.

Mainframes may also be interconnected using Token Ring (Figure 4.21). In this case, the interconnection may be used as a replacement for channel coupling which was previously the norm.

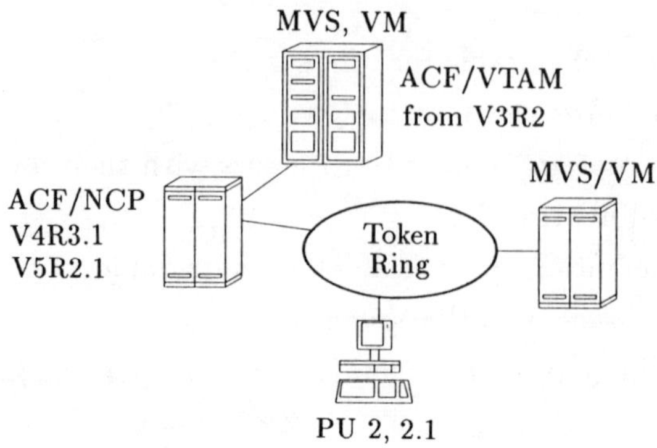

Figure 4.21 Prerequisites for connecting Token Ring to VTAM.

IBM's first strategic SAA product, Office View, is also fully supported by Token Ring. Figure 4.22 shows an example of how electronic mail or other data may be exchanged between two spatially separated LANs.

Mail may be exchanged not only between two identical systems but also between different IBM systems (Figure 4.23).

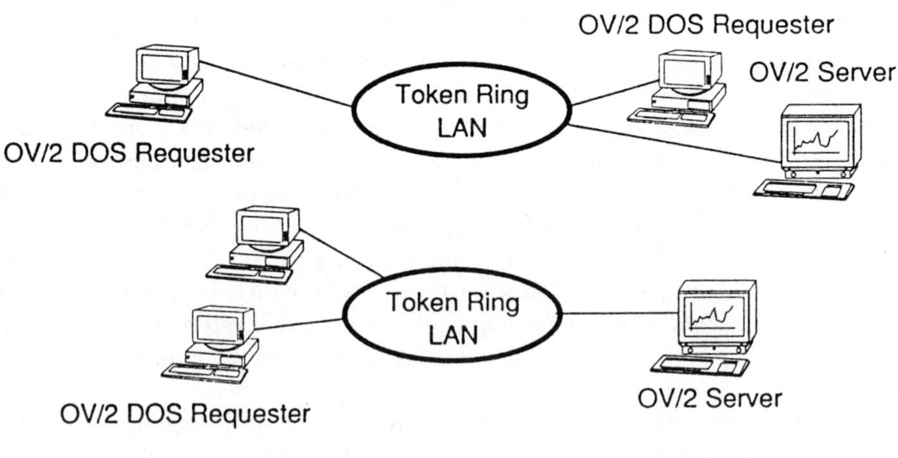

Figure 4.22 Mailing between LANs and Office Vision.

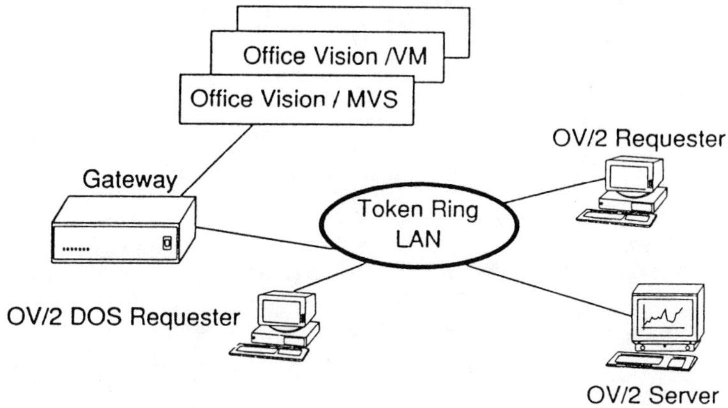

Figure 4.23 Mailing with Office Vision.

Office Vision covers almost the whole of the IBM hardware spectrum. Using Office Vision, /370 systems with the VM and the MVS operating systems, AS/400 systems, DOS and OS/2 may be interconnected to form a unified office environment.

Chapter 5

PC LAN software in Token Ring

What would a LAN be without the integration of PCs and workstations? Token Ring is no exception to this. Its province is the linking and integration of PCs in an SNA/SAA environment; however, pure PC–PC interconnection is also increasingly frequently implemented using Token Ring and even a combination of PC–host interconnection and PC–PC interconnection using Token Ring is now the rule. In a pure UNIX environment, TCP/IP-based protocols now provide the means for the integration. We have already given examples of this. NFS and X-Windows (OSF/Motif) are the dominant products. In a PC environment, network operating systems based on DOS or OS/2 still predominate.

5.1 Basic aspects of PC LANs

PCs in the LAN use operating system extensions to facilitate communication amongst themselves and with the server of a selected, particularly powerful workstation in the LAN. The PC operating system of this workstation is still a standard microcomputer operating system. In Token Ring, it is usually now no longer important whether the operating system on the workstation is DOS, OS/2 or UNIX.

Very different implementations are currently available. However, some network operating systems only support DOS systems. Consequently, workstations and servers use the same operating system. This restriction to a single operating system also means that the additional costs of the network software and the main memory requirements in the workstation and the server are relatively low. The software costs often run into less than three figures (in DM) and the main memory requirements may be less than 20 kbytes for the workstation and less than 60 kbytes for the server (for example, Artisoft's Lantastic).

The classical network operating systems OS/2 LAN Server (Microsoft/3Com LAN Manager), Banyan Vines and Novell NetWare permit various operating systems on the workstations. Thus, the server is often dedicated, with its own operating system (NetWare, Vines) and provides very user-friendly facilities for constructing and managing networks with well over 100 workstations.

Novell NetWare, for example, supports DOS PCs, OS/2 PCs and Macintosh PCs as workstations and Intel 80286, 80386 and 80486, together with UNIX and VMS (DEC) systems as servers. UNIX has been increasingly in the foreground since the introduction of the 80386/80486 processor. SCO UNIX with PC NFS under DOS plays the role of a demonstrator. The UNIX machine becomes a proper DOS server. Data may be stored in the DOS format in the UNIX system. UNIX data may be used in DOS applications. Up to five DOS sessions per PC workstation may be simulated under UNIX (DOS merge). Applications such as Lotus 1-2-3 and Microsoft

Word operate as before, without restrictions, directly under UNIX. There are no surprises as to who is making the running, namely Novell with its large market potential and OS/2 with IBM and Microsoft as sponsors. Or is UNIX the happy third party, since UNIX is now supported by all main suppliers including IBM and since, thanks to X/Open, some agreement on a UNIX standard is becoming apparent in the market place?

In particular, public authorities in Europe have come down heavily in favour of UNIX, in order to be manufacturer independent.

5.2 Servers

What distinguishes a server? A server provides other stations in the network with services which the stations do not have to manage locally. The server also secures and controls access to the desired services implemented by them. The server implements monitoring functions which control who accesses which resources when and with what priorities and access rights. The differences between the various network operating systems now on the market relate to the resources which are made available, the data protection and data security mechanisms, the capabilities of the network operating system and the user-friendliness of the user interfaces.

Servers may also be classified according to their functions and tasks, as follows:

- print servers,
- file servers,
- mail servers,
- broadcast servers,
- gateway servers,
- teletext/telex servers,
- electronic mail/X.400 servers,
- directory servers,
- program servers,
- boot servers for PCs without a disk drive,
- database servers,
- other servers.

As a rule, several of these logical server functions are combined in a single physical machine. It is usual to combine file servers, print servers, broadcast servers and boot servers in a single program. Other functions are add-on products (gateway, teletex, telefax, etc.) or standalone products (for

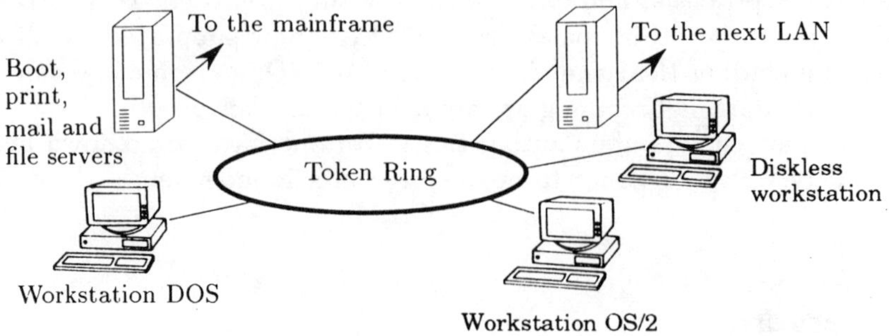

Figure 5.1 Server in Token Ring.

example, database server) which build on to the network interfaces (for example, APPC) (Figure 5.1).

A number of general performance characteristics of servers are particularly noteworthy. We list the most important of these:

- The number of similar servers supported per Token Ring LAN (here, we speak of a domain, when the user does not need to know on which server his application is located).
- The number of servers of different types supported in the Token Ring (manufacturer, type, etc.).
- The number of operating systems supported by the server.
- The number of different workstations/servers.
- The numbers and types of the devices supported by the server.
- The number of servers which may be simultaneously addressed from a workstation.
- Error handling (recovery management).
- Networking facilities of servers using public networks (Datex P, ISDN, Datex L, etc.).
- Global network management.

What LAN software should one now choose? There is no clear and unambiguous answer to this question. As in the case of LAN hardware, every network operating system has its advantages and disadvantages, which also make it possible for the user to acquire a network product tailored to his needs.

The simple case of the networking of a small number of PCs with a view to the use of programs stored centrally in the server, files and information or attached printer peripherals will not be discussed in further detail here.

The crucial factors are:

- The price of the software.
- The storage requirements, above all in the server. For example, for cost reasons, in a network of three PCs, the server may also be used as a workstation.
- The simplicity and speed of installation of the software.
- The cost of training those in charge of the system and the users.

Ideally, no training should be necessary for the user. He should not have sight of the network functions, since their execution is concealed (for example, in AUTOEXEC.BAT) and a user-controlled Logon to the network functions is not usually required. Programs of this type include Lantastic, Network OS, 10Net and IBM/3Com's PC LAN Program (base version).

5.3 IBM PC LAN Program

The PC LAN Program is based on the Microsoft LAN Program and belongs to the group of powerful network operating systems. It was the first network software produced by IBM; it is now available in an extended version (Extended Services) and provides functions which are needed to construct and manage larger networks with various functions and security mechanisms. Unlike the machine-oriented base services, the extended services are user oriented. They include a number of extra services needed to manage larger networks.

The basic idea behind this network software was to construct a domain for management of the available resources in the LAN. This idea is also found in IBM's corresponding OS/2 product, the OS/2 LAN Server (OS/2 LAN Manager).

In a domain, several servers are brought together into a LAN. The smallest domain consists of a single server, which at the same time controls the domain and is called the domain controller. All the resources in a domain are uniformly managed and administered. The user, working at any workstation, which is not itself a component of the domain, accesses the resources made available to him in a uniform manner. Which programs are on which servers within the domain is a matter of no importance to him. He identifies himself to the domain with a user number and a password. These are again components of the domain. The user with system administrator rights defines the user numbers, assigns passwords and allocates resources and access rights to individual users or user groups.

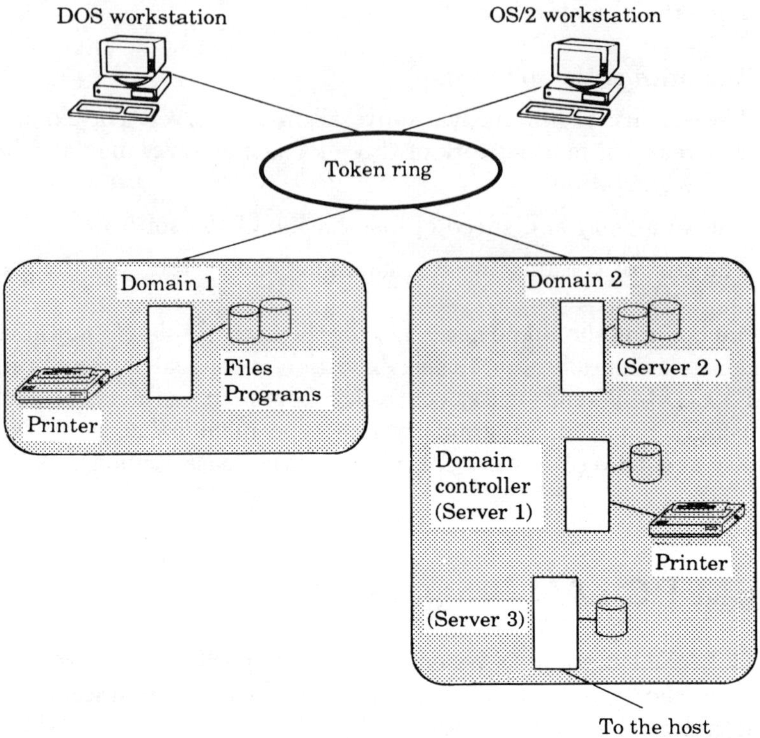

Figure 5.2 Domains.

Several domains may be defined within a LAN. Thus, names which are allocated within a domain must be unique in the LAN as a whole. The name of the domain must be the same as that of the domain controller (Figure 5.2).

A chosen user, the system administrator, is responsible for the management of the domains and their resources. Only he has direct access to all the functions of the domain controller and only he manages the network. His tasks include:

- Installation of the programs on the servers.
- Definition of the domains and their management, including the allocation of user IDs and passwords.
- Definition of resources allocated to users.
- Definition of additional servers in the domain.
- Definition of RIPL (Remote Initial Program Load) servers over which

diskless systems may load their operating systems.

- Allocation of user access rights to file sets.

Using his authorized number, the system administrator is able to manage the domains from any workstation.

Users may login to the domain using the user number and password assigned by the system administrator. The domain controller then constructs the system environment specified by the system administrator, which is specially tailored to the needs of the user. After a successful Logon to the system, the user is faced with a screen menu from which he may select an application, including a number of PC LAN functions such as display and selection of current disk and printer allocations.

Which network functions are implemented on the workstation and which on the server depends on the nature of the generation of the workstation software and its configuration. If the workstation has a disk the menus are stored on the workstation's disk; if the station only has a floppy disk drive the menus are loaded over the LAN by the server. In the case of a diskless workstation, as previously mentioned, the operating system is also loaded by the server. This controlled loading of the workstation by a central RIPL server means, amongst other things, that the workstation set up is continuously controllable and that all attached stations have the same software. Thus, software modifications may be implemented centrally and uniformly.

Requirements on the workstation network card include a special additional boot ROM which diverts the procedure of loading the PC operating system via the server.

This form of workstation is increasingly popular. Not only does it ensure the presence of uniform software across the network, but it also prevents viruses, gremlins and bugs from being slipped into the system accidentally or on purpose by users and prevents illegal copying of programs or data. Thus, it is ideal for banks, insurance companies and security-related areas where intelligent workstations are necessary or desirable and where there should be no additional input/output devices.

Even in Germany, so-called LAN stations are increasingly available. Here, the Token Ring card is already built in. This type of LAN station comes with a colour display and at least 2 Mbytes of main memory (extendable to 4 to 16 Mbytes) as standard.

Returning to the management of resources in the LAN, we distinguish between internal and external resources of the LAN. Internal resources are defined, managed and used within the domain. These include programs, files and printers, amongst other things. External resources may be either defined within a domain and used from outside or made available in other domains or servers and used by the users of the local domain.

After the Logon each user is presented with his own menu which is predefined by the system manager and may be added to by the user to include private applications. The following functions are predefined by the system and the system manager:

Logoff ends the network session.

PCLP provides access to the functions of the network software.

OLR is the Online Reference Manual.

Overview provides an overview of the most important LAN functions.

Adminsrv Printdd is only available to users with administrator rights.

DOS allows DOS commands to be entered. EXIT should be used to return to the main menu.

Lanmsg calls the Base Services Messages function.

xyz is used for user entries.

After a user exits from the system using Logoff the next user must log on again before he can use the workstation PC. Additional functions are often built into the Logoff function by the system manager (for example, the automatic saving of user files or the closure of any open resident DOS applications which the user has forgotten to close). We shall not go further into the individual security functions and access-protection mechanisms at this point; these will be explained in more detail in our discussion of the OS/2 LAN Server (Section 5.4).

For larger installations in which several PCs access a single shared server, it is advisable to modify the default parameters for starting up the server software together with the corresponding parameters in the CONFIG.SYS file. The number of buffers in the server which DOS uses for disk access should be set to be as high as possible. The storage requirement varies between around 55 kbytes (simple workstation with no auxiliary functions) and up to 350 kbytes (server). Every server may carry out network management functions within a certain area. IBM's PC LAN Support Program (or compatible) is a prerequisite for use of the software.

5.4 OS/2 Extended Edition and OS/2 LAN Server

IBM's OS/2 Extended Edition contains the database manager and the communications manager which are not in the standard version.

The database manager, which conforms to SAA, works with an SQL interface and has conversion facilities for existing databases (Lotus, dBase). The IBM OS/2 database manager is compatible with the database interface of the mainframe.

The communications manager provides all the necessary communications interfaces for OS/2. A basic system with a communications manager and a database manager requires at least 6 Mbytes of main memory. The memory requirement is composed as follows (base OS/2 version 1.2)

OS/2 including DOS	
Compatibility box	2.9 Mbytes
Communications manager, basic system	0.1 Mbytes
3270 emulation (DFT)	0.3 Mbytes
3270 host print	0.3 Mbytes
File transfer	0.3 Mbytes
APPC	0.4 Mbytes
Database manager	1.8 Mbytes
Query manager	1.6 Mbytes
LAN requester	0.4 Mbytes
Total	8.1 Mbytes

Without a database, but with an SNA gateway, the requirement is still 4.8 Mbytes.

In general, the following recommendations should be followed:

- If possible the requester should not occupy less than 5 Mbytes.
- If possible the server should not occupy less than 8 Mbytes.

The communications manager contains the following as standard:

- Asynchronous communications interfaces
- 3270 emulation, including printer support
- IBM 5250 support
- APPC interface
- X.25 SNA support
- LAN support for IBM LANs and Ethernet LANs (Etherand)
- Gateway support

It does not contain the additional hardware which may be required.

It is only sensible to install the communications manager in its menu-driven form. This may optionally take place when the overall system is installed or is easy to carry out subsequently. OS/2 automatically sets up all the necessary directories and checks them for completeness. There are standard configuration files which facilitate system-specific configuration of the system. This is carried out by the system manager who enters the user-related and system-dependent parameters and transmits them to all other systems. Active features of the communications manager may be displayed and modified at any time. Errors on connection establishment or during the connection itself are automatically notified (including installation errors).

The 3270 emulation under OS/2 enables the user to establish up to ten simultaneous sessions (using the Distributed Function Terminal function). File transfer is menu driven or may also be possible from the OS/2 session. When SRPI is required it must be separately generated and connected. It uses 300 kbytes of memory. The PC keyboard is adaptable to the national language. Unfortunately, APL is not yet supported, instead drivers for IBM graphics software (GDDM) are also provided under OS/2.

The gateway functions under OS/2 are very distinctive. Up to 255 LUs may be defined per gateway. Of these 64 may be active at any one time. Seen from the mainframe, the gateway behaves like a PU 2 with up to 255 LUs (1, 2, 3, 6.2). Seen from the workstation, the gateway is transparent and behaves like a front-end processor on the host. LUs may be assigned to groups and pooled. If desired, links which have not been active within a preset time interval may be immediately cleared down automatically by the gateway, thereby freeing resources for other users (Figure 5.3).

OS/2 workstations attached to Ethernet LANs are also supported by the gateway software. A prerequisite for this is that the PCs incorporate Ethernet cards which are supported by IBM (3Com, Ungermann Bass, Western Digital). As the figure clearly shows, which IBM software is used in Token Ring is unimportant to the gateway. It is 'IBM transparent' in the truest sense.

IBM also supports the asynchronous VT100 and IBM 3101 terminal emulation under OS/2. Only one of three possible links may be active at any time. In this case, file transfer is also possible via IBM-compatible protocol converters under TSO or CMS and via the X-Modem protocol (fixed block length of 128 bytes). Dedicated and switched links are supported with speeds between 300 bps and 9600 bps.

Under OS/2, five programmer interfaces are supported for applications development:

- 802.2 (LLC)
- NetBios
- ACDI
- APPC
- SRPI

The LLC or 802.2 interface has been taken over practically unaltered.

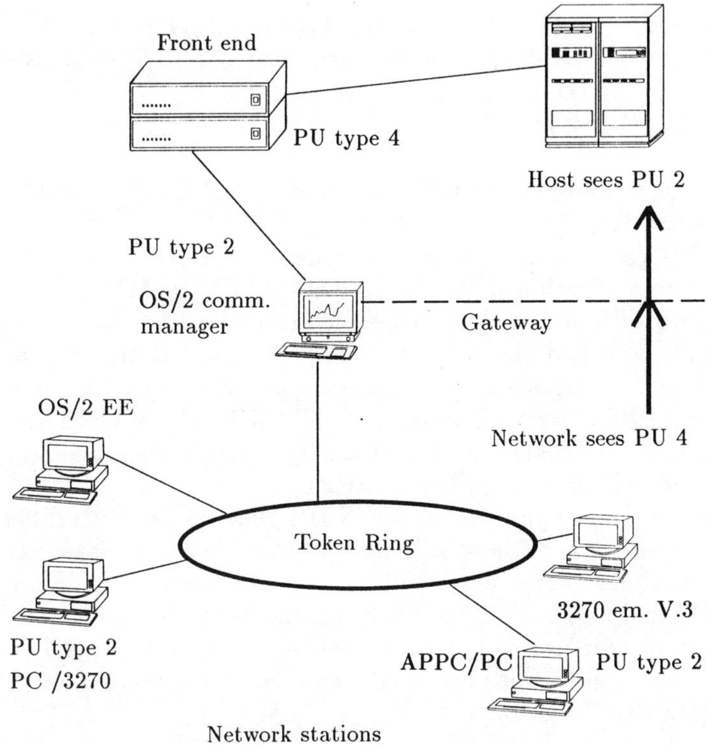

Figure 5.3 SNA gateway.

According to the adaptor type, up to 254 so-called link stations are supported per adaptor. The interface is called under OS/2 using CALL and not using the DOS INT 5C function.

ACDI (Asynchronous Common Device Interface) is only available under OS/2. ACDI may be used by several applications at the same time. It may also be used as the basis for developing one's own terminal emulation. ACDI is device independent.

The OS/2 EE implementation APPC is based on the SNA LU 6.2 rules.

- Several transaction programs may share an LU.
- Several parallel sessions may be established between two partner LUs.
- The session management and the data-flow control can only be carried out by the LU.

- APPC applications do not require 3270 emulation and thus do not require an IBM host in the network.
- According to the LU 6.2 rules, links may also be established between two PCs or workstations, provided that one partner is able to carry out the functions of the mainframe SSCP (System Services Control Point) (PU 2.1).

The dynamic link libraries APPC.DLL and ACSSVC.DLL are prerequisites for the use of APPC.

SRPI (Server Requester Programming Interface) is normally only used for communication between IBM hosts (VM or MVS/XA) and IBM PCs. The server function is implemented on the host and the corresponding PC program is called the requester. This interface is still the most user-friendly interface between mainframes and PCs; however, it is not as flexible as APPC. Every program can call SRPI. If two or more requester programs use the SEND_REQUEST verb simultaneously the requests will be processed one after the other by SRPI.

If concurrent applications over SRPI place requests via different 3270 links at the same time, these will also be processed at the same time. IBM ECF (Enhanced Connection Facilities) is available as an add-on for VM, MVS, DOS and OS/2. This relatively expensive product, which is based on SRPI, provides for use of the /370 host as server in the LAN, automatic control of host applications by the PC and automatic conversion of host file formats into PC file formats.

5.5 OS/2 LAN Manager

Microsoft, the developer of DOS and OS/2, produces the LAN Manager for OS/2. This LAN Manager is a standalone entity, the first versions of which were very different from the competitor product IBM's OS/2 LAN Server. In the meantime, there has been an alignment of the two systems so that they now differ primarily only in their communications interfaces (to IBM's SAA world). OS/2 LAN Manager products are supplied by 3Com, Ungermann Bass, Siemens, etc. These products differ in terms of the available add-on products and other interfaces and the aids to integration into the appropriate manufacturer world. However, the basis for all the products is the same and is described in brief below.

Like the network program under DOS, the OS/2 LAN Manager supports the shared use of the disks and printers which are attached to the server. Unlike the DOS network software, the OS/2 LAN Manager uses the multitasking facility and the extended memory area which is available under OS/2. Up to 12 tasks may be executed simultaneously. The server becomes a multi-functional system for all attached systems. The window surface of the presentation manager also helps when serving unpractised users. Functionally, the server in the LAN is a competitor to DP systems based on office computers.

This is also shown by the general trend towards increasing networking of PCs in professional environments. Already around 15% of all PCs and workstations are attached to LANs. In the future, it is thought that up to 50% will be integrated into LANs.

Amongst the greatest advantages which the OS/2 LAN Manager offers the user and the software developer are the new facilities for user communication and information exchange between processes which may run in a distributed fashion in the LAN. Two basic mechanisms are available: named pipes and mail slots.

Named pipes are principally used for remote interprocess communication. Named pipes permit simplex and duplex communication and extend the functions of normal pipes under OS/2 in that they may be used both locally and remotely. Unnamed pipes are already known in DOS, but only in relation to the local environment. They may be used, for example, to divert a normal command such as DIR (list the directory entries on the screen) into another program and store the result in a file.

The command DIR|SORT> HUGO.DAT has the effect that the output from the DIR command is stored in sorted form in the file HUGO.DAT.

Named Pipes have unique names in the network. Their names are assigned when they are generated. With the introduction of named pipes into OS/2 it is now possible to access the computer resources over a standard interface, regardless of whether they are installed on the local computer (the workstation), on the server or distributed across both these computers simultaneously. Use of this interface alone for applications development permits uniform program development. It no longer makes any difference whether an application program is stored on a workstation or on the server or is distributed across both systems.

Thus, named pipes are ideal for constructing the known client–server applications in the LAN. Database applications with the server as back end and the client as front end are easy to implement, particularly when a common language, SQL, is used for access to the server. The procedure to search for a given data record (passing of the search criteria to the server, receipt of the results) may now be implemented using named pipes.

'Threads' are used in OS/2 to grant several clients simultaneous access to the server; they may be used to parallelize operations within a single process. For this, a predefined number of named pipes of the same name are created and made available in the server. The next free area of the named pipe is now always assigned to the front-end process. Thus, this gives the user the impression that the data is processed in a quasi-parallel fashion on the server. The actual area assigned is unimportant to the applications developer since the assignment is automatic.

NetBios and the so-called mail slots provide other facilities for interprocess communication. NetBios, which we have already met, is the interface from the DOS environment. It is very network dependent but also very user-friendly and transfers data at enormous speeds.

Mail slots on the other hand provide a very simple means of distributing short messages in the network. Mail slots operate in connectionless mode, are unidirectional and have no security mechanisms. They may be compared with datagrams. If necessary, mail slots may also be acknowledged, following the procedure for recorded delivery letters, in which the recipient must acknowledge receipt. This does not by any means imply that the information is actually processed again. Mail slots are ideal for transmitting messages to groups or to all attached subscribers (broadcasting).

Let us consider the specific example of the IBM OS/2 LAN Server which should be by far the most common product.

IBM's OS/2 LAN Server is based on two independent software packages. One package contains the so-called requester function (workstation functions) which is included in OS/2 EE and the other package (which must be ordered separately) contains the server functions and uses OS/2 EE as a basis. One major difference from the PC LAN functions under DOS is already apparent, since in the latter case the PC LAN programs must be bought for and installed on all the systems including the workstation.

The server need not be dedicated. For example, it is sensible when the server is not heavily used to install the OS/2 LAN Manager on the system as well. In most cases, additional use of the server as a workstation is not advisable for security reasons and since the performance may be affected. Service errors in this workstation/server combination may in certain circumstances result in the blocking of all the stations in the LAN. As in the case of the PC LAN Program, servers may, if required, be combined into a logical system, the domain. As before, the system administrator (ADMIN) defines users and user groups, usable disk areas for users, network applications and printer queues together with terminals with asynchronous interfaces which may be accessed by appropriately authorized users or user groups. Every user may login to the overall system from any workstation in the network. If prescribed by the administrator, the user must also enter a password which he may change himself. Should a user forget a password only the administrator is able to read or change it. Overall the user management, with the presentation manager surface, is considerably more user-friendly than under DOS.

The OS/2 LAN Server may also be used from DOS workstations. From version 1.2 of the LAN Server, the PC LAN Program is no longer needed for this. The DOS Requester and the IBM LAN Support Program are delivered with the server program. Most LAN Server functions and commands are also available under DOS, with minor exceptions. Thus, for example, users of DOS workstations cannot themselves execute a program on the server (batch processing). Terminals which are serially connected to the server cannot be accessed (except for printers with serial interfaces) and Ethernet LANs are not supported (in our view this is an advantage rather than a disadvantage).

The LAN API is also available to DOS users (although there are restrictions in comparison with OS/2 workstations) for the development of distributed applications in the LAN. From LAN Server version 1.2, this includes the possibility of interprocess communication via named pipes and mail slots, various network management functions and additional network utilities and data-protection mechanisms (such as password encryption). The LAN API may be called from the popular programming languages and permits automation of many procedures from automatic logging in to the application on the server to automatic data transfer according to predefined options.

The network itself and its functions are started up manually or automatically (using API) using the network start commands, for example:

- Net Start Workstation (computer name)
- Net Start Server (computer name)
- Net Start Netrun
- Net Start Alerter

A user attached to an OS/2 LAN Server also has access to older servers or to DOS servers, when the entries here are treated as EXTERNAL resources in the server. This ensures that migration is possible.

The administrator defines:

- which network applications may be used by which user (start-up menu),
- the allocation of network disks and directories,
- the assignment of printers,
- the assignment of terminals to serial interfaces.

The OS/2 LAN Server has distinctive access-protection mechanisms. The following may be protected:

- individual files or groups of files,
- application programs,
- access to printer queues,
- access to serial terminals,
- access to external resources.

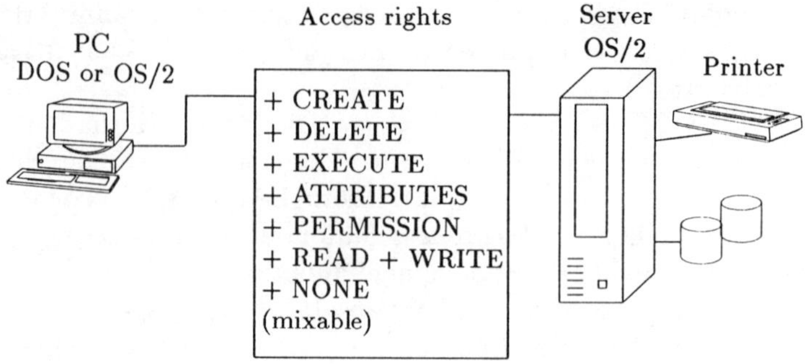

Figure 5.4 Access facilities in the OS/2 LAN Server.

Users may be combined into user groups in which they are easier to manage. In addition to the user profiles, the administrator also defines the profiles for each application on the server.

The protection mechanisms for the LAN Server provide for different access rights to its files and groups of its files which may be combined together. Access rights are allocated on a per user, per group and global basis (Figure 5.4).

If a user's authorization level is not specified, the user has no access to the corresponding resource. Files may be protected in such a way that they cannot be copied by the user; this is not unimportant as far as the licensing rights for software on the server are concerned. The OS/2 LAN Server itself can manage up to 8000 files simultaneously. This does not restrict even large database applications.

A number of facilities for network monitoring are available. If required, all accesses in the LAN can be logged. Every access from a workstation with a false user number or false password is automatically recorded together with the time.

Processes which may be started automatically on the server may be used, for example, for automatic back up of the disk. The process or program may be time controlled and activated at fixed intervals (for example, every night at 0.00 hours for witching-hour back up to erasable CD).

Several printers are supported in parallel. The printer assignment may be automatic or manual. Each user may inspect and influence the printer queue in respect of his own print jobs. The administrator has special rights and can modify all outstanding print requests. The user is notified when a print request is executed or when a printer error occurs.

Printers may be combined into groups (by the administrator) so as to improve the distribution of the load. A single print queue may serve several printers or several print queues may serve a single printer (for example,

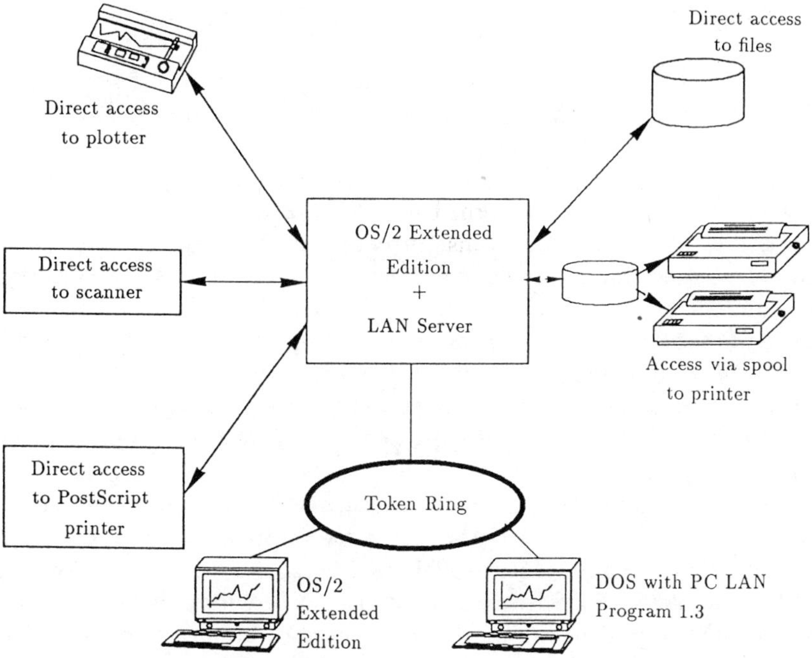

Figure 5.5 A typical OS/2 LAN Server environment.

when the printer has to be preloaded with different fonts, paper types, etc.), according to requirements.

Direct access to serial or parallel interfaces provides for access to systems such as digitizers, high-performance plotters, scanners, etc. attached to the server, under the control of each application program and without spooling (Figure 5.5).

The LAN API may also be used to automate or control access to serial terminals. Several similar terminals may be combined into a pool and jointly managed, so that a number of applications may have simultaneous access to terminals in the pool via queues. The following API calls may be used to control serial terminals via an application program:

- List all available devices in a pool.
- List all device pools.
- Request information about special devices.
- Delete unexecuted commands in a queue.
- Change the state of a queue on the server.
- Delete requester requests which for some reason have not been executed in full.

- Stop a device when it is being used by an application.

We shall not discuss other functions of the OS/2 LAN Server here (see IBM OS/2 Extended Edition Version 1.2 Cookbook). The table in Table 5.1 lists the most important commands.

All in all, the OS/2 LAN Server from Microsoft and IBM is an almost perfect network operating system. Under OS/2 with the LAN Server, it is now possible to execute programs directly on the server and to define a tiered access mechanism for access to the individual files. The definition of several queues per terminal and the assignment of several terminals to one queue facilitates user access to these devices and increases the throughput. The presentation manager simplifies the operation of the system and at last provides for a sensible representation of several processes on the screen, similar to the facility which has now been available from Apple and Xerox for some years.

The forthcoming months and years will show whether this leap forward will be sufficient or whether competition from Novell and UNIX will again leave OS/2 behind. Microsoft is assuming the further development of OS/2 for the 80386/80486 processor and also provides the LAN Manager for the UNIX operating system. The chances of gaining a greater market share of this promising future market are not slim. But the battle is not yet fought. Sun, Locus, AT&T and even IBM and co. are continually extending their network functions under UNIX both downwards (to DOS, OS/2) and upwards (IBM SAA, DECnet, ISO/OSI networking, etc.). As major network manufacturers, Novell and Banyan ensure that the user will still be spoilt for choice in the DOS, OS/2 and UNIX areas. Thus, we shall now give a brief description of the two network operating systems.

5.6 Novell NetWare for DOS, VMS, UNIX and OS/2

Novell NetWare was one of the first true network operating systems. It was developed as a file server operating system and since its introduction in 1983 it can point to over a million users who are now connected to around 150 000 NetWare file servers. In 1990, its market share in the USA was at least 70%. Its multiuser and multitasking architecture enables the system to process various requests from workstations simultaneously and to support several different operating systems.

In the NetWare system the file server manages the shared resources and coordinates the network activities. Depending on the version of the operating system the server may be used as a workstation (not dedicated) or simply as the network controller (dedicated). The operating systems of all other workstations (for example, OS/2, Macintosh OS, MS-DOS

Table 5.1 Commands.

OS/2 LAN Server	*Command functions*
AT	Execution of time-controlled tasks
Net	Call the start-up or main menu
Net Admin	Execution of administrator commands on the server
Net Audit	Display/delete audit trail
Net Comm	Control device queues in the LAN
Net Config	Control/alter configuration parameters of a workstation or server
Net Continue	Continue interrupted function
Net Copy	Copy files from LAN Server
Net Device	Control/display status of terminals
Net Error	Display/delete error indications
Net File	Display status of server files and close these files
Net Forward	Forward messages to another user
Net Help	Clarification of network commands
Net Log	Display messages in the network log
Net Logon	User log in to a domain
Net Logoff	User log out of a domain
Net Move	Move a file on the LAN Server
Net Name	Display names/messages
Net Pause	Interrupt server, workstation or other functions
Net Print	Display server print queues
Net Run	Execute a program in the server memory
Net Send	Send messages
Net Separator	Definition of a cover page for print jobs
Net Session	Display/close user sessions
Net Share	Make drivers, printers or other devices available on the server
Net Start	Start up specific network services (server, receiver, etc.)
Net Stats	Display network statistics
Net Status	Display resources made available by the server and configuration parameters
Net Stop	Stop servers, workstations or other services
Net Use	Use network resources
Net View	Display network servers and resources

or Windows /386) are extended by the so-called NetWare shell, which, depending on the operating system and the LAN adaptor, requires between 50 kbytes and 100 kbytes of main memory.

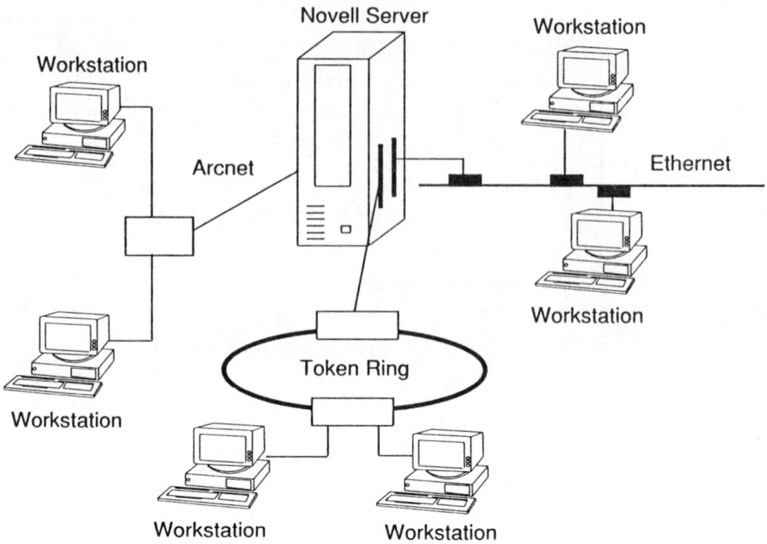

Figure 5.6 Novell server as a bridge.

Unlike the IBM products, NetWare is designed to be a hardware-independent operating system. There are corresponding network drivers for various network cards. Currently, about 80 different manufacturers of network hardware support the Novell operating system. Thus, the user may choose from a range of networks with various physical characteristics, covering the whole gamut of speeds, cable types, maximum distances, security levels and structural possibilities. Almost all manufacturers supply Novell drivers for their network cards. Several network cards may be incorporated per server. These cards need not come from the same manufacturer and may even use different LAN protocols (Figure 5.6). NetWare now supports five interfaces for the network and application software. These bridges reside at different levels of the ISO seven-layer model; three of them are special NetWare interfaces:

IPX (Internetwork Packet Exchange Protocol) is located at level 3 and permits direct addressing from the application. IPX does not guarantee error-free transmission of packets, which must be provided for at a higher level. It is fully supported on all LAN topologies which run under Advanced NetWare V2.0 or higher.

SPX (Sequenced Packet Exchange Protocol) is located at level 4 of the ISO model. SPX provides mechanisms to check for error-free communication. It falls back on the simple send and receive properties of IPX.

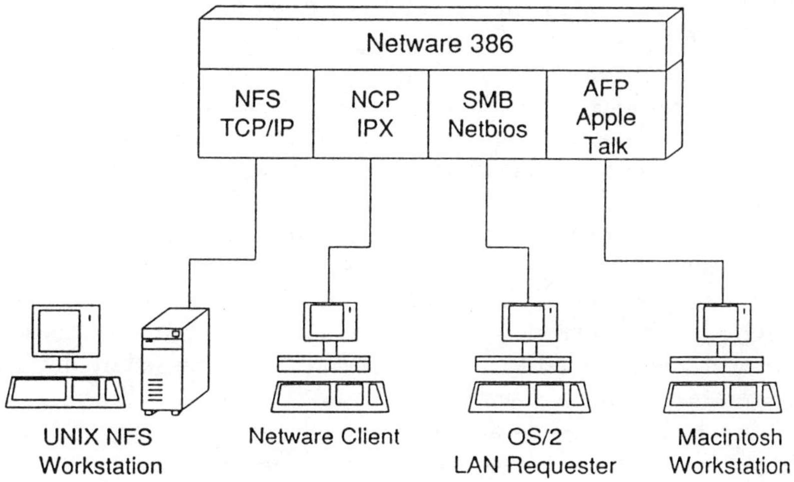

Figure 5.7 NetWare 386.

The NetWare shell corresponds to layer 6 of the ISO/OSI model and is an extension of the functions present under DOS. The shell handles access requests to fixed disks which are not located on the workstation together with all commands unknown to DOS. It forwards these via the network card to the file server for further processing.

Naturally, the standard LAN interface NetBios is also supported by Novell. Novell provides a NetBios emulator which enables one to use all the software and hardware developed for the network IBM PCs and Token Ring under NetWare. Thus, in Token Ring, workstations may, if necessary, access a Novell server and an OS/2 server simultaneously.

NetWare also supports TCP/IP and NFS, and allows workstations on the Novell network to access end systems which use TCP/IP for communication. Conversely, it also allows TCP/IP workstations to access the Novell server (Figure 5.7). As Figure 5.7 shows, more recent versions of NetWare also support Apple systems.

The NetWare operating system is available at several different configuration levels. The cheaper ELS NetWare (Entry Level Solution) is suitable for small PC networks. Up to eight users may access a server, which need not be dedicated. The user surface is the same as in the versions for larger networks. Advanced NetWare versions 2.x are suitable for networks with up to 100 workstations per server. Up to 3 Gbytes disk capacity per server is supported. From Version 3, it is virtually impossible to make better use of Intel 80386/80486 processors, since the operating system, unlike the previous OS/2 versions, makes full use of the features of these processors to improve performance. These versions support up to 250 users per server, up to 4 Gbytes main memory and up to 32 Tbytes disk capacity. Thus, a Token Ring with a fast, well-built 486 server is more than capable of replacing a medium-to-large DP system.

These versions are available with or without Novell's SFT (System Fault Tolerant), a considerably extended add-on which guarantees the data integrity in the network and thus provides an alternative to the security mechanisms in mainframes.

SFT provides schemes and techniques for resolving the most common sources of error in DP systems and LAN servers including outage of the shared storage media due to disk error, outage of the disk controller and ultimately the total breakdown of a server. First of all the directory and file assignment tables, the most commonly used parts of a disk, are duplicated. SFT generates two file assignment tables (FATs) and two directory entries for a disk, which it stores on different disk cylinders. A consistency check of the directories when the server is switched on ensures that they are correct and available. A disk write is followed by a read access to the same point to ensure that the information has been correctly stored. Thus, disk errors are detected and corrected as quickly as possible.

Data security mechanisms may be increased if several disks and disk controllers are built into the system. Disks and controllers may be shadowed; in other words, information is simultaneously written to two physically separate disks over different access paths. At any given time the two disks contain the same information and one disk is a mirror image of the other. If now a disk or a controller breaks down due to a defect this has no effect on the operation of the server. The users may carry on working unhindered and the defective disk may be exchanged at a convenient moment and updated. The presence of two disks with identical contents is also used to improve read access to the data. Since disk reads do not alter any information, simultaneous read access by several applications may be optimized. For read access the software picks up the disk with head nearest to the data position.

In database applications the so-called Transaction Tracking System (TTS) may be used to combine all the individual steps needed to modify a database into a single logical transaction, as a feature of the operating system. Transactions are always executed in full; faulty transactions are always automatically resolved (even in the case of system breakdown). The dreaded undefinable state of a transaction, in which some parts of a database have been altered and others have not, may thus be almost ruled out. Provision can even be made for power failures. So-called interruption-free emergency power supplies, specially designed for Novell operating systems, are now available from various manufacturers. If there is a power cut, depending on the system, operation may continue for up to 2 hours and the system is automatically taken down so that all files are correctly closed and data integrity is preserved.

From version 3 of this network operating system, these functions are contained as standard. From version 3.1, it is possible to shadow a whole server in the LAN. Two completely separate systems may be operated as mirror images. The probability of an outage is reduced even further. This provides for a level of reliability that is only otherwise achieved in expensive systems (for example, TANDEM).

All SFT functions are automatic and do not impair the normal operation of the network. Menu-driven service programs for the service manager are used to maintain and control the network. In the latest versions, provision is made for the menus to be linked in via a windows surface. It is possible to manage the server from any workstation (supervisor function). Directories or files which are not required by users or user groups are not made visible to them, according to the Lord's prayer 'lead us not into temptation'.

As in the case of the OS/2 LAN Server, there is a tiered access mechanism which protects individual directories against access from users or user groups. The possible restrictions on the access rights are more flexible than in the case of the LAN Server/Manager and may be applied to individual files.

Even the network access facilities available to a user (namely, when and at which workstations he may work in the network) may be specified precisely by the supervisor. Jokers must already have made a fool of their network administrator by only allowing him access to a particularly inconvenient workstation on Sunday mornings between 2 and 3 o'clock. Thus, the supervisor's password should, if possible, only be known to the administrator, since only he can make changes to the configuration of the network. It is in one's own interests to activate the facilities provided for and compel users to choose passwords of at least N characters which should be changed every X days.

The generation of special profiles for the user permits direct user command even in the application itself. For the user the network is non-existent. Novell functions are invisible to him. The file structures needed for his applications are automatically allocated.

Services provided by the server may be accounted for with Novell as for mainframes. Every individual service (for example, access to a file on the server) has a particular cost. The user is given an account of points with which to pay for services. Quotas are imposed on the server disk space. Every individual user has an overall view of his available disk quota and the proportion of it which is unused.

It is particularly worth noting that printers need not be attached to the server for them to be used by workstations in Token Ring. Every printer in the network, including those on workstations, may be managed centrally by the server. This means that the installation of printers is more flexible. Printer interfaces are supplied for well-known printers. Even DEC systems may be used as servers (compare ECF, 3Com) under VMS. In our opinion, this is only advisable when another DEC system is available which is also to be used for this task.

Novell offers a variety of additional gateway server functions. Internal or external servers which communicate with the main frame using

- switched, dedicated, ISDN or multidrop lines,
- transmission rates of from 1200 bps to 64000 bps,
- BSC, MSV, SNA/SDLC or ISO protocols,

are all possible in a Novell environment. Novell also supports direct connection of Token Ring to the IBM channel via a local controller or front-end processor.

Anyone who is not attached to the LAN may use the network services from outside via the public network without restrictions. This requires a special server in the LAN based on an 80386 processor. The PCs dial up this gateway. After verification (possibly more than entry of the password and the telephone number) communication with the server is established. To ensure reasonable response times over these slow lines essentially only the keyboard and the screen of the PC are used. The processor of the external PC is simulated in the gateway PC (the 80386 processor has the ability to emulate several 8086 processors). Up to 12 simultaneous links may be supported.

Novell also offers considerably more functions and add-on products than can be described here. For example, there is a database (Btrieve) which amongst other useful add-on products also contains the (almost) complete user manual. Add-on products may be linked into the server software as NLMs (network loadable modules). However, we have described the most important functions of the operating system briefly, to give an impression of the capabilities of the system. NetWare's strength lies not in its operating system but in the hundreds of add-on products and applications produced by software houses for the NetWare environment. Everything is available from programs for general practitioners, bakers, chemical laboratories, tilers, to programs for customer management, store management, contract management, order management, including the much-loved software to explain taxation and programs for dental surgeons. If only for this reason NetWare will not be quickly driven out of its leading position by the OS/2 LAN Manager or by UNIX with NFS.

5.7 Banyan Vines

Banyan Vines plays a special role. This network operating system originally required a Banyan UNIX machine (Motorola processor) as server, but now operates with Intel processors. Vines stands for Virtual Network

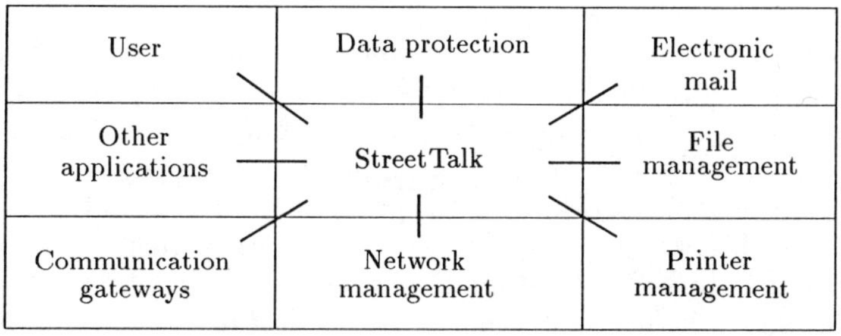

Figure 5.8 Structure of Vines.

operating system. It supports most network applications which use NetBios or TCP/IP as interfaces. Vines is above all suitable for companies which maintain several networks in different cities or countries and wish to operate these as a single logical network. For this Vines uses a distributed directory system StreetTalk which forms the basis of the Vines architecture. The Vines operating system is based on StreetTalk (Figure 5.8). StreetTalk is most easily described as a database which contains the description and location of every part of the network. This includes disks, files, printers, host gateways and also LAN users. Programs and users access this information in order to access the resources they require, without knowing where these are located in the network. What distinguishes Vines from other networks is not the database itself but its distribution across the whole network, which consists of several servers in different networks. Every server contains a part of StreetTalk. Every name used in StreetTalk which describes a user, a device or a network service consists of three parts: the object (user, printer, gateway, server, etc.), the group and the organization. For example, the following are normal StreetTalk names:

- HGG Göhring@CommunicationsEngineering@Company XYZ
- Printer1@CommunicationsEngineering@Company XYZ
- 370Gateway@Sales@Kauffels PLC

Groups describe logically related objects which are managed by a single server in the network. The detailed information about the group is also managed by this server. The detailed information about a user includes, for example, his encrypted password and his login profile (the latter ensures that the user always finds the same environment, whether he logs into the

Token Ring LAN in Bonn or into the same network in Sydney). To avoid the need to use one's full name when logging into the system or sending a message to someone, aliases may be used as shorthand. All the necessary definitions in the network may be menu driven.

StreetTalk always covers the whole network which may involve a large number of servers. The way in which the servers are interlinked is less important. Every possible connection method may be used (X.25, TCP/IP, dedicated lines, switched lines, etc.). As previously mentioned, every server contains part of the network (up to 25 groups). This information is uniquely available on this server. When a server receives a request for a service which it cannot provide it automatically forwards this request to the next correct server. The user does not need an 'attach or mount' command for this. Changes in the network (for example, the introduction of a new server or user) are automatically detected by the network and dynamically entered in the StreetTalk database without the need for intervention by the administrator. The user need not even know these names. StreetTalk has a menu system in which all the services which a user may request are entered.

As in other network operating systems, profiles are defined for each user which make the network appear transparent to that user. Unlike in other networks, these profiles are valid throughout the network without the need to define a resource as external (OS/2) and without the need for a guest logon (Novell).

The establishment of worldwide unified networks also requires uniform user interfaces. Thus, StreetTalk supports several languages (English, German, French, Italian) simultaneously in the network. Every user is served in his own language.

Thus, Vines is a suitable candidate for constructing and managing unified networks consisting of several LANs in different branches of a concern. All users everywhere login to their own environment to which they are accustomed and may access the same resources even when these are not in the same LAN.

5.8 Examples of programs with networking capabilities

At this point, a brief explanation of the expression 'program with networking capabilities' is required. There are very different interpretations of this expression. Most manufacturers interpret this in a different way to users, and problems are therefore often inevitable. Thus, we now describe the three most important distinguishing features:

(1) The standard method. The programs are not specially adapted. The programs are copied in full when called from the workstation and,

provided overlays are not being used, may only be used by a single user at a given time.

(2) Adapted program systems such as Word, WordPerfect and Harvard Graphics with few (at most about five) users. The adaptation consists of providing an individual working area for each user. The program is still copied in full over the network into the workstation memory.

(3) SQL database applications (client–server). For the first time, these applications make proper use of the LAN and the intelligence of the server. The workstation only sends commands (SQL) to the server which processes these sequentially according to their priority and authorization. Thus, the volume of data transferred in the LAN decreases drastically. Only what is actually required is transmitted. The server becomes a classical pseudo-host. The actual preparation, processing and representation of the data takes place independently on the workstation in the form desired by the user. The server software no longer has any influence on this. Thus, user surfaces may be individually tailored to the user. Almost all these applications use named pipes. Mailing (X.400) network software also operates according to this principle.

Chapter 6

Management and monitoring of networks

Only a few subareas of computer science and computer technology have undergone such massive development over recent years as the technologies of computer and system interconnection.

The interaction of computer science, telecommunications and messaging technology has been a catalyst for new forms of communication between digital information-processing devices, including, for example, high-speed data transfer over LANs and remote connection via satellite channels.

The network requirements are growing in at least two dimensions:

- The number of stations per network is permanently increasing.
- The logical complexity (functional level) of the functions to be performed by the network is increasing.

Moreover, there are additional problems associated with the connection of largely heterogeneous networks.

While the communications engineering side of networks is on the whole clear, in the area of operation-supporting functions there are uncertainties similar to those associated with the general formulation of the application-oriented aspects of computer networks.

In Section 6.1, after a basic analysis of the problem, we give a general introduction to the most modern network management schemes. Token Ring networks are currently principally used in IBM environments. Because of the broad distribution of compatible products it is appropriate to consider other network management architectures, since, in the future, Token Rings may also be used in conjunction with these. This is particularly true of FDDI. Section 6.2 is particularly concerned with management tools in the Token Ring network area.

6.1 Network management: problems and solutions

The logical complexity of network systems varies and ranges from terminal networks through server-oriented networks and open systems to distributed systems. In many cases one finds a confused mixture of differently organized subnetworks. The demands on the management of such network systems vary accordingly. However, there are certain commonalities.

The usual classification of networks according to the technical structure and the distances involved is only useful in the network management context when we are actually dealing with communications engineering resources. Above a functional layer such as layer 3 of the ISO reference model there is another logical function layer which takes into account the tasks of the network and the capabilities of the components.

For the classification of networks from the logical–function viewpoint

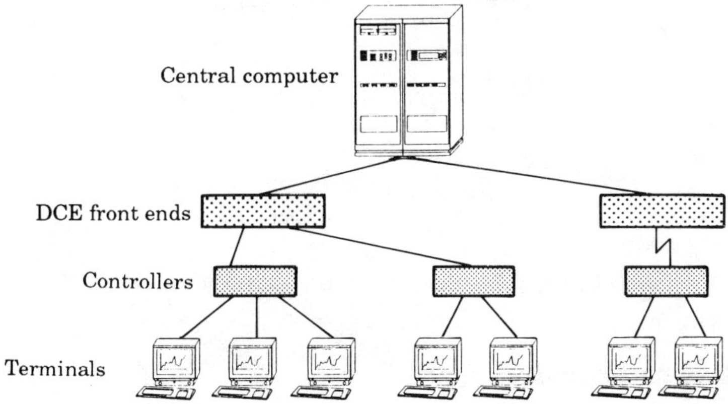

Figure 6.1 Class 1 network: terminal network.

we form four classes. This subdivision into classes is a mixture of statistics (which will be the most common system classes today and in the future?) and necessary didactics (how can one fight one's way through the various facets of the network management?) and represents a confused mix of functional and device-specific characteristics. Nevertheless, it appears to the authors to provide an appropriate cross-section.

Class 1: terminal networks

The network consists of a central computer, remote data-processing computers and terminal controllers together with the terminals and the hardware components which connect these components (lines, LANs, data switches); the control is central and the nodes have limited capabilities. Example: SNA network with one domain (Figure 6.1).

Class 2: server networks

Here, two groups of nodes (workstations and servers) are connected by a message transport system. Servers provide services which may be used by the workstations. All nodes have their own independent control: from a workstation viewpoint the cooperation with the server is controlled by the latter; there is no network control, however, a server may take on control tasks. Example: PC networks with NetWare (Figure 6.2)

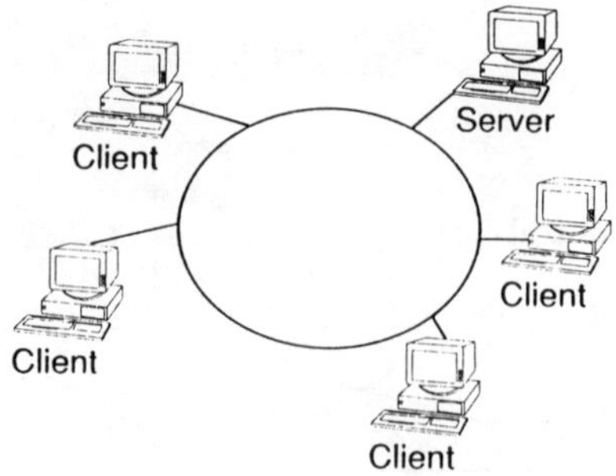

Figure 6.2 Class 2 network: server network.

Class 3: open systems

Computers may belong to these systems if they adhere to a set of hardware and software agreements, provided they are connected to the computers already in the system by a communication link. They may then use a range of services provided in the system and may also provide services. Users are normally connected to these computers indirectly via class 1 networks. Control of the individual nodes is carried out by the nodes themselves, while control of the network installations is in most cases carried out by a network operator. A user of a service is in the main subordinate to the control of the service provider. Example: DFN (Figure 6.3) or other research networks.

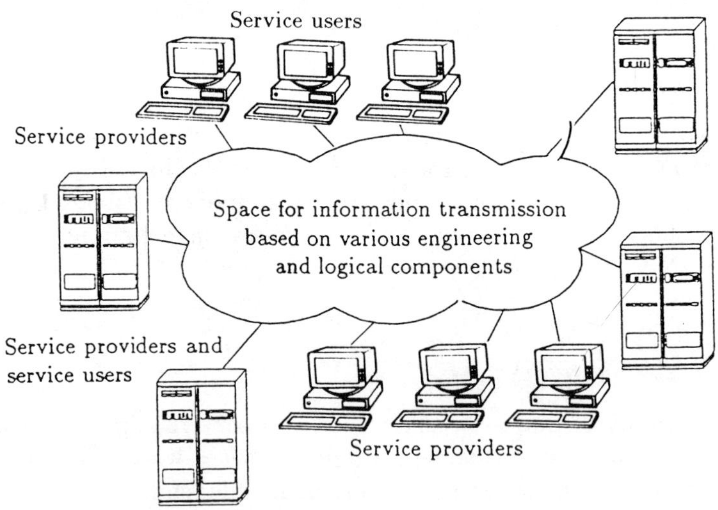

Figure 6.3 Class 3 network: open systems.

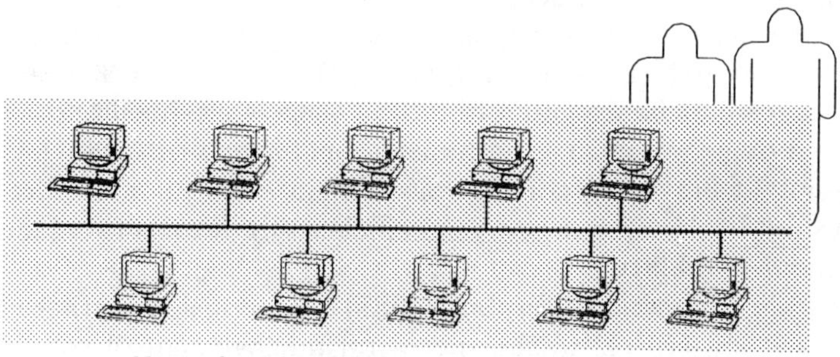

Network and computers fused into a unit
Distributed system transparent to the user

Figure 6.4 Class 4 network: distributed systems.

Class 4: distributed systems

A distributed system consists of a set of computers (nodes) and a system of connections which permits the exchange of messages between the points. The main characteristics of a distributed system are (Figure 6.4):

- Variety of components.
- Several processors.
- A system-wide operating system.
- Transparency.
- Distributed control based on the principle of cooperative autonomy.

In a real networked environment an increasing number of heterogeneous mixtures of the above classes will occur over a period time. For example, a system may begin as a class 1 network such as an SNA network with a single domain. With the introduction of Token Rings and PS/2 as end systems instead of terminal clusters a new class of systems will essentially be formed, namely that of class 1 networks with class 2 subsystems in the end area. The control of the previously pure class 1 network must adapt itself to this. Then, when someone thinks of an X.25 connection to permit access to an X.400 service, there will be a new class of system comprising class 1 networks with class 2 subsystems in the end system area in very large class 3 integrated networks. Finally, the core computer of the class 1 network might be replaced by a distributed system.

If one now concentrates on the management, there are commonalities between the classes and features specific to each class, and it may be assumed that in a mixture of two or more network types, the class-specific characteristics add together.

Firstly, we must describe the tasks of network management more exactly. If we consider the management of a networked system globally, there is a division into external and internal functions. The external functions are those which cannot be executed in full by the system itself and which must be executed by people such as administrators or repairmen, with the system itself playing at best a supporting role. The internal functions are executed by the system itself and guarantee its efficiency in terms of its functionality, reactions and reliability.

In this connection, Terplan (1987) also notes that there are three factors which are critical to the successful management of communication networks: methods, tools and human resources.

All three must be valued appropriately. The methods of network management depend very heavily on the network and its structure. However, they should not depend directly on the size of the network, since then the network manager encounters problems when the network grows.

For those who want to deny everything possible about networks, one thing they do with certainty is grow! Here, in Germany, networks are still comparatively small. Thus, we can take advantage of the fact that others before us (for example, in the United States) have already had to manage even larger networks. Nevertheless, one should not labour under false illusions: with the rapid advance of the personal computer a tenfold increase in the number of networked computers must be reckoned with in the next five years. This tenfold increase means that we can no longer 'manage by hand' as many today still believe.

Network management tools are also becoming more powerful. Where previously a network manager had to be content with a few terminals and consoles, he now has powerful systems available to him.

To a first approximation, there are five groups of network management functions for the currently existing communication networks with a more classical tree structure (see for example, Sloman (1984)):

- **Operational management** This describes the group of functions which are used in the operational area to prepare and manage the network resources.
- **Maintenance** This includes all functions which may be used for error prevention, error detection and error recovery in the network.
- **Configuration management** This incorporates utilities and functions for planning, extension and modification of the configuration and maintenance of the configuration information.
- **Performance management** This involves utilities and tools to measure and improve the network performance.

- **User administration** This group contains means of ensuring that the usage of the network is properly managed (including access management, control of usage, accounting utilities and information services).

As far as the general structure of computer network systems is concerned, the ISO reference model (DIN (1982), Effelsberg and Fleischmann (1986), Beyschlag (1988)) and the resulting standards provide a reference point for the status of the technology and form part of the development work.

Since, however, according to this, only protocols which are needed to control the exchange of information between systems are candidates for a standardization, only those management activities which imply an actual exchange of information between systems will be seen as belonging to the architectural framework. Other management activities which are local to a system will not be considered in this context.

Since such a division cannot always be uniquely drawn up (for example, the enforcement of a user authorization may be viewed as local to a system or network wide, according to the type of the network and the application), this standpoint is in many cases inappropriate to a closed consideration of the overall problem.

As far as Token Ring LANs are concerned, OSI network management, SNA network management and network management in TCP/IP environments are of particular interest.

6.1.1 OSI network management

The environment for an OSI protocol world and thus for the necessary management is becoming increasingly specific. The various common and special application service elements (CASEs and SASEs) support a distributed system environment. For this, they use protocols and service elements of layers 1–6. In the lower layers there is a large choice of alternative transmission technologies which may be used to create subnetworks with varied qualities, transmission speeds and costs.

Unlike in the case of previous proposals, the standardization bodies are now concentrating more specifically on the formulation of tasks and on the available aids.

The OSI protocol environment provides for direct communication and supports distributed execution environments. Every protocol layer has the ability to monitor and control an individual instance of a communication link (in other words, the interworking of the entities involved in the logical link). In time, this will lead to a requirement for an extended mechanism with the ability to observe, control and monitor all the OSI resources which provide the communication and execute auxiliary functions.

Another task for this mechanism is to create and maintain the boundary conditions for efficient communication (for example, flow control).

Working Group X3T5.4 of the American Standards Committee (ASC) is charged by ISO with the responsibility for developing the OSI management standards. Corresponding activities in other standardization bodies are coordinated by X3T5.4.

The conceptual management framework has reached the first step of international standardization.

6.1.1.1 Structure of the management framework

Together with the information processing, the management is viewed as the facility to plan, organize and control the resources which the user has available to meet his information-engineering needs.

One problem with this perspective is that 'the user' is not defined in any greater detail. There are very different users. They should at least be provided with mechanisms which are sufficiently powerful for them to make structural modifications in an information-processing environment.

The needs of the users are covered by the appropriate active and passive components and objects of the (possibly networked) system environment. Ideally, the physical implementations of the components are not apparent to the users and thus not liable to misuse or damage due to clumsiness.

In an OSI environment, a resource is also conceptually described as an OSI resource, which, at the end of the day, is an abstract object on which certain operations are specified. Examples of such resources include a generic electronic mailbox, a generic directory and a file description.

In most cases these operations have boundary conditions which are described by the protocols of the OSI layer containing the resource (this is usually layer 7, the application layer). One of the most important operations is the incarnation of a resource which, for example, generates a real system 'object' mailbox, tied to a user, from an abstract generic description of an electronic mailbox. It is clear that this generation process is a management function, while the emptying of a mailbox is a function which is carried out by a single user (or by a small number of authorized users) and mailing to a mailbox may be carried out by almost any user.

An incarnation of an OSI resource is an object. Such incarnations are also called entities in the standards documents. As already mentioned, this is nothing mysterious. OSI resources are only templates from which deductions about 'reality' are made. Logical links may also be described in this way. A management function is a sequence of parameterized operations on an object (Figure 6.5).

As far as the ISO reference model is concerned, there are three different management layers: protocol management, layer management and system management.

The protocol management consists of those protocol-internal mechanisms within one of the seven layers which are used to monitor a

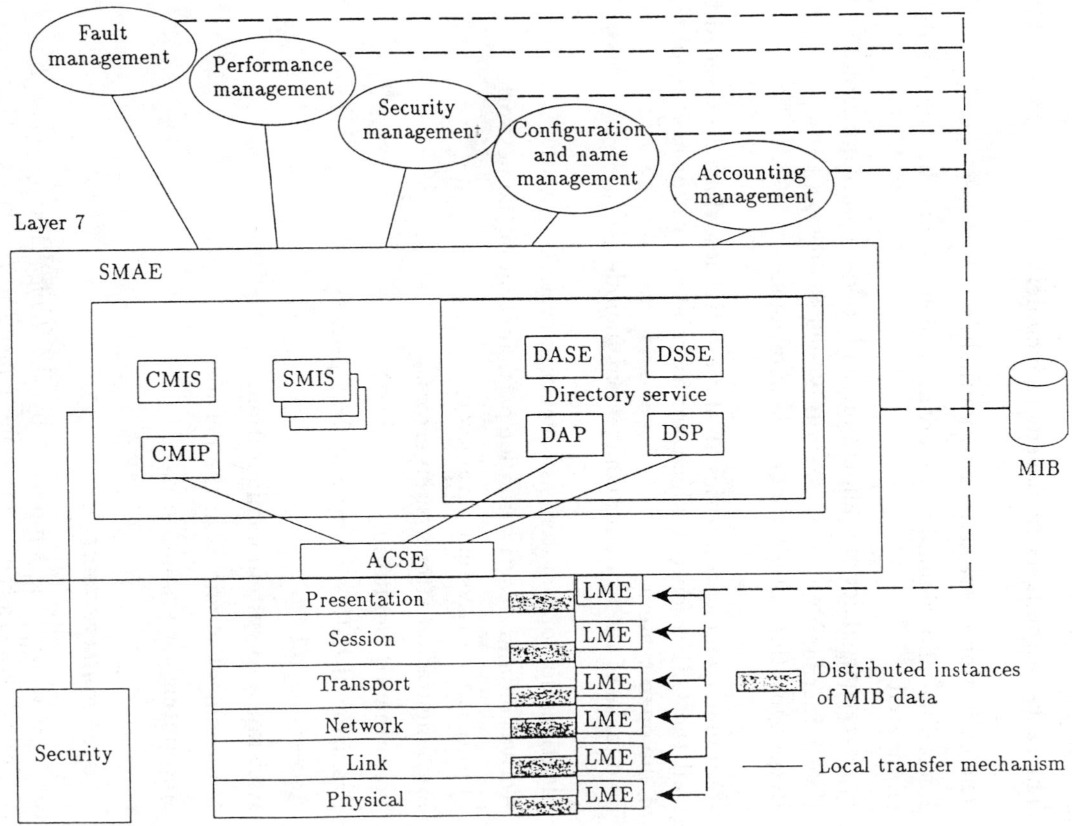

Figure 6.5 Layer management and layer management entities.

specific instance of a communications link. One example of this is flow control in various layers. The protocol management is specified and described in the standard for the protocol and services of each layer.

The layer management may concern various instances of communication links. It comprises all the activities which are needed to monitor all OSI resources belonging to a particular protocol layer (for example, routing in layer 3).

The tasks of the layer management include:

- The collection of statistics and journaling.
- Recording and signalling of errors which cannot be immediately eliminated.
- Registration, deletion, allocation and release of communications resources on behalf of the system management.
- Reconfiguration under abnormal conditions.

The system management comprises all those activities which are needed to manage all the OSI resources which are associated with one or all of the layers of the open system.

The tasks of the system management include:

- Identification of a system as a network system.
- Activation and deactivation for participation in the network.
- Maintenance of system parameters.
- Reconfiguration after system errors.
- Performance monitoring.
- Provision of data security and data protection.
- Access control.
- Assistance to system configuration.
- Management of names in the network.
- Accounting for system services.

6.1.1.2 Layer management

The layer management is supported by the *Layer Management Entities* (LMEs). The LMEs together control the *Layer Entities* (LEs). There is one LME per protocol layer, which has a view of this layer. The LME permits the observation of layer-specific information such as state variables, protocol operations, events (errors, thresholds, changes of state) and parameters for performance analysis. The LME provides a facility for loading protocol parameters and activating and controlling resources. An LME supports the layer-specific decision taking which may be based on the observation either of local components and parameters or of foreign LMEs belonging to other incarnations of this layer.

As conceived by the working group, the communication between LMEs in a specific layer should be executed using system management protocols of layer 7, which use all underlying layers. However, where not all seven layers are implemented a layer-specific management protocol may also be installed.

6.1.1.3 System management

The system management is supported by *System Management Applications Entities* (SMAEs) in layer 7. An SMAE is a 'tool box' of management services and protocols for exchanging management information between open systems. There is an SMAE for every incarnation of the seven protocol layers.

The SMAEs intercommunicate using system management protocols. X3T5.4 is currently developing a protocol specification and the associated service specification (Common Management Information Protocol, CMIP, and Common Management Information Services, CMIS). There is also a group of specific management information-passing services (SMISs) which relate to the following five areas of system management:

- Error management
- Performance management
- Security
- Configuration and name management
- Accounting

CMIP uses the services and protocols of the underlying protocol layers.

Decisions in the framework of an overall OSI system are taken by a set of centralized or distributed management processes. These processes are applications which lie above layer 7 and thus outside of the scope of the ISO reference model. This is a serious change from earlier OSI management proposals which led to major conflicts between the operating system tasks and communications subsystems control tasks, since layer 7 was assigned tasks for which it is actually not responsible.

The management processes receive their input from appropriate personnel and/or from automated software agents together with local and remote SMAEs and LMEs.

The name management may be supported by SMAE-resident directory services and protocols:

- DASE (Directory Access Service Element)

- DSSE (Directory System Service Element)
- DAP (Directory Access Protocol)
- DSP (Directory System Protocol)

6.1.2 IBM's Network Management Architecture

Today, the management of larger networks requires more than the administrator's intuition, in particular, in the case of IBM, SNA networks. SNA networks have developed from centralistically oriented systems with a single host from a single supplier to distributed DP environments with many hosts and devices from various manufacturers. Thus, the management problem for SNA networks has taken on new dimensions.

IBM has been forced to develop its Network Management Architecture (NMA) (also known as CNM–Computer Network Management or MSA–Management Services Architecture) continuously in order to keep up with progress in SNA networks.

6.1.2.1 The situation of SNA networks

The basic structure of a traditional SNA network is a class 1 network. The overall power of control lies with the *System Services Control Point* (SSCP, also abbreviated to CP). All interaction between terminals and application programs is controlled by the access methods, the database software and the communications software in the host. The control elements are in part logically broken down by the host into the cluster controllers and the communications controllers (see also Figure 6.6).

Every message flow relates to the host. Thus, message sizes, the overall message envelopes and intermediate arrival distributions may be very safely predicted. The intermediate arrival time is the time between the beginning of the transmission of one message and the beginning of the transmission of the next message. If the average message length (for example, in units of time; a message field of 12 000 bytes on a 9600 bauds communications channel has length approximately 10 s) and the distribution of the intermediate arrival times are known, it is easy to calculate the average load and the average empty time and much more (according to the mathematical structure). This is a great help in planning, as one might imagine.

Because of its restricted areas of visibility and influence and also because of its largely predictable behaviour, an IBM network of the old class 1 structure is very easy to manage.

Figure 6.7 shows an example of a highly ramified, complicated, multi-domain SNA network consisting of several subnetworks, with products from various manufacturers. The upper half of the figure shows an SNA Network Interconnection (SNI). Here, two multi-domain SNA networks are connected

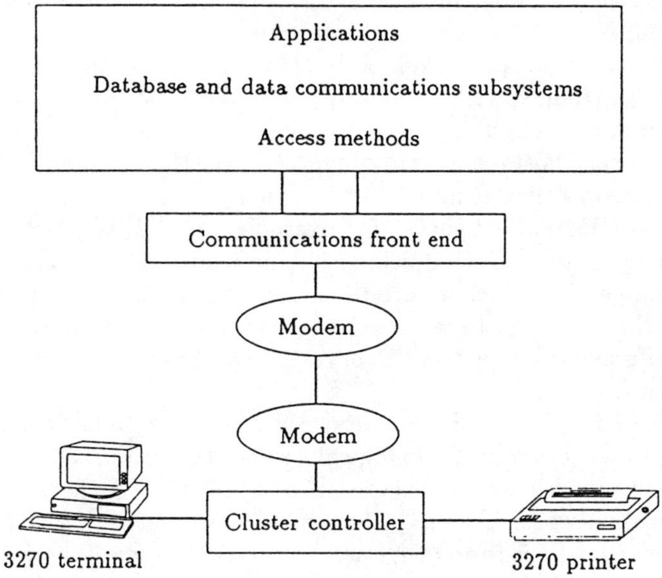

Figure 6.6 Traditional SNA network.

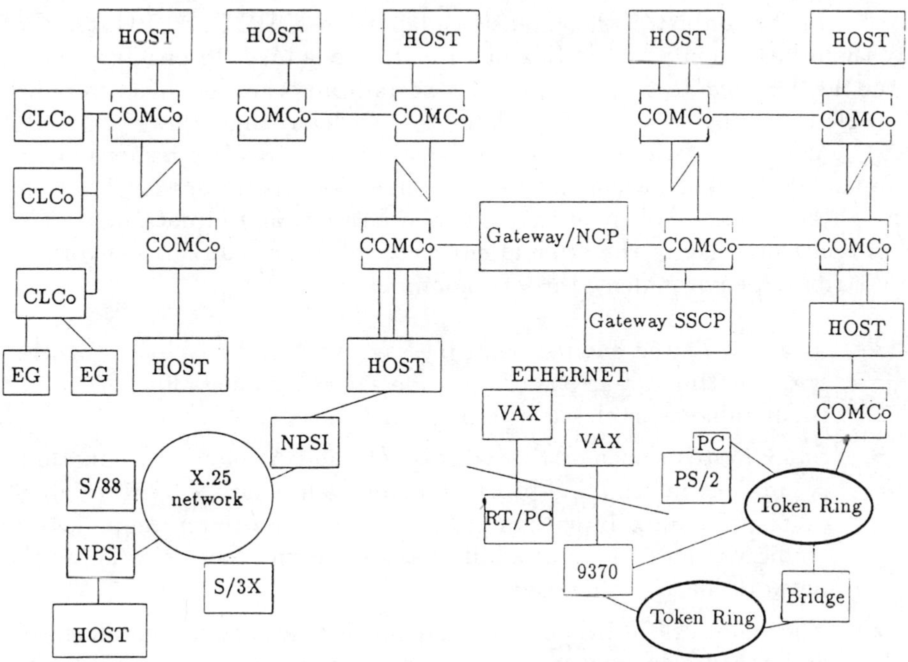

Figure 6.7 Modern SNA network.

together via the gateway SSCP and the gateway network control program (gateway NCP). A CP controls the functions of the resources of a node. Every SNA host is locally or remotely attached to various communications and cluster controllers, with point-to-point and multidrop connections being found in similar numbers.

Moreover, hosts may be connected together via packet-switching WANs, PBXs or Token Ring networks. Finally, in many cases, connections between non-IBM subnetworks (for example, from DEC, HP, TANDEM, Wang or Siemens) are created using SNA networks. This is largely because, while the range of networking products meeting the ISO standards remains extremely thin, SNA is today one of the very few common denominators between different subnetworks. 'Everything can have a little SNA' from the PC to the host.

The management of a modern SNA network today corresponds to navigation through a complex of logical and hybrid networked environments. Lower down on Figure 6.7 there is a typical SNA host and cluster controller subnetwork. The IBM System /36 subnetwork is characterized by the Advanced Peer-to-Peer Networking (APPN) feature which is based on the physical node type 2.1 LEN (Low Entry Networking). APPN generates distributed dynamic directories and executes special functions for intermediate nodes. The subnetworks of third-party manufacturers on the other hand in most cases involve central control and usually appear to the SNA hosts as PU 2.0 cluster controllers.

In the context of the extensive adaptation of IBM's APPC standard by the other manufacturers this picture will be subject to ongoing change over the next five to ten years, so that hosts from other manufacturers will be able to communicate with SNA hosts at logically higher levels.

We now restrict ourselves to the status quo. SNA is responsible for the management of logical end-to-end connections in the session layer and the physical management of routes in the network and of data links. This was relatively easy in the original environment of an old SNA network. In a distributed environment, this is a good deal harder:

- In a distributed environment, message sizes and envelopes together with the times of arrival of some messages in some buffers are not as predictable as in classical terminal networks.
- Small systems such as PCs, PS/2s, /36 and AS/400 may operate as standalone information-processing units and emulate 3270 terminals or transfer files. In so doing, they create even more unpredictable traffic volumes and thus additional uncertainty factors as far as the network load is concerned.
- The traces of LU–LU end-to-end sessions which are used for diagnosis and other purposes must run over gateways if necessary. Whether this operation is sensible, successful and efficient depends on the

extent to which the administrators of various subnetworks and user organizations are willing to cooperate.

- The performance of a packet-switching WAN cannot normally be controlled by the external users.
- The management of the host domains and controller subareas is usually carried out on the PU 2.0 node type.
- Non-IBM devices and environments may collect (possibly locally) a great deal of current management information. However, this information is not necessarily comprehensible to the SNA host, if indeed the latter receives it at all.

6.1.2.2 Network Management Architecture

In current (classical) IBM installations, the *Network Management Architecture* (NMA) specifies the management services which are needed to plan, organize and control the functions within an SNA network (Table 6.1). Problem management is the process of handling problems in the network, from determination to solution. As far as problem determination is concerned, problems in the hardware, software or firmware are detected by an automatic process or by hand. Diagnosis determines the cause of the problem. In many cases, it will not be possible to eliminate the cause of the problem immediately and initially attempts must be made to simply bypass the problem and to recover from any errors resulting from the problem. The solution of the problem consists of corrective measures which settle the problem for good. In many cases we will not be dealing with isolated or isolatable problems, but with chains of problems which must be resolved one by one. Moreover, often, an internal problem may be hidden by an external superficial effect. In the end, tracking is an important conclusive procedure: it records the history of the problem, from its inception to its solution. The inclusion of tracking is particularly important for the solution of problems which may be related. If one is thinking of using knowledge-based systems in the future for network management, one must also recognize the particular importance of tracking in the generation of the knowledge base.

Performance and accounting management is that part of NMA which quantifies, records, controls and balances the use of network components. The monitoring of response-time measurements involves the generation of problem messages when predefined thresholds are exceeded. The recording of the load and availability of network resources and servers together with the measurement of the delay in network components may involve the generation of corresponding alarms when predefined values are exceeded or fallen below. Performance tuning involves the modification of critical network performance parameters in order to increase the overall performance. This also involves tracking and monitoring with messages issued at fixed values. Accounting is concerned with deriving a proper,

Table 6.1 SNA computer network management.

SNA NMA			
Problem management	*Performance and costs*	*Configuration management*	*Change management*
Problem determination	Monitoring of response times	Determination of relationships between physical resources	Software modification
Problem diagnosis	Monitoring of availability	Determination of relationships between logical resources	Microcode modification
Problem bypass	Monitoring of load	Relationships	Hardware modification
Restart	Monitoring of delays		
Problem solution	Performance tuning		
Problem tracking	Performance tracking		
Problem control	Performance control		
	Accounting		

adequate and use-dependent distribution of the overall costs over the units in use.

Configuration management controls the information which is needed to identify networked resources and their dependencies and interactions at any given time. This applies both to physical and logical network resources such as hosts, communications front ends, cluster controllers, modems, multiplexers, concentrators and protocol converters and to their software and firmware. Resources are identified according to their line types, serial numbers, inventory numbers, telephone numbers, real and virtual memory allocations and program numbers. Logical resources are characterized by the information generated by the operating system, such as SSCP, LU or PU names, addresses, domains and capabilities. The resource relationship identification is the process of identifying and recording the physical and logical configuration of the network resource topologies.

Change management is the process of planning and controlling changes (introduction, removal and modification of networked hardware, microcode and software). Software change control looks after software updates, including the installation, removal and modification of modules which are only installed temporarily. The microcode and hardware change controls are responsible for journaling installation, removal and structural, functional or other modifications of the microcode or the hardware, respectively.

6.1.2.3 The structure of NMA

NMA makes a constructive distinction between focal points, entry points and service points. This is shown in Table 6.2. Usually, the focal point resides in a System /370 host. It makes processed and sanitized network management data available to central network management applications. Entry points are points which make network management services available to themselves and to the SNA resources and devices connected to them. Service points provide management services to support access by non-SNA units to SNA. Service points are, so to speak, network management servers: they collect network management data from non-SNA units, convert this data into SNA network management service data and forward the information to a focal point. The communication between the non-SNA resources and the service points is not managed by SNA protocols.

NetView Rel. 1, which was announced in mid 1986, is the strategic implementation of a focal point within SNA. It combined elements of IBM's previous most important network management products. In mid 1987 came Rel. 2 for the most important /370 operating systems MVS/XA, MVS/370, VM and VSE.

6.1.2.4 The host perspective

NMA pieces the scattered pieces of SNA together. It specifies the management services which are needed to plan, organize and control functions in SNA networks. However, NMA also has drawbacks. Most NMA products are host and cluster controller based and reflect the philosophy of central control; but this philosophy contributes to the overheads and reduces the throughput. Moreover, the standstill of a critical network management host may cripple the network management and thus also the recovery process. What is more, with central control, the process of restart after errors may disrupt data traffic which is not involved (for example, resulting in considerable slowing down of sessions or lost or modified data).

NetView, the current base incarnation of NMA implementations, belongs primarily to the System /370. It is powerful in its field, but has clear limitations. It is not oriented towards fundamental requirements such as are commonly found in small system environments networked with SNA. Although gateways to subnetworks with small systems such as a System /36

Table 6.2 NMA. Architectural units.

Focal point	Performs central network management control
•	NetView
•	NetView distribution manager
•	NetView performance manager
•	NetView file transfer program
•	NetView network billing system
•	NetView traffic engineering line optimization system
•	NetView tariff database
•	Information management
Entry point	Performs management services for itself and attached units
•	System /36
•	System /38
•	System /88
•	Series /1
•	3174/3274 cluster controllers
•	3710 network controller
•	3708 network conversation unit
•	3220/3725 communication controllers
Service point	Supports the network management of third-party devices and non-SNA devices and environments
•	NetView/PC
•	Token Ring network
•	ROLM CBXII, 9750, 8750
•	OEM PBX
•	OEM SNA and non-SNA devices
•	Non-IBM devices

are possible, these subnetworks do not possess any management facilities which would be independent of a System /370.

6.1.2.5 NetView

NetView currently represents the core of the IBM network management products. The basic component of NetView is the command facility. It is descended from the Network Communications Control Facility (NCCF). In practice, NCCF was extended by the facilities to interwork with other new NetView components and to support new network products such as IBM 586X/38XX modems, 3710 network controllers and Token Ring networks. One element of the command facility, the Terminal Access Facility (TAF), supports various terminal screen sizes from 1920 to 65 025 characters per screen page. The command facility helps in configuration (for example, of modems) and in load balancing.

The network hardware monitor is an extension of the Network Problem Determination Application (NPDA) and runs under the command facility. It checks whether preset thresholds have been exceeded or fallen below and generates corresponding alarms to the network operator (a person or a program). Alarms may be sent dynamically to selected operator stations. They relate to the problem areas described earlier. Statistics about alarms and events are continuously extrapolated.

The Link Problem Determination Aid (LPDA) is used in conjunction with the hardware monitor TEST command to test local and remote IBM terminals. The LPDA tests include a test of the remote DTE interface and of the state of the link and the execution of a self-diagnosis on remote modems. The signal-to-noise ratio of a link and the state of a link to a modem may also be tested. Lastly, a send/receive test requires modems to send themselves predefined bit patterns and report the results of a comparison.

In addition, the hardware monitor is able to monitor attached Token Ring networks via controllers such as the 3725. For this controller, the Token Ring connection is via the line attachment base type C using ACF/NCP V4 R2 or higher. The 3745 controller is designed to support all levels of Version 5 of the NCP. The NCP Token Ring interface (NTRI) interprets and records unresolved alarms, events on lines and problem determination statistics.

Another important core component of NetView is the session monitor. Like almost all other important components, it is also a further development of an existing product, namely the Network Logical Data Manager (NLDM). It also runs under the command facility. The session monitor is designed to implement software problem determination, and configuration and performance management (using monitoring and recording mechanisms) for SNA LU–LU links. The monitor observes sessions, both in isolated SNA networks and through gateways (Figure 6.8).

The configuration data of the NetView session monitor includes the names of the primary or secondary half sessions, subarea and element addresses, a domain name, the name of the subnetwork, the node type (SSCP, PU, LU, link, cluster controller), node names and addresses

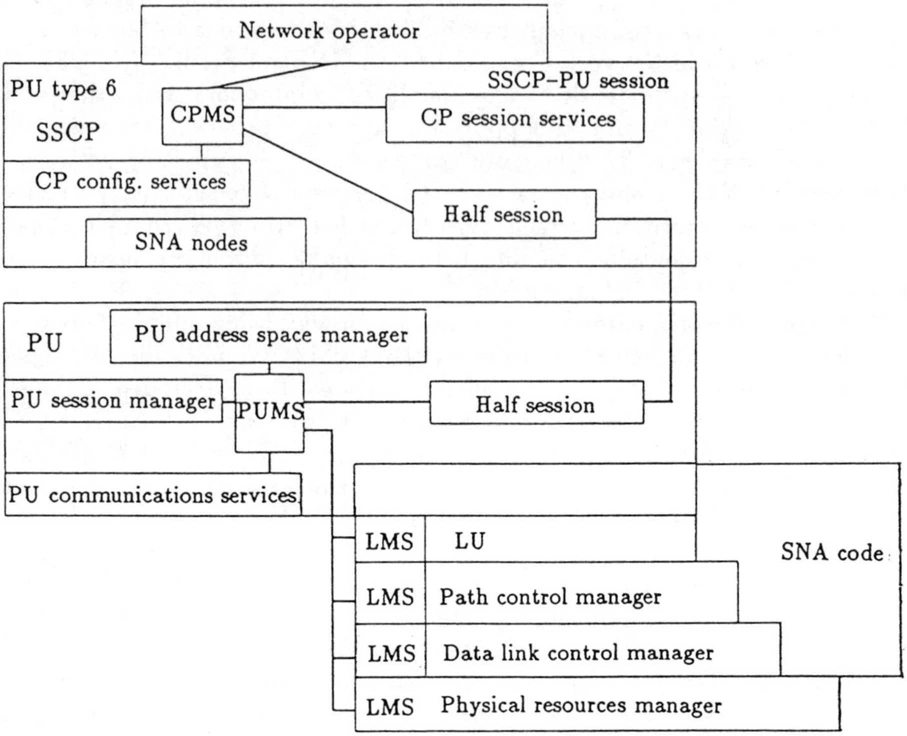

Figure 6.8 Interplay of SNA management components.

together with node identifiers (many objects in SNA have several identifiers, depending on how they are viewed). Other configuration data for a session includes: the virtual route number, a number representing the transmission priority, the number of the explicit route, the number of the explicit route in the opposite direction, an indication of the operational status of the route in the opposite direction, the name of the service class and the log-mode name which is issued by the SSCP.

The session monitor generates a status for the Virtual Route (VR), consisting of the following elements: domain name, network identifier, name of the VR and of the end-point PU, subarea address of the end-point PU, PU type, VR pool counter, VR pool limit, VR status, buffer status, smallest, largest and current VR window sizes, sequence numbers of the last packets exchanged, system time, description of the VR status (for example, VR active, route busy, VR blocked due to various known conditions, unexpected blockage of VR, VR permanently blocked).

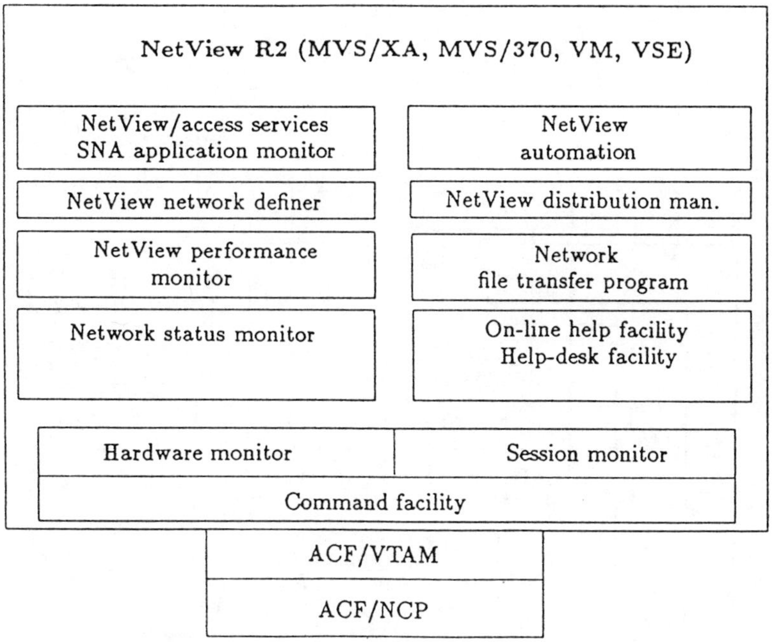

Figure 6.9 NetView computer centre.

In order to perform its tasks, the session monitor must carry out extensive further data processing. However, currently, the complicated interworking of its internal components (and this is a criticism of many NetView users) occasionally generates a totally unrepresentative variety of results the automatic reappraisal of which still leaves much to be desired.

The NetView status monitor STATMON is an extension of the VTAM Node Control Application (VNCA). It returns the status of the domain and a hierarchical view of the network resources and enables the network control to control the resources. It also permits occasional updating of the domain status indicator field, skimming of the NetView log and an automatic reactivation of network components when they become available after breakdown. In addition, STATMON has a filter for critical messages which are forwarded immediately from the command facility by the hardware monitor, VTAM or TAF to the operators (usually people).

The NetView on-line help and help-desk facilities are an extension of the Network Management Productivity Facility.

The on-line help facility simplifies the installation of the command facility and of the hardware, session and status monitors and their

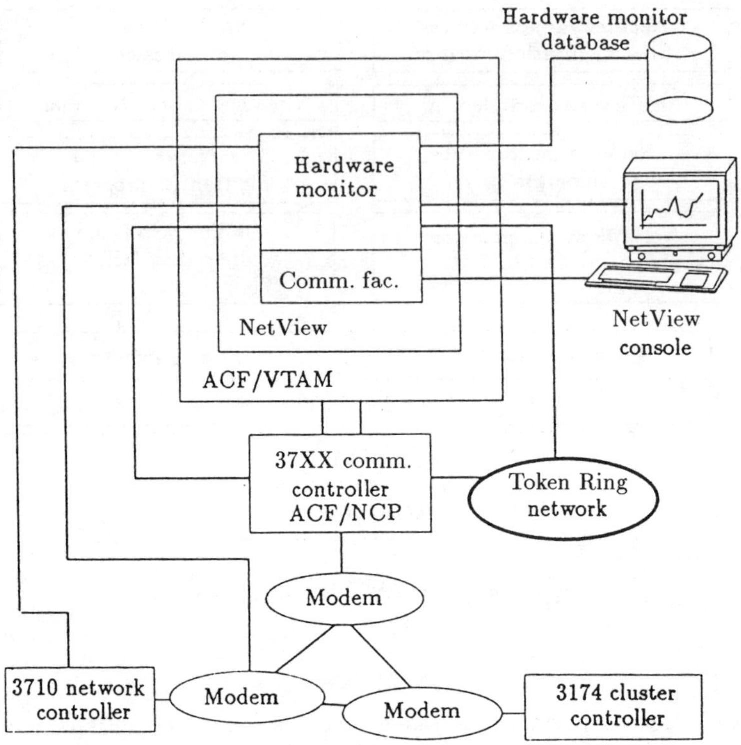

Figure 6.10 Alarms: interworking of the components.

adaptation to the client. This facility is augmented by tutorials, a full screen editor to read network-specific description files, and command lists (CLISTs) to automate frequently used operator and network functions. CLISTs are high-level execution statements which cause the execution of a number of statements in a high-level language or assembler in order to accomplish a specific task (or a number of tasks). It is also possible to incorporate the results of tests that have just been executed together with other conditions.

The help-desk is an on-line driver through procedures for diagnosing network faults. It helps one to detect and (if necessary) reactivate non-operational terminals, transactions or applications, to notice slow reaction times, to deal with problems detected by the monitor and to process system messages.

The performance monitor R3 is a VTAM application which monitors, records and graphically illustrates the network performance and load. It runs under the MVS and VM operating systems and is activated from the operator console via TAF under the command facility.

The NetView performance monitor R3 supports the extended accounting mechanisms which were provided in NCP 5.2 on 3745/3720 machines and in NCP 4.3 on the 3725 on a per session basis. When primaries in the context of an LU 6.2/PU 2.1 run on a peripheral node, accounting data which was previously mainly generated in host-based applications is provided for such node combinations and is forwarded to the performance monitor in the host. This data and the corresponding control information include, for example:

- Session accounting for primary, secondary or all LUs.
- Immediate or delayed collection of the accounting data.
- Thresholds for data entered group-wise.
- The presence of back-up sessions.
- The number of half sessions to which the session accounting applies.

The NetView file transfer program for MVS is a VTAM application which is a strategic product for the transmission of bulk data in a /370 MVS, VM/SP or VSE system environment. NetView FTP MVS is delivered as a base product and as a product with additional facilities (Advanced Function Feature, AFF). Both variants support the previous product FTP Version 2.2 MVS which provides the following basic functions:

- Direct file transfer without spooling.
- File handlers for various file system access methods such as VSAM or QSAM.
- Checkpoint/restart.
- Data compression.

The NetView FTP MVS base product has various extensions, such as queue management, server mechanisms, parallel transmission, operator console commands and the identification of remote NetView FTPs. AFF refines these facilities further.

The network definer runs under VM/SP and is used for interactive creation and updating of the definition tables for VM-based SNA networks, including the 9370. Its configuration management is based on ACF/VTAM definitions which support locally connected SNA and non-SNA devices and an integrated communications adaptor for dedicated and switched connections. In addition, it can handle X.25 adaptors, channel connections, connected Token Ring networks and SNI connections. In the light of the more recent extensions with TCP/IP it is certain that this protocol suite together with the 9370 connections will likewise also be supported soon.

The configuration definition is used by the NetView command facility, the hardware, session and status monitors and the operators.

The NetView distribution manager for MVS/XA, MVS/370 and VM/SP operating systems provides functions for change management within the framework of centrally controlled distribution of data and software in the SNA network. For this, it implements the VM end-node support, System /36 intermediate node support APPN and PC-DOS end-node support (provided these are connected via S/36), together with System /36, VSE, 4680, Series/1, System /88, 8100 and other directly connected end nodes.

According to the environment, the SNA change management is supported by SNADS, DDM or AIX; it will surely also soon be supported by OS/2 EE.

The NetView access services for MVS permit simultaneous access to several VTAM applications from a single screen via parallel sessions. They automate logon/logoff procedures based on user profiles and implement an interface to SAMON, the SNA application monitor which reports the status of all active VTAM applications, and links terminals to a VTAM application.

The NetView automaton is a subsystem which automates various key functions in NetView under MVS, VSE or VM. We see three basic areas of this automaton: the message table, the task and the hardware monitor alert. Essentially, the automaton on its own activates CLISTs (which were previously activated manually) according to prescribed conditions.

The message table allows one to specify criteria which imply automatic CLIST activation. The task links NetView responses to the operating system or a subsystem together with NetView messages to the corresponding sinks, without the need for manual intervention. The hardware monitor alert extends the facilities of the NetView hardware monitor. It starts an automatic scenario by activating predefined CLISTs after it has been notified of alarms or network events. Within the NetView Inter-System Control Facility (ISCF) application and ISCF/PC, the automaton provides automated console operations, which allow it to control and monitor target operating systems and hardware control consoles and also to execute initial program loads and initial warm starts from a focal point.

The NetView automaton is not a knowledge-based or self-learning system, but simply an automaton with very restricted capabilities and facilities. Nevertheless, it clearly characterizes further developments in this direction and the functions which will be implemented by corresponding systems in the first instance.

NetView Rel. 3 forms the basis for the handling of all network alarms in VM/SP, VM/XA, MVS/370 and MVS/ESA environments. It allows a focal point to record alarms of its own or any connected domain. Rel. 3 provides language support for PL/1, C and interfaces to knowledge-processing tools. The IBM LAN Manager which is responsible for management tasks in a Token Ring environment is also supported. NetView Rel. 3 command lists may be formulated in the SAA-compatible high-level procedural language REXX.

NetView/PC is a strategic NMA service point implementation. It is an extension of the NetView services and is designed to extend the NetView network management over IBM LANs and ROLM PBXs (perhaps also soon Siemens PBXs) and over non-SNA and non-IBM communications equipment. In Token Rings, NetView/PC may, for example, connect a LAN to NetView over a gateway PC.

NetView/PC was issued prematurely and is above all designed to enable third-party manufacturers to implement their products with communications-monitoring parts which communicate with the entry point to which they are attached.

NetView/PC is defined by base system services, which are an extension of DOS. These include a help facility, initialization aids, a session manager, a dialogue manager and a remote console facility which allows NetView/PC stations to control one another.

The Token Ring network manager is a NetView PC LAN application. The LAN Manager informs NetView of faults in the Token Ring, the exceeding of error limits, the self-healing of the Token Ring and other events. The IBM LAN Manager also supports PC LAN broadband installations and the bridge program assists in the management of interconnected LANs.

NetView/PC accepts service point commands from NetView and forwards them to the corresponding application.

However, there is much criticism of NetView/PC, which is directed against its lack of performance under DOS, its lack of sufficient features and the fact that its interfaces are difficult to program. NetView/PC was intended to open the IBM SNA world to third-party manufacturers, as far as management is concerned. However, because of the construction, all the actions of NetView/PC hang at the service point and it is some time before the focal point NetView does anything, if at all. Thus, many manufacturers are now working on a direct focal point linkage.

IBM itself complains that the interface has often been misunderstood. The OS/2 EE version of NetView/PC was intended to overcome the performance bottle-necks. However, this seems not to be the case, since users are already complaining.

In its performance and development, NetView/PC is far behind NetView. NetView is used in more than 2000 large US host environments. According to a market evaluation by IDC, NetView/PC has only made it to 30–50 installations. Third-party developers who have relied on the NetView/PC specifications are particularly affected by this.

The original purpose of NetView/PC included, for example, the control of remote LANs. In the meantime, the manufacturers of LAN operating software, such as Novell, Microsoft and 3Com, have designed better utilities for the management of autonomous LAN subsystems.

NetView is an important tool for the control of large networks. Its centralistic approach is appropriate to the structure of a modern SNA network, provided there are enough components which may be correspondingly relocated.

In addition to basic functions, it also contains a collection of utilities the possible uses of which are strongly moulded by each host environment. In the end, this leads to a confusing variety of systems.

NetView will surely develop further in the direction of distributed processing and gain an appropriate place even in the SAA spectrum.

One problem today is that NetView generates too much information which cannot be sensibly evaluated by the normal set of operators. The development of the system must involve a further automation of all the functions if it is to have a chance of succeeding.

According to the application there are alternatives to NetView, of which we shall name only a few.

Net/Master from Cincom works directly with VTAM, so that neither NetView nor NCCF is used. According to experts and users, Net/Master has two major advantages over NetView: easier management of resources and a fourth-generation language as user interface.

Other products, such as Net/Center from USWest, refine the surface of NetView.

All in all, the use of alternatives is always associated with a certain risk, as far as the reaction to extensions of the IBM SNA concept is concerned.

Other details of the embedding of Token Ring networks in an NMA environment are given in Section 6.2

6.1.3 Simple Network Management Protocol

The Simple Network Management Protocol (SNMP) stemmed from the TCP/IP suite. It was originally conceived as a simple and fast facility for performance and error monitoring for Internet. However, in the first half of 1990, it received a considerable boost from commitments by large manufacturers such as IBM, DEC and Sun and from practical window-oriented network management products.

SNMP is intended to provide network managers with a central point for observation, control and management of their installations. As such, it is fully independent of manufacturer-linked concepts.

Products based on SNMP facilitate the upkeep of complex internetworks and the reconfiguration of a broad spectrum of devices in the network from routers to workstations, depending on actual requirements. These products, which have been announced and in some cases delivered by a large number of manufacturers, are based on powerful workstations with a graphical user interface. Thus, the network manager may journey in comfort through the network and inspect weak points, ideally before errors occur. It is also important that the manager only needs to use a single central workstation and not devices distributed everywhere.

SNMP is based on the TCP/IP suite and was designed for use in the framework of distributed data processing with PCs, workstations, minis and mainframes in the commercial office environment and in administration. In the US it is widely implemented in place of manufacturer-dependent programs to manage LANs, bridges, routers or servers.

SNMP is swimming on the TCP/IP wave. The relationship between SNMP and CMIP (the ISO/OSI information protocol) is coarsely analogous to the relationship between TCP/IP and ISO/OSI themselves. Ideally, one would like to base communication between heterogeneous installations on the OSI standard. However, TCP/IP is installed because it is more compact, simpler, cheaper and more available and may be implemented without grossly affecting the most immediately important performance characteristics.

The relationship between SNMP and NetView may be viewed in the same way. NetView is a tool for network management in closed SNA environments. SNMP controls open TCP/IP Internets. There are clearly points of contact between SNMP and NetView domains. It is important that the two management systems should obtain information from one another, since this would bridge the isolation at the most effective point. IBM is prepared to implement exactly this in the framework of the increased TCP/IP activities.

6.1.3.1 The structure of SNMP

The SNMP protocol itself is only one aspect of the overall management structure, the other parts of which form the *Management Information Basis* (MIB) and the *Structure of Management Information* (SMI) specifications. The MIB is a collection of objects, which abstractly represent the devices in the network and their internal components. SMI is a set of rules to define the characteristics of network objects and how management protocols obtain information about these objects. The *Network Management Station* (NMS) is a central component, usually a workstation, which provides the administrator with an overview of the state of the network and with facilities for intervention. The individual network devices contain *agents*, small programs which execute the most important network management functions such as the recording of state values on the spot (Figure 6.11).

In the narrow sense, SNMP is the protocol for interworking between the agents and the NMS. All SNMP systems use both the connectionless UDP and the connection-oriented TCP to exchange messages. The management software in the NMS monitors and controls devices by querying values which the agents assemble. The most important task of an agent

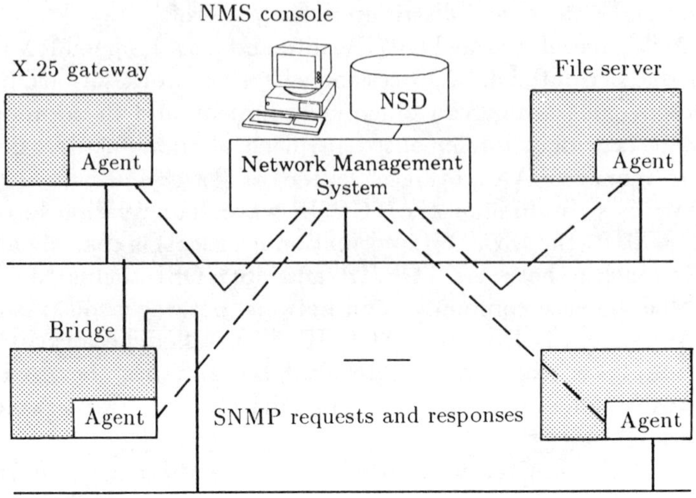

Figure 6.11 SNMP. The central management model.

program is to provide information about objects which correspond to the critical parts and actions of the device for which the agent is responsible (for example, the state of a Token Ring card or the number of collisions in the Ethernet over a given time span). The agents store this information and deliver it to a management program on request. Unrequested signals (alarms) are only issued by agents in critical circumstances such as unusual errors or power failures.

The SMI specifications are rules governing how network variables or objects should be defined for use via the network management protocol, how the protocol accesses the objects and how objects in the MIB are implemented. The OSI description language ASN.1 is used to describe the data formats for objects corresponding to an object information model.

In order to permit future extensions in addition to existing objects and functions, SMI contains four classes of objects: directory objects, management objects, experimental objects and private objects.

The SNMP MIB is a database-like collection of objects in the agents which may be observed and controlled from the management workstation. Thus, the MIB is distributed. These objects are mostly of a statistical nature; they include counters of packets sent, connections used and connection-establishment attempts, together with the numbers of faulty packets and collisions in a LAN segment.

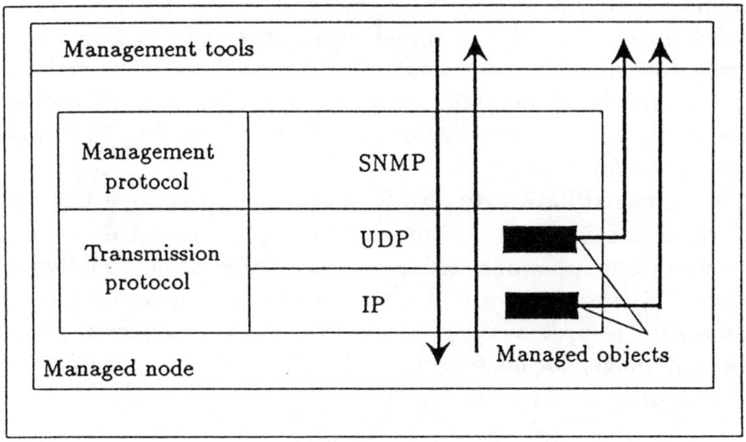

Figure 6.12 SNMP. Managed nodes.

The MIB defines 126 groups of objects some of which are permanently or temporarily obligatory. The objects themselves are hierarchically arranged; naturally, the same numerical identification cannot be allocated to several objects. The individual objects themselves form the lowest level of the hierarchy. At the highest level are tables composed of entries.

In an SNMP implementation, the NMS manager code runs on a management console (for example, a Sun SPARC workstation, which turns out to be the device most used for this purpose). The administrators and network managers perform their observation, monitoring, control and installation functions from the central point of the workstation.

In SNMP, observation of the network involves the polling of the devices, where information is continuously fetched from the agents and collected in the NSD for the purposes of correlation and planning. The network administrator may determine the polling rate. The agents reply to the polling queries, thereby using up all the data they have collected; whence, the storage space allocated to them remains small.

If a device ceases to function and thus is no longer reachable, an alarm condition or a 'trap' is tripped. There are five important events which lead to a trap: the going down of a connection; the restart of a connection; the initialization of an agent; the restart of an agent; and an authentication error when an unauthorized user attempts to gain access to an agent. SNMP allows the manufacturers to define other trap conditions. These might be events connected with the use of X.25, DECnet or 802.1 protocols.

Polling with traps is the SNMP method of isolating sources of error. The method is very effective and fast.

The data collected by polling or the reaction to certain events may stimulate network managers to modify certain network parameters. Parameters are essentially modified using the SET command, which, analogously to the GET command, may be used to set variables in the tables. For example, if a duplicated address is identified as the source of error in routing, this source of error may be eliminated by entering one or more new addresses.

The collected data may also be used to support long-term planning tasks. Here, the manufacturers may naturally provide their clients with extensive first-hand planning assistance using this data. Finally, *Artificial Intelligence* (AI) programs are also conceivable which would use the NSD data (amounting to previous experiences and rules) to generate proposals to the network manager for his further work. This will be of particular interest for large networks.

6.1.3.2 SNMP products

SNMP is simply the biggest surprise on the network management market. Scarcely any well-known manufacturer has gone over completely to this protocol.

Typically, a supplier first develops SNMP agent software for his products, leaving the development of an NMS product until later. Many manufacturers have opted for the first operational agent software codes from MIT, Carnegie Mellon or NetLabs as a basis. Some OEM products are made for special environments, such as, for example, UNIX. Others, such as SNMP Rel.2 from Epilogue or XNetmon from SNMP Research, are ported and may run in various environments such as Sun-OS, DEC VAX VMS, IBM AIX, DOS or Xenix. They are mostly written in C. These products are often supplemented by a range of utilities, such as, for example, an MIB compiler which generates SNMP MIB data from manufacturer-specific data. This may avoid time-consuming error-prone hand conversions.

The basic functions of SNMP may be refined for the user in a variety of different ways. Simple systems provide only network observation and error isolation. More complicated implementations also permit performance and configuration management. The same is true for the user surfaces: simple surfaces may be character based for the tough guys below the network manager. User-friendly surfaces use window techniques and coloured representations of the network which may be zoomed into step by step. Alarms and problem points are emphasized in colour.

What is the position of large DP manufacturers who in many cases have a network management concept for their own relatively homogeneous world which is different to SNMP? The answer to this question is surely the decisive key to the success or failure of this group of protocols.

IBM, DEC, HP and Sun have announced support both for SNMP and for OSI CMIP in their network management systems.

All four have their own network management systems with capabilities considerably more powerful than those of SNMP. However, each manufacturer sees the need to support standards which permit clients to use and control a wide range of devices from various manufacturers.

For OS/2 EE 1.2, IBM has announced TCP/IP complete with an SNMP agent. This implementation allows OS/2 EE servers to communicate with an SNMP NMS. The network manager receives information such as error statistics or packet counters from the agent MIB. In the near future, IBM is to extend the host-based NetView management system with a facility to control TCP/IP SNMP and OSI CMIP nodes. This should also be seen as a reaction to the feeble acceptance of NetView/PC. The agent software contains no IBM-specific MIB extensions. It supports the SNMP GET function, which allows an OS/2 client to ask other SNMP agents for their MIB data. However, IBM does not support the SET function and thus elegantly avoids the security obstacles.

3Com and Novell have both announced that they are to provide their servers and internetworking units (gateways, bridges) with SNMP agent capabilities. Banyan is still undecided. The role of IBM has already been discussed.

However, 3Com and Novell do not want to bring the SNMP capability to the workstations.

6.1.4 Summary

Apart from IBM's SNA, NetView and SNMP, all other network management architectures have a very small distinctive product base. Only the future will attest to the effectiveness of these schemes. However, it is clear that there will be a juxtaposition of OSI- and SNA-oriented communication. Correspondingly, in the world of heterogeneous networks, a true integrated network is scarcely conceivable in the foreseeable future.

6.2 Network management: IBM facilities in Token Ring networks

IBM has two different programs for monitoring Token Ring, namely the trace and performance monitor and the LAN Manager. The programs, which are normally installed on a dedicated PC in the ring, monitor the ring for hardware and software errors and provide facilities for controlling the throughput in the ring. Errors are notified to the operator together with advice on how to recover from them.

It is possible to monitor individual LANs and several LANs linked by bridges. Errors are recorded with the date and time on a diskette or disk. Stations may be logically removed from the ring in order to analyze errors in more detail. Here, other management tools, such as those from Proteon, are advantageous, since they also permit the physical removal of a station from the ring. In the case of logical (protocol-controlled) connection establishment, the user of this workstation can immediately attempt to access the ring again; if the ports are locked, as with Proteon and Ungermann Bass, this is not possible.

6.2.1 IBM LAN Manager

The LAN Manager is primarily used to record and analyze errors. Modifications of the ring configuration may be logged for security reasons. In a DOS environment, the LAN Manager is also linked to NetView/PC. NetView/PC uses the LAN Manager error messages to generate the typical alerts in IBM environments, which are then forwarded via SNA networks to the main system. System programmers may then carry out the error analysis centrally at the mainframe network management console. As a prerequisite, either a dedicated DOS PC with a real-time coprocessor interface card, which is connected to the central manager PC over a switched line for access to its data, or an OS/2 PC with a suitable adaptor (not necessarily dedicated) is required.

The monitoring functions may be executed in other subnetworks which are attached via a bridge (Figure 6.13).

When several Token Ring LANs are installed in a company or a concern, central control of the Token Ring manager DOS PCs using NetView/PC (respectively, the OS/2 EE PCs using the LAN Manager from version 2, when NetView/PC is not needed) is often the only organizationally sensible way of monitoring the network.

From version 2.0, the LAN Manager is able to forward the error messages to the host NetView via the normal Token Ring link without having to establish an additional line. However, this version requires OS/2 EE as operating system while the other version can run under DOS. This variant also has little to recommend it since errors in Token Ring in the area of the gateway to the host are detected but cannot be communicated onwards.

For small networks, it is sensible to install the LAN Manager on the OS/2 server so as not to increase the cost of the overall system unnecessarily.

The error analysis uses menu-driven evaluation programs. The individual stations may be assigned symbolic names which are stored in a special name file. Access to this program may be restricted by password entry. Permanent errors are recorded directly. Support functions in the program facilitate debugging. Temporary errors are only logged when a predefined threshold is exceeded; thus, the error statistics remain readable. Alterations to the Token Ring configuration may also be logged (Figure 6.14).

The control mechanisms for data protection in newer versions of

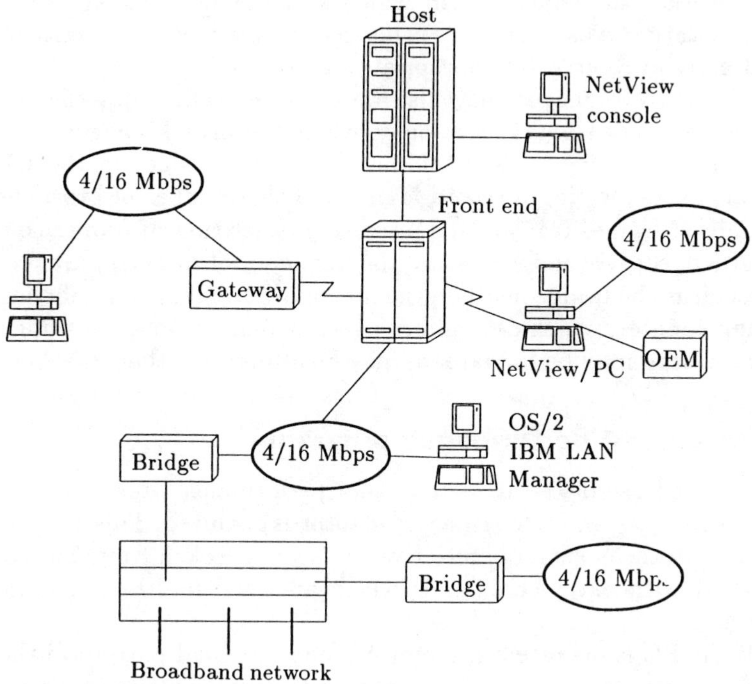

Figure 6.13 Extended network management.

The LAN Manager has control mechanisms for data protection:
Who was active when and where?
Selectable according to:

- Date, time
- Adaptor name, address
- Bridge
- Message number
- LAN segment

Unauthorized, unintentional access may be prevented by appropriate programming.
For all terminals, from a central point!

Figure 6.14 LAN Manager.

the LAN Manager are also important. It is possible to record exactly who has worked at what time in which segment of the LAN and which LAN workstation was used. Unauthorized or inadvertent access may be automatically prevented by appropriate programming.

The LAN Manager may also be used centrally from the NetView operating station or from the station on which the LAN Manager is installed to monitor and configure all IBM source routing bridges in the LAN. In particular, for every ring a record is made of the number of broadcast and non-broadcast frames transmitted into every other ring. If frames could not be forwarded, the reason for this and the frequency of this error are recorded. Entries such as the bridge number, the maximum frame size, symbolic names or the hop counter, which determines the maximum number of bridges over which a message may be forwarded, may be altered via the LAN Manager.

6.2.2 Trace and performance program

Only dedicated use of the IBM trace and performance program is possible and a special trace and performance adaptor is required. This adaptor may also be used in the normal operation of a station in Token Ring, but contains an EPROM with extra commands which are used for trace and monitor functions.

If the PC is operated in monitor mode, the load pattern in the LAN is recorded over a long period. If desired, the results can also be prepared in graphical form. This is only sensible when firstly an IBM-compatible printer is available and secondly when the recording time is at least several hours. The instantaneous load is shown directly on the PC screen in the form of a bar chart. Here, the average waiting time of a station, which again depends on the overall load in the LAN, is also of interest.

The examples in Figures 6.15 and 6.16 illustrate two typical behaviour patterns in the Token Ring LAN. In Figure 6.15 the load pattern in the LAN is analyzed over an interval of two minutes only. Several PCs were attached to the LAN and accessed a common server in Token Ring. The load of the LAN was around 10%. The amount of control information (MAC frames, 2 frames per second) is negligible in comparison with the number of LLC frames (148 frames per second). Since we must also distinguish between control information and data for frames at the LLC level, these frames were analyzed more closely. Just 10% of the overall load in the LAN was again control information and more than 90% was data. Considerably more small LLC frames than (large) data frames were transmitted. 81% of all frames were less than 128 bytes long.

The second example (Figure 6.16) shows a LAN in which the PCs only use Token Ring as a vehicle for communication with the mainframe. Here, the monitoring took place over a longer interval and breaks in use (breakfast, midday, etc.) were also considered when determining the average load. It is immediately clear that the load on the Token Ring is scarcely

PERF01.CT0

PMON performance analysis summary

DATE 01/04/1989 Start 10:43 End 10:45 Sample period is 1 minute.
Number of intervals with unreliable data 0.

	Frames/s	Bits/s	Utilization %	& Non-MAC
Total	149	394 557	9.86	
MAC frames	2	625	0.02	
Non-MAC frames	148	393 932	9.85	100.00
LLC control	77	37 466	0.94	9.51
User data	70	356 467	8.91	90.49

Frame size distribution as a percent of total frames

0–128	128–256	256–512	512–1024	1024–2048	2048–32 767
81	3	0	2	14	0

Figure 6.15 PMON performance analysis summary, taken over two minutes only.

PERF031.CT0

PMON performance analysis summary

DATE 01/11/1989 Start 09:57 End 16:11 Sample period is 1 minute.
Number of intervals with unreliable data 0.

	Frames/s	Bits/s	Utilization %	& Non-MAC
Total	11	11 395	0.28	
MAC frames	2	620	0.02	
Non-MAC frames	9	10 775	0.27	100.00
LLC control	8	9280	0.23	86.13
User data	1	1495	0.04	13.87

Frame size distribution as a percent of total frames

0–128	128–256	256–512	512–1024	1024–2048	2048–32 767
81	3	0	2	14	0

Figure 6.16 PMON performance analysis summary, taken over several hours.

worth talking about (0.28% on average). Moreover, most of the frames transmitted in the LAN contained control and check information for the token protocol, as described in Chapter 5.

This clearly lays to rest the fear frequently expressed by users that the Token Ring LAN could lead to bottle-necks if it is used as a bus for terminals communicating with the mainframe in the 3270 mode. At least 50 PCs were attached to the LAN in the example. Measurements using the trace and performance monitor in large configurations with more than 1000 terminals in a 4 Mbps LAN have confirmed this result.

The bottle-neck was never Token Ring, but the gateway to the host (3174 establishment controller or front-end processor) which impeded the overall throughput. Measurements show that, for example, an IBM 3174 01L has a maximum throughput of 40 kbytes per second, which corresponds to a load of 2.5% in a 16 Mbps Token Ring.

The Token Ring trace and performance monitor is now more often used to locate protocol errors than in its above function as monitor. Filter functions permit deliberate searches for protocol errors in Token Ring or in SNA protocols. Even sporadic errors or errors which cannot be exactly located may be isolated in this way. This is an indisputable aid when you are developing system-oriented applications or looking for the source of errors in a heterogeneous environment.

Trace functions of this type with extensions and additions (mostly connected with the analysis of other protocols such as TCP/IP or IPX/SPX (Novell)) are offered by several other manufacturers (for example, the Sniffer from Spider and the LAN Analyser from Excelan) as alternatives to the IBM product. However, these products are very expensive. Anyone who does not also need to support non-IBM protocols in the LAN will be best served by the trace and performance monitor.

An IBM network management centre for Token Ring might look like Figure 6.17.

6.2.3 The Token Ring administrator

There is another network manager who is certainly more important than the program described above. This is the person who is responsible for and manages the LAN. Functionally, a Token Ring LAN operates like a conventional computer centre, and must be managed in the same way. Thus, in large Token Ring installations, it is an absolute must to name a manager in chief who is responsible for the LAN management. His most important tasks are summarized below:

- Planning of the routing of the physical ring, taking into account distance and transmission media handicaps.
- Integration of new terminals.

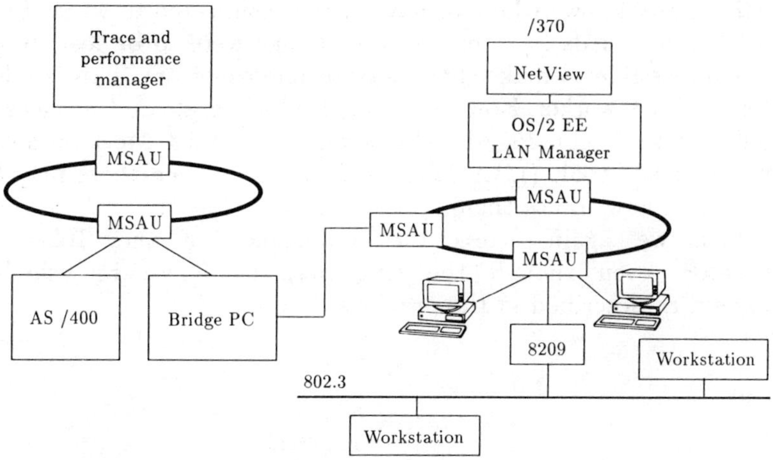

Figure 6.17 IBM network management centre for Token Ring.

- Performance measurement.
- Design of bridges.
- Definition of gateways and layout to other LANs.
- Address management for terminals in the ring.
- Allocation of access priorities to servers.
- Management of the network operating system.
- Error tracking and analysis.
- Updating of hardware and software.
- Compatibility tests (of terminals and Token Ring components).
- Implementation of gateways to SNA, DECnet, Transdata, ..., (terminal emulation, file transfer, APL, graphics, APPC, X.400, FTAM, SRPI, ...).

The function of the network manager is still relatively new. This task requires a qualified person, since the ideal candidate should have a knowledge of the world of mainframes and their network components, workstations and PCs, public networks, services and regulations and naturally also of the LAN hardware and software; in addition, he should be able to take part in technical discussions with the specialist departments and users concerned.

The continual growth of LANs shows how important the administrator is.

At some stage, the point will be reached where nothing works any more and nobody knows where or how what is connected to what. Imagine that all the plugboards in a telephone exchange were to be lost. It would be almost impossible to make changes or to remove errors. This is a horror vision for the PTT worker. However, many LANs operate on this basis, with the belief that the technology is reliable and never fails. Most do not even have the necessary tools (LAN Manager), and even then there may be no one who knows how to use them.

Thus, we again stress the importance of the Token Ring administrator, even though the ring may be a secure vehicle for transmission, as described in the previous chapters.

Chapter 7

Token Ring versus Ethernet

7.1 Ethernet: basic technology

7.2 Ethernet standards and formats

7.3 Comparison of Ethernet and Token Ring

This book on Token Ring networks would not be complete without a comparison with the other important LAN concept, Ethernet. This comparison could be made on a theoretical basis, but that is not our aim here since famous papers by Bux (1981) and Spaniol (1982) already exist. Readers with a flair for mathematics should refer to Kauffels (1989a–c) or Suppan *et al.* (1987).

An important paper for practical considerations is Suppan (1989).

We shall now restrict ourselves likewise to practical considerations only. Although we discussed Ethernet in Chapter 1, we shall now give a brief description of it to save the reader from having to look up the details elsewhere.

7.1 Ethernet: basic technology

Ethernet was first marketed in 1980 by DEC, Intel and Xerox, long before the first Token Ring protocols were available. Ethernet has just managed to hold on to this home or time advantage, at least until now. Ethernet has been modified several times; thus, today's Ethernet is no longer the original Ethernet. In fact, some of the protocols are not even mutually compatible. This can often lead to problems when different protocol versions are used in a LAN. The following is a list of known variants:

- Ethernet version 1
- Ethernet version 2
- The 802.3 standard
- Ethernet based on twisted pair (10baseT)
- Ethernet based on fibre-optic cable (10baseF)
- Thin wire Ethernet (10base2) or Cheapernet

Thus, Ethernet denotes a class of similar systems all of which largely correspond to the standard. The main advantage of Ethernet until now is its very broad distribution and acceptance in industry, and in research and development. In what follows, we shall use the term Ethernet to refer to the overall family, unless specific variants are listed.

Ethernet is normally a bus system with a random-access access procedure. The CSMA/CD (Carrier Sense Multiple Access/Collision Detection) protocol forms the basis for all these variants (Figure 7.1).

When a station wishes to transmit information, it first checks to see whether the medium is free (carrier sensing). If there is no other transmission at that time, it transmits immediately, without having to wait for a free token as in the Token Ring procedure. Every station attached to the bus is

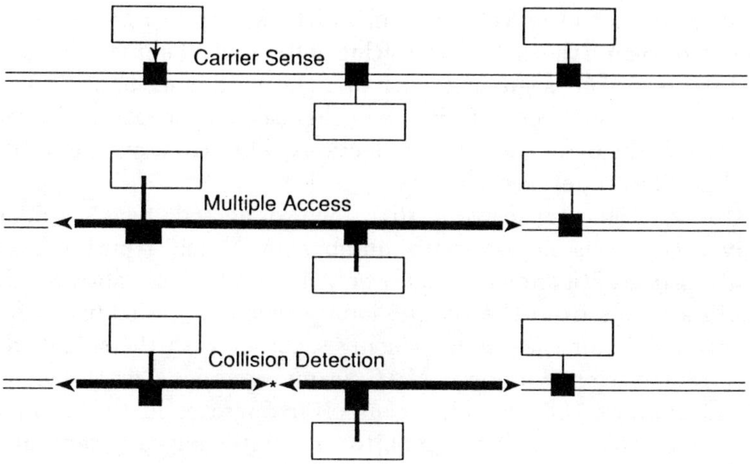

Figure 7.1 CSMA/CD procedure.

passive (not active as in Token Ring). The station for which the message is intended removes it from the network.

Resistances at both ends of the bus prevent the message from being reflected in the LAN. If now two stations attempt to insert information on the apparently free transmission medium at the same time the two sets of information collide. This collision is detected by the sending stations. The stations involved abort their attempts to transmit and try to transmit the information on the LAN again after a random timer elapses.

If there are a lot of active stations attached to the LAN, there may be further collisions, this time involving other stations. If the load is high, the number of collisions may increase exponentially, in some cases (error cases) leading to the mutual blocking of all the stations in the LAN.

The individual stations then abort their attempts to transmit (after the fifteenth attempt) and notify the error to the next higher protocol layer in the station. This error situation is impossible in Token Ring networks since the token guarantees access to the transmission medium even when there is a heavy load.

In addition to its use on the yellow 50 ohms baseband cable, Ethernet is now used, for example, on broadband systems in fibre-optic and telephone networks.

Ethernet versions 1 and 2 together with 802.3 operate with a transmission speed of 10 Mbps and use coaxial cable as transmission medium. Passive terminals are connected via transceivers with a minimum separation of 2.5 m, which transmit the information bidirectionally (Token Ring is unidirectional) on the bus. Corresponding markings on the cable are provided for this. The maximum distance between two transceivers, if regenerators are not used, is 2.5 km, in which case up to 1024 terminals may be connected to an Ethernet (Token Ring 260). The 50 ohms cable is divided into individual cable segments with a maximum length of 500 m. The connection to the next segment involves the use of a repeater. This prevents a phase-wise addition of the signal reflections. The signal attenuation should be less than 8.5 db per segment.

Up to 100 transceivers may be connected per segment. The transceiver (there is no opposite number in Token Ring) provides for regeneration-free data transmission over at least 500 m of cable, receives bit-serial data streams from the coaxial cable, executes the collision detection and is responsible for the carrier sensing together with the so-called jabber control (transmission window). MAC frame emissions must last at least 20 ms and at most 150 ms. The transceiver operates in the normal mode and in the monitor mode. In the monitor mode it is logically separated from the medium.

The transceiver cable (the lobe cable in Token Ring) links the transceiver with the Ethernet controller in the terminal. It may be up to 50 m long. At most six transceivers may lie between any two stations. The signal cycling time must be less than 3.08 μs.

The Ethernet controller of the terminals to be connected covers the lowest two layers of the ISO model, but may, according to the manufacturer, include functions up to and including layers 4 and 5 (NetBios, TCP/IP). It is based on two different VLSI chips, the MEC (Manchester encoding chip) and the LANCE (LAN controller for Ethernet).

The (multiport) repeater connects two (or more) Ethernet segments together.

A local repeater is a normal regenerator. It has two transceiver connections and the maximum distance between two segments is 100 m. The remote repeater consists of two spatially separated devices. Here, the maximum possible distance between two segments is around 1000 m, when fibre-optic cables are used between the repeaters. Buffered repeaters have a special role. They permit intermediate storage of frames and thus may be used to bridge large distances.

Bridges are also used in Ethernet to construct larger networks. The so-called MAC level bridge functions as a bridge between two network segments with identical LLC protocols. The physical levels and, if necessary, the MAC levels may be different. Intelligent MAC level bridges use the worldwide unique Ethernet addresses to create an address book for the network management system. They automatically enter the addresses in the network into their address book. Destination addresses which lie in the same segment of the network as the sender address are not entered in the address book. This provides for a decoupling of the loads in the two separate segments since frames only cross the bridge if their destination address lies in the other segment. The address book may be managed dynamically or statically by the network manager. The latter enters inter-segment or internetwork connections in the tables. Thus, he can ensure that only certain authorized connections between two segments can be established. This prevents unauthorized and uncontrolled access between systems in different subsegments.

Bridges are now used to create worldwide LANs. Like repeaters, bridges may be used locally or remotely. Remote bridges use all conceivable public networks, from dedicated links at 9600 bps and PCM30 routes (2 Mbps) via X.25 and ISDN links, to fibre-optic links in the Bundespost's VBN network.

Because of their load-decoupling and address-filtering facilities, bridges may be used to construct backbone networks and permit the construction of redundant network structures (unusual for Ethernet). According to protocol, Ethernet only admits explicit links, and at most two repeaters may be installed between two terminals.

7.2 Ethernet standards and formats

The ISO 8802.3 standard defines CSMA/CD for rates from 1 to 20 Mbps. The following procedures have been specified:

- **10base5** This was the first procedure to be specified; it is a 10 Mbps Ethernet based on 500 m segments.
- **10base2 or Cheapernet** This is a 10 Mbps Ethernet based on 200 (185) m segments.
- **10baseT** CSMA/CD for twisted pair cables.
- **10baseF** CSMA/CD for fibre-optic cables.

Figure 7.2 shows the structure of an Ethernet frame. The following explanations are necessary:

- SFD (Start of Frame Delimiter): identifier of the start of a frame B'10101011' as in Ethernet version 2, but individual field.
- The address field may be 2 or 6 bytes long, but always uniform addresses within a LAN.
- The LLC data length indicates the length of the subsequent data field. In Ethernet versions 1 and 2, this field is used as a type field

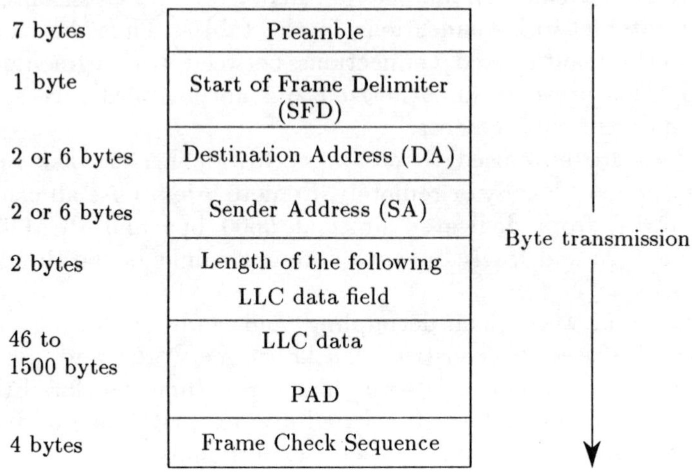

Figure 7.2 Structure of an Ethernet frame.

for higher protocols, which may lead to irremovable protocol errors if the field is interpreted in different ways.

- PAD. Filler bytes to fill to a minimum data field length of 46 bytes.

The standard Ethernet versions 1 and 2 also differ in the electrical properties of layer 1. Refer to the relevant literature for details.

7.3 Comparison of Ethernet and Token Ring

In this section we attempt to compare the properties of these two LAN worlds. This comparison, insofar as it is possible at all, considers the usual technologies employed in these LANs today and focuses on aspects such as topology, capacity, flexibility and performance.

7.3.1 Topology

802.3 The greater the distance between two stations, the greater the time interval in which conflicts (collisions) may occur. This leads to restriction of this distance to 2700 m (fibre-optic cable, 4700 m), in the case of operation without bridges, whence without dividing the LAN into two separate self-sufficient networks.

802.5 The procedure does not lead to any restrictions on the coverage of a ring (access time is increased).

Thus, Token Ring has clear advantages.

7.3.2 Transmission speed

CSMA/CD The minimum transmission length must not be less than the signal propagation time (danger of additional collisions). For a given speed of 10 Mbps, a packet must be at least 68 bytes long. If the speed is increased the minimum packet length also increases or the segment size must be shortened. However, this would be ineffective for interactive applications. For a gross message transmission speed of 100 Mbytes/s on the medium, the average packet length would have to rise to 64 kbytes (this was already established in the seventies) to achieve the efficiency of the current 10 Mbps system (ratio between protocol overheads and effective load). However, this value is unrealistic for standard applications. The development of Ethernet appears to have come to an end, as far as speed is concerned. This can be seen from the fact that none of today's high-speed developments (FDDI, ATM, DQDB, etc.) use a CSMA algorithm. Even the conflict-free variant CSMA/CA used by the company Network Systems in its HYPERchannel is not being developed any further.

802.5 Token Ring depends only on the medium and not on the access procedure. Speeds of 4, 10 and 16 Mbps are implemented. Speeds of up to 2 Gbps are conceivable, although this will lead to an increase in the access time in the case of large distances and it is not yet technically possible to implement an essentially delay-free duplex protocol with a storage capacity of 1–2 bits per station cost effectively. Important modern high-speed networks such as FDDI are based on the flexible token principle.

Thus, Token Ring again has clear advantages.

7.3.3 Performance

802.3 When a lot of stations are active in the ring at the same time, the LAN load may reach around 40% before the number of collisions (and thus also the mean delay time) increases disproportionately. For transaction-oriented traffic (terminal emulation), this may even occur for a load of 20%. This case, which we make no attempt to conceal here, occurs relatively rarely in current applications. If only a few stations (ideally only two) are active the load may increase to almost 100% without anything happening. Of more concern than these numbers is the fact that one usually does not know the load levels that will occur in a network. Today, the picture is still relatively homogeneous. The use of distributed storage techniques such as NFS and even fully distributed operating systems (possibly in comparatively harmless client–server applications) gives rise to a relatively unknown spontaneous inner-system load in addition to the load induced by the user (which lies

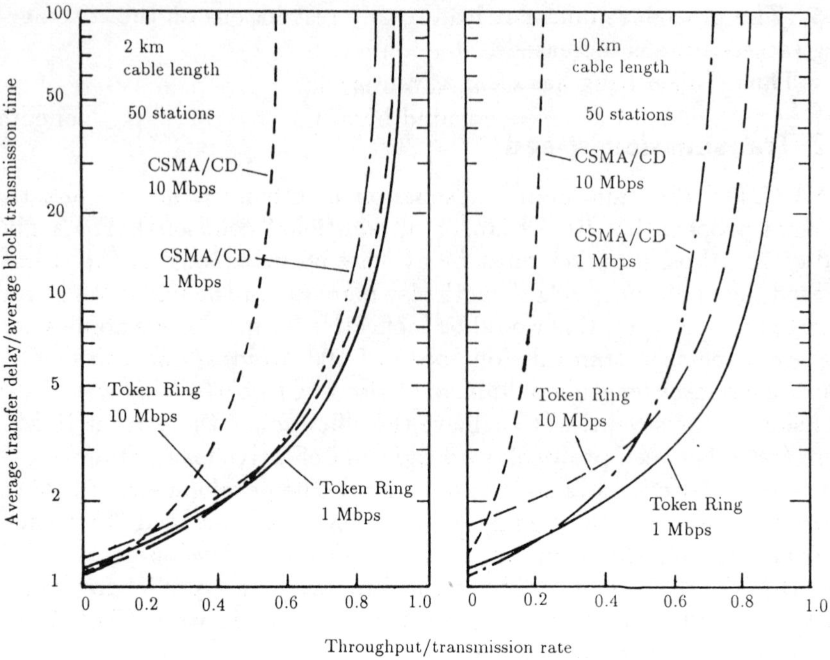

Figure 7.3 Graphs of LAN performance.

within predefinable limits). This may lead to unpredictable degradation of performance (Figure 7.3).

Manufacturers of workstations with limited system-oriented connections, such as Sun with SunOS, who now use Ethernet as standard are now thinking (aloud) of providing for FDDI Token Rings as standard. Others (Apollo domain) long since took steps in the Token Ring direction.

802.5 The throughput in Token Ring is almost totally independent of the number of stations simultaneously active at a given time. It is possible to achieve a ring load of over 90% with a large number of active stations without noticeably affecting the response time behaviour perceived by the individual stations. Above all, the 16 Mbps Token Ring with its early token release protocol offers advantages for large LANs with a small number of active stations.

Token Ring also has advantages in this area.

7.3.4 Suitability for various media

802.3 These LANs are now suitable for all known media. However, bidirectional transmission causes problems. When fibre-optic or 4-wire lines are used, the bus takes on a multistage star structure and the advantages of the bus structure (minimum cable length) are lost. Transitions from one medium to another require special adaptors (for example, passive or active star couplers or multistation access units similar to the IBM MSAUs). Since different technologies are implemented here, the individual components of a LAN cannot always be mixed.

802.5 All the usual transmission media are suitable for use in Token Ring. Since the stations are active in the LAN, it is possible to operate with different transmission media on the individual physically separate link sections (MSAU↔MSAU and MSAU↔terminal) without having to change the topology. With the directed mode of transmission, fibre-optic cables may be used without problems. Even coaxial cable or broadband networks may be used together. The only restrictions are due to the differences in performance of the individual transmission media. In fact, 16 Mbps links have also been implemented using unshielded 4-wire cables.

In this case Token Ring is also clearly advantageous.

7.3.5 Flexibility of use

802.3 All large manufacturers now offer Ethernet products. This fact has not escaped IBM which supplies Ethernet controllers for some of its systems.

802.5 Token Ring is not yet supported by all major manufacturers (for example, DEC and HP). The question is how long can these companies last before sacrificing important market segments?

Thus, 802.3 still has advantages.

7.3.6 Management

802.3 Various manufacturers now provide relatively good facilities for central network management for their Ethernet products. However, these are in many cases mutually incompatible and, above all, not tied into the mainframe environment. Some manufacturers use SNMP, others such as Ungermann Bass provide interfaces to the IBM network management system.

802.5 IBM has a number of tools for network management in Token Ring. The latest variants (for example, OS/2 LAN Manager) permit central monitoring of all components attached to Token Ring from the mainframe, providing the latter uses NetView.

Because of the duplication of the ring, which has been provided for since the beginning and which makes it possible to continue working despite errors, 802.5 versions are considerably more failsafe than 802.3 versions. In the latter case, if the transmission medium is destroyed in error (for example, if an excavator cuts the bus), the whole network will be blocked.

Token Ring again has advantages.

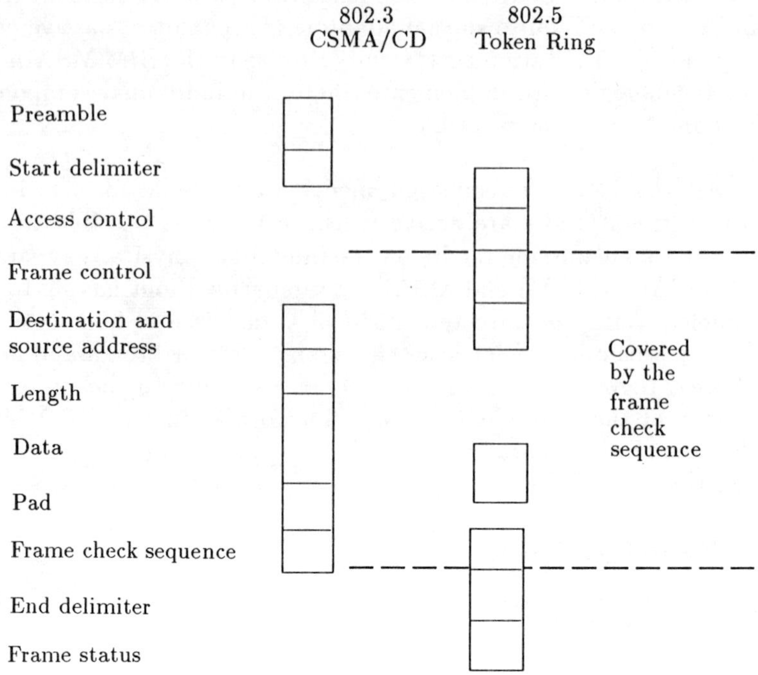

Figure 7.4 Differences in the structure of Ethernet and Token Ring frames.

7.3.7 Complexity

802.3 procedures are technically simple to implement. Chip sets are produced by various manufacturers. Only Texas Instruments chip sets are currently available for Token Ring, and there are insufficient of these. Thus, Ethernet cards are usually cheaper and the user has a larger choice.

802.3 has advantages here.

7.3.8 Summary

802.3 and 802.5 both have advantages and disadvantages. The number of Token Ring installations is now increasingly considerably faster than the number of 802.3 installations. The 802.3 is currently more suitable in a heterogeneous environment with a lot of systems from various manufacturers. Even the connection costs for Ethernet are lower than those for Token Ring (above all for Cheapernet, which is based on a cheap 50 ohms RG 58 cable rather than the more expensive BNC T plugs). In all other respects Token Ring is now superior to Ethernet, particularly when working in an IBM mainframe environment. Figure 7.4 shows the main differences between the structures of Ethernet and Token Ring frames.

Table 7.1 Comparison of Token Ring and Ethernet.

	Token Ring	*Ethernet*
Protocol support APPC XNS NetBios TCP/IP ISO TP4	 IBM etc. e.g. Novell IBM IBM, FTP ?	 e.g. Novell DECnet 3Com, etc. almost all ISOLAN, CMC
Asynchronous connection	IBM asynchr. conn. server, Ungerm. Bass	various manufacturers
3278 direct connection	Ungermann Bass HOB	e.g. Ungermann Bass
3174 direct connection	IBM, ...	?
/370 channel interface	IBM, Telex	IBM, Nixdorf Interlink
Central network management	NetView LAN Manager	? Sniffer?
UNIX support	IBM	IBM, DEC, Sun, HP, etc.
Based on standard	802.5	802.3
Medium	4-wire screened unscreened FO 50/125 62.5/125 9/125	10base2 10base5 10baseT 10baseF
Transmission speed theoretical effective now possible	 4 Mbps (16 Mbps) ≈ 3.6 Mbps (≈ 14 Mbps) 80 Mbps, 100 Mbps	 10 Mbps ≈ 4 Mbps
Max. connectable terminals	≈ 260 per ring	1024 200 per segment
Extensible to larger networks	arbitrarily with bridges	arbitrarily with intelligent bridges
Remote bridge (router)	Proteon, Vitalink IBM (up to 1.5 Mbps)	2400 bps – 1.92 Mbps (also over X.25)

Table 7.1 summarizes the properties of the two competing LANs.

Chapter 8

Appendix: SNA primer

IBM Systems Network Architecture (SNA) is the communications architecture and strategy of the market leader, IBM. This appendix to the book on Token Rings is no substitute for an SNA manual. Rather it is intended to facilitate the introduction to SNA of interested readers who until now have had nothing to do with SNA. It is also designed to help further understanding of the book.

In its initial stages more than ten years ago SNA contributed to the replacement of a variety of incompatible individual solutions by an overall communications scheme, thus enabling clients to create their own private networks on a host or a subnetwork basis.

Since SNA is not just an architectural proposal but a conversion of that into practice, it is relatively difficult to gain a homogeneous picture from the wealth of detailed information.

SNA was primarily initially designed for the systematic construction of terminal networks. Over the course of time, features and capabilities have been added which have turned SNA into an architecture for computer networks. Today, it might even be said that there is no longer an invincible chasm between SNA networks and those based on the ISO reference model.

8.1 Tasks and development of SNA networks

In an IBM system without SNA, the application programs are unit dependent and the network management must be individually coded into each application program. This is both annoying and expensive.

With its different functional distribution, SNA provides for shared use of the network components including simultaneous use of a line and access to several programs. The functions which a network user needs in order to access an application program in a host computer are as follows:

- Polling.
- Control of units and data preparation.
- Addressing and forwarding.
- Control of the data flow.
- Control of different types of application programs.
- Control of an uneven volume of message traffic.
- Line control.

These functions and a number of others are made available by SNA functional components.

When a computer centre equipped with SNA components is extended with new devices the integration is completely problem free.

The original structure of an SNA network is that of a tree with a host computer as root and terminals as leaves. This was introduced some ten years ago. However, terminal structures have changed completely since then and SNA has had to take account of these developments.

The next extension made it possible for an SNA network to contain several hosts each of which was a root of a tree. However, communication between trees was only possible at the roots. Nevertheless, this enabled users to access programs which were not implemented in the host belonging to their own tree.

The 1979 version dropped these restrictions and permitted more general communication. This phase also provides for the opening to public networks, which was only in the offing in phase 2.

With the introduction of personal computers as possible terminals, the further development of SNA had to cater for a network with distributed intelligence.

The introduction of APPC provided a convenient interface for the communication of transaction programs. The communications objects used here are so-called verbs, which may be viewed as an extension of a higher-level programming language. Any node in the SNA network which implements this interface can, regardless of its complexity, communicate over a logical link (conversation) with any other node which also has this interface.

This is a revolutionary advance from the historical, strongly hierarchically oriented control structure of SNA networks. APPC opens up opportunities for SNA in the office communication, LAN and distributed system sectors.

In its second stage of development in 1986, Token Ring extended the IBM LAN concept in such a way as to permit an integration of the main terminals into SNA under the control of SNA management components. Thus, this advanced technology can also be used in SNA networks.

Other extensions of SNA relate to the use of satellite transmission links to create global SNA systems.

Finally, within the SNA framework, there are also recommendations for a Document Content Architecture (DCA) and a Document Interchange Architecture (DIA). The SNADS transactions software package (SNA distribution service) provides the tools for asynchronous communication, based on the APPC interfaces and provides a basis for document interchange. The SAA strategy draws these extensions together.

8.2 SNA node types and NAUs

An SNA network consists of a collection of devices, known as nodes, and links between these nodes.

There are four different node types which may be described as follows.

8.2.1 Host nodes

The host node usually consists of a CPU (mainframe) with an operating system (for example, OS/MVS or DOS/VS), an access method (for example, ACF/VTAM) and application programs. As far as SNA is concerned, the host node usually contains a software central control point (SSCP: systems services control point). Examples of host nodes include computers of the IBM 4300, IBM 3081 or IBM /370 families controlled by OS MVS SP and the TP (teleprocessing) access method ACF/VTAM (advanced communication facility/virtual telecommunications access method). ACF denotes an extension of a method of accessing the facilities of the SNA network.

8.2.2 Communications controller node

This is a front-end processor which is attached directly to the host node. It controls the remote network configuration which is attached to it. It does not have an SSCP. The software for such a node is ACF/NCP (network control program), which contains the following functions:

- Control of the data exchange over the cable connection or lines, using the SDLC (synchronous data link control) line protocol (similar to HDLC, see Section 1.4.3).
- Execution of error-handling procedures.
- Introduction and removal of line header information.
- Generation and verification of a block check digit for the message together with the hardware.
- Modification and verification of the transmission counter.
- Receipt and forwarding of line control information to the network address management system.

8.2.3 Cluster controller node

This enables a remote station to access a host. In the case of the programmable cluster controller node (for example, the IBM 8100 communications system), the applications programs may be divided between the host node and the cluster controller so as to provide for optimal use of the network. This node represents a distribution of the functions and the processing within the SNA network. Examples include the IBM 3600, the IBM 3650, the IBM 3360 and the IBM 3790. Cluster controller nodes are often referred to as controllers and may serve very different terminals.

8.2.4 Terminal node

This is a slimmed-down version of the cluster controller node, which, unlike the latter, can only serve terminals. Such a node is very dependent on its limiting function which is predefined by the host or the communications controller and restricts its possibilities. The capabilities of such a device could be integrated into a terminal. On the other hand, these devices usually serve up to 64 terminals in that they provide logical interfaces to the network.

The nodes are also referred to as Physical Units (PUs), where a host node is a PU type 5, a communications controller node is a PU type 4, a cluster controller node is a PU type 2 and a terminal node is a PU type 1.

These are the node types which occur in a classical tree-structured SNA network. However, we have already referred to an extension which permits more general communication, namely APPC. APPC is supported by a new node type, the PU 2.1.

A PU 2.1 node may be directly subordinate to a PU 5 or a PU 4 node and is controlled by the SSCP. On the other hand, PU 2.1 nodes (for example, in a Token Ring LAN) may be directly linked together without calling upon the services of an SSCP, which can only reside in a type 5 node.

A PU 2.1 node consists of a physical unit (device), one or more logical interfaces to the network and an SNCP (Single Node Control Point) which corresponds to a highly reduced SSCP. Thus, the PU 2.1 node in this structure is an autonomous object which may therefore be linked into either a hierarchical or a decentralized symbiotic network. The classical implementation of such a node is the PC.

Each node contains one or more Network Addressable Units (NAUs). An NAU is a piece of software which allows a process to use the network. An analogy is helpful here: imagine a building with a telephone line in each office, in which every line has its own hardwired address which is permanently assigned to it. To use the telephone system a user plugs a telephone handset into the line and may then be reached at the address of the line. Similarly, each NAU has a network address. To use the network, a process must connect to an NAU. In this way it becomes reachable and may itself reach other processes linked to other NAUs.

There are logical and physical NAUs:

- **Logical Unit (LU)** This is the usual interface to which user processes go and which we have referred to implicitly above.
- **Physical Unit (PU)** Such an NAU is associated with every node and is used by the network to couple, uncouple and test nodes and to execute various similar administrative functions.
- **Central controlling SSCP** This has complete knowledge of and control over all front ends (communications controller nodes), all

controllers (cluster controller nodes), all terminal nodes and all terminals which are attached via the network to the host.

- **PU 2.1 control component SNCP** This is able to control a node autonomously in the framework of the APPC services, if the node is not controlled by an SSCP.

The collection of hardware and software which is controlled by an SSCP is called a *domain.* An SNA network may consist of one or more domains. There is a different subdivision into domains for routing and flow-control purposes. An SNA network may be subdivided into subareas, each of which consists of a subarea node and all the peripheral nodes attached to it.

A subarea node may receive messages from any origin and transport these towards any given point in the network, assuming that there is a group of lines to this given point. A peripheral node can only send message units to its subarea node. It follows immediately that most of the routing can be executed over the subareas, analogously to the hierarchical address procedure for the telephone system.

A subarea node may be a PU 5 or a PU 4 node. Since only PU 5 nodes contain SSCPs, a domain may stretch over several subareas. The other PU types can only be peripheral nodes, except in the case when PU 2.1 nodes are directly interconnected without being controlled by an SSCP. The term subarea is used since the routing is restricted to the PU 2.1 nodes.

Subarea nodes may be interconnected via System /370 channels or SDLC point-to-point lines. Subarea nodes may be linked to peripheral nodes via System /370 channels, point-to-point or multi-point SDLC dedicated lines or point-to-point SDLC switched lines. The IBM cable system and more recent LANs provide alternative connection schemes.

8.3 The functional layers of an SNA system

Architecturally, SNA is subdivided into functional layers which do not always correspond to the ISO layers. However, it is clear that this subdivision into layers is very useful.

8.3.1 Overview

8.3.1.1 Physical layer

The lowest layer contains the tools for transmitting a bitstream, including descriptions and specifications of lines, physical transmission procedures, modems, adaptors, switching networks, distributors, etc.

8.3.1.2 Data link layer

This layer constructs a packet communications resource, based on the physical transmission of the lowest layer. It forms frames and detects and removes transmission errors without involving the higher functional layers. The SDLC protocol of this layer corresponds, apart from a few modifications, to HDLC. As far as the use of LANs is concerned, the medium access-control mechanisms reside in this layer, where they are supplemented by a logical link control.

8.3.1.3 Path control layer

This functional layer monitors the overall use of the (remote) data processing line resources of the SNA network and routes message elements over the lines. The path control routes message units between NAUs through the network and makes the transport path between the NAUs available. For this, message units from the transmission control are transformed into path information units.

Globally, this layer corresponds to the ISO network layer, but it has rather more work to do, since it also takes on some of the tasks of a transport layer.

8.3.1.4 Transmission control layer

The next higher layer is the transmission control layer, which is responsible for creating the management and clearing transport links (known as sessions in SNA). It provides the higher layers with a uniform interface abstracted from the realities of the actual transport network. When a session is established it regulates the data flow rates between processes, controls the allocation of memory, manages the various message priorities, is responsible for multiplexing and demultiplexing data and control messages on behalf of the higher layers and carries out encryption and decoding if necessary. The transmission control layer has two components, the manager for the point-to-point links and the session control.

8.3.1.5 Data flow layer

This has nothing to do with control of the data flow in the usual sense, but controls the sessions from the point of view of the LUs. A session from the point of view of an LU is also called a half session. This layer controls whether the half session can send, receive or send and receive at the same time. It groups related request/response messages into message chains, restricts transactions with a bracket procedure, controls the blocking of requests/responses according to the control mode specified on system activation, generates sequence numbers and cross-references request/response messages with one another.

8.3.1.6 NAU services layer

This makes two classes of services available to the end-user layer, namely presentation services (for example, text compression, code conversion, encryption) and session services for the establishment of logical links.

There are also network services which have to do with the operation of the network as a whole. The services are provided by the LUs in the corresponding devices. The boundaries are flexible according to the application; thus, we shall not give a further breakdown at this stage.

8.3.1.7 End-user layer

Just as in the ISO reference model, this layer cannot be specified exactly since its functions depend largely on the application. On the other hand, there are various basic mechanisms, which we shall come to later. The main anchor of the network management is to be found in this layer; moreover, management has a much greater importance in an SNA network.

In what follows, we discuss the details of the layers insofar as they are of interest to us and in some sense typical of SNA.

8.3.2 The end-user layer in SNA

End users are sources and sinks of information outside of the SNA network. They may be programs, operators, I/O devices, storage devices or users. Most of these users may be represented by code which is accessible through the LU mechanism. An LU must know either the LU partner address or a synonym for it which is then converted back into the LU partner address by the SSCP or the SNCP.

The most general form of user is a program. This may be a simple application program or a program with a ramified structure which is not fully visible to the SNA network. The program may access devices which are not in the SNA area. Each program end user interworks with the NAU services. This interworking covers data exchange and the transmission of commands and acknowledgements for the use of SNA functions.

In an SNA network, interconnected subsystems are used for two types of distributed applications: execution of jobs in the network and distributed transaction processing.

As far as the execution of jobs in the network is concerned, processing requests are sent to a subsystem from where they are forwarded to other subsystems for execution. The results are then returned to the initial subsystem.

This procedure is used to equalize the use of computers in the network or to access programs or files in a different computer system. In this case, the work unit is the batch job. This is a collection of one or more application programs and files which are transmitted and processed together.

In distributed transaction processing the transactions from the terminal server are processed by several application programs under the control of a number of cooperating subsystems. A transaction-processing system is a subsystem which monitors the shared use of resources so as to process several transactions simultaneously. Transaction-processing systems are built to support dialogue-oriented applications.

Here, requests from terminal users are processed directly on receipt and the results returned to the user within as reasonable a time as possible.

When transaction-processing systems are linked via an SNA network they may use each other's resources. This simplifies and supports the introduction of corresponding applications.

In the framework of the PU 2.1/LU 6.2 (APPC) services, a PC SNA application can communicate with another PC SNA application or a host application via Token Ring or other media. APPC is an application program interface based on transactions.

Other forms of end users include operators who carry out various administrative functions in connection with the network and thus have certain interfaces to the NAU services, media end users such as disk packs, card readers and tapes and application subsystems which use various message streams (for example, the Information Management System (IMS), the Customer Information Control System (CICS)).

8.3.3 NAU services layer

LUs, PUs, SSCP and SNCP are NAUs. So as not to expand the distinction unnecessarily, we shall consider SNCP as a special SSCP and will no longer distinguish between the two. The NAU services then break down into LUNSs, PUNSs and SSCPNSs according to the type of the NAU which provides them. There are six main categories of services:

- Configuration services
- Session services
- Maintenance services
- Measurement services
- Network operator services
- Presentation services

The primary functions are the configuration services in the SSCPs and PUs and the session services in the SSCPs and the LUs.

Configuration services are responsible for the control of the network structure, including the activation and deactivation of links, PUs and LUs.

Over a special interface to the operator, an SSCP provides facilities for restarting the whole network, activating parts of the network after outages or taking down some or all of the network. With these facilities, the control of a possibly highly ramified network is concentrated on a reasonable spatial scale.

Session services support the activation of a logical link between two logical entities. They are largely SSCPNSs and to a lesser extent LUNSs. The ability of LUs to accept connections may be restricted. This is a service of this layer. Other services include the establishment, execution and termination of a logical link, where considerable distinctions in the functionality must be made according to the network structure. We shall not discuss this further here and we now proceed to the actual session establishment in the transmission control layer.

Maintenance services, network measurement services and operator services support the network management with corresponding functions. Since this has been discussed in detail, we shall not go into it any further.

Presentation services mostly reside at both ends of a session. In a centralized network, these services mainly relate to the communication between the centre and devices. The transformation from a common format to the device format may be carried out in the destination NAU. Then the device can change the representation to suit itself without affecting the rest of the network. The conversions undertaken in classical data processing are not particularly educational (the formats for certain header fields are given and it is a question of changing the code).

On the other hand, there is a noticeable recent trend, with advances in graphical data processing and office communication, for IBM to consider developing services with regard to typed objects. DCA and DIA are a first step in this direction.

8.3.4 Data flow layer

Contrary to the otherwise usual practice, this layer obtains its information not from its own message headers but from parameters set in the headers of the layer below.

Although the data flow rate in a session is determined by the transmission control layer, the direction of the flow is determined here. This function is called dialogue control and corresponds in its basic functionality to that of the session layer in the ISO reference model. In order to understand the necessity for dialogue control, one should bear in mind that sending a message does not necessarily shut down a process and that messages and ACKs from the other end may arrive and cause interrupts at arbitrary, inappropriate times.

The dialogue control provides a facility for grouping requests into chains for restarting after errors or for other purposes (chaining). It can be arranged that an error in the middle of the chain leads to the whole chain being repeated. Similarly, a process may request that acknowledgements of packets at the beginning of a chain should not be sent until the whole chain has been sent. This leads to alternating chains between senders and recipients.

SNA distinguishes between requests which require acknowledgements and those which do not. Senders and recipients should agree on the semantics of an ACK (for example, message received, message received and processing started, message received and processing complete).

Thus, since the processing of messages may take some time, there is a danger that ACKs to messages sent much later and processed more quickly may arrive earlier. The dialogue control is then able to ensure that NAU ACKS arrive in the same sequence as the requests were transmitted. This provides for a considerable simplification of user programs.

Another feature of the dialogue control is the facility to include a number of requests and responses for each direction within a bracket. Bracketing may, for example, be used to preserve consistency, so that a user does not interrupt another user in a transaction before the latter has finished (database area).

Session management and dialogue control are supported by the RH and by special transport protocol messages. The header contains information about the data flow and message chains, indicators of the type of response desired, data flow control indicators and indicators for special cases.

Finally, there are also facilities for ending a logical link from this layer (shutdown).

8.3.5 Transmission control layer

This layer controls the creation, execution and termination of sessions between LUs.

When a process wishes to communicate with another process, it turns in its existing session with the local SSCP (LSSCP) to the latter with the connection request. The two ends of a session are not symmetric, there are always two different partners, one of which is called the primary and the other the secondary. By definition, the primary has more facilities and more responsibility, down to layer 2.

The details of a session establishment depend on, amongst other factors, whether or not the source and sink are in the same domain, whether the connection is requested by the primary, by the secondary or by a third party and whether both ends are available should the connection be established.

In addition to initiating and clearing down sessions, the transmission control layer also ensures that in the higher layers data is delivered in the correct order, unless otherwise specified on linkage. The sequence numbers are not contained in the response headers (RHs) for this layer but are given as parameters with the path control data.

The flow control mechanism used by the transmission control is the same as in the path control layer except that it is applied to each individual session and not to a set of sessions. Flow control in the transmission control layer is independent of flow control in the path control layer. Details of the algorithm are given in the next section. To obtain authorization to send further messages the sender alters a bit in the RH. If the partner station alters the corresponding bit in the ACK, further messages may be sent.

This mechanism, which is known as pacing, and which like almost all functions is executed by the connection point manager controlling the half session, prevents local overloading of a participating NAU, while the mechanism of the layer below prevents overloading of the network as a whole.

8.3.6 Path control layer

This layer monitors the shared use of the remote data processing resources of the SNA network and routes messages through it. The main function here is the so-called session routing.

As previously mentioned, the SNA network may be divided into subareas, each of which contains one or more NAUs. Each NAU has a two-part address comprising the subarea address and the address within the subarea.

Every subarea is controlled by a node which is either a host or a communications controller node. The subareas form a framework in which nodes of a lower type (peripheral nodes) are embedded. When a session is established the source chooses a virtual route for the session.

A virtual route is an ordered list relating to the path from the source to the destination subarea. The decision as to which route to select from those available depends on the load on the routes and the class of service desired for the session. The possible service classes are:

- Interactive
- Remote job entry
- File transfer
- Secure
- Real time

Service classes differ in terms of the delay, the throughput and the security requirements. Up to eight alternative routes may be made available for each service class.

Different unrelated sessions may use the same virtual route.

This layer carries out flow control for each virtual route without taking into account the number of sessions using the virtual route. The flow control mechanism is known in SNA as pacing.

Layers 1 and 2 are formed by SDLC and physical specifications.

8.4 SNA and OSI

Unlike the ISO reference model SNA has historically developed in the interests of data processing practice. Thus it does not have such clear lines as the ISO model, although there are a number of commonalities.

These are most apparent in layers 1–3, since the HDLC and SDLC implementations are very similar; when local networks based on IEEE 802 or MAP are used there are scarcely any differences and the path control layer is a practical implementation of the network layer.

The tasks of an ISO transport layer are performed by a combination of the services of the path and transmission control layers, where the path control is responsible for the end-to-end reliability and transport connections are made available and released by the transmission control. The data flow layer adds a number of user-oriented services to the transport connection. The end-user level, like in ISO, only supports applications when these could also be interpreted initially in a different way by SNA.

When business consultancy groups consider the world of data communications, they come to the conclusion that in the nineties only two types of network implementation will have a significant market share, namely SNA networks and ISO-oriented implementations such as MAP or the latest version of DECnet.

IBM is taking this trend into account by extending the strategic SNA lines and providing software support for the ISO/OSI protocols for open communication systems.

The newest product in this direction is the OSI Communications Subsystem, OSI/CS.

Abbreviations

ACF/VTAM	Advanced Communication Facility/Virtual Telecommunications Access Method
AFF	Advanced Function Feature
APPC	Advanced Program-to-Program Communication
APPN	Advanced Peer-to-Peer Networking
CMIP	Common Management Information Protocol
CNM	Computer Network Management
CP	Control Point
CPU	Central Processing Unit
CSMA	Carrier Sense Multiple Access
CSMA/CA	Carrier Sense Multiple Access/Collision Avoidance
CSMA/CD	Carrier Sense Multiple Access/Collision Detection
DAP	Directory Access Point
DASE	Directory Access Service Element
DCA	Document Contents Architecture
DFN	Deutsches Forschungsnetz (German research network)
DIA	Document Interchange Architecture
DLC	Data Link Control
DMA	Direct Memory Access
DNA	Digital Network Architecture
DNS	Domain Name Service
DQDB	Distributed Queue Double Bus
DSAP	Destination Service Access Point
DSP	Directory System Protocol
DSSE	Directory System Service Element
FDDI	Fibre-Distributed Data Interface
FTAM	File Transfer Access and Management
FTP	File Transfer Protocol
HDLC	High-level Data Link Control
HPPI	High-Performance Parallel Interface
ICMP	Internet Communication Message Protocol
ICS	IBM Cable System
IP	Internet Protocol
IPX	Internetwork Packet Exchange
ISCF	Inter-System Control Facility
ISO	International Standardization Organization
LAN	Local Area Network

LEN	Low Entry Networking
LLC	Logical Link Control
LME	Layer Management Entity
LPDA	Link Problem Determination Aid
LPDU	LLC Protocol Data Unit
LSAP	Link Service Access Point
LU	Logical Unit
MAC	Medium Access Control
MEC	Manchester Encoding Chip
MIB	Management Information Base
MSA	Management Services Architecture
MVS/XA	Multiple Virtual Storage/Extended Architecture
NAU	Network Addressable Unit
NCCF	Network Communications Control Facility
NCP	Network Control Program
NLDM	Network Logical Data Manager
NMA	Network Management Architecture
NMS	Network Management Station
NPDA	Network Problem Determination Application
NSP	Name Service Protocol
ODA/ODIF	Office Document Architecture/Office Document Interchange Formats
OSF	Open Software Foundation
OSI	Open Systems Interconnection
OTF	Open Token Foundation
PAD	Packet Assembly/Disassembly
PU	Physical Unit
QSAM	Queued Sequential Access Method
REXX	Restructured Extended Execute (Language)
RH	Request/Response Header
RISC	Reduced Instruction Set
RJE	Remote Job Entry
SAA	System Applications Architecture
SAP	Service Access Point
SDLC	Synchronous Data Link Control
SMAE	System Management Application Entity
SMI	Structure of Management Information
SMIS	Specific Management Information Passing Service
SMTP	Simple Mail Transfer Protocol
SNA	System Network Architecture
SNCP	Single Node Control Point
SNI	SNA Network Interconnection
SNMP	Simple Network Management Protocol
SSCP	System Services Control Point
STATMON	Station Monitor
STM	Station Manager

STP	Shielded Twisted Pair
TAF	Terminal Access Facility
TKO	Telelommunikationsordnung (Telecommunications office)
TP	Teleprocessing
UDP	User Datagram Protocol
UTP	Unshielded Twisted Pair
VM	Virtual Machine
VNCA	VTAM Node Control Application
VR	Virtual Route
VSAM	Virtual Sequential Access Method
XNS	Xerox Network System

Bibliography

Bennett (1990). The simple network management protocol. *Telecommunications* (2)

Beyschlag U., ed. (1988). *OSI in der Anwendungsebene.* Datacom Verlag

Boell H.-P. (1989). *Lokale Netze – Momentane Möglichkeiten und zükunftige Entwicklung.* McGraw Hill

Bux W. (1981). Local area subnetworks – a performance comparison. *IEEE Tr. Comm.* (29), 1465–1474

Chylla P. and Hegering H.-G. (1989). *Ethernet LANS. Planung, Realisierung und Netz-Management* 2nd edn. Datacom Verlag

DEC (1985). *DNA und DECnet Informationsschrift*

Deitel and Harvey M. (1984). *An Introduction to Operating Systems.* Reading: Addison Wesley

DIN (1982). *ISO 7498 Informationsverarbeitung – Kommunikation Offener Systeme, Basis Referenzmodell.* Beuth Verlag

Effelsberg W. and Fleischmann A. (1986). Das ISO Referenzmodell für Offene Systeme und seine sieben Schichten. *Informatik Spektrum* (9), 280–299

Erhard (1990). Netzwerk Philosophie, I: Offene Kommunikationswege als Infrastruktur der Firmenkultur. *Datacom,* (4)

Glaser G., Hein M. and Vogl J. (1990). *TCP/IP. Protokolle, Projektplanung, Realisierung.* Datacom Verlag

Göhring H.-G. and Jasper E. (1990). *Der PC im Netz* 2nd edn. Datacom Verlag

Gora W. and Speyerer R. (1990). *Abstract Syntax Notation One* 2nd edn. Datacom Verlag

Hegering H.-G. (1987). Benutzeridentifikation und Abrechnungsdienste in einer verteilten Systemumgebung. In *Proc. GI/NTG Tech. Conf. Kommunikation in Verteilten Systemen,* Aachen, 1987. Springer

Heigert J. (1988). Directory und Netzwerk-Management. In (Beyschlag, 1988)

Huntington J.A. (1989). OSI-based net management. Is it too early, or too late?, *Data communications* (3)

IBM (a). *SNA format and protocol reference manual: management services* (SC30-3346-0)

IBM (b). *IBM Token Ring network architecture reference* (SC30-3374)

IBM (c). *IBM local area network technical manual* (SC30-3383)

IBM (d). *IBM OS/2 Extended Edition version 1.2, cookbook* (GB05-2195)

IBM (e). *Installation guidelines for IBM Token Ring products* (GG24-3291)

IBM (f). *IBM Token Ring network bridges and management* (GG24-3062)

IBM (g). *IBM TCP/IP* (GG22-9125)

IBM (h). *An introduction to programming APPC* (GG24-3034)
IBM (i). *IBM enhanced communications facilities, technical review* (GG24-3001)
IBM (j). *IBM Token Ring network administrator's guide* (GA27-3748)
IBM (k). *IBM Token Ring network optical fiber options* (GA27-3747)
IBM (l). *IBM Token Ring network telephone twisted pair guide* (GA27-3714)
IBM (m). *IBM personal computer seminar proceedings, OS/2, Token Ring and interfaces volumes* (G360-xxxx)
IBM (n). *IBM Token Ring installation guide* (GA27-3678)
IBM (o). *IBM Token Ring network adapter, technical reference* (SC30-3383)
IBM (p). *NetView general information and planning* (GC30-3463)
IBM (q). *NetView program products general information* (GC30-3350)
IBM (r). *NetView primer* (GC24-3047)
IEEE (a). *Token Ring Access Method. ANSI/IEEE Standard.* Wiley Interscience
Kanyuh D. (1988). An integrated network management product. *IBM Systems Journal* 27(1)
Kauffels F.-J. (1989a). *Einführung in die Datenkommunikation* 3rd edn. Datacom Verlag
Kauffels F.-J. (1989b). *Lokale Netze. Systeme für den Hochleistungs-Informationstransfer* 4th edn. Datacom Verlag
Kauffels F.-J. (1989c). *Kommunikation unter OS/2.* Verlag Markt & Technik
Kauffels F.-J. (1990a). *Personal Computer und Lokale Netze.* Verlag Markt & Technik
Kauffels F.-J. (1990b). *Rechnernetzwerksystemarchitekturen und Datenkommunikation* 3rd edn. Mannheim: BI
Krall (1990). SNMP opens new lines of sight. *Data Communications Spec. LAN Strategies* (3)
Maekawa, Oldehoeft and Oldehoeft (1987). *Operating Systems Advanced Concepts.* Menlo Park: Benjamin Cummings
McCann (1989). OSI-based network management. In *Datapro Network Management.* McGraw-Hill
Melchard W. (1990). Strategisches Netzwerkmanagement in SNA-Netzen, IV *Datacom* (4)
Popek G. *et al.* (1983). The LOCUS distributed operating system. *ACM Operating System Review* 17(5)
Popescu-Zeletin, Le Lann and Kim, eds. (1987). *Proc. 7th Int. IEEE Conf. Distributed Computing Systems*, Berlin 1987. Los Angeles: IEEE
Preshun (1990). Considering CMIP. *Data Communications Spec. LAN Strategies* (3)
Rose and Fuss (1990). OSI Netzwerk Management. *Datacom* (4)
Ross R.W.Jr. (1989). Integration of the physical layer into network management: AT&T's approach. In *Proc. Datacom Congress*, Cologne, 1989
Routt T.-J. (1988). SNA network management: what makes IBM's NetView tick? *Data Communications* (6)
Ruland Chr. (1988). *Datenschutz in Kommunikationssystemen.* Datacom Verlag
Scott (1990a). Taking care of business with SNMP. *Data Communications Spec. LAN Strategies* (3)

Scott (1990b). SNMP brings order to chaos. *Data Communications Spec. LAN Strategies* (3)

Sloman M., ed. (1984). *COST: Management of Local Area Networks*, Final Report of COST 11bis, LAN Group, Part II

Spaniol O. (1982). Konzepte und Bewertungsmethoden für Lokale Rechnernetze. *Informatik Spektrum* (5), 152–170

Strauss P.R. (1989). NetView/PC: users are just saying 'no'. *Data Communications* (1)

Suppan J. (1989). Ethernet gegen Token Ring: wer muss ins Museum? *Data Communications* (2)

Suppan J. (1990). Wirtschaftlicher Einsatz von Netzwerksystemen. *Proc. Network Management Forum*, Cologne 1990

Suppan J. *et al.* (1987). *Ethernet Handbuch.* Datacom Verlag

Suppan-Borowka J. (1986). Netzwerkmanagement in MAP. *Data Communications* (3)

Tanenbaum and Renesse (1985). Distributed operating systems. *Computing Surveys* 17(4)

Terplan K. (1987). *Communication Networks Management.* Prentice Hall

Terplan K. (1989). Allgemeine Konzepte des Netzwerkmanagements. In *Proc. Datacom Congress*, Cologne, 1989

Terplan K. and Huntington-Lee J. (1990). Can third parties change SNA management's stripes? *Data Communications International*, April 1990

Tripathi (1987). Distributed operating systems. In (Popescu-Zeletin, Le Lann and Kim, 1987)

Wakid, Brusil and La Barre (1987). Coming to OSI: network resource management and global reachability. *Data Communications* (12)

Documents, test systems and leaflets from the following companies (in alphabetical order):

3Com	Fuba	Philips	Racal Milgo
Ascom	HOB	Proteon	Racore
Apple	IBM	Schneider & Koch	RAD
Banyan	Madge	SEL	Retronika
Compaq	Microsoft	Siemens	Telemation
Crosscom	Microware	Simpact	Telonik
DCA	NCR	Spider	Thomas Conrad
DDS	Nokia	Startek	Ungermann Bass
DEC	Novell	Stemmer	Western Digital
Ericsson	ODS	Sun	Wetronik
Fibronics	Olicom	SynOptics	and other companies.

Index